INTEREST GROUPS IN
ITALIAN POLITICS

INTEREST GROUPS IN
ITALIAN POLITICS

BY JOSEPH LA PALOMBARA

PRINCETON, NEW JERSEY

PRINCETON UNIVERSITY PRESS

1964

320.945
43

To Richard, David, and Susan
with fond wishes
that they may some day fully experience
the beauty and the mystery
that is Italy

CONTENTS

CONTENTS

PREFACE

MY concern with organized interest groups in Italy goes back fourteen years, to the time of my first intensive field work there. *The Italian Labor Movement: Problems and Prospects*, published in 1957, emanated from this early phase of my research. Since that time, I have returned to Italy at frequent intervals and have had the opportunity to add to my understanding of the Italian political system, and particularly to the impact on it of such major aggregates as organized labor, business, agriculture, and religion. The present volume represents an effort to relate to the Italian situation the work of several American and European scholars whose intellectual concern has been the organization and behavior of interest groups.

Between my first extended field work in Italy and the publication of the present volume, I became intimately involved in the work of the Social Science Research Council's Committee on Comparative Politics. It was this Committee—in conjunction with the Conference Board of Associated Research Councils—that provided the funds to make possible the year of field work, during 1957–1958, on which the major portions of this volume are based. Even more important, however, has been the intellectual stimulation and concern for theoretical problems and formulations that my colleagues on the Committee managed to engender. Although this may be far from an adequate application or testing of the theoretical ideas of Gabriel Almond and others on the Committee, my debt to all of them is as deep as I hope it is apparent. I am convinced that the empirical information presented here will be better understood and evaluated if it is seen in the context of the broader theoretical concerns against which it is cast.

Initially, it was my intention to do a study in depth of the interaction between a very limited number of interest groups and a single Italian bureaucratic agency. Several considerations served to lead me to modify this approach. First, the Committee on Comparative Politics encouraged a number of scholars to devise a somewhat broader research prospectus that would make possible the accumulation of somewhat comparable data on interest groups in a number of countries. In this sense, what I have to say here should be compared with the findings of the important volume edited by Gabriel Almond and James Coleman [1] and with the excellent study of Indian interest groups written by Myron Weiner.[2] Although these works are not strictly comparable, they raise many of the same questions and are concerned with many of the same problems involving the theory of political systems.

Second, because a significant general or specific literature on Italian interest groups does not exist, I felt compelled to draw some of the broader contours of interest group organization and behavior in Italian society. Thus, while Chapters V and VI are not exhaustive inventories of this subject, they will provide a useful general orientation. The sample of interest groups on which these chapters are based is probably a reasonably accurate representation of those groups in Italian society that are the most intimately and intensively involved in the political process.

Third, the focus was broadened to include more than the bureaucracy, because it was found in the field that the social scientist's desire to find behavioral phenomena neatly compartmentalized rarely conforms to empirical realities. For example, to have limited the analysis of Italian Catholic Action and the General Confederation of Italian Industry strictly to a single bureaucratic agency— or even simply to the bureaucratic sector—would have resulted in a serious distortion of the nature of the inter-

[1] *The Politics of the Developing Areas* (Princeton, 1960).
[2] *The Politics of Scarcity: Public Pressure and Political Response in India* (Chicago, 1962).

vention of these groups in the political process. The impact of any organized group in politics can be adequately gauged, in the final analysis, only if one takes account of its intervention in several governmental sectors, as well as of the kind of related intervention engaged in by groups other than those under intensive study. Thus I devote only three chapters to groups in the bureaucracy, while other chapters attempt to depict group responses to the general political culture and to the national legislature.

Last, as I have suggested above, my participation in the work of the S.S.R.C. Committee on Comparative Politics led me to take a broader systemic view of the interest-group process in Italy. It was in this enlarged context that follow-up research in Italy in the years since 1958 was conducted. It is my hope, therefore, that this volume will add to our knowledge of the important political functions of interest articulation, interest aggregation, political socialization, and political communications.

The data accumulated during the initial field stages were derived from several sources. Because of my primary concern with Italian Catholic Action and the General Confederation of Italian Industry, the publications of these organizations, for periods ranging from ten to fifty years, were intensively scrutinized. This work was carried on in Italy primarily by Dr. Gianfranco Poggi, now at the University of Florence, whose contribution to the entire enterprise was at all times substantial. Dr. Poggi also assisted me in the initial phases of my own data analysis. Intensive work on one of the major publications of the General Confederation of Italian Industry (Confindustria) was conducted by Dr. Giuseppe DiFederico, who served as my graduate assistant at Michigan State University.

General data on Italian interest groups were solicited through a questionnaire mailed to a selected sample of 129 interest groups. Sixty-eight groups returned completed questionnaires, and an additional eighteen provided various kinds of documentary information concerning themselves. These findings are reported in Chapters V and VI.

As is normally the case, the field work included an intensive reading of several newspapers and periodicals, as well as discussion of the project and its problems with dozens of "informants" or "knowledgeables" in the field of government, business, labor, and the professions. This activity was of inestimable value in terms of providing a backdrop against which all of the other data could be evaluated.

Finally, and most critically, focused interviews lasting from one to three hours were conducted with almost 130 carefully selected respondents. These included twenty-nine high-level bureaucrats, twenty-four leaders of Confindustria, twenty-three leaders of Italian Catholic Action, thirty-four officials of other interest groups, and eleven political party leaders. Those remaining fall into a miscellaneous category.

Let it be said at once that I did not use a "set schedule" interview and that I did not attempt to compel my respondents to reply to a rigidly constructed pattern of questions. My previous experience in Italy, coupled with conversations with colleagues, such as Henry Ehrmann, who had recently completed field work in Europe, served to reinforce my own convictions concerning the extreme and fascinating complexities of interviewing the educated and highly articulate Italian elite. For all of my wisdom, however, a number of my respondents were surely amused and possibly dismayed by some of my "probes"—or by my "scientific" demeanor. One of them remarked to my assistant the day following a long interview, "Il professore è un registratore!" "The professor is a tape recorder!" I trust that my own limitations as a field researcher, as well as my practice of simultaneously translating responses into English, have caused only insignificant distortions. In general, I was satisfied that the methods I used were probing those dimensions of the interest-group phenomenon that were of primary concern to me. I should add that my respondents were always assured of their complete anonymity, that this assurance greatly facilitated conversations, and that I assume their anonymity is adequately protected by my practice of referring to the interviews by number, date, and place where conducted.

I am not certain how an author goes about extending adequate recognition to all of those who, over a period of several years, help to make possible a book of this sort. Informants and respondents, whose good will and cooperation make the field work possible in the first place, must remain unknown to the reader. With a strong expression of gratitude extended in their direction, I can turn to record my debt to several persons and organizations—in Italy and the United States—who provided more than an ordinary amount of assistance at several stages in the book's evolution.

I have already recognized the Social Science Research Council and the Conference Board of Associated Research Councils, who provided the initial funds for the field work in Italy. Early work on the research design was facilitated by my association with the School of Labor and Industrial Relations at Michigan State University. In Italy, I was able to draw on the assistance of the Fulbright Commission, and particularly my friend Dr. Cipriana Scelba, its Director, who can open many doors. The Facoltà di Scienze Politiche Cesare Alfieri of the University of Florence provided credentials that made access to many people less arduous than would otherwise have been the case. In the United States, the All-University Research Grant Program of Michigan State University provided needed funds to aid in the work of data analysis.

Access to Italian Catholic Action was graciously facilitated by Mons. Luigi Cardini, Ecclesiastical Assistant to the General Presidency at Rome, with whom I conducted an initial conversation concerning the research project. Mons. Cardini, as well as Professor Luigi Gedda, then A.C.I. President, made possible subsequent interviews in various Catholic Action branches. Others in that organization who liberally assisted include Dr. Giovanni Fallani, Mons. Giuseppe LaNave, and Don Claudio Bucciarelli.

Dr. Ugo Sciascia, Director General of the National Civic Committees, was cooperative beyond my most optimistic expectations.

The Honorable Fiorentino Sullo, then Minister of Industry and Commerce, greatly facilitated access to his ministry, as did my friend and colleague Professor Guglielmo Negri. Within the Italian bureaucracy, I wish especially to recognize the assistance and courtesies of Dr. Rino Onofri, Dr. Domenico Macri, Dr. Enrico Lubrano, Dr. Antonio Padellaro, Dr. Giovanni Palmieri, Dr. Carlo Urcioli, Dr. Antonio Marino, Dr. Ugo Cevoli, and Dr. Francesco Tortora.

Dr. Camillo Benevento and Dr. Italo Viglianesi of the Italian Union of Labor, the Honorable Vittorio Foà, the Honorable Fernando Santi, and Dr. Bruno Trentin of the Italian General Confederation of Labor, the Honorable Bruno Storti, Dr. Franco Archibugi, and Dr. Pietro Merli-Brandini of the Italian Confederation of Workers' Unions were all helpful in bringing me up to date on developments in the Italian labor movement.

I was accorded complete cooperation by the General Confederation of Italian Industry. I am particularly indebted to Avv. Giacomo Guglia, Director of the Press and Propaganda Section, for his important help on several occasions, and to Dr. Lidia Barbera, Confindustria's librarian, without whose willing and valuable collaboration documentary research would surely have bogged down. In addition, I owe a debt to Avv. Giovanni Battista Codina, Avv. Rosario Toscani, and Dr. Zirano. To Dr. Emilio Gilardi must go my special thanks for his willingness to recount in minute detail aspects of the history of Confindustria with which he was intimately acquainted.

Professor Alberto Spreafico of the University of Florence provided more specific services than I can enumerate here. Suffice it to say that he seems to know everyone in Italy and possesses that unique ability to lead the sometimes hapless researcher to exactly the person who can help to resolve a major field problem.

The manuscript was read by members of the S.S.R.C. Committee on Comparative Politics, several of whom were kind enough to offer constructive suggestions. My wife, Lyda, was patient enough to read an early version of the work, and she managed to point my attention to several important problems. She is also primarily responsible for the index. Exhaustive critiques of the work were provided by my good friend Professor Giovanni Sartori of the University of Florence, who several times saved me from serious pitfalls, and by Mr. Sidney Tarrow, a graduate student at the University of California (Berkeley), whose candid objections to particularly obscure prose helped to improve many parts of the manuscript. Regarding all of those who offered suggestions, I enter the customary caveat that the responsibility for the manuscript's imperfections is my own.

Portions of this manuscript have appeared in the *Journal of Politics, Tempi Moderni* (Rome), *Revista de Estudios Politicos* (Madrid), *Rassegna Italiana di Sociologia,* and *Politische Vierteljahresschrift* (Heidelberg). I am grateful to the editors for permission to reproduce these materials here.

I might never have completed this book had not the winds of good fortune brought me an extraordinary year at the Center for Advanced Study in the Behavioral Sciences. My full year of work and study in an atmosphere ideally designed to that end provided the time, the intellectual stimulation, and the impetus to conclude a study that had dragged along considerably beyond the limits of my earlier expectations.

J. LaP.

East Lansing, Michigan
Spring, 1963

INTEREST GROUPS IN
ITALIAN POLITICS

CHAPTER I · INTRODUCTION

THE STUDY OF ITALIAN INTEREST GROUPS

ITALY is one of the more recent countries to "discover" the presence of interest groups in the political process. This fact does not mean that, prior to the present, the impact of organized interests on governmental decisions has been a totally neglected subject. For example, the reports of the Committees of the Constituent Assembly constitute a rich source of historical information on the political role of organized business and finance. Although some of these data are used from time to time for polemical purposes, they have never been systematically mined for the light they would shed on the important relationship between economic and political power.[1] Or one might turn to the pages of the important weekly newspaper, *Il Mondo,* which throughout the postwar years contain innumerable articles pointing to the many ways, frequently of questionable political probity, in which interest groups intervene in the political process. Beyond this, one might consult the works of Ernesto Rossi, a prodigious researcher, who understands Italian politics as few Italians do, but whose books are sometimes marred in their accuracy and objectivity by Rossi's quite genuine zeal for reform and his fear of the growing threat of clericalism in Italy.[2]

Postwar Italian literature is also rich in books and other

[1] The more interesting and important studies are the following published by the Ministero per la Costituente: *Rapporto della Commissione Economico V, Finanza I Relazione* and *II Appendice alla relazione; II Industria I Relazione* and *II* and *III, Appendice alla relazione.* All these volumes, now difficult to secure, were published in Rome in 1946 by the Istituto Poligrafico dello Stato.

[2] Among Ernesto Rossi's many works, see *Lo Stato industriale* (1953), *I Padroni del vapore* (1955), and *Il Malgoverno* (1955), all published at Bari by Editore Laterza. On the important subject of the pressures surrounding the issue of the exploitation of petroleum and the development of the petroleum industry in Italy, see Ernesto Rossi, Eugenio Scalfari, and Leopoldo Piccardi, *Petrolio in gabbia* (Bari, 1955).

writings that point to the massive role in politics of organized Catholicism. Some of these works, such as the important study of Church and State by Arturo Carlo Jemolo,[3] are serious pieces of history or political science. Most of the writing, however, is clearly polemical, even sensational. It is designed to call attention in an alarmist way to the impact of the Catholic Church on Italian schools, or to ring out warnings about the undemocratic consequences implicit in the relationship between the Vatican and an Italian government dominated by Christian Democrats, or to focus a spotlight on the allegedly unsavory way in which the powers of the Church succeed in imposing their will on the government, thereby assuring themselves control of the temporal as well as the spiritual world in Italy.[4]

Although much of the literature extant provides important information and insights that are of utility to the researcher, scholarly attention to the interest group phenomenon remains scant. The materials available tend to be exploratory,[5] philosophical,[6] juridical,[7] or theoretical.[8] It is evident that Italian scholars are just beginning to feel their way along a path that is now much more well

---

[3] *Chiesa e stato in Italia negli ultimi cento anni* (Milan, 1955).

[4] A prolific antagonist of the Vatican is Carlo Falconi, an ex-clergyman. Among his writings, see *La Chiesa e le organizzazioni cattoliche in Italia, 1945–1955* (Milan, 1956); *Gedda e l'Azione Cattolica* (Florence, n.d.); *Il Pentagono vaticano* (Bari, 1958). Like Ernesto Rossi, Falconi possesses a wealth of information, but some of his factual presentations are open to serious doubt.

An important and critical work on the relationship between Church and State is Vittorio Gorresio (ed.), *Stato e chiesa* (Bari, 1957). An interesting short volume on the impact of the Catholic Church on Italian public education is Luigi Rodelli, *I Preti in cattedra* (Florence, 1958). An extreme exposé of the relationship between Catholic Action and Italian Fascism, published almost two decades after it was written, is Francesco Luigi Ferrari, *L'Azione Cattolica e il "regime"* (Florence, 1957). A typical left-wing polemic on the totalitarian implications of organized Catholicism in Italian politics is Lelio Basso, *Due totalitarismi: Fascismo e Democrazia Cristiana* (Milan, 1951).

[5] For example, E. De Marchi, "Introduzione ai 'pressure groups'," *Occidente*, 12 (1956), pp. 105–12; U. Piazzi, "I Gruppi di pressione nella democrazia moderna," *Quaderni di Azione Sociale*, 10 (September–October

traveled in countries such as Britain and France. But the willingness to set off in this direction is clearly on the rise, and we can anticipate that over the next decade there will be a great proliferation of interest group studies.

One important reason for the striking growth in Italian attention to the problem of interest groups is that the general subject of the impact of organized groups on political parties and government was specifically and dramatically raised in the debates during the 1960 Congress of the Christian Democratic Party, held at Florence.[9] The spirited discussion by delegates to the Congress served to underline what any observant person already knew, namely, that there exists an enormous discrepancy between political reality and what the formal structure of constitutional government might lead one to expect.

Because of the national attention to interest groups engendered by the Christian Democratic Congress, *Tempi Moderni,* a political journal brilliantly edited by Fabrizio Onofri and supported by some of Italy's more able young social scientists, devoted one of its "Round Table" discussions to the subject of interest groups in the country. Contributions, in response to a questionnaire prepared by the editors, were requested from a wide range of Italian scholars, political officials, journalists, and publicists, and

1959), pp. 666–91; Joseph LaPalombara, "Gruppi di pressione e pubblica amministrazione," in *Problemi della pubblica amministrazione* (Bologna, 1959), pp. 141–59.

6 Vittorio de Caprariis, "Gruppi di pressione," *Nord e Sud,* 3 (December, 1956), pp. 66–69; and "Gruppi di pressione e società democratica," *ibid.,* 8 (May, 1961), pp. 16–27.

7 G. D'Eufemia, "Aspetti giuridici dei gruppi di pressione," *Nord e Sud,* 6 (March, 1957), pp. 69–71.

8 An article of great theoretical importance is Giovanni Sartori's "Gruppi di pressione o gruppi di interesse," *Il Mulino,* 8 (February, 1959), pp. 7–42. Cf. G. Manzocchi, "Appunti sul fenomeno dei gruppi di pressione," *Vita e Pensiero,* 43 (January, 1960), pp. 48–51; Joseph LaPalombara, "I Gruppi di interesse in Italia," *Studi Politici,* 7 (January–March, 1960), pp. 11–35.

9 For an interesting statement by a leader of the Christian Democratic Left, see Giulio Pastore, "I Gruppi di pressione," *Concretezza,* 6 (January, 1960), pp. 3–5.

their replies occupy portions of three 1960 issues of the journal.[10]

One striking aspect of the replies provided by *Tempi Moderni's* respondents is that they are unanimous in the view that interest groups (the Italians prefer the nomenclature "pressure groups") exercise a significant influence over the political life of the country. Beyond this, however, many of these same men emphasize that, in theory at least, interest groups are not to be viewed as pathological but, rather, as physiological—as a necessary organic part of a pluralistic democracy. Rather than treat the interest group as an aberration, as was done at the turn of the century when interest groups were "discovered" in the United States, there is an explicit recognition that organized groups are ubiquitous in political systems, that they tend to be manifested in relatively greater numbers in pluralistic democracies, that in these latter types of political systems they have important functional roles to perform, and that, indeed, it is both unrealistic and unthinkable to assume that the democratic polity can function well without the presence of organized interest.

However, *Tempi Moderni's* respondents are equally vigorous in the assertion that, for various reasons, interest groups in Italy are pathological for the system. The most fascinating type of analysis concerning this point is offered by Giuseppe Maranini, who warns that interest groups will be compelled to operate *outside* of government as such only so long as political power in the country is strong and organized. Where, as in Italy, political power is weak or in a state of collapse, the situation changes radically; attempts to regulate or to limit the activities of interest groups fail and "the most immoral and corrupt methods come to prevail." When this occurs, the state disintegrates, branches of government begin to operate as

[10] See Centro Italiano di Ricerche e Documentazione, "I Gruppi di pressione," *Tempi Moderni*, 3 (April–June, 1960), pp. 43–55; "I Gruppi di pressione," *Ibid.* (July–September, 1960), pp. 13–33; "I Gruppi di pressione in Italia: Conclusioni," *ibid.* (October–December, 1960), pp. 103–12.

interest groups, and, cautions Maranini, ". . . pressure groups affirm themselves as the protagonists of one of the worst kinds of feudalism that can corrupt and mortify a society." [11]

Maranini believes that the situation he describes represents the realities of contemporary Italy, and, as we shall note in detail in later chapters, he is at least partially correct. The Italian bureaucracy, the locus of attention of major aggregations of organized interest, is correctly identified as a series of feudal holdings in which those in Italy who are theoretically empowered to make the rules are strikingly at the mercy of others whom the rules are supposed to control or regulate.

Another sign of pathology is said to be the tendency of branches of government to behave like interest groups. Such groups serve to create great confusion and disorientation in a democratic polity when they become so closely allied with *associational* interest groups that it is impossible to know when a governmental branch is speaking or acting as a unit of government or as a segment of organized interest. To cite the most salient example treated in this volume, it is frequently difficult to detect whether the Ministry of Industry and Commerce is functioning in a regulatory capacity or merely as the mouthpiece of the General Confederation of Italian Industry, with which it maintains intimate ties. Other examples such as this could be cited; the point is that what Italians ominously call *il sottogoverno* now involves a network of relationships in which it is not always easy to detect when the bureaucracy—or some other branch of government—is acting as a part of an authoritative governmental structure or merely as one of the many competing interest groups that characterize the society.

So much has the Italian bureaucracy become the instrument of organized interest that even a person identified with Catholic Action's Civic Committees is moved to com-

[11] *Ibid.* (April–June, 1960), p. 49.

ment unfavorably on this state of affairs. Giovanni Baget-Bozzo, who edits the Civic Committees' *Ordine Civile,* insists that Italy's political parties have not succeeded in eliminating privilege but have instead served to reinforce it. Moreover, he says, the bureaucracy itself has become a pressure group, indicating that the political parties fail to serve as buffers between organized groups and the state. In short, whereas political parties should serve to filter and to aggregate the demands on the political system, they function instead as instruments of the groups, transmitting to governmental structures demands that are selfish and that do not in any way represent a willingness to compromise. This circumstance, too, serves seriously to weaken the Italian state.[12]

One derives from observations such as these the impression that the Italian government is to a marked degree the helpless object of interest group manipulation. This is exactly the point that is intended by the respondents, for, as Ugo La Malfa insists, Italian government simply does not possess that system of manifest and subtle checks and balances that is true in the United States or Great Britain. La Malfa frankly suggests that in Italy the interest groups constitute primordial forces in direct competition with the state. His argument, which gives one fair reason for pause, is that in Italy the interest groups are not a *consequence* of political democracy but are actually prior to it, and are therefore in a position of extraordinary power vis-à-vis the democratic state. It is precisely in these circumstances, he says, that organs of the state tend to become interest groups themselves, rather than regulators or arbiters of group conflict.[13]

Another indication of pathology in the interest group sector is said to lie in the overt interference of the Catholic Church in political affairs. Ignazio Silone considers the Vatican's interference in the nation's political affairs a direct assault on free government. In this regard, he says,

[12] *Ibid.* (July–September, 1960), pp. 13–14.
[13] *Ibid.*, pp. 17–18.

8

"Given its frequency and the state of paralysis in which it has placed the D.C. [Christian Democracy], the intervention of the clerical hierarchy in our political life now constitutes the most serious problem of our democracy." [14]

As we shall observe minutely later, it is obvious that one of the major forces in Italian politics is Catholicism. One response to this fact is simply that it is inconceivable that the Catholic Church could refrain from massive political involvement on the Italian peninsula. To which the rejoinder might appropriately be that offered by Franco Simoncini: "The difficulty is not so much that certain pressure groups are uncommonly strong; it is rather that Italian democracy is still extremely weak." [15]

Interest groups, then, are viewed as omnipresent in government and as serving to undermine the stability of the polity. The major protagonists in this political drama are generally conceded to be such organizations as the General Confederation of Italian Industry (Confindustria); the General Confederation of Italian Agriculture (Confagricoltura); the National Confederation of Direct Cultivators (Coltivatori Diretti), large industrial enterprises such as Italcementi, Edison, Fiat, Montecatini, and the sugar cartel; public corporations like the Ente Nazionale Idrocarburi (E.N.I.); Italian Catholic Action and other manifestations of organized Catholicism; powerful national labor confederations, such as the Communist-Socialist Italian General Confederation of Labor (C.G.I.L.), the Christian Democratic Italian Confederation of Workers' Unions (C.I.S.L.), and the Social Democratic Italian Union of Labor (U.I.L.). By and large, those who replied to *Tempi Moderni's* questionnaire consider that the most pernicious influence on Italian politics is exercised by organized business and organized religion. One cannot escape the general feeling that while groups are probably necessary in a democracy, their presence in Italian society today constitutes a fundamental source of weakness and instabil-

[14] *Ibid.*, p. 26.
[15] *Ibid.* (April–June, 1960), p. 53.

ity in Italian democracy, and that something ought be done about it.

There are those who demand a series of restrictive laws. Such legislation would regulate industrial monopolies and limit their profits, compel political parties to reveal their sources of finance and financial outlays, make public the financial structure of the Italian press, regulate the activities of syndical organizations, provide more penetrating and public control of public corporations and governmental ministries, effect an over-all reform of the Italian bureaucracy, and so on. Although some of this legislation (e.g., bureaucratic reform) is desperately needed in Italy, it is doubtful that it would have the anticipated impact on the organization and behavior of interest groups. Experience in the United States would suggest, for example, that regulatory laws have the result of worrying but not seriously inhibiting the ability of the groups to operate. Interest groups will gravitate to the critical points of political power. Legislation alone will not prevent patterns of group organization and behavior that may be considered damaging to democracy. Moreover, as the editors of *Tempi Moderni* wisely recognize, it is possible that, if carried too far, regulatory legislation could destroy the very freedom of association that is conceded to be a premise of pluralistic democracy. Such legislation may be defective not merely in the sense that it tends to treat symptoms rather than cause, but also in the sense that a wholesale, massive, and indiscriminate attack on the unsavory symptoms of interest group behavior may succeed in killing rather than curing the ailing democratic patient.

The notion of essentially repressive legislation rests on the assumption—hazardous in Italy—that those who control political power will not abuse it to serve their own ends. The situation might be somewhat different if the Italian political elite, like their counterparts in India,[16]

[16] For the very conservative way in which the Indian government has used existing repressive legislation against interest groups, see the excel-

had been deeply socialized in the central values of British politics. But, as I shall try to portray in later chapters, it is precisely the fragmented, nonbargaining nature of the Italian political culture that makes such legislative proposals as dangerous to democracy as they are unrealistic.

As an alternative to regulatory legislation, a few Italians specify the need to treat the causes of political pathology. Giuseppe Maranini, for example, flatly states that the problem is not with the groups as such, and therefore cannot be resolved by attempts to control them. Rather, some effort must be made to restore the unity and integrity of the state: the executive must be strengthened, the bureaucracy reformed and constrained to limit its interest-group activities, the various branches of government made to understand that they have roles to perform that in the final analysis must be independent of the groups, even if somewhat influenced by them.[17]

In a similar vein, Ugo La Malfa sees the problem of pathology growing out of the extreme ideological fragmentation that characterizes contemporary Italy. In this type of setting, he notes, interest groups tend to view the state as something to be conquered by some groups to the disadvantage of all others. Government is simply never seen as functioning in the general interest, but only as an instrument of aggrandizing a limited segment of society. La Malfa, therefore, would use legislation as a means of strengthening governmental institutions—and as a way of reducing ideological fragmentation and bringing about an impersonal government, a government which would serve as a guarantor of basic rights, and as a means of aiding the development of all of the country's productive, moral, political, and social forces. He holds that it is only when this problem is solved that one will be able to speak of Italian interest groups as structures that are similar in their behavior and political consequences to the kinds of

---

lent study by Myron Weiner, *The Politics of Scarcity: Public Pressure and Political Response in India* (Chicago, 1962).

[17] *Tempi Moderni*, 3 (April–June, 1960), p. 49.

interest groups that exist in Britain or the United States.[18]

For many reasons, as will be apparent in the chapters that follow, the prescriptions of Giuseppe Maranini and Ugo La Malfa are much easier suggested than implemented. There are forces in Italian society—some of them recent, others buttressed by decades of historical experience—that would make it tremendously arduous, if not impossible, to bring into existence the kind of political system these men advocate. It will also be made relatively clear that much of what one discovers about the actual behavior of interest groups in Italy is not unlike what one would except to find in most complex and relatively democratic societies.

In this effort to shed empirical light on the organization and behavior of Italian interest groups, I also hope to provide an additional basis upon which certain theoretical and hypothetical formulations concerning the interest group phenomenon can be appraised and evaluated. The major propositions that are examined in the study are enumerated later in this chapter.

Although the reader will find in the pages that follow information regarding a wide array of interest groups, major attention is accorded Confindustria (the General Confederation of Italian Industry) and Italian Catholic Action. Any attempt at a full understanding of the role of interest groups within the Italian political system must take these two massive organizations into careful account. Indeed, our résumé of responses to *Tempi Moderni's* questionnaire clearly indicates that few Italians would exclude either organization from a list of the three or four most powerful groups in Italy. In any case, in a society deeply torn by ideological and religious conflict, organized business and organized religion necessarily loom as major protagonists.

The analytical chapters, which seek to delineate patterns of group interaction with the legislature, and par-

18 *Ibid.*, 3 (June–September, 1960), pp. 19–20.

ticularly with the bureaucracy, are set off against several chapters in which the social, political, and governmental settings of Italy are described. The empirical data which serve as the basis for analysis and generalization become meaningful only when understood within the broader cultural context from which they are abstracted. An evaluation of both these data and the generalizations concerning them should help make future discussions of the interest group phenomenon in Italy less tentative and speculative than is presently the case.

A NOTE ON DEFINITIONS

I do not consider the political process to be characterized exclusively by group behavior or by group-oriented decisions. Yet it is obvious that no political process, no matter what the nature or stage of development of the political system may be, can be understood without according serious attention to the role of interest groups. To be sure, the interest group approach—particularly if it is based on sweeping and simplistic claims emanating from the work of Arthur Fisher Bentley—might become a conceptual and theoretical trap, limiting the researcher to highly dubious explications and interpretations of political phenomena.[19] However, one does not need to adhere to the tenets of simplistic group "theory," or claim that the "theory" constitutes a general theory of politics, in order to derive empirical utility from the approach. As Gabriel Almond appropriately puts it: ". . . we turn to the comparative study of interest groups not with the hope that these rather than parties or governmental institutions

[19] On the various difficulties associated with the interest group approach to the political process, see Joseph LaPalombara, "The Utility and Limitations of Interest Group Theory in Non-American Field Situations," *Journal of Politics*, 22 (February, 1960), pp. 29–49; Stanley Rothman, "Systematic Political Theory: Observations on the Group Approach," *American Political Science Review*, 54 (March, 1960), pp. 15–33; Roy E. Macridis, "Interest Groups in Comparative Analysis," *Journal of Politics*, 23 (February, 1961), pp. 25–45; W. J. M. MacKenzie, "Pressure Groups: The Conceptual Framework," *Political Studies*, 3 (October, 1955), pp. 247–55.

will yield *the principles* of discrimination between types of political systems, but rather with the expectation that the systematic examination of interest groups in their complex interrelations with public opinion, political parties and formal governmental institutions will enable us to differentiate more accurately between political systems as *wholes*. In other words, the growing concern among scholars with interest groups and public opinion is the consequence of a search for a more complete and systematic conception of the political process as a whole, rather than a search for an approach which is an *alternative* to the present emphasis on formal governmental institutions." [20]

Thus the interest-group approach would use the concept of the interest group as an analytical tool, or as a system of describing some but not all aspects of the political process. It is in this manner that the concept is utilized in this volume, and it is toward a further refinement of some of the propositions concerning the role and function of interest groups in complex political systems that the analytical chapters are directed.

In the broadest sense, a group may be understood to be any two or more individuals interacting with each other. At this level of generalization, very little of human behavior can be viewed outside the group context. To apply such a broad definition is simply to confirm an obvious observation of John Dewey, namely, that the individual, as a social animal, behaves on the basis of his associations and interactions with others, and that it is difficult to explain or describe human behavior outside the associational environment.[21]

There are many ways in which groups can be classified,

[20] Gabriel A. Almond, *A Comparative Study of Interest Groups and the Political Process*, mimeographed by the Social Science Research Council (New York, April, 1957), p. 5.

[21] I am trying to avoid here a problem that besets David Truman, whose definition of a group evidently requires an unspecified and, perhaps, unspecifiable "frequency of interaction." See his *The Governmental Process* (New York, 1951), p. 24. What Truman calls a "casual" group is still a group as far as I am concerned.

and just as many vantage points from which they might be analyzed. Factors such as size, nature of membership, geographic location, sex, age, and occupation are only a few of the possible bases of classification that immediately come to mind. Other possibly useful classification bases would include frequency of interaction among member, purpose, style, or tactics, and so on. In Chapter III, I utilize a broad classification of groups that divides them into institutional, nonassociational, associational, and anomic categories.[22] This book is concerned essentially with certain secondary *associational* groups that are intimately and frequently involved in the political process and that have other important characteristics in common. The relative frequency of political intervention is an important reason for choosing such groups for analysis, but this choice should not be understood to mean that the significant groups in Italy are *only* those that fall into the categories to which I devote major attention.

What makes a group a *political interest group* and therefore worthy of the political scientist's attention? If, as one student of Arthur Fisher Bentley claims, the concept "interest group" is redundant in the sense that the group is also the interest,[23] we have very little to guide us in our search to understand which groups are significant in the political process, and in what ways. Similarly, if we accept the Truman view that an interest is any "shared attitude,"[24] we are led to conclude that every form of human

[22] The classification used in Chapter III is taken from Gabriel Almond in Gabriel A. Almond and James S. Coleman, eds., *The Politics of the Developing Areas* (Princeton, 1960), pp. 33–45. A very similar classification is expounded by George I. Blanksten, "Political Groups in Latin America," *American Political Science Review*, 53 (March, 1959), pp. 106–27. Similarly, Myron Weiner, "Interest Groups in India," mimeographed paper presented to the Annual Meeting of the American Political Science Association, St. Louis, Missouri, September, 1958.

[23] See, for example, Charles B. Hagan, "The Group in a Political Science," in Roland Young, ed., *Approaches to the Study of Politics* (Evanston, 1958), pp. 38–51; Phillip Monypenny, "Political Science and the Study of Groups," *Western Political Quarterly*, 7 (June, 1954), pp. 183–201.

[24] Truman, *op. cit.*, pp. 33–34. In Truman's words, "The shared attitudes, moreover, constitute the interests."

association and interaction implies the existence of an interest group. Moreover, Truman's discussion leads us into the conceptually very foggy, badly illuminated labyrinth of "latent interest" and "potential group." Escaping from it involves a degree of shifting that has been the subject of several trenchant criticisms.[25] As Giovanni Sartori says, ". . . in Bentley's or Truman's usage, 'interest' means almost everything, and *everything* is too much; it is close to being nothing." [26]

It seems to me quite legitimate to require, as Sartori says, that the concept of interest group imply the existence of disinterested groups. It is for this reason that I prefer to think of interest as something that has some relationship to the political process. It may very well be that any group, as I have defined the term, would manifest at least a minimum amount of shared attitudes. Nevertheless, I would suggest that many such groups, most of them perhaps, are essentially disinterested in the political process.

As I use "interest," it means a *conscious* desire to have public policy, or the authoritative allocation of values, move in a particular general or specific direction. I use *interest group* rather than *political interest group* because my conceptualization of "interest" requires a set of attitudes toward public policy. Insofar as any group, for whatever part of the time, does not consciously articulate (or in some symbolic way manifest) desires and attitudes regarding the authoritative allocation of values, it is by definition simply not an interest group for my purposes; it is something else.

David Apter suggests that, in the final analysis, all such attitudes or desires—all such interests—are attempts to modify the social stratification system of a society. For Apter, political groups are those that, in any way, seek to

---

[25] *Ibid.*, p. 35. For a critique of Truman's use of the "potential interest group" concept, see the excellent article by Stanley Rothman, *op. cit.* Truman's response to Rothman is "On the Invention of Systems," *American Political Science Review*, 54 (June, 1960), pp. 494-95.

[26] Sartori, *op. cit.*, p. 16.

bring about changes in the stratification system.[27] While this formulation is close to what I intend, the definition of political groups seems to exclude those whose desires or activities are oriented to the system's maintenance. As far as I am concerned, a group's *interest* may very well be (and, in fact, often is) that of maintaining an existing configuration of public policy. It is not merely for the future performance of authoritative functions that interest groups organize and intervene; many of them are vitally attuned to the preservation of the consequences of previous rule-making, rule-application, and rule-adjudication.

This definition of interest avoids the problem of whether the concept is too broad or too narrow. In its narrow sense, interest is often taken to mean *economic* interest. As Sartori aptly remarks, the narrow connotation quickly relates interest to the concept of *utilitas*. In its broadest sense, interest tends to become something as vague and amorphous as "shared attitudes." My formulation of this concept permits the broadest or the narrowest kind of interest, provided that its expression involves desire regarding public policy. Thus the basis of the interest may be economic, religious, ideological, social, or psychological, or any combination of these factors. Desires concerning public policy or the authoritative allocation of values may grow out of a more basic wish to aggrandize one's economic position in society. Or the interest may be the expression of an emotional or intellectual commitment to a particular ideology. In this sense, ideas are not "spooks," as Bentley claimed, but important factors in human behavior. Psychologically, interest may be nothing more than a manifestation of a need to exercise power for its own sake. In short, what underlies an interest is a subject for empirical investigation, insofar as that is possible, and not something to be assumed on an a priori basis. Moreover, it is important to bear in mind that if interests in the final analysis are *individuals'* interests, any

[27] David E. Apter, "A Comparative Method for the Study of Politics," *American Journal of Sociology*, 64 (November, 1958), pp. 221–37.

interest manifested by an organized group will be the result of a highly complex interplay between an accommodation of these individual desires. To understand fully *how* an organized group arrives at a particular formulation of the group's interest would require an intensive examination of the dynamics of the group itself.

To summarize, an interest group is any aggregation of interacting individuals who manifest conscious desires concerning the authoritative allocation of values. This definition tells us absolutely nothing about the relationship of such groups to other groups in the society or to the formal institutions of government. Nor is there anything implicit in the definition regarding whether an interest group does in fact seek to communicate its desires to others and, if so, the manner in which such communication of demands takes place. It is entirely possible for groups to manifest conscious desires regarding public policy while doing little or nothing to translate such desires into demands. Nevertheless, a sensitive government may seek to discover what such desires may be and to make public policy partially responsive to them. The notion that there must be some sort of formal organization—or at least some kind of overt activity—through which interests are translated into demands seems to me to place too great an emphasis on purposive political behavior. It also seems to reflect a model of the interest group that is too narrowly tied to the structure of pluralistic democratic societies. While I agree that such societies are not conceivable without a considerable amount of interest articulation through primary and especially secondary associations, I prefer a definition of interest group that permits us to understand why and how interest groups can exist in any society, regardless of its ideological basis or organizational configuration, or its level of political structural differentiation.

This study, then, devotes major attention to Italian Catholic Action and Confindustria, two associational interest groups that are continuously and intimately involved in the Italian political process. This type of involvement is not true of all secondary associations in Italy. As our general survey of Italian interest groups will show, some organized associations express desires concerning public policy only intermittently and, according to my definition, are therefore not always interest groups. I am also aware that, in order to draw a complete picture of the interest group phenomenon in Italy, it would be necessary to research not only *associational* interest groups but also such institutional groups as the armed forces, and anomic groups such as mobs. Not only is such an analysis beyond the intended scope of this work; my broad hypothesis is that the most significant kinds of interest groups in a pluralistic democracy are those that intervene politically in a frequent and highly institutionalized way.

There are some students who are dissatisfied with the use of the concept "interest group" and who prefer instead to use the term "pressure group." I have rejected this usage because it unnecessarily circumscribes the *method* whereby an organized aggregate intervenes in the political process. Pressure usually implies the threat of a sanction, an ability of the interest group to retaliate in some way if the governmental or political unit to which demands are communicated does not respond in the expected way.[28] Pressure understood in this way is certainly included in the arsenal of many interest groups. However, it is only one of many weapons. Under some circumstances it may even be the most important or efficacious weapon that an interest group can utilize, but it certainly is not the only one. The central difficulty in accepting such a formulation is that it limits the field of analysis—so much so that the observer may be led to overlook patterns of interaction between interest groups and government that are, on the whole, much more significant in the determination of the

[28] Sartori, who prefers pressure group, intends to use the concept in this way. See *op. cit.*, p. 23. Cf. S. E. Finer, "Interest Groups and Political Process in Great Britain," in Henry Ehrmann, ed., *Interest Groups in Four Continents* (Pittsburgh, 1958), p. 118, and *Anonymous Empire* (London, 1958), pp. 3–4.

amount of real leverage the groups exercise over public policy. Thus, in this volume, pressure is used not as a generic concept, but only as one of several modes of interest group behavior. Where it seems to be particularly relevant to the Italian political process we will cite and examine it; where it is relegated to a minor position alongside other patterns of interaction, we will want to be aware of that important fact as well.

THE USE OF PROPOSITIONS TO BE TESTED

As I conceive of interest groups and understand the partial role they play in a political system, I think it is useful to formulate middle- or lower-level propositions about groups and to ponder the degree to which the propositions are valid for one or more societies. I would suggest, therefore, that if we can present a roll call of each proposition that can be tested empirically, there is every reason why the propositions that emerge in the United States might be tested in Europe and vice versa. It is precisely because we do not yet know enough about the validity of interest group propositions, because we do not have a general group theory or know if one is viable empirically, that we should insist that some of our notions be tested in political systems other than that of the United States. If we discover, not a priori but as the result of empirical, tightly organized research, that propositions about interest groups in politics do or do not apply to other political systems, we will have won a major skirmish in the campaign to sharpen our capacities and understanding as social scientists. The field of comparative government is likely to make better progress if some effort is devoted to the question that is central to any science, namely, to what degree are hypothetical statements about the nature of political organization and behavior universally applicable.

There is no dearth of interesting propositions that might be examined. Almost everyone who has written on interest groups in recent years has explicitly or implicitly suggested reasonably operational propositions that can and perhaps should be tested in several settings.[29] David Truman's ground-breaking book, notwithstanding that it was written essentially for the United States and that it fails to work out a thoroughly developed or consistent conceptual scheme, abounds with operational propositions and keen insights to guide further study. His excellent chapter on "The Web of Relationships in the Administrative Process"[30] is a mine of clues for anyone who wishes to research the role of interest groups in the public administrative sector. Truman has much to say on the importance of administrative discretion as an inducement to group intervention, on the vital role of administration in the initiation and promotion of legislative policies, on the complex and reciprocal clientele relationship between interest groups and administrative agencies, on the double-edged consequences of formal group representation in administrative agencies, and on the degree to which an administrator's response to interest groups will be conditioned by the role he occupies. Even where insights such as these are not translated into propositions to be tested, they serve a critically important function in alerting the

[29] In addition to works already cited, the reader may fruitfully consult the following: Henry Ehrmann, *Organized Business in France* (Princeton, 1957), "French Bureaucracy and Organized Interests," *Administrative Science Quarterly*, 5 (March, 1961), pp. 534–55, "Les Groupes d'intérêt et la bureaucratie dans les democraties occidentales," *Revue Française de Science Politique*, 11 (September, 1961), pp. 541–68; Harry Eckstein, *Pressure Group Politics: The Case of the British Medical Association* (Stanford, 1960); Joseph LaPalombara, *The Italian Labor Movement: Problems and Prospects* (Ithaca, 1957); Joseph LaPalombara and Gianfranco Poggi, "I Gruppi di pressione e la burocrazia italiana," *Rassegna Italiana di Sociologia*, 1 (October–December, 1960), pp. 31–55; Jean Meynaud, *Les Groupes de pression en France* (Paris, 1958), "Essai d'analyse de l'influence des groupes d'intérêt," *Revue Economique*, 2 (1957), pp. 3–46, "Les Groupes d'intérêt et l'administration en France," *Revue Française de Science Politique*, 7 (July–September, 1957), pp. 573–93, "I Gruppi di interesse in Francia," *Studi Politici*, 4 (July–September, 1957), pp. 404–34; J. D. Stewart, *British Pressure Groups* (Oxford, 1958); and Allen M. Potter, *Organized Groups in British National Politics* (London, 1961).

[30] Truman, *op. cit.*, Ch. 14, pp. 437–78.

researcher to the kinds of data that are important and that must in some reasonably systematic way be analyzed or otherwise accounted for.

Some of the specific propositions that were abstracted from the literature and which serve to set the framework for ensuing chapters of this volume are these: [31]

1. An interest group's influence *vis-à-vis* its competitors will vary with the proportion of the total membership in its specialized area that it is able to organize or mobilize. (Meynaud)

2. Although formal organization is not essential to an interest group, other things being equal, organization is in itself an independent variable affecting the degree of success a group will have in influencing decisions or policies. (Latham, Meynaud)

3. A group's ability to intervene efficaciously in authoritative decision-making varies directly with the nature of the group's access to decisional information and to the centers of decisional authority. (Truman)

4. Bureaucratic agencies differ in the degree to which they are penetrable by organized interest groups. Maximum responsiveness to group demands will come from those agencies that are newer and more functionally specialized. (Meynaud)

5. Other things being equal, decision-makers in the bureaucracy will favor those group representatives or negotiators who evidence life experiences (e.g., social origin, social class, education) similar to those of the decision-makers themselves. (Truman, Meynaud)

[31] The sources from which the propositions are derived are indicated in parentheses following each statement. The studies not previously cited in this chapter, which are also responsible for propositions, are: H. Simon, D. Smithburg, and V. Thompson, *Public Administration* (New York, 1950), esp. pp. 461–65; H. Simon, *Administrative Behavior* (New York, 1947), Ch. 10; Earl Latham, "The Group Basis of Politics: Notes for a Theory," *American Political Science Review*, 46 (June, 1952), pp. 380 ff. My own early formulation of the research prospectus is summarized in Joseph LaPalombara and John T. Dorsey, "On the French and Italian Bureaucracies," *PROD*, 1 (September, 1957), pp. 35–40.

6. Wherever the "public interest" is a strongly held myth or value of the decision-makers, it will act as an important factor limiting the ability of interest groups to make successful particularistic demands. (Ehrmann, Meynaud)

7. Increases in delegated legislation or in welfare state activities will serve to shift the major locus of interest group intervention from the legislative to the administrative branch of government. (Beer)

8. The administrative role, as such, limits the amount of influence that interest groups can exercise because, like all roles, it involves required, permitted, and forbidden behavior. (Simon, Truman)

9. The power over authoritative decisions of any sample of interest groups (on any given series of issues) will vary with a) the political "styles" of the group, b) the nature of group leadership, c) the reference groups of the bureaucrats, and d) the structure and processes of the bureaucracy. (Ehrmann, Truman, Simon)

10. Among the many weapons that interest groups can utilize in attempts to exert pressure on administrative agencies, the most significant, from the standpoint of maximizing responsiveness, is the administrator's perception of the *power* of the group. Power in this sense is understood to mean the ability to affect adversely the bureaucrat's career or professional status. (My own proposition)

Many of these propositions are related to each other. Most of them have to do with interest group relationships to the administrative sector of government, where the field research was primarily concentrated. By intervening in this area, most groups intend to influence not merely the rule-application function but also that of rule-making, insofar as administrative agencies are also involved in that process. The findings concerning these propositions are interspersed throughout later chapters.

It would also be possible to lay out here a complete set of propositions regarding the relationship of interest groups to other formal branches of government, to political parties as a specialized kind of interest group, and to other kinds of interest aggregations with which the groups compete, cooperate, or otherwise interact. Or one could specify some hypotheses about the way in which salient social, economic, or political characteristics of Italian society impinge on group organization and behavior. Although this volume is not primarily a systematic study of either of the above types of problems, they are important enough to be treated, even if somewhat impressionistically and on the basis of incomplete data. Thus in Chapters II, III, and IV an effort is made to define the context of Italian interest group activity and to suggest what gross consequences for the functions of interest groups derive from contextual conditions. This procedure is in keeping with the contention stated above that interest groups cannot meaningfully be studied in isolation, on the Bentleyan assumption that to describe them adequately means to describe everything that is relevant about the political process.

Nor have I attempted to enumerate here the many less significant hunches and what appear to be minor propositions that one takes into the field. For example, it was one of my hunches, resoundingly confirmed, that some Italian interest groups exercise considerable leverage over the bureaucratic agencies with which they interact because of their relatively disproportionate control over technical information. We were therefore vitally interested in pursuing this hunch by accumulating as much interview and other data as possible concerning it. Another hunch, equally confirmed, was that notwithstanding the relative failure of the Italian administration to decentralize decisional power in conformance with the reform law of 1956, a great deal of de facto discretion exists, on the basis of which groups can be rewarded by attempts to intervene at lower levels of the administrative hierarchy. An equally important surmise concerning peak associations is that they are likely to be less effective in the bureaucratic sphere than interest groups whose memberships are more homogeneous and whose goals or purposes are more consistent and narrowly defined.[32] As it turns out, this proposition seems to be true in many cases in Italy, but there are important exceptions, as in the case of Catholic Action where, notwithstanding its peak associational character and the existence of serious internal tensions, the ecclesiastical authorities can, if they wish, establish a monolithic set of interests for the organization. A last hunch that might be mentioned, suggested by the work of Robert Dahl, is that one cannot easily speak of a distinct, cohesive, and relatively stable political elite, but that the nature of the elite tends to shift over time on the basis of such factors as the nature of the issue involved, the types of groups mobilized in connection with an issue, the place in the formal political structure in which the mobilized groups seek to intervene. Again, this speculation is only partly confirmed by our field data, but we seem to know enough to disagree with those who, for any system, rigidly posit the existence of *the* elite in the power structure.

It is hardly necessary to emphasize, in conclusion, that some of the generalizations this volume contains emerged a posteriori from the field investigation itself. The particular structure of Italian interest-group intervention in the bureaucracy, which is spelled out in Chapters VIII and IX, emerged *while* the field interviews were being conducted. One might, perhaps, have guessed or had hunches about the basically different approaches of the Confindustria and of Catholic Action to the agencies of public administration, but the general impressions concerning interest-group behavior in this sector failed to alert me to important variations in behavioral patterns. Similarly, the typology of identification between Italian administrators and interest groups is, perhaps, implicit in some of the

---

[32] My colleague Charles Adrian suggests this as a basic axiom of interest-group analysis. A similar formulation is presented by Henry Ehrmann in "Les Groupes d'intérêt," *op. cit.*, p. 547.

literature but never formulated exactly as I depict it in later pages. Before turning to the wide array of empirical findings and emergent generalizations, however, let us go over the basic contours of the milieu in which the Italian interest-group phenomenon takes place.

CHAPTER II · THE SOCIAL
AND ECONOMIC CONTEXT

WHILE the organization and behavior of voluntary associations—interest groups—is a critically significant aspect of the Italian political system, the context in which the group phenomenon evolves has an important bearing on what the groups do, what belief systems they develop, how they interact with one another, and how they seek to intervene in the formulation and implementation of public policy. This study does not represent an effort systematically to analyze the manner in which characteristics of the context, as independent variables, impinge upon group behavior. Yet it is obvious from the data that Italian interest groups are to some unspecified degree influenced by the salient characteristics of the social, economic, and political systems. These characteristics, the contextual ingredients, set the tone of interest group activity; they help us to understand why the Italian group behavioral configuration is similar to what one finds in, say, a country like France, and is considerably different from what one knows about group behavior in a place like the United States. Later chapters will clearly delineate why what is done by Confindustria and by Italian Catholic Action cannot be adequately understood except with reference to some of the realities of Italian society, as well as to the manner in which these realities are perceived and interpreted by group leaders and representatives.

Three general characteristics of Italian society are worth particular attention. First, Italy is undergoing rapid economic and social change. Second, notwithstanding the marked economic improvement in recent years, Italian society remains a startling example of extreme class conflict and ideological fragmentation. Third, both growing economic stability and the persistence of extreme ideological differences are reflected in the voting behavior and political institutions of the country. The first two of these are treated in this chapter; the last in Chapter III.

ECONOMIC CHANGE

There are numerous ways of depicting the tempo and magnitude of economic growth. Historically, from the birth of the Italian nation until the advent of Fascism, Italy's economic development moved along quite gradually, roughly duplicating the evolution of other Western European countries, even if at a somewhat less pronounced rate, particularly in the area of industrialization. Economically (and culturally) the nation was predominantly agricultural. Industrial development, significantly stepped up during the years of World War I, was largely concentrated in the Industrial Triangle formed by Milan, Turin, and Genoa. Uneven industrial development served to intensify the many differences that continue to create tensions between the North and the South.

Contrary to the proud claims of the Fascists and their apologists, the period from 1922 to 1945 was marked by economic stagnation and regression and culminated in destruction of an unprecedented magnitude as a result of Allied strategic bombing and invasion, occupation by the Germans, and a civil war that was bitterly fought between die-hard Fascists and members of the Italian Resistance.[1] Under Mussolini's regime, total agricultural production barely moved ahead and actually declined in the South; industrial production at the time of Italy's entrance into World War II was essentially what it had been two decades earlier. To be sure, one cause of this stagnation was the economic depression that engulfed all of Europe in the 1930's. Yet, it is apparent that Fascist economic and political policies themselves did little or nothing to move the country forward. Indeed, the disastrous consequences of agricultural policies in the depressed South and of au-

[1] On the history of the anti-Fascist resistance, see the first-rate work of Charles F. Delzell, *Mussolini's Enemies* (Princeton, 1961).

28

tarchic industrial development are too well known to require a detailed analysis here.[2]

Nor is this the place to recount the minute particulars of the economic devastation suffered by Italy in World War II. Suffice it to say that by 1945 the economy was moribund. National wealth had fallen to one-third of its prewar level; 60 percent of the available highways and over eight thousand bridges were damaged or destroyed; 90 percent of port facilities were rendered unusable, as were 40 percent of the railroads; a once proud merchant fleet was reduced by 90 percent. Both agricultural and industrial production had fallen to perilous lows. Only emergency assistance in the immediate postwar months managed to keep the country from going under completely and irrevocably.[3]

Italy's early recovery from these conditions was dramatic in the extreme. From 1945 to 1949, in many productive sectors, the country managed to return to the most favorable prewar levels. In the era of good will (1946–1947), while Communists and Socialists were still in the government and the nation acted in concert in the confrontation of its problems, truly extraordinary strides were made in the reconstruction of roads, railroads, and transport, in the mending and replacement of industrial complexes, in the provision of new sources of power, in the desperate business of setting both the industrial and agricultural productive sectors back into motion.

The year 1948 saw the beginning of massive American economic intervention, without which meaningful recovery could not have proceeded beyond the levels reached in

[2] See Daniel Guérin's classic *Fascism and Big Business* (New York, 1939), translated into Italian as *Fascismo e grande capitale* (Milan, 1956). For a sympathetic view by an insider, see Felice Guarneri, *Battaglie economiche* (2 vols. Milan, 1953).

[3] The data on the economic cost of World War II are contained in Istituto Centrale di Statistica (hereafter referred to as ISTAT), *Annuario Statistico Italiano, 1952* (Rome, 1953), Part IV. The reader should also consult Centro di Documentazione della Presidenza del Consiglio dei Ministri, "La Rinascita dell'Italia, 1945–1952," *Documenti di vita italiana,* 3 (January–February, 1953).

the first years following the war. It was apparent that further economic progress would be necessary if Italy, like other Western European countries, was to avoid the fate of Czechoslovakia. With the extreme Left out of the government and uncompromisingly opposed to the Marshall Plan, economic strides forward would have to be made under the difficult circumstances of a politically divided country on the brink of revolution. Many frankly doubted that violent revolution could be averted. Unemployment was rampant, particularly in the dislocated South but in all of the urban centers of the North as well; migratory escape valves for a rapidly growing population had been cut off by Fascist policies and the war; abject poverty characterized both the cities and the countryside; organized labor was largely concentrated in Communist-dominated labor unions; and over one-third of the population supported the extreme Left at the polls in the elections of 1946 and 1948.[4] It is generally conceded that only the extraordinary effort of organized Catholicism in 1948—the successful creation of a "Christ or Communism" alternative for the voter—prevented the extreme Left from coming legally to power in the elections of that year. It was widely understood that the reborn democracy was on very unsure footing and that only some rapid and dramatic changes in the social and economic sectors would provide the minimum conditions of survival.

Economic developments since 1948 are usually described as a miracle of reconstruction. Certainly, from many vantage points, startling and unexpected advances are demonstrable. The general index of industrial production shows an increase in excess of 100 percent since 1953. Production in areas such as fuels and combustibles, hydrocarbons, chemicals, transportation, synthetic fibers, and plastics has increased as much as three or four times.[5] Although gains

[4] See Joseph LaPalombara, "Left-Wing Trade Unionism: The Matrix of Communist Power in Italy," *Western Political Quarterly*, 7 (June, 1954), pp. 202–26.

[5] See ISTAT, *Compendio statistico italiano, 1963* (Rome, 1963), p. 165.

in the general index of agricultural production are not nearly as impressive, important developments are noteworthy in the mechanization of agriculture, especially in regions of the North.[6] Of equal interest has been the recent growth of the important tourist industry, which manages to keep Italy's balance of payments in a favorable or near-favorable position.

Rapid economic change is also reflected in national income statistics. In terms of constant lira values, annual national income rose from 47 to 146 billion lire between 1861 and 1939. Between 1945 and the present, however, national income, drastically reduced by the war, rose from 71 to 270 billions. During the last fifteen years, per-capita income registered a level of increase more than double that of the period between 1861 and 1938. Changes which in many other countries required several decades of evolution have taken place in Italy in just a few years. These changes, while reducing the threat of violent revolution, brought in their wake the kinds of social transformations and problems that now have a greater impact on Italian society than did previous centuries of gradual development.[7]

The growth of national income reflects primarily industrialization. Whereas, in 1861, agriculture contributed 57.8 percent of national income, today that figure has fallen to 21.3 percent.[8] A basically agricultural and strongly traditional society is now experiencing a rate of industrialization and urbanization that is reflected in all sorts of social disequilibrium. Extreme dislocation is most characteristic

[6] See *ibid.*, p. 130. Cf. ISTAT, *Annuario, 1959* (Rome, 1960), pp. 154–169.

[7] For a documentation of these economic changes, consult the issues of ISTAT, *Annuario,* for the years since World War II. See also Roberto Tremelloni, *Storia recente dell'industria italiana* (Milan, 1956). It should be noted, however, that the gains in per-capita income were most unevenly distributed geographically, the North benefiting more than the depressed South. See Comitato dei Ministri per il Mezzogiorno, *Relazione al parlamento* (Rome, 1960), p. 261.

[8] It should be noted, however, that over 40 percent of Italy's labor force remains occupied in agriculture. Large sections of the country, particularly in the South, are still essentially agricultural in character.

of the South where thousands of peasants, weary of the stagnation of hidden unemployment and underemployment on the land, are leaving for urban centers elsewhere in the South and in the North. For the metropolitan areas to which they migrate, these peasants—"terroni," as they are called in the North—create unprecedented economic and social problems. Efforts at land reform of the South, designed in part to alleviate bad economic conditions and to keep the peasants productively occupied on the land, have had mixed results thus far. Thus, while it is certainly reasonable to point to many indicators of economic progress—to more jobs, more industry, agricultural mechanization, production indexes, more automobiles and television sets, important changes in habits of consumption—one should not leap to the conclusion that, as a result of changes registered, Italian society is more integrated, the Italian political system more stable, and the future of Italian democracy more secure. To some degree all such observations are valid. But it must be underscored that many of the old problems persist and that economic change, in itself, has carried along with it some new problems and dilemmas that were unanticipated a few years ago.

UNEMPLOYMENT AND DEMOGRAPHIC IMBALANCE

Until very recently, Italy's most nagging economic problem was that of unemployment. Official figures for January, 1959, placed the labor force at 20,523,000 persons, or approximately 40 percent of the population. Of these, 1,150,000 were classified as unemployed and another 433,000 persons cited as in search of first employment. These latter were presumably young people entering the labor market for the first time or housewives compelled by economic pressures to augment family income.[9] As of May 10, 1963, the official unemployment figure had fallen to 227,000 and those in search of first employment had

9 See ISTAT, *Annuario, 1959*, pp. 312–16.

been reduced to 199,000.[10] Quite obviously, the marked tempo of economic growth over the last three years had greatly alleviated the unemployment problem, so much so, in fact, that Italian economists could actually begin talking about full employment within a few years.

These figures, however, depict the most favorable possible picture. They fail to convey, for example, the wretched economic conditions that beset many of the Southern Italians who have ventured to northern cities to find employment but whose actual living conditions do not provide as much security as they may have known in the economically depressed South. Nor do these statistics tell us very much about the extent to which agricultural sectors continue to harbor serious underemployment and hidden unemployment. In order to understand the full scope of this problem it would be necessary to ask how it is that Italian agriculture, with approximately one-third of the labor force accounts for less than one-fifth of the officially unemployed. One would also wish to know whether Southern Italian peasants, who work less than 200 days per year, are considered employed. The point is that, as far as the South is concerned, the country, even in the years of its most striking economic growth, had a partial unemployment problem of depression proportions. All of the recent frenzied talk concerning the need for economic planning aimed at removing the continuing and widening economic disequilibrium between North and South is dramatic evidence of this persistent problem.

It is perhaps superfluous to point out that serious economic distress contributes to political extremism and instability. Survey research data clearly indicate that support for the Italian Communist party is often strongly provided by those who are in the most disadvantaged economic conditions. Moreover, analyses of voting patterns in such industrial cities as Bologna, Turin, Genoa

10 See ISTAT, *Rilevazione nazionale delle forze di lavoro (10 maggio 1963)—Supplemento all'annuario di statistiche del lavoro e dell'emigrazione* (Rome, 1963), p. 22.

and Milan show unmistakably that the Communist party is the major beneficiary at the polls of the wretched conditions in which Southern migrants find themselves there. We are thus confronted with the grim prospect of having the Communist vote increase roughly in proportion to the significant movement from rural to urban areas which is now in full swing. Unfortunately, this problem cannot be met simply by the marked and increasing ability of the Italian economy to provide new jobs. Several million new jobs have been created in the last ten years, and yet there remain large sectors of the society in which existence remains marginal.

Moreover, the situation can quickly become desperate again if the rate of economic growth should diminish. For Italy, despite one of the lowest birth rates in Europe, continues to register a net annual gain in population that exceeds 400,000 persons. This is the combined result of continued heavy birth rates in the South and of greatly improved medical care that has reduced mortality during the first year of life and added significantly to average life expectancies.[11]

Where emigration was once a critical means of lowering Italy's population pressure, it has diminished considerably in importance since World War II. To be sure, approximately 350,000 persons have emigrated each year in recent years. On the other hand, roughly 200,000 emigrants return each year, so that the net average annual emigration does not exceed 150,000 by very much.[12] This means that the Italian economy is called upon to absorb net yearly population increases of essentially 250,000 persons. During the most recent economic upswing, the economy

[11] See ISTAT, *Annuario, 1959,* pp. 30–53. See also Robert E. Dickinson, *The Population Problem of Southern Italy* (Syracuse, 1955).

[12] For recent data see ISTAT, *Annuario statistico italiano, 1962* (Rome, 1963), p. 55; ISTAT, *Compendio statistico italiano, 1963,* p. 58. Note that in 1913 alone 872,598 Italians emigrated and only 188,968 repatriated themselves. See ISTAT, *Annuario, 1952* (Rome, 1953), pp. 432–33. These tables contain complete statistical summaries of emigrations and repatriations by major country from 1901 to 1951.

has done much better than this; during the greater portion of the postwar years, however, it has barely held its own against this demographic pressure. In the future, either greater economic expansion, or sharper drops in the birth rate, or greater effective emigration (or all of these working together) might remove the pressure of employment and underemployment.

However, it is necessary to be cautious about emigration as a modern escape valve. For obvious political reasons, Italy cannot permit its citizens to migrate to places where the interests of Italians are not adequately protected. This involves not only Latin American countries, but also some of the countries of the Common Market. For another thing, it is certainly debatable whether a country gains very much by sending abroad young workers in whose education and training the country has made a considerable investment. One can go all the way back to Adam Smith for support for the idea that the export of young people involves adverse economic consequences for the country of origin.[13] Indeed, the current truth is that Italy desperately needs trained manpower and that it is for the illiterate, semi-literate and technically untrained that the economy is currently not able to provide very well. These are precisely those Italians who are not good candidates for emigration abroad; host countries, too, are in search of skilled manpower. It is equally apparent that not all Italians favor the mass migration of Southerners to the North, and essentially for the reasons adduced by Adam Smith. The point is that the rapid depletion of the South's skilled manpower creates a great danger that that part of the country will fall even farther behind the North in social and economic terms.[14]

Thus, while on the one hand it is possible to speak of an extraordinary economic "miracle" of recent years, it is

13 *The Wealth of Nations* (London, 1950), I, pp. 27-32, 294-98.
14 For an exhaustive treatment of this and other problems concerning the South, see the special issue of *Il Veltro* devoted to southern problems, Vol. VI, December, 1962.

necessary, on the other hand, to recognize that Italy is still a long way from solving some of the economic problems that make for political instability in the country.

DUAL CULTURE AND ECONOMY

Other age-old problems should be cited in depicting the context of interest group behavior. There exists, for example, continued socio-economic differentiation between North and South. Northern Italy differs from the South on almost every significant variable. Culturally, the North is European, the South is Mediterranean; the North was exposed directly to the forces of eighteenth- and nine-teenth-century European thought; these ideas permeated to the South much later and most imperfectly. Large sections of the North, as we have noted, are industrialized. This fact accounts for the concentration of national wealth in the Industrial Triangle. It is also responsible for conveying to the northern rural countryside a value system that one associates with a modern, urbanized society. Politically and administratively the North was strongly influenced by the values of the French and Austrians who occupied or otherwise ruled the northern states well into the nineteenth century. The South, on the other hand, acquired the less dynamic ways of the Spanish Bourbons, who contributed little to economic development and who encouraged the rigid preservation of class and caste that is apparent to this day.

By comparison with the North, the South is desperately poor.[15] Industry provides only a small fraction of the region's net product. On the one hand, highly fragmented farm lands are cultivated by poverty-ridden small proprietors, the *coltivatori diretti;* on the other hand, larger and often neglected holdings are still worked by agricultural day laborers, the *braccianti,* whose desperate economic plight would rival that of peasants in some of the least

---

[15] There are, of course, agricultural regions of the North where life is as mean and primitive as in the South. The phenomenon is not as pervasive, however.

36

developed countries of Asia. Carlo Levi, in his classic *Christ Stopped at Eboli,* movingly portrayed life in a typical southern rural area. Except in those places where public programs of land reform have brought some changes, the situation is not substantially different today. The meaner conditions of the South are reflected in higher death (and birth) rates, fewer schools, inferior teachers, bad roads, inadequate public services, primitive housing, rampant truancy, and the wholesale failure adequately to enforce and administer social welfare legislation aimed at relieving the poor of a considerable burden.

The discrepancies in the goods and services—the amenities—available to the Southerner compared to his northern countryman touch every facet of human existence. Whether one thinks of diet or recreation, public transportation or agricultural tools, indoor plumbing or medical care, the per-capita availability of these things is always heavier to the north of Rome than in the southern provinces. Only with regard to impressive public buildings and monuments do the cities of the South manage to hold their own against their northern counterparts. The notion, expressed in travel posters and motion pictures, that the southern Italian sings happy ballads in the face of misery and backwardness is as misleading in its distortion as the idea that Mussolini's Fascists got the trains to run on time. The bedeviled southern peasant is much more likely to develop a serious case of anomie or, in his desperation, invade untended and untilled land. If he is still young and vigorous, he may migrate North, creating other problems that I shall touch upon below.

The fact is that Italy represents two distinct cultures, the relatively dynamic and industrial North and the relatively stagnant and traditional South. The South, still deeply tied to tradition, moves slowly and painfully toward economic development. The whole of southern society—economy, politics, religious practices, belief systems, and associational activities—is typical of what one will find in any of the less-developed societies currently undergoing change. Primary associations are still dominant; family, kinship, neighborhood, village are still the associational forms that have the first and greatest call on individual loyalties.[16] As we shall see in a later chapter, secondary associations that are economically or politically based, such as interest groups, have failed to attract Southerners except in the rarest cases.

North and South are hostile toward each other. The Northerner is prone to consider his countrymen to the South indolent and shiftless, crafty (*furbo* is the Italian expression) in commercial dealings but not reliable as business executives or industrial managers. Corruption and inefficiency in government and administration are often explained in terms of the Southerners who dominate public administrative agencies and the Southern notables, supported by captive and illiterate clienteles, who maneuver in the halls of parliament. While, as in all stereotypes, there are considerable elements of truth in these observations, the Northerner is prone to overlook the fact that the administrative system was an extension of Piedmont *cum* Napoleon and that political *trasformismo*, that bane of Italian legislative practice, was perfected by that eminent northern statesman Giovanni Giolitti.

In any event, antipathy is fully reciprocated by the Southerner. With some justification he can claim that, until recently, the problem of southern economic development was largely ignored by a succession of northern-dominated governments.[17] To be sure, this neglect was strongly abetted by gentlemen southern deputies who had no real interest in social and economic change and who were the willing tools of northern politicians who viewed

[16] I am aware that this statement is not in keeping with the major finding of Edward Banfield's *The Moral Basis of a Backward Society* (Glencoe, 1958). I can only suggest that his village is not, to my knowledge, typical of large sections of Southern Italy with which I am acquainted.

[17] The literature on "the Southern Question" is as vast as has been the neglect of the region. The reader can fruitfully consult Bruno Caizzi, *Antologia della questione meridionale* (2nd ed. Milan, 1955). For a more recent treatment, see the special issue of *Il Veltro* cited in note 14, *supra*, p. 35.

the South as a place to exploit rather than to develop. Nevertheless, considerable reason is on the side of those many southern students who have alleged that the industrial development of the North took place at the South's expense, that the economic imbalance has involved a continuous flow of southern capital to the northern cities, and that generations of governors and entrepreneurs did little or nothing to redress the balance.

What is of interest to us here is both the North-South syndrome of distrust and hostility and the fact that the Italian peninsula is genuinely split across the middle culturally. Generalizations about interest group organization and behavior are not easy in such a context. What the group does, what it means to its membership, how it intervenes in local politics and administration, and how effective it can be as an independent source of power will vary enormously from group to group, depending on the part of the Italian peninsula in which the interest group is present. This caveat should be borne in mind when, in later chapters, we examine Confindustria, Italian Catholic Action, and other interest groups.

SOCIAL STRATIFICATION

A fairly rigid system of social stratification and a very high degree of class conflict is also characteristic of Italian society. As one would expect, recent economic development has to some degree made the social system more fluid. Yet class rigidities tend to be modified slowly, particularly when they reflect a situation that has evolved over several centuries. To be sure, the North manifests greater social mobility than the South. In that region, the forces of industrialization and urbanization, the greater incidence of literacy, the progressive improvement of the economic lot of workers in cities like Turin and Milan, the superior conditions of agriculture, and the higher incidence of physical mobility have served to create some opportunities of social mobility. In contrast to the South, a strong middle class does exist, consisting of highly skilled workers, independent artisans, small businessmen and shopkeepers, clerical workers engaged in service occupations, and intermediate bureaucratic personnel. This group is still relatively small, but growing. In addition, however, there are the tens of thousands of semiskilled or unskilled workers, poorly paid clerks and public employees, peasant sharecroppers, the agricultural day laborers of the Po Valley, the desperately poor peasants who occupy the hilly and mountainous regions, and the unemployed.

At the top of the North's social hierarchy are found the upper-level bureaucrats, members of the liberal professions, owners and operators of large-scale agricultural enterprises, and industrial owners and managers. The last, with few exceptions, have not evolved into the "enlightened" type prominent today in the United States. In many cases they manifest the same attitudes toward labor that are characteristic of the southern landlord. In popular Italian parlance, both are referred to as *padrone,* and the social distance of the rural, semifeudal South can be quickly and readily transferred to the industrial plant. In many instances management's attitude toward labor is at best condescending; the factory is viewed as personal, inviolable property; trade unionists are considered social upstarts and dangerous revolutionaries; and a rigid discipline over workers is upheld as the sanest and most efficacious means of conducting industrial enterprise. Even where the trade unions have succeeded in compelling industrial management to make concessions, the latter often view these changes as paternalistic largesse rather than a *quid pro quo* resulting from negotiations among bargaining equals. In most of their behavior, the industrial managers evince the same commitment to the idea of irreconcilable class conflict that one finds among workers led by Communist- and Socialist-dominated trade unions.

As one of Italy's most perceptive sociologists puts it, rigid class differences in industrial management grow in part out of the extreme fragmentation of Italian industry. Excepting the giant industries such as Fiat, Pirelli, Montecatini, Edison, Italcementi, and a few others, Italy's industrial workers are largely concentrated in small, family-managed enterprises. The 1951 census revealed that Italy's 4,300,000 industrial workers were employed by 680,000 firms! Of these industrial enterprises, 490,147 employed fewer than three workers each, 121,547 employed under eleven, and 33,617 employed under one hundred. Only 2,000 firms employed more than five hundred workers; a mere 312 employed over one thousand. Of the nearly 700,000 firms, only 11,700 were classified as joint stock companies or cooperatives. The remaining 89 percent were listed as the property of a single proprietor.[18]

Thus, while Italian industry is clearly dominated by a handful of industrial giants, most of the industrial workers are exposed to the kind of labor-management relations that are tailor-made for the Marxist propagandists. Ferrarotti points to three types of paternalistic management. The first is the *authoritarian* variety, wherein a single family owns and manages the enterprise and is therefore the sole source of power in the firm. The family demands absolute loyalty from the workers, the same kind of relationship that one would encounter between landowner and sharecropper. Efforts by the workers to organize or to insist that social welfare legislation be applied in the firm are considered acts of personal betrayal of and disloyalty to the family. The worker is expected to know his place and to maintain the social distance between himself and the *padrone*. The system of social stratification is more important to the latter than greater productivity or higher profits. About this tendency, Ferrarotti remarks: "In order not to lose absolute control over all of the essential operations of the enterprise, one prefers to sacrifice possible increases in the productive cycle and in the volume of

[18] Franco Ferrarotti, "L'Evoluzione dei rapporti fra direzioni aziendali e rappresentanti operai nell'Italia del dopoguerra," in Atti del IV Convegno Mondiale di Sociologia, *Aspetti e problemi sociali dello sviluppo economico in Italia* (Bari, 1959), pp. 137–38.

business, not to proceed to new activities. The key value, in this first type of relationship, is obedience or pure subordination." [19]

Ferrarotti cites *manipulative paternalism* and *democratic paternalism* as additional types, but their evolution requires the breakdown of single-family ownership and management.[20] It is reasonably clear that most of Italy's industrial workers, concentrated north of Rome, continue to be exposed to work situations that reflect the class structure and conditions of a pre-industrial society, and of authoritarian family enterprises. In this kind of situation both the managers and the workers have a strong belief in, and a commitment to, class war and differentiation.

The class configuration of the South is even more rigid. Nowhere else in Western Europe except, perhaps, in Spain and Portugal are the extremes of wealth and poverty as distant and pronounced as in the provinces south of Rome. The feudal social structure pervades the entire region, in striking contrast to the more socially heterogeneous industrial North. In this kind of rigidly structured, traditional society, everyone knows his place and is expected to reinforce the hierarchical system. The social distance in the South between workers or peasant, on the one hand, and the salaried clerk or small shopkeeper, on the other, is greater than anything comparable in most Western countries. Between worker, peasant, clerk or shopkeeper, and the southern nobility or landowners, the gap would have to be calculated in social light years. Class differences are clearly identified in the way people dress, the way they speak, the manner in which they address each other, the kind of food they eat, and the recreation they enjoy—through the entire roll call of social behavior. Titles may have been formally abolished under the Republic, but the entire array of them, from *commendatore* to *eccellenza* is still in widespread use. Those who are entitled to the appellation "don" (and many who are not) insist that it

[19] *Ibid.*, p. 142.
[20] *Ibid.*, pp. 142–44.

be used; established artisans still expect to be addressed as "maestro." Peasants remove their hats before gentlemen, and they stand in conversation while the latter sit. The system of deferential behavior, established over centuries, remains strong in the countryside and displays an amazing power of survival in such urban centers as Naples and Palermo.

It must be stressed that the class structure of the South provides considerable security and integration and is for this reason widely accepted by many of the southerners. For this reason, the class-conflict notions advanced by political parties and voluntary associations of the extreme Left have met with considerably less favorable reception in the South than in the North. It is obvious, of course, that these ideas are slowly spreading, and that they attract a considerable following in urban areas, where the transition from traditional to legal-rational institutions is most pronounced. It is also true that, from time immemorial, the southern peasant has occasionally engaged in violent behavior against landowners and the nobility. However, such behavior should not be confused with the highly class-conscious and class-oriented violence that has sometimes occurred in the industrial sectors of the North. It is true that in the postwar years the southern peasant and worker has had considerable exposure to left-wing ideology. But the transitional nature of the situation is dramatically depicted by the fact that when so-called "red" peasants have forcibly occupied land in the South, they have been known to carry red flags and pictures of Marx side by side with pictures of Garibaldi and paintings of Christ and the Virgin Mary. The dominance of a traditional culture still serves to make it difficult for secondary structures, such as interest groups, to evolve. In any case, as I have said before, voluntary associations in the South do not necessarily have the same meaning, or perform the same functions, as they do in the North.

Unlike the North, the South does not have a well-developed middle class. This is owing in part to seriously retarded industrialization, in part to the system of agriculture that, unlike the central and northern regions, does not include much sharecropping (*mezzadria*). Thus there exists a very small upper class consisting of the nobility, large landowners, a few industrialists, the political "notables," and the upper-echelon bureaucrats. Below them exists a small middle group of shopkeepers, middle-level bureaucrats, teachers, and a few highly skilled artisans and workers. These are followed, at the bottom of the pyramid, by the legions of clerks, government workers, unskilled labor, small proprietors, agricultural day laborers, and the unemployed. In some places, like Naples, Bari, Palermo, and Catania, where new industrial activity has grown markedly in recent years, the elements of a new middle class are visible but still essentially embryonic. Even under the very best of circumstances, it will be several decades before the social structure of the South is reasonably similar to that in the North.

Our brief depiction of the social system would be incomplete if something were not said about the distribution of wealth and the place of the Catholic Church in Italy. An overwhelming proportion of Italy's wealth belongs, as one writer put it, to the approximately 30,000 individuals who are large landowners and stockholders in the 1,500 joint stock companies that control most of Italy's industrial output.[21] These are the people who have succeeded in having the nation retain a basically regressive tax structure, who have ignored the education of the peasantry, who have fought land reform every inch of the way, and who greatly fear any political "opening to the Left." This is the group that strongly opposes trade unions, is suspicious of free speech, manages to harness the so-called independent press to its own interests, and supports the most conservative groups and political movements in the country. In earlier years, members of this group, or their forebears, supported Mussolini's rise to power. In recent

[21] Massimo Salvadori, *Italy* (New York, 1951), p. 14.

years many have helped to finance and to further the Monarchist and neo-Fascist movements. In their ability to concentrate the nation's wealth and to buttress economic and political conservatism, they help to perpetuate social conditions that result in considerable inter-class rivalry and conflict. The fact that some of them are liberally inclined, and actually favor a political shift to the Left, does not remove the basically reactionary impact that the group as a whole has had on Italian society.

Catholicism, as we shall later see in detail, is also essentially a conservative social force, as well as an important divisive element in the social system. While it is reasonably accurate to say, as do representatives of the church, that Italy is an overwhelmingly Catholic country, such a statement obscures the virulent anticlericalism that one detects throughout the peninsula. The conflict between organized Catholicism, on the one hand, and anticlerical and laical groups, on the other, permeates all aspects of society. It is manifested in differences over education, economic organization, civil rights, administrative organization, the development of the visual arts, the evolution of industrial and agricultural worker organizations. Thus, cutting across all other kinds of social conflict and tensions in the society is the fundamental difference of opinion regarding the role that organized Catholicism should play in spheres other than the strictly religious. This conflict, too, is a centrally vital aspect of the milieu of voluntary associations.

URBANIZATION AND ITS CONSEQUENCES

In addition to these economic and social problems of long-standing significance, we must also recognize that the rapid transformations have created newer problems with which Italian society has had limited experience. We will touch here only on three of the most important and closely linked of these: urbanization, the industrialization and transformation of the South, and education.

Urbanization has been a greatly accelerated process since World War II. The migration to the cities from the countryside is everywhere apparent, although the cities of the industrial North have been particularly affected by it. Over the last two decades, cities of over 100,000 inhabitants registered population increases in excess of 30 percent, while the general increase in population was only half that much. The phenomenon of urbanization is even more marked if one considers not so much official administrative units, such as municipalities, but the broader metropolitan areas of which the cities form the central core.[22] Migration from the countryside has been such in the major cities of Italian provinces that increases in population there have been twenty-nine times greater than in the lesser municipalities of the country. The problems of providing jobs, housing, roads, and other services for these new arrivals are enormous. They severely tax the capacities of the places to which the Italian peasants migrate.

There are several important aspects of the phenomenon of urbanization that must be noted. First, there has been an enormous movement of southerners to cities of the North such as Turin and Milan. Many of these migrants are ill-educated and hardly able immediately to be absorbed into increasingly complex industrial communities. They are also dirt poor and extremely insecure outside of their native southern villages. As a result, they tend to congregate in peripheral slums, where squalor is omnipresent and city services nonexistent. Languishing there, severely disappointed by the absence of immediate good fortune at the end of the migratory rainbow, relatively unsophisticated about matters of political ideology, they fall prey to the promises and solicitations of extreme political parties and groups. This tendency is true not merely

---

[22] See Manlio Rossi Doria, "Aspetti sociali dello sviluppo economico in Italia," in Atti del IV Congresso Mondiale di Sociologia, *op. cit.*, pp. 9–35. Note particularly the table on page 25.

for the southern migrants but also for northern peasants who leave the land and the hills for the central city.[23]

Residents of the northern cities toward which most of the migration from the South has been directed are anything but pleased by the influx of new neighbors. Newspapers have protested these arrivals. The host city citizens resent the intrusion, are fearful of competition for jobs, look with alarm on increased costs of social welfare, and are anything but disposed to take the communal action which is necessary to alleviate the often terrible conditions into which the migrants fall. There is great concern with aggravated problems of public health, crime, education, and unemployment; and acts of extreme hostility and discrimination against the hapless peasants are not uncommon.[24]

Because this problem is relatively so recent in Italy, serious research efforts concerning it date only since 1958. Yet the need to know more about the process, about its social, economic, and political implications, is certainly very great. Even less is known about the consequences of this vast migration for the areas from which the migrants depart. There are some, of course, who view any encouragement of migration from South to North as an insidious means of circumventing the problem of southern economic development.[25] Certain it is that more than merely surplus farm labor is leaving the countryside of many

[23] See the important and perceptive study of Achille Ardigò, "Il Volto elettorale di Bologna," in Alberto Spreafico and Joseph LaPalombara, eds., *Elezioni e comportamento politico in Italia* (Milan, 1963), pp. 801–49.

[24] For an eloquent depiction of some of these problems by one of Italy's most avid students of the problem, see Francesco Compagna, *I Terroni in città* (Bari, 1959). See also Goffredo Fofi, "Meridionali e settentrionali attraverso lo 'specchio dei tempi'," *Nord e Sud*, 8 (June, 1961), pp. 81–105. The motion picture "Rocco and His Brothers" also depicts some aspects of this flight from southern agricultural lands. As one might expect, migrants from specific regions of the South tend to congregate in the same northern cities—those from Foggia and Bari at Milan, those from Puglia at Turin, etc.

[25] See Giuseppe Galasso, "Le Aree povere del Mezzogiorno e la ripresa dei movimenti migratori," in Atti del IV Congresso Mondiale di Sociologia, *op. cit.*, pp. 71–101.

southern provinces. Many of those who move North would be able to make a strong contribution to the economic development of the South. At the very least, as Francesco Compagna points out, it is necessary to investigate the consequences and to effect whatever beneficial changes in patterns of land-holding and cultivation that might be facilitated by the large-scale sale of small pieces of land by departing peasants.[26]

Second, the urbanization of the South should not be confused with industrialization. What has developed there —and it is a movement that has been in progress for many decades—is the "peasant city," about which Francesco Compagna comments: "As is known, the characteristic of 'peasant cities' is that of hosting, like a true 'dormitory,' a high percentage of agricultural population, always greater, and sometimes much greater, than 50 percent of the active population."[27]

These "dormitories" are literally that; peasants sleep there and leave each morning to work the several small pieces of land that they either own or rent. Sometimes they travel great distances on foot, or by donkey, or bicycle if they are relatively affluent, to reach the lands they till. The peasant cities are also labor and produce markets. Peasants or landowners recruit day laborers there, land contracts are negotiated, land is exchanged. There also exists a high degree of social differentiation between the peasants and the "permanent" residents, consisting of shopkeepers, bureaucrats, artisans, merchants, tradesmen, and sometimes small-scale entrepreneurs.[28]

The increased migration to the central cities, then, is not the result of industrialization and economic expansion but the extension of a social pattern that is strongly grounded in southern culture. Those who have moved into the cities in recent years do so because of historical

[26] Francesco Compagna, "Dopo i primi anni di esodo rurale," *Nord e Sud*, 8 (October, 1961), pp. 6–10.

[27] *Ibid.*, p. 12.

[28] See Riccardo Musatti, *La via del Sud* (2nd ed. Milan, 1958).

precedent, and because greater numbers of peasants are now in search of more complex administrative, economic, and civic services. Such congregations become parasitic, living off the land and serving to delay rather than to spur economic modernization. It is for this reason that some students of the South strongly favor the development of smaller service centers that might lead to some deconcentration of urban population.

Such hopes seem futile, however; trends now fully in progress will be difficult to reverse. The problem is that of coping, in the short run, with the conditions of expanded urban populations and, in the long run, of providing the kind of industrial development that would change the basic character of the cities themselves. Not much industrialization is underway. It is significant that Italy's major postwar industrial expansion has occurred in those zones that were already industrialized, thus perpetuating and aggravating the economic imbalance that characterizes the country.

In any event, programs of agricultural reform, some industrialization around cities like Bari, Catania, Naples, and Palermo, and the large-scale movement from countryside to city have served to create greater social mobility than previously existed. New sources of income have been created, the communications revolution has helped to generate new canons of taste and patterns of consumption. Urbanization itself, whatever its causes, tends to change associative patterns from the traditional and affective to the secondary and voluntary forms that are typical of industrial societies. The South in this sense is clearly in ferment, undergoing fairly rapid transformation. The family is not as important in many places as it once was. Nor are kinship groups, the Church, or townsmen. Secondary structures take on a new importance in both the work and leisure-time situations. It is reasonable to suppose that the basic trend is irreversible and that the South will constitute a fertile field that competing interest groups can in the future cultivate.

EDUCATION

Finally, something must be said about education. The economic and social transformations evolving in Italy require major changes in the educational system. For example, there must be greater emphasis in the lower grades and middle schools on vocational training. The school system, particularly in the underdeveloped South, must produce the skills that are needed by an industrializing society. Equally important would be a modification of university curricula, away from the classics, humanities, and the liberal professions, and toward the kinds of training that a modern industrial society would demand of its university graduates. There are pressures for reform manifested in Italy, but the school system, particularly the university system, shows amazing capacities to resist change.[29]

Despite the considerable progress that has been made since the war in the construction of classrooms, the training of more teachers, and the development of vocational schools,[30] the general situation leaves much to be desired. Illiteracy, for example, remains a major problem in the South, and throughout the country it is a major factor influencing the social and economic conditions of the chronically unemployed.[31] Equally significant is the fact that educational opportunity—a critical determinant factor in social mobility—is not equally distributed. Just a few years ago, for example, a government pilot study revealed that as many as ten percent of school-age children, from six to eight years old, were not in school in several southern provinces. Theoretically, all children between the ages of five and fourteen should be found in school because this is required by law. But in many areas, par-

[29] See Giuseppe Galasso, "Qualificazione e istruzione professionale: introduzione ad una inchiesta," *Nord e Sud*, 8 (February, 1961), pp. 46–47. Cf. Giuseppe De Rita, "Evoluzione e prospettive dell'attività scolastica in Italia," in *Atti del IV Congresso Mondiale di Sociologia, op. cit.*, pp. 245–60.

[30] See the summary table produced by De Rita, *op. cit.*, p. 248.

[31] Domenico Tarantini, "L'Analfabetismo in Italia," *Nord e Sud*, 6 (February, 1959), pp. 55–89.

ticularly in the South, the law is an expression of a pious hope rather than an index of realized public policy. To be sure, the present situation is better than it was in the early postwar years, when only slightly over half of the youngsters who should have been entering elementary schools in the South actually did so. In those years, only 25 per 100 youngsters in the appropriate age bracket entered the lower middle schools and as few as 12 per 100 entered the high schools. Another way of putting this is simply to point out that only 5 percent of Italy's southern young people managed to complete high school training.[32]

Relatively impressive public investments in education have effected improvements over this earlier situation. Yet much more must be done to alleviate the serious classroom shortage,[33] to remove the poverty that forces youngsters in agricultural regions to go into the labor market at immature ages, and to reduce the illiteracy and semiliteracy that besets those tens of thousands who, until recent years, found it impossible to take advantage of free public education. More must be done, too, to permit greater numbers of students who get through the elementary grades to move into the high schools and universities. Italy's educational pyramid is still a dramatic portrayal of the uneven life chances that the society produces.[34] It makes it valid to repeat at this time the words of one observer: "The class system was strong and secure even before Fascism; morally, at least, it persists to this day. The system has historically resisted educational opportunity, equality, and democracy." [35] It is to this lingering rigid social stratification and inequality of opportunity that many of Italy's extreme political parties and voluntary

[32] For an excellent survey of this early situation, see SVIMEZ (Association for the Development of Southern Italy), *Survey of Southern Italian Economy* (Rome, 1949), p. 17 and *passim*.

[33] See George F. Kneller, "Education in Italy," in A. H. Moehlman and J. Roucek, *Comparative Education* (New York, 1951), Ch. 8.

[34] See ISTAT, *Annuario, 1959*, graph facing page 91.

[35] Kneller, *op. cit.*, p. 257.

associations point accusing fingers. It is also among these less privileged masses that groups and movements that favor revolutionary changes seek adherents. The structure of education, therefore, is a strong factor making for political instability as well as for continued economic disequilibrium.

CHAPTER III · THE ITALIAN POLITICAL CULTURE

THE interest-group phenomenon in Italy also evolves within a broad political institutional and behavioral context—that is, within a political system.[1] The groups treated in this volume are important to us primarily as they seek to translate their interests into public policy. In doing so, they play a central role, in the political system, in the performance of the functions of interest articulation and aggregation, political socialization and recruitment, and political communication. As we shall see, the boundary maintenance between society and polity in Italy is quite poor, so that some of the groups are also intimately involved in the performance of the authoritative functions of government. Indeed, these latter functions of rule-making, rule-application, and rule-adjudication are empirically performed in such a way that often interest groups can be, at best, only analytically separated from them.[2] In their operations, interest groups not only help to characterize Italy's political culture but are also strongly influenced by other aspects of that culture to which they are exposed.

It is widely recognized that the nature of group organization and behavior will be greatly influenced by the character of the political culture in which it takes place. It is apparent, for example, that the group phenomenon differs significantly when one views it in a highly traditional setting, on the one hand, and in a strongly legal-

[1] The theoretical orientation of this chapter is strongly influenced by Gabriel Almond's introductory essay, "A Functional Approach to Comparative Politics," in G. A. Almond and J. S. Coleman (eds.), *The Politics of the Developing Areas* (Princeton, 1960), pp. 3–64.

[2] This fact creates something of a problem for the Almond conceptual scheme in the sense that it is far from clear when an interest group crosses the line from the performance of an "input" function to the performance of an "output" function. See *ibid.*, p. 16 and *passim*.

rational setting, on the other.[3] Similarly, when formal institutional arrangements are considered, it is assumed that the nature of interest-group intervention in the rule-making process is different when one compares, say, the British House of Commons with its extremely limited and generalized committee system, and the United States Congress with its greatly proliferated and specialized committees. Where formal effective rule-making power is highly concentrated in the executive, as it is in the Fifth Republic of France, one would expect interest groups to be less active—certainly less effective—in the legislature than they were in the French Third and Fourth Republics, which were dominated by legislative supremacy. By the same token, one can say that differences in patterns of interest articulation and aggregation are certain to be detected as one moves from a totalitarian to a democratic political system; from a system dominated by one party, or two major parties, to another characterized by many parties; from a system that enshrines the power of judicial review to one in which the courts have little control over the activities of the legislature or the executive.

Once again it should be understood that no effort is made here to lay out in a systematic and exhaustive way how each and every aspect of the Italian political culture or system impinges on interest-group organization and behavior. Sufficient data to permit this are simply not at our disposal. To some extent, however, in this and the case-study chapters that follow, we can trace the interrelationships between certain political and governmental arrangements, on the one hand, and group behavior, on the other. In the present chapter, my purpose is primarily that of sketching the primary outlines of the Italian political culture in which the groups operate, how this culture affects them, and how they constitute an integral part of it.

[3] For many perceptive and insightful illustrations of this fact, see the case-study chapters in *ibid.*, by Lucian Pye, Myron Weiner, George Blanksten, James Coleman, and Dankwart Rustow.

POLITICAL CULTURE: SOME GENERAL CHARACTERISTICS

One would rightly be led to infer from the previous chapter that Italy's political culture is highly fragmented and isolative. Fragmentation into many subcultures is a function of many factors—of the basic differences between North and South, the rapid urbanization of the country in recent years, the strong ideological and social class divisions that characterize all sectors of the country, the basic division of Italians over the question of organized Catholicism, as well as the particular conditions surrounding the unification of Italy and her early evolution as a single state. This type of extreme social diversity, which is marked by low political and social communication, is a strong factor making for fragmentation.

It is of vital importance to recall that Italy's unification was never a mass movement. The *Risorgimento* attracted not the man on the street but primarily elements of the northern middle and upper classes. Moreover, even among those who favored a united Italy, there was considerable difference of opinion concerning the kind of cohesive state system that should be created or how it should be led. What emerged under the guiding spirit of Count Cavour and the House of Savoy was the Italy wanted neither by Giuseppe Mazzini nor by Giuseppe Garibaldi, both of whom played vital roles in the *Risorgimento*. Thus the new state came into existence without the substantive participation of the masses, despite the virulent hostility of the Catholic Church, and with only the half-hearted support of those south of Rome, who little understood that the ballots they cast in the plebescites would help to usher in a period of Piedmont hegemony over the entire peninsula.

It is true that the House of Savoy managed to "Piedmontize" Italy within a relatively brief period. This was accomplished primarily by means of two important and connected strategies. First, the essentially Napoleonic administrative system, with its centralized ministries extending their power and influence downward from the center through the system of provinces and prefects. Second, in exchange for a central governmental policy that left the South pretty much alone, Piedmont was able to buy the support of the southern gentlemen—the notables—whose illiterate and politically unsophisticated clienteles continued to return them to the legislature in Rome even after manhood suffrage was expanded.

To be sure, with the exception of southern riots in the early months following unification Sicilian restiveness following World War II and the more recent problem of the South Tyrol, there has never been a serious separatist movement since 1861. This should not be misconstrued to mean, however, that Italy evinces a relatively high degree of political integration. In an oft-quoted remark, Massimo D'Azeglio, a leader of the *Risorgimento*, is supposed to have said, "Fatta l'Italia, bisogna fare gli italiani"—Having made Italy, we must now make Italians. The chore has been more arduous than many imagined. As we have seen, little was accomplished between unification and Fascism to alleviate the total imbalance that characterized North and South. Fascism, while providing some stronger sense of nationhood and promising to recapture the glory that was Rome, plunged the nation into tragicomic economic enterprise and a devastating and unwanted war. Perhaps the most significant consequence of the latter is that, in its last years, it gave rise to the Resistance Movement, yet another major event in Italy's history, which was primarily a northern phenomenon that served further to impede the growth of understanding between North and South.

We thus encounter, at a most basic level, political identification and allegiance that is local and parochial rather than national. Parochialism, while strongly evident in the traditional South, is also amazingly present in the North, where the localizing influences of the city-states and independent duchies are still very much in evidence. In Tuscany, for example, ancient hostility among the cities of Florence, Pisa, and Lucca is still much in evidence. Residents of these communities are Florentines, Pisans, and Luccans first, then Tuscans as opposed to other regions of Italy, then Northerners as opposed to Southerners, and finally—perhaps divinely—Italians. While such provincialism is probably more intensive in a place like Florence than elsewhere, it is present throughout Italy. It is the product of centuries of political fragmentation; of important and sometimes impressive—even glorious—cultural and political traditions; of inadequate means of communication among city-states and regions; of forced occupation of the peninsula by quite different groups ranging from Arabs, Normans, and Spaniards in the South to Barbarian hordes, French, and Austrians in the North. Even linguistically, Italy has been long divided, with the Italian language indigenous only to the regions of Tuscany and Umbria and only slowly managing to penetrate into rural areas, where the basic language spoken is a dialect often quite radically different from the Italian that seeks to replace it. The graduates of the modern educational system can, of course, communicate in Italian. But with striking regularity—even among middle-class strata—the language spoken in the home, in the village, or in the neighborhood is still the indigenous dialect. When D'Azeglio spoke of "making Italians," he was referring to the entire complex of human behavior and not merely to one or two political aspects of it.

To all these factors which help to create a fragmented and isolative political culture one should add extreme ideological fragmentation. Some of this is based on the historic conflict between Church and State. One can go all the way back to St. Paul for a statement of the Catholic position that, except in rare circumstances, "the powers that be are ordained by God," and the Church does not take a stand on the particular form that a political system may take. But it is apparent—and will be heavily documented in later chapters—that organized Catholicism has never been politically neutral in Italy. At the time of unification, opposition to the New Italian state was framed in terms of Catholicism's general battle with European liberalism, seen as a direct threat to the Church's spiritual, and overriding, mission on earth. In the years since World War II, the political intervention of Catholicism has been rationalized on the basis of the threat to its spiritual ends presented by Marxism, as articulated and fostered by the Italian Communist Party in particular, but by the Italian Socialist Party as well. One recent writer put the matter as follows: "The only case in which the Church, by reason of its doctrine, descends to the level of ideology is when She finds Herself confronted by systems in which the principles of the promotion of the common good, of the salvation of the person, of the extra-terrestrial end of all human action, of the origin and substance of natural law and authority, are replaced by a philosophical, ideological, and therefore political platform that excludes all idea of God. This is the reason that leads to the condemnation of liberalism, for example, and of Communism, systems, however opposed they may be to each other, which are both naturalistic conceptions of human destiny." [4]

Prandi goes on to say that, even where this is the case, the Church condemns the principles of the system and not the "empirical structurings" of the political system as such. According to him, it is clericalism—the aggressive behavior of the Church's representatives—that leads to Catholic condemnation of specific political institutions and behavior. I do not wish to debate here whether one can speak of "distortions" of Church doctrine or whether an institution can be understood apart from the behavior of its representatives.[5] The fact is that organized Catholicism is deeply involved in Italian politics in every conceivable way short of electing priests and nuns to legislative and executive bodies. This fact is widely understood and resented. It gives rise to fundamental and essentially irre-

---

[4] Alfonso Prandi, "L'Insegnamento politico della chiesa," Il Mulino, 11 (February, 1962), p. 130.

[5] This is the burden of Prandi's argument. Ibid., pp. 130–31.

concilable clashes between those Italians who support the Church in politics and others who see such involvement as threats to democratic institutions, or at least to their own interests.

Counterpoised against the political ideology and involvement of Catholicism is that of Marxism in its many organizational variations. This is not to suggest that the Italian ideological struggle is exclusively bipolar. The Marxists range all the way from mild revisionists to extreme revolutionaries. In addition, there are some Christian Socialists, Republicans, Radicals, Monarchists, neo-Fascists, and others who have worked out their particular ideological orientations. Even within the Catholic movements one learns that there is a "hard" and a "soft" line, that Jesuits and Dominicans in the Vatican are at odds, that the political party and voluntary associations that represent Catholicism do not constitute an ideological monolith.[6] The point here is that Marxism is massively involved in the basic ideological division of the country and that this basic division is in turn further exacerbated by the proliferation of other ideologies. In such a context the dominant value is one of relatively unremitting hostility and conflict, with little predisposition to engage in bargaining and political compromise. It is possible that a number of recent developments may serve to modify the situation. In this category would fall the political "Opening to the Left" initiated by the Christian Democrats and participated in by a major portion of the Italian Socialist Party. In the same vein, the seemingly milder attitudes toward the opposition manifested by Pope John XXIII and by Paul VI may move organized Catholicism toward a less intransigent position. Even the transformation of the Italian Communist Party from a revolutionary to an electoral instrument may contribute to such a change, but all this is speculative, looking toward possible future development rather than reflecting present reality.

6 This latter is an important and valid point to which we shall return several times in this study.

In addition to extreme social and ideological fragmentation, Italian political culture is highly differentiated structurally. A wide variety of structures exist for the performance of both the input and the output functions of the political system. As one would expect of this kind of society, some of the structures—the family, the schools, industrial firms, some voluntary associations, the mass media—are only intermittently involved in the political process. When they do become so involved, they may do so with regard to any of the political functions, although they tend to be of primary importance regarding the functions of political socialization and interest articulation. Extensive structural differentiation also exists in the formal governmental sector. While this does not imply a complete separation of functions (or powers), it does mean that a very high degree of division and specialization of governmental labor has evolved, so that, unlike the case of less-developed, more structurally undifferentiated systems, one can point to particular institutions that are associated with the rule-making, rule-application, and rule-adjudication functions. Such differentiation implies that the process of government is most complex and that a complete explication of all the relevant variables and relationships that characterize it would require careful empirical observation over an extended period. It is for this reason, among others, that the present study focuses primarily on the role of certain voluntary associations in the performance of some—but not all—of the political functions.

As a final general point, we might make explicit what has been clearly implied about Italy's political culture, namely that it is mixed or dual. This is, of course, the case with old political cultures, since, to my knowledge, neither the "traditional" nor the "legal-rational" ideal types exist in empirical reality.[7] What we find in all political systems

[7] The terminology here is essentially Max Weber's. It is also used by Gabriel Almond in Almond and Coleman, *op. cit.* Other efforts to give nomenclature to the taxonomies of political systems might be cited, notably that of Fred W. Riggs, who divides bureaucratic (and presumably political) systems into "agrarian" and "industrial" types and, more re-

is a combination of structures, some reflecting particularism, some universalism; some reflecting ascription, others achievement; some essentially sacral in content, other secular; some that ascribe major importance to primary groups and loyalties, others that accord such importance to secondary groups and associations. One would like to say something precise about the particular "mix" of these characteristics that exists in an entire nation-state. However, at that level of generalization we can only be approximate, understanding that when looking in greater detail at specific interest groups and sectors of the governmental structure, we may be able to deal more meaningfully with the configuration of traits that confront us.

It is obvious that southern Italy is still overwhelmingly traditional and that, in politics, traditional structures still count for more than the legal-rational ones, notwithstanding that the formal setting for the political process itself appears to be almost entirely legal-rational. Particularly in this part of the country, it is necessary to go behind the formal façade to ask what role in the political process is played by the family, by obligations of friendship, by ties to one's village or region or to one's religious group. It is certainly reasonable to state, for example, that these factors are of much greater import south of Rome than they are in the provinces of the industrial North. One important indication of this is the relative use of the preference vote in national elections, which gives the voter the opportunity to cast votes for individuals as well as for political parties. Evidence of the use of the preference vote in the South shows that it is used several times for every occurrence in the North.[8] The Southerner votes particular-

cently, into "fused," "prismatic," and "refracted" types. See his "Agraria and Industria—Toward a Typology of Comparative Administration," in W. J. Siffin, *Toward a Comparative Study of Public Administration* (Bloomington, 1957), pp. 23–116, and his "Prismatic Society and Financial Administration," *Administrative Science Quarterly* 5 (June, 1960), pp. 1–46. In the terminology of Riggs, all systems are necessarily "prismatic."

[8] See Giovanni Schepis, "Analisi statistica dei risultati," in Alberto Spreafico and Joseph LaPalombara (eds.), *Elezioni e comportamento politico in Italia* (Milan, 1963), pp. 329–406.

istically for the man—the notable of whose clientele he is a part—while the Northerner votes for the political party as such. One could multiply these indirect indexes of southern traditionality. They include such varied things as the greater incidence of crimes of honor, the place of the woman in society and politics, the marked influence of what is defined as political corruption in places like Naples and Sicily, to name only a few. Some years ago, I happened to be talking with a Neapolitan who had gone to Rome to have his military pension adjusted and who had met with the completely frustrating indifference of Rome's bureaucracy. Undismayed, he assured me that everything would be taken care of because, through his deputy, he was forwarding his personal petition and photograph to Premier De Gasperi, just as one would have done with the king, he said, and as one would do if he wanted equitable redress from the local padrone.

Needless to say, the North is not nearly as traditional, although traditional structures are found in the rural sectors. But, as Achille Ardigò points out, the rural institutions have been strongly influenced by the urban, industrial, secular, and legal-rational centers that surround them.[9] In other words, the traditional, primary structures have been strongly penetrated and modified by the more important secondary structures of a modern, industrialized society. The impact of this has been to make the political behavior and organization in the North more characterized by achievement and universalistic norms, more secular and rational, more reflective of and responsive to the interests of voluntary associations.

Italy's division into essentially two political subcultures is a critical datum. Not only do we find a dual or mixed system there, but also a combination which is neither fused nor fluid but fractured and highly crystallized. The two cultures, the old and the new, are antagonistic to each

[9] Achille Ardigò, "Le Trasformazioni interne nelle campagne settentrionali e l'esodo rurale," in *Aspetti e problemi sociali dello sviluppo economico in Italia* (Bari, 1959), pp. 39–54.

other. They maintain at best an armed truce; at worst, open hostility. Only the continued removal of the sources of disequilibrium is likely to bring about an improvement in this unfortunate situation. In the meantime, the basic difference will intensify misunderstanding and the lack of adequate intercultural communication. This in turn, like other factors touched upon, will continue to make the Italian political system quite volatile and unpredictable.

POLITICAL SOCIALIZATION

All political systems, it has been noted, tend to perpetuate their cultures and structures through time. This is not a static but a dynamic process. That is, if the society in general is undergoing rapid change, these changes are likely to be reflected in the kind of political socialization that the individual experiences. However, we can anticipate that there will be a lag between the actual development of change and the kinds of socializing experiences, particularly in primary associations such as the family and the school, to which the individual is exposed. Indeed, a critical problem for any political elite bent on bringing about rapid change is that of transforming the primary associations to the point where they are producing values and belief systems consonant with the new society that is desired. This explains, for example, the concern of Italy's Fascist regime with the school system, or the massive Bolshevik effort to remake Soviet schools to the point where they would produce the kind of people who would make dreams of rapid industrialization reasonable of achievement. It also explains why there are many in Italy who do not feel that liberal democracy or industrialization are viable goals as long as the Italian educational system remains basically unchanged.

Political socialization is not a process that is limited to one's exposure to nuclear family and the schools. It is rather a process that, in the early years, involves a great deal of latent socialization that becomes more manifest as secondary and more openly political associations become a major part of each individual's existence.[10] Whatever attitudes the adult maintains toward the state, what he feels about the political system and process, how he reacts to other groups, the reactions he manifests toward political authority—all of these are things that he first learns indirectly in childhood and that are more openly reinforced or challenged in adulthood. In any case, it is apparent that the forces of socialization define the limits, or set the parameters, within which political organization and behavior evolve.

What we know about the primary socializing institutions of Italian society is not encouraging for those who wish to see a liberal democratic system take root. It is a commonplace to say that Fascism was alien to the Italian personality, that it never really took firm hold in the society, that Italians tended to be scornful about Fascism's boasts, pretentions, and attempts at creating totalitarian control.[11] Yet, if one stops to consider what has been said in this and the previous chapter, it is fairly obvious that primary institutions are of vital importance in political socialization in vast sectors of the country and that the kinds of values and orientations these institutions inculcate is anything but reassuring.

The most obvious point to make here—I have already alluded to it—is that in many parts of Italy the most important claims on the loyalty and allegiance of the individual are the family, the kinship group, the neighborhood, and the village. In his perceptive study of a southern Italian village, Edward Banfield argues, indeed, that what characterizes that part of the peninsula is "amoral familism," which is based on the axiom: "Maximize the material, short-run advantage of the nuclear family; assume

[10] On the point of continuous socialization, see Herbert Hyman, *Political Socialization* (Glencoe, 1959).

[11] For a sobering commentary on the more fundamental meaning of Fascism for Italians, see Costanzo Casucci, *Il Fascismo* (Bologna, 1961), which is perhaps the most interesting anthology on the subject ever put together. An interesting commentary on the volume is provided by Gianni Sofri, "Il Fascismo," *Il Mulino*, 11 (February, 1962), pp. 159–62.

that all others will do likewise." [12] In this kind of society, Banfield found that "no one will further the interest of the group or community except as it is to his private advantage to do so," that the individual citizen neither takes an interest in public affairs nor is expected to do so, that politics constitutes a sphere of activity outside the ken of most people, that political organization is almost impossible to achieve, that politics is essentially corrupt business, and that, on the whole, the situation favors strong and authoritarian regimes.[13]

One may want to quarrel with the finding that, in the South, political cognition and involvement does not extend beyond the nuclear family. But the evidence is fairly strong that, in the southern regions of Italy, extreme political illiteracy is rampant, knowledge of national issues or policies is fragmentary at best, national political parties are unimportant, and elections turn primarily on local and particularistic issues.[14] Thus it is relatively apparent that, even where the concept of citizenship and political participation is inculcated, socialization fails to provide tens of thousands of Italians with a coherent view of the *national* political system and with a sense of efficacious involvement concerning it. Most of these persons are to be found in the rural, underdeveloped and traditional South, but one can imagine that the situation does not differ markedly in the poorer and more isolated regions of central and northern Italy. Only in the urban, industrialized areas would

[12] Edward C. Banfield, *The Moral Basis of a Backward Society* (Glencoe, 1958), p. 85. As I have already noted, Banfield's formulation is too restrictive and not accurately descriptive of loyalties in the South.

[13] *Ibid.*, pp. 85–97. The whole of Chapter V is a fascinating commentary on southern local politics.

[14] International Research Associates, Incorporated, conducted a study of 76 communes in connection with the elections of 1953. These were places where the vote had shifted substantially compared with the 1948 results. The study found that the voters were motivated by strictly *local* and personal economic issues, that ideology and national issues played little part in determining voting behavior, and that many shifts were simply the result of *clientelismo*, voters following a personal leader from one party to another.

the situation be much different, as it is on almost any dimension one can imagine. It is true that exceptional crises, such as that surrounding the Trieste issue a few years ago, can give the impression of strong identification with the nation as such, but crises are by definition exceptions to the normal; they do not serve to define the general degree to which one's sense of participation and involvement extends beyond the primary and local institutions of immediate concern.

One may also consider the kinds of basic values that are likely to emerge from experiences in the primary socializing institutions. Such speculation is admittedly hazardous, since it is difficult to demonstrate how one's early experience in the home and schools gets translated into later political behavior. The difficulty is immediately apparent when one stops to consider that out of a basically similar family or school system a fairly wide-ranging pattern of orientation to politics can and does emerge. Thus, while some suggestive generalizations can be offered, it must be understood that later and intervening political socialization experiences can and probably do serve to modify adult political behavior.

In general, both the Italian family and the educational systems are essentially authoritarian in character. Both the rural and the urban family is organized around the central idea of unquestioning respect for and obedience to parents and grandparents. Hierarchical authority is fairly clearly structured, particularly in rural centers, with authority descending from parents to oldest male sibling, and so on through the entire family membership. While the Italian is noted for the loving and overt affection he bestows on his offspring, he is also capable of administering physical punishment, sometimes quite severely. It would be misleading, however, to view the Italian family as essentially patriarchal. At the formal—and public—level, authority appears to reside in the father. Yet, despite her formally inferior role in the family, the mother is of utmost importance, and Italians in the countryside or city will frankly explain that, as a matter of fact, much of what occurs in the family situation revolves around the functions and authority of the mother. Hers is a major role in the education of the children, in introducing them to the first chores to which they are assigned, in seeing to their religious needs and observances, and in managing the household economy. It is not merely coincidence that Italians seem so preoccupied with the woman. Religiously, it is the Virgin Mary who occupies the foremost position; politically, the country is seen not as the Fatherland but as the "Madre Patria," the Mother-Fatherland. In any case, if sexual traits transfer into the political realm, it is possible that the difference in intensity and rigidity in politics that one can detect in going from, say, Germany to Italy is owing in part to the moderating role of the mother in the Italian family. But because the family structure remains essentially authoritarian, we should also expect to see the values instilled there transferred to attitudes toward political authority and interaction.

Whatever authoritarianism is instilled by the family tends to be reinforced by Italy's educational system, both public and parochial. Rigid discipline characterizes the schools from the earliest years. Except in those few elementary schools in the country that have tried deliberately to experiment with the methods of Dewey or Pestalozzi, pupils are exposed to patterns of pupil-teacher interaction in which the latter is the unquestioned and unassailable authority. The social gap maintained between teacher and pupil is enormous—and it grows even wider as one moves up through the middle and high schools into the universities. In the last, the professor is generally a remote and austere person who makes periodic classroom appearances, where he casts his pearls of wisdom and retreats to his office, home, or outside professional interests. His well-made lectures, often genuinely brilliant in conception and delivery, are not meant to be interrupted by student questions. His command of the subject is thought to be complete and perfect, and questions or challenges are viewed as both dilatory and impertinent. If the student has a problem of whatever nature or concern, it is usually handled by a professorial *assistente,* and frequently just as dictatorially.

This is not to suggest that this standard of behavior is universally followed. Some changes are at work in several of the universities. Additionally, the situation is often markedly different in some of the specialized schools of advanced training that have emerged since the war. Some of the younger academics are experimenting with the lecture-discussion method and find it to be no threat to status or psychological security. Nevertheless, as many Italians themselves have publicly remarked in recent years, the school system, from the early grades through the university years, continues to reflect the values that were institutionalized under Fascism and is hardly an impressive means of preparing the Italian to perform the role of the active and questioning citizen in a liberal democracy.

The system retains a strong Roman Catholic orientation. Highly centralized under a Ministry of Public Instruction in Rome, it still serves to inculcate a system of values that is more attuned to conservative Catholic, even Fascistic, doctrine than to the central idea of the "new deal" approach to social, political, and economic problems that is favored by the left wing of Christian Democracy. It need scarcely be added that the schools—largely staffed with teachers who are pro-Catholic—are anything but breeding grounds for the political ideas of the extreme Left. Three quotations from official elementary school texts may serve to illustrate the kind of political socialization to which Italian youngsters are sometimes exposed:

"The fourth commandment—honor thy father and thy mother —orders us to respect and love our parents and all who have authority over us, that is, our superiors: the Pope, the bishops, the priests, the civil authorities and our teachers."

"On the Trans-Siberia Railroad one rides for days and days, passing through the Urals and over the immense Siberian steppes to enter into immense and mostly unexplored forests, where the few primitive inhabitants live like animals."

"There is much social change because parents fall prey to stupid ambitions for their children. The shoemaker wants his son to become an accountant; the sausage vendor wants his son to become a physician. Just imagine such foolishness." [15]

These quotations suggest some aspects of the type of orientation to politics that the school system fosters. Italy's fragmented political culture suggests as well that other factors are at work in the process of political socialization. Authoritarian values of the family and the schools are, of course, greatly reinforced by the organized Catholic Church. Catholicism clearly purports to exercise full power over its members both in things spiritual and in those things temporal that, in the view of the Church's representatives, have a bearing on the attainment of man's spiritual salvation. While canonical scholars carefully distinguish the things about which the Catholic Pope speaks with infallibility, the fine distinction is lost on the millions of Catholics, young and old, who listen to priests and nuns expatiating on the relative merit of political parties, on the nature of obligation to public authority, on political policies that fall into the social and economic spheres, in short on the entire spectrum of items that are of concern to man as citizen. For the millions of Italian women who take their political leads from their confessors, and from the additional millions who are members of Catholic secondary associations, the basic process of political socialization serves to enshrine the kind of cognition, values, and attitudes that only accidentally reinforce democratic institutions. The attitudes toward authority and toward other political groups that emanate from this source serve to reinforce and to perpetuate the isolation and fragmentation that is so typical of Italian political culture.

In addition to the primary associations, there exists a

[15] From John Clarke Adams and Paolo Barile, *The Government of Republican Italy* (Boston, 1961), p. 234.

wide variety of secondary socializing structures in the society. Some of these, like the political parties, trade unions, and professional associations are more or less continuously involved in the socialization process. As we shall see later in some detail, the voluntary associations barrage their memberships with a constant stream of publications, hold frequent conferences and training and informational meetings, and generally use a wide variety of communicative devices designed to set and reinforce a particular orientation to the political system, political issues, and groups with which the associations cooperate and compete in an effort to influence political decisions. Within many of these associations the ideological content is very high, and socialization tends to strengthen the combative and isolative political positions of the membership. Moreover, to a striking degree, the image of the political system and process fostered by the groups is negative. Government is viewed as in the hands of "the enemy," the bureaucracy is portrayed as a haven of corrupt practices (for which the Italians have coined the term *sottogoverno*), and political parties are described as equally corrupt forces impeding progress and the attainment of the common good. Internally, the organizations tend to be run by tight oligarchies, thus tending to reinforce basic attitudes about the nature of authority and the essentially passive role of the individual in the face of it.[16]

One might expect the mass media to be of great importance in counteracting some of these patterns of political socialization. For example, the great expansion of radio and television in recent years might be viewed as broadening the political horizons of the individual considerably beyond his family and village. Similarly, one might expect the press to bring the individual meaningfully into contact with the political system and process at the national level. To some degree, both are true; certainly the penetration

16 This is certainly true of the trade unions. For a discussion of the problem, see Joseph LaPalombara, *The Italian Labor Movement: Problems and Prospects* (Ithaca, 1957), Ch. 3.

of the mass media into the remoter parts of the country has served to increase the Italian's spatial milieu. We know that new patterns of taste and behavior have emerged from the technological revolution the country has experienced during the last decade. But, in looking at the mass media from the standpoint of political socialization, one must bear in mind three basic caveats.

First, it must be noted that radio and television in Italy are state monopolies. This fact, in itself, does not tell us very much, because the same thing is largely true of Great Britain, where the British Broadcasting Corporation has set very high standards and is considered one of the best public corporations in the world. The same cannot be said for Italy, particularly in the use of mass media for political purposes. In the elections of 1958, for example, pressures to allow the competing political parties proportionate time on radio and television were rejected by the Christian Democratic government. It was said that radio and television would not be available for *any* partisan purposes but would instead restrict themselves to an objective reporting of the news. For the month preceding the election, we had a group of university students monitor the newscasts. The slanting of the news to favor the government, to highlight activities of the Christian Democrats, and to place the opposition (particularly the extreme left) at a disadvantage was plainly apparent. The most minatory statements from speeches of Communist and Socialist leaders were reported; the most insignificant ceremonial activities of Christian Democratic candidates were accorded wide coverage. No one in Italy who paid even the most cursory attention to radio and television would argue with the statement that the mass media were being utilized to orient the electorate in a particular direction. Although this policy was somewhat liberalized during the electoral campaign of 1963, a wide gap continues to separate Italy from places like Great Britain in the use of the mass media in political campaigns.

Catholic organizations, as we shall see in later chapters, are quick to admit that they seek to bend the state-controlled mass media to the furtherance of the Catholic viewpoint. This effort involves not merely radio and television but also the production and distribution of Italian motion pictures over which the government—and increasingly Catholic Action—has considerable influence and control. Views regarding the kinds of things to which the masses should appropriately be exposed are explicit; it certainly does not involve the use of the media to provide the kind of objective political information on the basis of which the Italian can generate a high degree of political wisdom and maturity.

Second, it is important to recognize that the structure of Italian newspapers is such as to intensify, for those who read them, the highly divisive quality of political socialization in Italy. Fourteen of the eighty-five dailies are owned by political parties; three others are essentially front-publications. Of the remaining sixty-eight, nineteen are owned by important industrial groups, twenty-one are controlled by Confindustria, thirteen are the property of Catholic groups or Christian Democratic exponents, four are the property of or controlled by quasi-public corporations, and the remaining eleven, including not a single one with a circulation in excess of 100,000, are difficult to classify but maintain a basically pro-government policy.[17] The so-called independent press is not independent at all, but highly partisan in its presentation, generally reflecting the viewpoint of the interest group or, more often, the single families, that control it. This is true even of such relatively excellent newspapers as Turin's *La Stampa* and Milan's *Corriere della Sera*. The Italian reader is therefore exposed to highly biased presentations by newspapers that work to reinforce the hostility and antagonism that characterize the society. It is almost impossible to read any Italian daily without encountering constant references to political scandal and corruption and to class war, even

[17] See Ignazio Weiss, "Proprietà e finanziamento della stampa quotidiana italiana," *Tempi Moderni,* 3 (July, 1960), pp. 3–12.

when the papers involved are purportedly condemning either or both of these things.

Third, one should note that the circulation of daily newspapers in Italy is very low; estimates of the total range from 4,700,000 to 7,000,000.[18] It is true, of course, that in addition to daily newspaper there are dozens of weekly newspapers and magazines, all of which are to some extent involved in the socializing process. Like the dailies, however, they are often read by sectarian groups, and many of them—such as *Il Punto, Il Mondo, L'Espresso*—are read by only a restricted group of intellectuals. The masses read very little, and in some sectors of the South the number of persons who never read any newspaper at all reaches high proportions, ranging from 30 to 43 percent.[19] Thus it is necessary to conclude not only that the newspapers tend to entrench political divisiveness when they are read, but also that there are large regions of Italy where the press is not in any way operative as an instrument of political socialization.

POLITICAL RECRUITMENT

Political recruitment in Italy is a highly structured process in which political parties and interest groups play central roles. Obviously, these are not the only structures that are involved in the complex process. There are certainly areas of the country in which such institutions as the family and church are primarily responsible for recruitment to political roles. It is also apparent that, in the bureaucratic sector, recruitment is handled primarily through formal procedures established by law and conducted by the bureaucracy itself. Nevertheless, when we

[18] *Ibid.*, p. 6. See also the Weiss reply to a criticism by Giorgio Galli, who opts for the 7,000,000 figure. *Ibid.*, 3 (October, 1960), pp. 101–02. Newspaper circulations are nowhere officially reported in Italy, so we have only educated guesses.

[19] See Pierpaolo Luzzatto Fegiz, *Il Volto sconosciuto dell'Italia* (Milan, 1956), p. 802. This report on ten years of survey research findings by DOXA, the organization directed by the author, contains valuable information.

think primarily of the rule-making positions—and even of many of the rule-adjudication and rule-application positions—it is apparent that the political parties and interest groups are intimately involved.

Italian legislation carefully defines the procedures whereby persons are formally recruited to legislative office. Currently in use is a list system of proportional representation which is reasonably accurate in giving political parties representation in the lower chamber in proportion to the relative number of voters they attract at the polls.[20] Both the party lists and the rank ordering of names on them are established by the political parties themselves. There are no primary or other nominating elections such as exist in the United States. The voter may not split his ballot but must cast it for one or another of the party lists that appear there. Basically, after the electoral quota is determined in each district, parties elect one deputy for every electoral quota, or fraction exceeding fifty percent of the quota, that the district-party votes represent. Remainders are transferred to a national electoral college, where seats unassigned at the district level are allocated. The electoral law gives the voter limited opportunity to modify the parties' listings in the sense that each elector can cast three or four preferential votes for individuals, depending on the number of deputies to be elected.

Within this legal framework, the basic contests pertaining to recruitment center on the formation of electoral lists and on the use of the preferential vote. The parties differ considerably in the procedures they follow in list formation. Some, such as the Italian Socialist Party (P.S.I.), accord great leeway to the party's regional federation. In the Christian Democratic Party (D.C.), the basic work is done at the provincial level. As one would expect, the

[20] The electoral system is described by Joseph LaPalombara, "The Italian Elections and the Problem of Representation," *American Political Science Review*, 47 (September, 1953), pp. 676–82. See also the Italian Constitution of 1948, Article 56. The electoral system for the Senate combines a majoritarian with a proportional system. The details are spelled out in Article 56. See also Article 57.

procedure in the Italian Communist Party (P.C.I.) is much more centralized. In all cases, however, there is a fairly high degree of centralized control, and the national party authorities can generally keep unwanted candidates off of district lists.

Within whatever party, individuals or groups interested in influencing the choice of candidates work intensively at both the local and central levels. Struggles among the disparate groups that function within the D.C. have received considerable press coverage in the past. Some of these—Catholic Action is a good example—have been aligned against those such as Amintore Fanfani who have tried to give the party bureaucracy itself a greater voice in the naming of candidates. Even within the P.C.I., particularly following the crises that emerged after the Hungarian Rebellion and the Twentieth Congress of the C.P.S.U., there has been considerable local jockeying for position in the naming of candidates.

One significant factor distinguishing interest groups is whether they have more or less official access to the parties in the naming of candidates. It is widely recognized, for example, that Confindustria has considerable influence in this regard within the Italian Liberal Party (P.L.I.). Youth groups, women's associations, agricultural associations, trade unions, religious groups, and so on, have more or less effective access in the other parties. The relative influence of the constituent groups is in part reflected in the party personnel who sit in the legislature. On this dimension, it is apparent that the trade unions have scored notable successes in gaining direct representation in the D.C., P.C.I., and P.S.I. The unions sometimes pay a heavy price for this influence, in that they lose organizational autonomy and tend to become merely the instrumentalities of the political parties through which they achieve political positions.[21] Despite this danger, the group com-

[21] See Joseph LaPalombara, "The Political Role of Organized Labor in Western Europe," *Journal of Politics,* 17 (February, 1955), pp. 59–81.

petition to influence the choice of candidates—and through them other aspects of political recruitment and policy making—remains quite avid.

Thanks to an exhaustive research project on the postwar legislature conducted by Giovanni Sartori and associates,[22] we have considerable information concerning the basic socio-economic characteristics of those recruited to national legislative office. One important finding is that those men who were associated with the Resistance Movement have gradually declined in importance from and in the qualitative influence they exert in the legislative halls. Early popular enthusiasm for those identified with the liberation of Italy from Fascism has continuously diminished; a newer breed of party bureaucrats has made its appearance. A similar fate has befallen women whose number in the Chamber of Deputies was cut in half between 1948 and 1958.[23]

Particularly striking is the fact that over 60 percent of the deputies come from families that resided in municipalities of 20,000 inhabitants or fewer. Approximately 40 percent of the deputies were reared and educated in rural communities that fall into this category. Only 30.7 percent of the deputies spent their formative years in cities with populations exceeding 100,000. It is most evident that the countryside has produced considerably more legislative leadership than the cities. In addition, the traditional South has been slightly overrepresented in the

[22] The Sartori study involved questionnaires sent to 1,358 deputies, former deputies, or their survivors. An amazing 1,150 questionnaires were returned. In addition, interviews and documentary searches were conducted to maximize the information obtained. Sartori is thus able to generalize on the basis of data representing ninety percent of those who have sat in the Chamber of Deputies since 1946. This pioneering work in legislative sociology is certain to become a classic of empirical social science in Italy. See his *Il Parlamento Italiano: 1946–1963* (Naples, 1962).

[23] A summary of the findings is found in Giovanni Sartori, "Parliamentarians in Italy," *International Social Science Journal*, 4 (October, 1961), pp. 583–99. A more detailed and analytical study is found in Giovanni Sartori, "La Sociologia del parlamento," *Studi politici*, 8 (April, 1961), pp. 131–59, and 8 (July–December, 1961), pp. 352–82.

Chamber of Deputies if one considers the place where deputies were born.[24]

As one would expect, the national legislature has recruited personnel primarily from the upper middle (53.4 percent) and the middle (28.5 percent) classes. The legislature has been the haven of lawyers, school and university teachers, professional politicians, upper-level officials, small entrepreneurs and middle-level employees in private and public service. Only 13.3 percent of the law makers originate in the lower-middle and working classes, and this representation is almost exclusively owing to the fact that approximately two-fifths of that party's representation has come from these categories. The Italian Socialist party, with only 3.6 percent of its deputies from the working class cannot rightfully claim to be a proletarian party. Nor can the Social Democratic party (P.S.D.I.) of Giuseppe Saragat which recruits almost 70 percent of its deputies from the upper middle class. Not even the D.C., which competes most effectively with the extreme Left for the mass vote can claim to be proletarian in this sense; only 6.4 percent of its parliamentary contingent comes from the lower-middle and working classes.[25] It is fairly obvious that how a party fares at the ballot box has little relationship to the social representativeness of its candidates.

While it would be possible to report in detail on the socio-economic structure of the postwar legislature, we shall limit ourselves to merely a few more interesting observations. Although lawyers represent the leading occupational group in the Chamber of Deputies (27.2 percent globally), they have continuously declined since 1948. Their places have been taken by professional party leaders and by trade union leaders. In the Constituent Assembly, lawyers accounted for 32.8 percent of the total representation; in the Third Legislature, elected in 1958, their num-

24 *Ibid.*, p. 587.
25 *Ibid.*, pp. 588–89. For the Communist Party the working-class percentage is 25.2, but is in decline. *Ibid.*

ber had fallen to 20.8 percent. Party and trade union leaders, on the other hand, went from 18.3 percent in 1946 to 29.7 percent in 1958. This change has been effected primarily in the northern and central provinces, with the South continuing to send very heavy contingents of lawyers to Rome. When we view this phenomenon by political party, we find that the occupational structure of the Communist Party has been extremely stable throughout the postwar period, while both D.C. and P.S.I. have tended to increase the number of party and trade union officials that they elect.[26]

This reflects what many Italian students describe as the increasing bureaucratization of the mass parties, so that they become less and less distinguishable from each other. The fact is that those recruited to rule-making political roles are increasingly middle-class and upper middle-class individuals who are semiprofessionals or professionals. These are men who, as Sartori rightly remarks, live "not only *for* politics but also *by* politics." [27] Fully 38.3 percent of the Third Legislature's membership consisted of strict professionals. Some of these, who are party chiefs, are highly independent and exercise central control over the decision-making process. Others, such as lesser party leaders and trade unionists, are considerably dependent in the sense that they have no alternative professions outside the party or trade union that elects them. Sartori estimates that fully one-fourth of the deputies are "active independents," or party bosses who hold top power positions.[28] It is with this restricted group that those who wish to influence the legislative process in the country must come to terms. This is the political leadership that, with few setbacks, has been able to maintain a dominant position since World War II.

[26] *Ibid.*, pp. 592–95. On the occupational structure of the legislature, see also Federico Mohroff, "Il nuovo parliamento," in Alberto Spreafico and Joseph LaPalombara, *op. cit.*, pp. 517–45.

[27] Sartori, *op. cit.*, p. 597.

[28] *Ibid.*, p. 599. This group represents less than one-fifth of all deputies.

INTEREST ARTICULATION

The functions of interest articulation and aggregation are treated in considerable detail in subsequent chapters of this volume. We can therefore restrict our comments here to some general observations that may be useful in helping to define and to understand the general contours of the political system. As much of the present chapter has suggested, the articulation of interests in Italy occurs through the operation of a number of structural arrangements. In the terminology of Gabriel Almond, Italian interest groups can be fruitfully divided into institutional, nonassociational, anomic, and associational types.[29] The first of these—the *institutional groups*—are structures established primarily for purposes other than interest articulation. They would include the Catholic Church, the bureaucracy (including the armed services), the political parties (which should, theoretically, primarily aggregate interests), and the various formal institutions of government. In all societies, for part of the time, such structures are likely to become involved in direct-interest articulation, either on behalf of themselves or of other groups in whose interest these institutions behave. However, where the incidence of direct-interest articulation becomes exceedingly heavy, we can agree with Almond that such behavior makes for poor boundary maintenance between the polity and the society.

Italy is clearly characterized by poor boundary maintenance. Although specialized structures for interest articulation exist, they are forced to compete with a heavy incidence of institutional interest-group behavior. The Catholic Church, for example, intervenes in the political process directly, as well as through the intermediary of its organized secondary associations. Priests campaign—and therefore articulate interests—from the pulpit and in the confessionals. Members of the clergy call on the ministries, even if the halls of the bureaucracy are not as crowded

---

[29] Almond and Coleman, *op. cit.*, pp. 33–34.

with black-robed messengers as some Italians suggest. Bishops, following a pattern that dates back several centuries, intervene directly in the political affairs of the diocese. Although this study does not present very much data on the political process at the local and provincial level, I am convinced that an adequate understanding of the interest-group phenomenon would require more information on the manner in which clergy and others seek to intervene in the decisions of prefects, provincial assemblies, mayors, chambers of commerce, field administrative agencies, and other decentralized formal institutions of government.

It is unnecessary to do more than recognize that other institutions such as the legislature, armed forces, and other sectors of the bureaucracy intervene in the political process in order to articulate expediency rather than principled interests. This phenomenon in Italy is not unlike that which we would expect to find in most western countries. It can occur with even greater impact and intensity in some of the less-developed countries, where the bureaucracy is overpowering, and associational interest groups are not well developed and are often nothing more than the mere instrumentalities of the bureaucracy itself.

Similarly, there are also evident in the Italian political process *nonassociational* and *anomic* interest groups that make intermittent demands on government. A typical nonassociational group might be a regional conference called to discuss the problems of the development of the South, or of civil liberties and their observance. Such conferences, which are fairly frequent in Italy, often recruit participants from a wide variety of formally organized groups. They are, however, essentially *ad hoc* affairs, out of which may emerge certain political policy resolutions or actual communications to governmental bodies demanding or requesting action. In many cases, the meetings are organized by a fairly cohesive, even associational interest group. Thus the labor unions, as part of their over-all strategy, will sponsor economic conferences or study groups to which a wide variety of citizens—representing other groups, the bureaucracy, the legislature and cabinet, journalism, and the universities—are invited as participants and performers. The hope is that greater prestige and authority will be lent to the sponsoring group's demands as a result of the broad and presumably expert and neutral participation in the formulation and appraisal of the demands themselves. Two loosely structured groups of intellectuals—those organized around the prestigious weekly newspaper *Il Mondo* and the equally important monthly journal *Il Mulino*—are particularly active in sponsoring study conferences of the type described. The results of these encounters are not only reported in the journals involved but often published as single volumes. Through this strategy, the intellectuals hope to have an impact on such varied policy matters as education, civil liberties, foreign policy, motion pictures, and television, even the formation of particular coalitions in the legislature.

Among the other nonassociational interests that might be cited we would include those that reflect the demands of particular geographic regions or linguistic groups. Where, as in Sicily, there is a highly developed system of regional government under the decentralizing provisions of the Constitution, the communication of regional demands is highly structured and flows regularly to Rome through formal governmental channels. On the other hand, where the nonassociational interest group has a linguistic base, such as the German-speaking Italians who live in the South Tyrol, the communication of demands is not as structured and tends to be more intermittent. The same intermittency is characteristic of families, single industrial firms, and minority religious groups, which from time to time, depending on the problems that confront them, seek to communicate demands for policy or administrative action to government at the local or central level. As one would expect in a society of great structural differentiation, the incidence of this type of demand communication is apparently not as high as in the less developed societies, where secondary associations have not taken firm hold. As a matter of fact, where a felt interest exists in Italy, there has been, since the War, an increased tendency to devise some associational pattern whereby the interest might be systematically articulated and communicated.

Italy is also a country that has experienced a great deal of *anomic interest group* behavior. In a strict sense, the articulation of interests by anomic groups—riots, demonstrations, revolutions—should be spontaneous. As a matter of practice, most such occurrences in Italy are the premeditated work of political parties or voluntary associations. Pregnant women, for example, do not spontaneously appear lying prone on roads leading from Montecatini sulphur mines in order to keep trucks from passing. Mutilated veterans who converge on Rome en masse to protest pension policies do not get there because, as if by magic, they all decided that a demonstration before the ministry might have some influence. Italians do not spontaneously riot to protest alleged germ warfare in Korea or the establishment of NATO missile bases on Italian soil. With rare exceptions even the desperate peasants who forcibly occupy land, or the workers who refuse to leave factories, take such anomic action because of the leadership provided by more than one group. There are, of course, some marginal cases. It is not clear, for example, that all the riots that broke out in 1959 at ceremonies to commemorate the Resistance Movement were carefully organized by neo-Fascist and Monarchist organizations. Similarly, some of the demonstrations that occurred when the issue of Trieste reached explosive proportions evidently bordered on complete spontaneity in the sense that people were reacting to information communicated by the mass media. But when students stone embassies, protest demonstrations are held over the execution of the Rosenbergs, or roughnecks invade political meetings indoors or in the public piazzas, it is reasonably certain that some organizational propelling force lies behind them.

It is difficult to be sure that anomic interest-group behavior is largely the result of the ineffectiveness of political parties and voluntary associations as interest articulators and aggregators. One is led to that easy conclusion because such behavior is primarily fostered by parties and groups of the political extremes who do not have great influence over governmental policy. It is obvious, for example, that the Communist and Neo-Fascist parties accord the riot and the demonstration a high priority in their arsenal of political tactics. The use of these and other means of articulating interests even for political matters that are considerably far removed from matters of immediate domestic concern has been very well documented in the postwar years.

Yet it would be a mistake to overlook the fact that such behavior is deeply ingrained in Italian history and culture, and that many groups from time to time have had recourse to violence. While Italy is not in the same category as many Latin American republics that seem unable to handle any political affairs except through anomic means, neither is she close to the traditions of Anglo-American democracy, where anomic behavior is a genuinely rare occurrence. The point is that in a fragmented, nonbargaining political culture such as Italy's, characterized as it is by ideological rigidities and absolute value rationality, all these qualities are transferred to the competing groups. Out of this kind of interaction emerge certain patterns of violence that are expressions of fragmentation, as well as unbelievably strong instruments for reinforcing the fragmentation itself.

To a considerable extent, the extreme consequences of anomic behavior are held in check by the existence of thousands of *associational interest groups*. A general survey of these is reported and analyzed in Chapter V. It is sufficient to stress here that a reasonable basis for reducing the amount of anomic, nonassociational, and institutional interest group behavior exists. If, as I would contend, the proliferation of strong and autonomous associational interest groups is vital to the establishment and maintenance of a liberal democracy, the relevant developments in Italy since 1945 are more promising than they are discouraging.

INTEREST AGGREGATION

Once interests or demands are articulated, they must in some manner be combined or aggregated before they are translated into public policy. In a sense, all legislation, executive orders, administrative action, and judicial decisions represent this interest-combining process. One source of stability in a political system will therefore be found in the relative capacity of the authoritative political structures to satisfy the demands of individuals or groups in the society. The capacity to satisfy is dependent on a host of conditions, such as the resources available to government, the tempo with which new demands are made, the efficiency with which demands are communicated to rule-making centers, the skills that rule-makers evince in dealing with demands. One critical factor conditioning ability to cope with demands is the extent to which the demands that reach the sources of authoritative decision are aggregated. If there is a reasonably high degree of aggregation in advance, the functions of rule-making, rule-application, and rule-adjudication can be performed with relative ease; compromise is facilitated and politics really becomes the art of the possible. If, instead, the demands that reach the legislature, executive, or judiciary are essentially raw and unaggregated, a tendency toward immobilism, dilatoriness, and temporizing with basic problems develops. When, in such a setting, authoritative decisions are taken, they tend further to polarize and to isolate the competing groups in the society.

A striking characteristic of the Italian political system is precisely that the authoritative structures are regularly called on to deal with unaggregated interests and demands. The most important reason for this is that Italian political parties, which should theoretically play a central role in interest aggregation, do not in fact aggregate interests but tend for the most part to function as interest articulators.

84

In other words, the functions of interest groups and political parties in Italy are not sufficiently differentiated. The parties, like the interest groups, are ideologically rigid, the social fragmentation we have noted is reproduced in most of them, and the parties become essentially transmission belts for introducing into the legislature and other sectors of government raw, diffuse, extremely particularistic and, in any event, unaggregated demands. The instability of the Italian political system is therefore owing in part to the failure of the party system adequately to perform a vital function that would be associated with it in a liberal democracy.

Let us look at some of the details of this important phenomenon.

There are at present eight significant political parties operating in Italy. Three of these, the Communists (P.C.I.), Socialists (P.S.I.) and Christian Democrats (D.C.), in 1963 succeeded in capturing 77.4 percent of the total votes to gain 81.4 percent of the seats in the Chamber of Deputies. The remaining five parties include the Social Democrats (P.S.D.I.), led by Giuseppe Saragat; the Italian Liberal Party (P.L.I.), which is very close to Confindustria; two Monarchist groups, which in 1963 were fused into P.D.I.U.M.; the Italian Republican Party (P.R.I.); and the Neo-Fascist Italian Social Movement (M.S.I.). The results of the elections for the Chamber of Deputies of May 25, 1958 and April 28, 1963, are given for each party in Table 1.

The first thing to note about Table 1 is that over fifty percent of Italy's voters are recruited by two political parties (D.C. and P.C.I.) that are utterly at odds with each other. The fact was made amply clear following the 1963 elections when Aldo Moro said to the National Council of the D.C., "Our essential political objective is to keep the Communists in opposition. Whoever joins us in forming a government must want the same thing." This kind of mutual antagonism characterized the relationship between the Socialists and Christian Democrats until the

"Opening to the Left" of 1962. Indeed, the fact that the P.S.I. under Nenni agreed not to oppose a government led by Amintore Fanfani, and actually joined a government led by Aldo Moro in 1963, represents only a partial thaw. It means neither that the strong Catholic forces within the D.C. have changed their hostile views toward socialism nor that the extreme left within P.S.I. wishes completely to disavow the former close ties of P.S.I. to the Communist Party. Indeed a portion of this latter group, led by Tullio Vechietti, bolted the P.S.I. in 1964 and formed the far left P.S.I.U.P. (Italian Socialist Party of Proletarian Unity.)

TABLE 1: Vote and Seat Distribution, by Political Party, Chamber of Deputies, Elections of May 25, 1958 and April 28, 1963 [30]

	Valid Votes				Seats	
	1958		1963		1958	1963
Party	Number	Per-cent	Number	Per-cent	Num-ber	Num-ber
P.C.I.	6,704,454	22.7	7,763,854	25.3	140	166
P.S.I.	4,206,726	14.2	4,251,966	13.8	84	87
P.S.D.I.	1,345,447	4.5	1,874,379	6.1	22	33
P.R.I.	405,782	1.4	420,746	1.4	6	6
D.C.	12,492,319	42.3	11,763,418	38.3	273	260
P.L.I.	1,047,081	3.5	2,142,053	7.0	17	39
P.D.I.U.M.	1,436,916	4.8	536,652	1.7	25	8
M.S.I.	1,406,140	4.8	1,569,202	5.1	24	27
Other	515,404	1.8	407,999	1.3	5	4
Totals	29,560,269	100.0	30,730,269	100.0	596	630

[30] Figures for 1963 are approximate, having been gleaned from newspapers. 1958 figures are from *Annuario Statistico Italiano, 1959* (Rome, ISTAT, 1960, p. 143. In 1958 the Monarchists ran as two parties—P.M.P. with 776,919 votes, and P.N.M. with 659,997 votes. In 1958 the Radical Party ran as one, with P.R.I. In 1958, the Comunità Party, sponsored by the now deceased Adriano Olivetti, received 173,277 votes and was awarded one seat. The figures for both elections include the Valle d'Aosta, where a majoritarian electoral system is used and where in both elections the single seat went to the left-wing *Unione Valdostana*. It should be noted that in January, 1964, a portion of the extreme left of P.S.I., in protest over Pietro Nenni joining the Moro Government, left P.S.I. and formed the P.S.I.U.P. (The Italian Socialist Party of Proletarian Unity.)

Thus, although there are profound changes under way in Italian society, these have not yet brought about in the political realm a lessening of the acute tensions that characterize inter- and intraparty relationships. This problem was dramatically demonstrated in the weeks following the 1963 elections, when Fanfani seemed to be losing his hold on D.C. and Pietro Nenni was unable to deliver a majority of his party leadership to support *any* kind of left-of-center government formed by D.C.

It is extremely difficult to interpret the 1963 elections or to predict with confidence their long-range impact on Italian political stability.[31] For example, if one were to minimize the deep and serious schism within the Socialist Party, it might be possible to argue that 59.6 percent (P.S.I., D.C., P.R.I., P.S.D.I.) of the voters supported the "Opening to the Left." Yet such a view is superficial, in that it is based on the quite erroneous assumption that the leaders and followers of P.S.I. and the D.C. are relatively and respectively cohesive on matters of ideology and governmental policy. Even a cursory analysis of the internal struggles within these two parties would dramatically depict how far from reality such a view actually is. The Nenni-centered "Autonomists" in P.S.I. have their hands full with the left-wing "Carristi," some of whom are now in P.S.I.U.P.) who clearly abandoned the Party in large numbers in 1964. The Christian Democratic Party is a complicated maze of individuals and voters who

31 The data on which these observations are based come from various sources. See, for example, Giovanni Schepis, *op. cit.;* Mattei Dogan, "Le Comportement politique des italiens," *Revue Française de Science Politique,* 9 (June, 1959); Elio Caranti, *Sociologia e statistica delle elezioni italiane* (Rome, 1954); Francesco Compagna and Vittorio De Caprariis, *Geografia delle elezioni italiane dal 1946 al 1953* (Bologna, 1954); C. Cervigni and G. Galasso, "Inchiesta sul Partito Socialista Italiano," *Nord e Sud,* 3 (March, 1956), especially pp. 126–47; Giorgio Braga, *Il Comunismo fra gli italiani* (Milan, 1956); Di Marco Cesarini, "La Grossa calamita," *Il Mondo,* 15 (May 14, 1963), pp. 3–4; Francesco Compagna, "L'Elettore meridionale," *Il Mondo,* 15 (May 21, 1963), pp. 1–2; Giorgio Galli, "L'Operaio abbandonato," *Il Mondo,* 15 (May 28, 1963), pp. 1–2; Mario Cesarini, "La Prova del nove," *Il Mondo,* 15 (June 11, 1963), pp. 1–2.

gravitate around such personalities as Fanfani, Giulio Pastore, Aldo Moro, Mario Scelba, and Giulio Andreotti, to name only a few of the more prominent party notables. The claims and counterclaims in these parties and others about the meaning of the April 1963 vote attest to the continuing and serious fractionation of the Italian political system.

It is also possible, therefore, to view the 1963 electoral results as representing a further and more radical political fragmentation and polarization of the society. The Communists, for example, ran an electoral campaign that was strongly critical of the P.S.I. and the "Opening to the Left," and the extreme left gained over one million votes over the 1958 results. However one tries to analyze or explain the strong Communist upsurge, it is certain that several hundred thousand new votes for the Communists came from Italians who had previously supported P.S.I. Similarly, the Liberal Party, which also campaigned vigorously against the left-wing thrust of Fanfani gained over one million votes over 1958. To be sure, some of these new Liberal votes came from a defunct Monarchist Party in the South, but considerable numbers must also have come from D.C., which suffered serious losses in general, and particularly in some sectors of the South such as Sicily. Although inferring the exact degree of social tension or integration purely from electoral data is admittedly hazardous, we can certainly suggest that nothing in the 1963 elections *clearly* demonstrates that the fragmentation of the Italian political system is significantly abated.

Indeed, when we consider the dogged persistence of several of the minor parties, it is apparent that great pains are taken to continue both ideological and organizational differentiation. P.S.D.I., for example, strongly feels the compulsion to provide a revisionist socialist alternative for the voter, as well as to demonstrate that a party can be Marxist and still support the Atlantic Alliance and the foreign policy of the West. The Republican Party, which perhaps lost its *raison d'être* in 1946 when Italy became a republic, holds on tenaciously to pockets of support in some sections of the Romagna and in some places in the South. The Liberal Party, increasingly opposed to the Left tendencies of D.C., continues to attract a conservative middle class, as well as some former Monarchists and Christian Democrats who are alarmed at the allegedly "soft" posture toward Communism manifested by some D.C. leaders and by elements in the Vatican under John XXIII and Paul VI. The Monarchists, now reduced to about one-half million followers, recruit voters who remain inexplicably nostalgic about the past or cynical supporters of Monarchist candidates who have local patronage at their disposal. M.S.I. demonstrates that there remain in Italy one and one-half million voters who are either new or die-hard Fascists irreconcilably opposed to democratic government. Whether the real cause of party fragmentation is historical accident, ideological rigidity, or contemporary power struggle, it is apparent that Italy now seems headed toward the kind of immobility and instability that was so typical of the French Fourth Republic before Charles de Gaulle came to power.

It will help us to understand how well or poorly the parties function as interest aggregators if we know something about the geographic, social, and organizational sources of their strength and make-up.[32] Communist strength, for example, is heavily concentrated in the central regions of Emilia Romagna, Tuscany, and Umbria, where the party vote can reach two-fifths of the votes cast and where, in some cities, it can approach an absolute majority. These regions constitute Italy's "Red Belt." Not only industrial workers there but also, and particularly, the peasants and sharecroppers have a strong tendency to vote left. Several of the leading municipalities in these regions have been administered by Communist mayors consistently since the War. It is noteworthy that in these

[32] See, for example, Luzzatto Fegiz, *op. cit.*, and Joseph LaPalombara's review of it in *American Political Science Review*, 51 (June, 1957), pp. 530–32.

more agricultural regions, and not in the more industrial areas of the Po Valley and Piedmont, P.C.I. finds its greatest support. In the 1963 elections, that party increased its vote in central provinces such as those named by almost four percentage points. On the other hand, it is also in the rural—but heavily Catholic—regions of the Veneto, Friuli-Venezia-Giulia, and Trentino-Alto Adige that P.C.I. registers its electoral lows.

Most Italian commentators on the 1963 elections concede that the Communist Party is the primary beneficiary of the processes of urbanization and in-migration that have been under way in Italy for some years. Studies conducted in Bologna, for example, clearly demonstrate that peasants who migrate to the city from the surrounding hills and mountains tend to vote for P.C.I. in proportions that were not previously the case. Similarly, P.C.I. draws disproportionate numbers of votes from the poverty-ridden areas on the periphery of large industrial centers in the North to which Southern peasants migrate. The Italian Communists have been good sociologists and have provided these displaced, insecure, and economically and socially frustrated masses with their first meaningful associations. It is possible to predict, therefore, that both urbanization and in-migration will in the short run aggrandize the party at the extreme Left, thus adding yet another source of instability to the political system.

Although the Christian Democrats remain the Italian party with the relative majority, it is generally conceded that they suffered a serious diminution in the 1963 elections. The heaviest losses were experienced in places like Sicily where the D.C. has had a major problem for some years. However, the depletion in strength is a generalized phenomenon, concerning which all sorts of explanations are possible. For example, there are those who argue simply that, after so many years in the seat of power D.C. must necessarily experience a falling-off of followers. Others, who are strongly opposed to the Fanfani left-wing experiment as well as to the new "Opening to the Left" under

Moro, stress that many previous D.C. voters went to the ranks of P.L.I. in 1963. The data suggest, however, that it was the left-wing within D.C. that made impressive gains in the last elections, and that those who are identified with Scelba, Paolo Bonomi, and Giulio Andreotti either were not elected or suffered significant losses in preference votes. From the Left in politics comes the explanation that D.C. lost votes because its program of reform is not sufficiently explicit, consistent, and comprehensive, because the Party and the government are riddled by scandals for which those responsible are not made to pay, and because the public has grown weary of shady deals and the other manifestations of *sottogoverno*.

Regardless of its recent losses, D.C. remains Italy's most significant major party. Its major support at the polls continues to come from the northern, agricultural, and strongly Catholic regions of the Veneto, Fruili-Venezia-Giulia, and Trentino-Alto Adige, and from the rural southern regions of Campania, Basilicata, Calabria, and Sardinia. In the central regions, where P.C.I. and P.S.I. are particularly strong, the D.C. vote falls off considerably, and is often under forty percent. In general, the Party is more successful in the less industrial and more illiterate regions of both the North and the South than in the urbanized and industrialized areas, where literacy is greater and political participation presumably more purposive and meaningful.

There are also significant geographic differences that characterize the electoral support of the other parties. P.S.I., helped perhaps in the past by P.C.I. organization and by the radical traditions of the regions, scores its best record in places like Umbria and Tuscany. Once very weak in the South, this party has made impressive strides there in recent elections, and in some southern provinces is clearly outdistancing the gains made by P.C.I. P.S.D.I. is primarily a northern and industrial phenomenon, with its votes heavily concentrated in the regions of Piedmont, Liguria, and Lombardy. In Milan, for example, P.S.D.I.

is a strong party that can rightfully expect to share in the government of that important city. P.L.I., partly because of its historical association, is stronger in Piedmont than in any other region. Its ties to the industrialist and educated classes also give it important followings in Liguria and Lombardy. In the 1963 elections, it is generally agreed that the gains registered by this party in the South are to be accounted for primarily in the diminution of Monarchist votes. The Monarchists, in turn, who suffered the greatest relative loss in 1963, constitute primarily a southern phenomenon, and one which will probably completely disappear after one or two more national elections. The Neo-Fascist M.S.I. is also primarily southern, although it manages to get above-average votes in a few scattered central and northern provinces.

There are also some striking contrasts to be noted when we take size of commune as the variable alongside which to gauge relative party support. Although the data represented by Table 2 refer to the elections of 1953 and 1958,

TABLE 2: Percentage of Electoral Support for Major Parties by Size of Community, 1953 and 1958

Size of Community	P.C.I.		P.S.I.		D.C.	
	1953	1958	1953	1958	1953	1958
Up to 3,000	16.23	15.71	11.57	12.52	48.78	52.38
3,001 to 5,000	19.80	20.12	12.70	13.80	46.03	49.68
5,001 to 10,000	22.84	23.26	13.44	14.42	43.04	46.18
10,001 to 30,000	25.22	25.17	13.86	15.57	38.17	41.67
Over 30,000	24.39	24.37	12.13	14.39	34.41	35.58
Italy	22.59	22.72	12.70	14.32	40.10	42.42

we can presume that the relationship holds true for 1963 as well. The most important point to make in this regard is that support for Christian Democracy varies inversely with the size of the community, while that of the Communist Party increases from small to large communities. Our previous observation regarding what happens to the party affiliations of those who leave the countryside should suggest that this relationship will become even more pronounced in the years ahead, with D.C. holding on to the remaining rural vote and P.C.I. gaining strongly among those recently urbanized.

It is apparent that although D.C. has managed to improve its strength in the more urbanized areas, its dominant position in Italian politics is dependent in part on the unchallenged electoral leadership it enjoys in Italy's smallest rural communes. In places that exceed 10,000 inhabitants the combined strength of P.C.I. and P.S.I. is equal to or slightly in excess of that of D.C. In communes of 5,000 inhabitants or less, which account for fully one-fourth of Italy's voters, the D.C. vote is from almost fifty to more than eighty percent greater than that for P.C.I. and P.S.I. together. Without the extraordinary D.C. vote in these geographic areas, Italy would long since have fallen to the rule of the extreme Left. It is this general knowledge that serves in part to keep the Italian political system in a relatively high state of tension.

This situation may change, of course, if the "Opening to the Left" under Moro works and if the D.C.–P.S.I. coalition now in force at the national level is extended downward to the provinces and communes. It is too early, however, to anticipate the effective creation of such a new center of gravity.

In order fully to understand why, with the possible exception of D.C., most of Italy's parties articulate rather than aggregate interests, we must know something about the groups that support them at the polls and that operate within party organizations. The data we have on party electoral composition is based on survey research data that are not always as reliable as one might desire.[32] Nevertheless, these data, particularly if interpreted with some caution, offer us the only information we have regarding the social and economic characteristics of those who support the various parties in national elections. It is on these sources, therefore, that the generalizations and observations that follow are based.[33]

Approximately two-thirds of Italy's industrial workers vote for Marxist parties (i.e., P.C.I., P.S.I., or P.S.D.I.), while only one-fourth of them support D.C. In the important Industrial Triangle, the data suggest that the three Marxist parties attract 72 percent of the vote. More unskilled workers filter into P.C.I. ranks than into any other party. Indeed, survey estimates disclose that approximately fifty percent of the P.C.I. vote is made up of manual workers and their wives. Thus, while it is possible to break down analyses to show that P.C.I. does not attract a *majority* of the skilled workers of the Industrial Triangle, or a *majority* of the manual workers, it is accurate to say that (1) P.C.I. attracts most of the *working class* vote in Italy, and (2) P.C.I. is clearly the most proletarian of the competing parties. This conclusion is supported not merely by analyses of party support by occupational category, but also by the educational achievement of the voter. It is significant, for example, that 90 percent of the supporters of the Communist Party have had no education or only elementary education. Only 2 percent of its supporters have been to upper middle school or the university.

P.C.I. also manages to attract considerable support in agricultural sectors, although it is not nearly as effective here as D.C. The latter party receives 49 percent of its votes in communes of fewer than 10,000 inhabitants; only 35 percent of P.C.I. support comes from such areas. Where

[33] For some examples of the treatment of survey research data see the chapters by Mattei Dogan, "La Stratificazione sociale dei suffragi," and "Le Donne italiane tra il cattolicesimo e il marxismo," in Spreafico and LaPalombara, *op. cit.*, pp. 407–94. Cf. Joseph LaPalombara, "Political Party Systems and Crisis Government: French and Italian Contrasts," *Midwest Journal of Political Science*, 2 (May, 1958), pp. 117–42; Joseph LaPalombara and Jerry B. Waters, "Values, Expectations and Political Predispositions of Italian Youth," *Midwest Journal of Political Science*, 5 (February, 1961), pp. 47–58; Murray Edelman, "Sources of Popular Support for the Italian Christian Democratic Party in the Postwar Decade," *Midwest Journal of Political Science*, 2 (May, 1958), pp. 143–59.

P.C.I. does attract agricultural votes, they come primarily from the sharecroppers (*mezzadri*), some of whom are affluent; the poverty-ridden agricultural day laborers (*braccianti*); and the agricultural lumpenproletariat. D.C. also recruits from these categories, but, more important, it manages to walk off with almost one-third of the votes of agricultural landowners and an overwhelming 79 to 83 percent of the votes of small and medium direct cultivators (*coltivatori diretti*). By way of contrast, it is noteworthy that D.C. manages to account for only 18 percent of the total industrial working class vote in the country.

P.S.I. shows some similarities to P.C.I. in the urban areas. Certainly most of its vote is working class. However, its working class supporters are better educated and more skilled than those of P.C.I. While it, too, has reason to think of itself as a proletarian party, it is obvious that it recruits in diminished degree among the poorest agricultural categories and that it is more successful than P.C.I. in attracting representatives of the lower-middle and middle classes. Moreover, despite its essentially working-class base, P.S.I. is not as successful as P.C.I. in reflecting this in the kinds of party members who achieve positions of internal leadership and who are sent to the legislature.

Neither P.C.I. nor P.S.I. is as popular among the middle class as are D.C. and the minor parties. Roughly one-fifth of the persons who fall into this category support the former parties, while it is estimated that as many as 50 percent of them fall into D.C. electoral ranks. One important category in which the latter is particularly strong is the elementary, middle, and high school teachers. But among white-collar workers in general, D.C. undoubtedly has considerable support. The same is true of many bureaucrats, small businessmen, and members of the liberal professions. In addition, it must be noted that the political dominance of D.C. is largely the result of its appeal to Italian women. Estimates suggest that the Party gets over 50 percent of the female vote and that women voters constitute two-thirds of the party's total electoral support.

In no other political party do female supporters exceed the males, and in cases like P.S.I., P.S.D.I., and P.L.I. the male-female ratio is at least two to one. In P.C.I., three-fifths of the supporters are male.

For the most part the minor parties are homogeneous and sectarian in their appeal. P.L.I. is strongly supported by employers, executives, large landowners, managers, and upper-level bureaucrats. P.R.I.'s supporters are almost exclusively recruited from those Italians for whom Republicanism and anticlericalism are strongly held values. This party's support, as we have already noted, is also concentrated geographically. P.S.D.I. is the Italian equivalent of the French S.F.I.O. It is the respectable, revisionist Marxist Party that appeals to the skilled worker elite, to artisans and clerical workers—even some employers and managers—who are in search of dignified and not too virulent leftism. It is also the party that provides a haven for elements of the middle class who find the clericalism implicit in D.C. unpalatable.

The Monarchist parties constitute a regionally isolated phenomenon in the South. There, landowners and members of the aristocracy provide strong support. Although the issue of the monarchy is undoubtedly dead, the Democratic Party into which the monarchists have merged provides the desired quantum of political and social conservatism. The Radicals constitute a small party with primary appeal to a middle class, intellectual, and anticlerical group who lean toward the Left, but not all the way to Marxism. Finally, M.S.I. is a party frankly based on nostalgia for Fascism and on such emotional symbols as "the nation," "order," and the "red menace."

In short, almost every Italian party shows extreme cohesion around a core that is based either on social class or on ideology. If class considerations are taken as the discriminating variable, the only party in Italy with any strong claim to being interclassist is D.C., which clearly recruits some substantial following from every socio-economic category. It is the only party that can dent the appeal of P.C.I. and P.S.I. for industrial workers, the conservative attraction of the monarchists in the South, P.L.I.'s strong appeal for the industrial and educated classes, and even the strong bid for support that M.S.I. can make within the public bureaucracy in Rome and elsewhere. What holds D.C. together is its confessionalism—and its control of governmental power—which seems to override the other ideological differences that separate conservative party notables from radical trade unionists, those who view interference from the Vatican from those who favor deep involvement of the Church in politics.

The homogeneity of each political party is understandably reflected in the interest groups that they harbor in their midst or with which they maintain close ties. Most of the parties maintain auxiliary organizations designed to provide a special place and voice for women, youth, intellectuals, workers, and so on. Thus members of the Italian General Confederation of Labor (C.G.I.L.) are prominent in P.C.I. and P.S.I.; leaders of the Italian Union of Labor (U.I.L.) militate in the ranks of P.S.D.I. and P.R.I.; those who lead the Italian Confederation of Workers' Unions are found primarily in D.C. Similarly, it is well known that close ties exist between Confindustria and P.L.I., between the fascist trade union confederation (C.I.S.N.A.L.) and M.S.I., between an intellectual interest group such as *Il Mondo* and the Republican and Radical parties, between the vast superstructure of Italian Catholic Action and D.C.

The point here is not that interest groups interact with parties but that each individual group tends to be identified with only one party, either as a structure conditioning what the party does or as a mere instrumentality and extension of the party itself. Thus the isolative character of the political culture is not strongly mitigated by the parties. For most parties there is little to aggregate because parties and constituent interest groups are in complete accord. D.C. constitutes the only partial exception to this generalization. Here there is clearly a conflict between employer and employee groups, agricultural and industrial labor associations, university students and old party notables, ardently Catholic groups and the party professionals themselves. This is one reason why the electoral language of D.C. tends to be vague and amorphous.[34] Nevertheless, the important aggregating role that D.C. might perform in Italy is considerably limited by the overriding nature of its confessional character. Any effort, such as the attempt at a rapprochement with P.S.I., is certain to cause considerable internal strain precisely because it threatens the vital link—Catholic antisocialism—that has held the Party together at all since 1946. Such internal tension was apparent in late 1963 when D.C. leaders of the right, such as Mario Scelba and Giuseppe Pella, threatened not to support the Moro Government because of the inclusion of P.S.I. on terms unacceptable to these men. Only intervention of the Vatican, in the name of Catholic unity, prevented an outright split in D.C.

I do not mean to suggest here that D.C. is the only party with internal factions,[35] or that the other Italian parties do not engage in any interest-aggregating activities. P.C.I., for example, has had to contend with the conflict between C.G.I.L.'s leaders and those in the Party who will not tolerate trade-union autonomy. Other internal crises have developed for the Party over the inferences to draw from the 20th Congress of the C.P.S.U. and de-Stalinization. P.S.I. has had difficulties reconciling factions born of the question concerning the proper degree of cooperation with P.C.I., on the one hand, and D.C., on the other. There also exists a generational conflict within P.S.I. of

[34] On the difficulty that D.C. experiences in articulating a coherent political philosophy, see E. Noether, "Political Catholicism in France and Italy," *Yale Review*, 44 (June, 1955), pp. 569–83. Cf. the interesting study on the evolution of Christian Democracy by Richard A. Webster, *The Cross and the Fasces* (Stanford, 1960).

[35] For an interesting view of party factionalism in Italy, see Raphael Zariski, "Party Factions and Comparative Politics: Some Preliminary Observations," *Midwest Journal of Political Science*, 4 (February, 1960), pp. 27–51.

considerable magnitude, as well as a rift between party bureaucrats and party trade unionists. However, intra-party conflicts, which in some countries are somehow resolved through compromise, tend to lead in Italy to party splits and to realignments that are ideologically more congenial to those who bolt. This fact is dramatically portrayed by the history of the ill-fated Action Party and by the tortured postwar odyssey of Italian socialism. It is also reflected in the schisms experienced by the Liberal and Monarchist parties, and even by some early splintering of D.C. itself. Where the expectation of each group is that the party will be simply the means of transmitting its demands intact to decisional centers of the government, the two most probable alternative outcomes are the party as mere interest articulator or the party as a continuously splintering phenomenon. Special considerations have prevented or delayed serious splintering in P.C.I. and D.C., but the price for this has been enforced ideological homogeneity and discipline in the former and an incredible amount of temporizing with basic problems in the latter. The truth is that Italy still lacks an orderly mechanism for the aggregation of demands before they get into the authoritative structures of government.

POLITICAL COMMUNICATION

I have already alluded to the most important characteristic of the political communication function in Italy, namely that it tends to be neither neutral nor objective. This is not to say that it is impossible for the interested Italian to learn what is transpiring in his society or in the broader international sphere. Isolation from the news is probably true of only a small, rural, and illiterate fraction of the population.[36] A highly developed communica-

36 How much political information the Italian actually has is quite another matter. Ignorance of things political and wholesale disinterest in political issues is particularly true of women, but it is a generalized phenomenon of striking proportions. See LaPalombara and Waters, op. cit., pp. 47-48. Cf. Paolo Ammassari, "Opinione politica e scelta elettorale," in Spreafico and LaPalombara, op. cit., pp. 733-79.

tions technology and the rapid spread of radio and television make it theoretically possible for the news-hungry individual to satiate his need. In addition, there are many other means whereby one would suppose that politically relevant information is transmitted. The pulpit, as I have noted, is one of these. So, presumably, is the vast bureaucratic apparatus that emanates from Rome and, at least intermittently, permeates even the remotest hamlet. Italian electoral campaigns involve not only the use of the mass media but the saturation of the country with roving loudspeakers, leaflets, brochures, agitprops, and the colorful speeches and debates in the public squares—the *comizi*. One should add to this the mountains of mimeographed and printed materials that interest groups make available for their members.

One might infer from all this activity that the Italian citizen is well informed. Yet, in a pre-electoral study conducted in 1958 in the city of Florence and four other communities in that vicinity—which are *not* isolated or underdeveloped—we uncovered some significant findings. For example, respondents were asked whether their opinion concerning the outgoing legislature and the political system was favorable, unfavorable, or nonexistent. The results of these two queries, by age group and sex, are summarized in Table 3.[37]

The most striking feature of the table is the difference between the sexes. It is certainly significant that well over half of the female voters have no opinion on the political system and almost as many have no opinion on the outgoing legislature. The men, who are more active and interested in politics, score much better, particularly on the work of the legislature. But the table suggests that there are considerable numbers in Italy who simply have little or no exposure to the media of communications. I would suggest, for example, that if the table reflects the situation

[37] See Ammassari, *op. cit.*, p. 748. This field study was conducted under the joint direction of the author and Alberto Spreafico. The technical details of it are discussed in pp. 781–84.

TABLE 3: Percentage of Voters Unable to Express an Opinion
on the Outgoing Legislature or Political System, by
Sex and Age

Voters without Opinion

	On Legislature	On Political System
Males		
21–35 years	16.6	29.8
36–49 years	15.6	16.6
Over 50 years	20.1	34.6
Females		
21–35 years	45.9	53.7
36–49 years	28.5	51.7
Over 50 years	50.5	68.3

in Tuscany and Emilia Romagna, where political contests
are most avidly and bitterly contested, the situation must
be appallingly worse in the South.

When these same people were asked to indicate which
of the various means of exposure to political information
attracted their attention, and whether they considered the
exposure sufficient or insufficient, the results given in
Table 4 were obtained.[38]

Our data clearly indicate that those who had experienced "sufficient" exposure to the media were more likely

TABLE 4: Exposure of Voters to Political Communication
Media

Exposure (N = 470)

Media	Sufficient (%)	Insufficient (%)
Meetings in public squares	32.1	67.9
Loudspeakers	34.0	66.0
Leaflets and posters	32.5	67.5
Brochures	15.9	84.1
Radio broadcasts	18.9	81.2
Documentary films	4.5	95.5
Telecasts	12.1	87.9
Newspapers and magazines	16.5	83.2

[38] *Ibid.*, p. 766.

to have opinions on the legislature and political system than those for whom exposure was insufficient. Similarly, those with exposure and opinions had also made up their minds in greater numbers on the matter of which party to support. Rather than become involved in the interesting implications of this type of analysis, however, it suffices for us to note that (1) considerable numbers of Italian voters go to the polls with little or no political information or opinions, and (2) one's level of political information and his political opinions are in part directly related to his exposure to the media and means of communication.

We must conclude that political communication in Italy is relatively limited and that much of it is highly fragmented, biased, and undoubtedly not designed to encourage rational choices in the electorate. To the extent that the society is imperfect regarding either the autonomy of the media or the degree of their penetration, the political system will lack a democratically effective citizenry and electorate. From the standpoint of the democratic polity, the state (i.e., party) monopoly of radio and television, the paucity of a genuinely independent press, and the generation of news and editorial comment by interest groups and others who are not professionally disinterested are not signs of political health. The structure of Italian communication, while it does afford some control of corruption and political excesses, and while it does provide the government with a reasonable degree of feedback from the governed, tends to reflect and to fortify the fragmented, isolative, nonbargaining character of the political culture.

CHAPTER IV · THE STRUCTURE
OF GOVERNMENT

THE Italian Constitution, drafted by the Constituent Assembly elected in 1946, was ratified by that body in December 1947 and went into effect on January 1, 1948.[1] Whereas the Constitution or *Statuto* obtained from Charles Albert of Piedmont in 1848 was flexible in the sense that it could be modified by ordinary legislation, the new basic law is rigid. The provisions of the Constitution cannot be modified except through extraordinary procedures,[2] and legislation that conflicts with the Constitution can be declared invalid by judicial authorities.[3] The Constitution also enshrines the abolition of the monarchy, provides for the establishment of a republican form of government, and specifies that the republican form of government cannot be made the subject of constitutional revision.[4]

The 1948 Constitution provides for a great deal of formal structural differentiation, in keeping with practice dating back at least a century. This should not be understood to mean that the document represents an effort to establish a clear-cut and rigid separation of powers. On the other hand, relatively firm lines are drawn that tend to separate the rule-making, rule-application, and rule-adjudication functions.

Before we examine the structures associated with these

[1] The "Committee of Seventy-Five" that drafted the document completed its work on January 31, 1947. The document was debated in general and then article by article. A great number of changes were made, many by the narrowest of votes. The final vote was 453 favorable and 82 opposed. An English translation is included in Norman Kogan, *The Government of Italy* (New York, 1962), pp. 188–215. A concise, carefully annotated version is produced by Ferruccio Pergolesi, *Lineamenti della Costituzione italiana* (Rome, 1956).

[2] *The Italian Constitution of 1948*, Article 138.

[3] *Ibid.*, Articles 134–37.

[4] *Ibid.*, Articles 83–91, 139.

functions, let us make a few further observations on the Constitution itself. The first twelve articles contain its fundamental principles. These include popular sovereignty (Art. 1), inviolable rights and concomitant duties (Art. 2), equality before the law (Art. 3), the obligation of the Republic to remove social and economic obstacles that limit liberty and equality or inhibit the development of the human personality (Art. 3), the right to work and the duty of the individual to work for the material and spiritual progress of the society (Art. 4), a call for maximum local autonomy and administrative decentralization (Art. 5). It should be noted that many of these (and other) provisions are *programmatic* and not *executory;* their implementation depends not on the Constitution alone but on the enactment of subsequent implementing legislation. Many of the political controversies among interest groups and political parties have centered on the failure of the government to implement the programmatic articles. Some scholars feel, with considerable logic, that some of the abstract principles and goals might better have been included in a preamble rather than in the corpus of the Constitution itself.

Pious hopes, clearly dependent on subsequent legislative and administrative action, are scattered about in other sections of the Constitution as well. Thus those who merit it are said to be entitled to the highest level of education they can reach regardless of means (Art. 34); the worker is to be compensated on the basis of the quality and quantity of his labor and in each case sufficiently to permit the free and dignified existence of his family (Art. 36); the right of workers to participate in the management of economic enterprises is recognized, within limits established by law (Art. 46); and the tax system is supposed to be informed by progressive criteria (Art. 47). These highly generic statements are present because the Constituent Assembly was dominated by Christian Democrats, Communists, and Socialists. Basic differences of ideology made it impossible to agree on executory provisions, with the result that compromises were taken and reflected in vague, programmatic pronouncements.

In addition, there are sections of the Constitution that seem to grant certain rights in one phrase and to limit them in the next. The right to strike is recognized, but within the limits of legislation that regulates it (Art. 40); freedom of trade unions to organize is granted, but they can be compelled by law to register, and registration can be made to turn on the internal democratic character of the organizations (Art. 39); private property is recognized and guaranteed by law, but it can be taken by the State in instances where monopoly or the public interest demands such action (Art. 43). There are even instances of seemingly outright contradiction. Thus, whereas freedom and equality of religious practice and observance are guaranteed (Arts. 8, 19, 20), the Constitution also provides that the relations between Church and State are regulated by the Lateran Pact of 1929. The latter contains, among many provisions, the following: "Italy recognizes and reaffirms the principle of the Albertine *Statuto* whereby the Catholic Apostolic and Roman religion is the only religion of the State." [5] That Palmiro Togliatti in the Constituent Assembly urged his followers to support this provision is taken by many to mean that he did not think the Italian Republic would survive many years beyond 1947. In any event, the vagueness and contractions of the Constitution have served not merely to provide the students of public law with a rich source of commentary and disputation but also to polarize further the parties and groups in Italy that develop esoteric interpretations and demands concerning implementation of the Constitution.

What Americans call civil rights are also granted in great profusion by the 1948 Constitution. These include rights of personal freedom (Art. 13); freedom and secrecy of communication (Art. 15); freedom of movement, except as restricted by law for reasons other than political ones (Art. 16); freedom of peaceful private and public assembly,

5 Pergolesi, *op. cit.*, p. 31.

except as limited for reasons of public security (Art. 17); freedom of association for ends not prohibited by law (Art. 18); protection from ex post facto legislation (Art. 25); freedom of the press (Art. 21); freedom to join political parties (Art. 49); and so on, through a long list of basic liberties. The Constitution, therefore, seems clearly to establish a liberal democratic government. That this does not always work out in fact is owing largely to the persistence of legislation enacted under Fascism and to the past and present failure of the Christian Democrats to implement many sections of the Constitution, some of them merely programmatic but others that go right to the structural heart of the constitutional system.[6] Alluding to one critical consequence of this, Gaetano Azzariti, who was named president of the Constitutional Court in 1957, said: ". . . the systematic neglect of the law by the major organs of the state and particularly by the legislature is extremely dangerous because it generates and diffuses a general distrust of the law and is a prime cause of lawlessness, of which in these recent years we have so often had reason to speak with sadness." [7]

RULE-MAKING

Authoritative rules are made by various sectors of government at both the national and local level. The most important formal rule-making body however is the bicameral Parliament, whose members are popularly elected for

[6] On this important problem, see John Clarke Adams and Paolo Barile, "The Implementation of the Italian Constitution," *American Political Science Review*, 47 (March, 1953), pp. 61–83. Cf. the important volume *Comitato Nazionale per la Celebrazione del Primo Decennale della Promulgazione della Costituzione*, Vol. V, *L'Attuazione della costituzione* (Milan, 1958). The four other volumes of this work are of basic importance to an understanding of the Italian constitutional system. They are: Vol. I, *Discorsi e scritti sulla costituzione;* Vol. II, *Studi sulla costituzione;* Vol. III, *Studi sulla costituzione;* Vol. IV, *I precedenti storici della costituzione.*

[7] Quoted by Adams and Barile, *The Government of Republican Italy* (Boston, 1961), p. 57.

fixed terms on the basis of population.[8] Members receive compensation that amounts to between $600 and $750 per month while the legislature is in session. Under the Constitution, both houses have almost equal power; legislation, to become effective, must be approved by both the Chamber of Deputies and the Senate. It is in this context that the most important debates over public policy occur.

The 851 legislators who make up the membership of the Chamber of Deputies and the Senate constitute a most important part of Italy's visible political elite.[9] It is from them, or from a segment of them, that interest groups must obtain a "yes" or a "no" before they can judge whether their attempts to influence the rule-making sector of the political system have been effective.

Various factors concerning the legislature are relevant to an analysis of the relationship between legislature and interest groups. One such factor is social-psychological; it involves the nature of role-taking on the part of the lawmakers. Giovanni Sartori, who has completed the only intensive political study of the Chamber of Deputies, suggests that it is necessary to analyze three major roles in the legislature, namely those of *parliamentarian, representative,* and *clientelistic.*[10] Within the last, there are several role subtypes, one of which involves interest groups as clients. Toward such groups, the lawmaker can behave as a *facilitator* of interests, as a *resistor* to the demands of interest groups, or as one who is relatively ignorant of or *outside* the group process.[11] One of Sartori's conclusions is: "In our parliament, for example, the outsiders, those who do not have a definite perception of the role and effect of

[8] For the major constitutional provisions concerning the legislature, see *Constitution,* Articles 55–82.

[9] On the important question of the "visible" and "invisible" elite, see Giovanni Sartori, "La Sociologia del parlamento," *Studi politici,* 8 (April, 1961), pp. 131–36.

[10] *Ibid.,* pp. 147–51.

[11] *Ibid.,* pp. 151, 153–55. The concepts used by Sartori were developed by J. C. Walke, H. Eulau, W. Buchanan, and L. C. Ferguson, *The Legislative System* (New York, 1962), Part IV.

the 'pressure group' clientele, are surely the most numerous group. This does not mean that the outsiders are neutrals, and that their outsideness must be interpreted as an involuntary means of facilitating pressure group influence. In effect, once the outsider is placed on his guard, it is more probable that he will align himself with the Resistors than with the Facilitators." [12]

Sartori's comment raises serious questions for those who might see all legislators as essentially the expression and instruments of one or another of society's competing groups. Such a typology of roles indicates that such a relationship is true only when it can be shown that the legislator engages in a *particular* configuration of role-taking. This suggests, as I have stressed in Chapter I, that it is inadequate to view any sector of the political process from the standpoint of simplistic interest-group theory. It also cautions us to the need for careful empirical examination of the legislative process before drawing firm conclusions regarding the role of interest groups in it.

Another factor of considerable importance in an examination of the relationship between interest groups and the legislature is structural. We may ask the general question: "What is it about the structural characteristics of the formal rule-making body that would seem either to inhibit or to facilitate group access and influence?" There are a number of statements to make about the Italian legislature that are relevant in this regard. The first of these is that nothing in the Constitution, laws, or practices concerning rule-making prohibits groups from seeking and obtaining direct representation in either house of Parliament. As a matter of fact, all of Italy's political parties have become vehicles for making such direct representation possible to some extent. Thus, if we look at the parliamentary contingent of Christian Democracy, it is apparent that it includes leaders of such constituent interest groups as Catholic Action, A.C.L.I., C.I.S.L., and the Col-

[12] *Ibid.*, pp. 154–55.

tivatori Diretti. The unions, female associations, and youth groups achieve representation through the Communist and Socialist Parties. To a very limited extent, Confindustria finds some spokesmen in P.L.I. and D.C. The fact is that, while it is not accurate to characterize the Italian Parliament as consisting merely of interest-group representatives, direct representation does exist and obviously has a bearing on what the legislature does and on the relative access of competing groups to an important decisional center.

The legislature also operates through a highly differentiated system of standing and investigating committees. There are fourteen specialized standing committees in the Chamber of Deputies and eleven in the Senate. These are the committees that normally consider bills introduced by the government, by private members, by regional assemblies, and by the National Council of Economics and Labor, which may also be authorized to initiate legislation. It should be noted, incidentally, that unlike most European legislatures, the Italian system places no limit on the number of private-member bills that can be introduced. As a result, an impressively high number of such bills pass initial legislative screening and are referred to standing committees for disposition.

One procedure open to the specialized committees is that of considering a legislative proposal and then reporting it back for action, with or without suggested amendments or modifications. Another procedure, more rarely used, is for the committees, themselves, to act as initiators of legislation. A third procedure, almost never found in western legislatures, is for the committee to sit in *sede deliberante* concerning a referred bill. In this capacity, the committee can actually pass the bill, making it law. There are, to be sure, classes of legislation (e.g., budgetary laws, constitutional laws, delegated legislation) to which the *sede deliberante* procedure may not be applied. Nevertheless, the use of the procedure is extensive, as indicated by the fact that it is normal for two-thirds of the bills introduced by the government and as many as ninety percent of the private-member bills to be turned into law in this way.[13] Thus, while one student emphasizes that little attention is paid to the development of a highly specialized committee system,[14] interest-group leaders and some legislators interviewed by the author frequently alluded to the importance of the *sede deliberante* as a means of giving organized interest considerable leverage over the legislative process. Certainly the fact that a proposal may be called from the committee through this operation of several mechanisms is not as reassuring as one would suppose in view of the very great numbers of bills adapted in committee sessions.

Several more structural observations are pertinent. No bill may be finally passed that is not approved in the same language by both houses. Thus a group defeated in one chamber can attempt to hold up passage in another. Legislation is shifted back and forth until differences are reconciled or until the legislative session terminates. Rules of the Chamber of Deputies require (and Senate practice frequently permits) that the votes on final passage of a bill be secret. It is theoretically not possible for any group or political party leadership to know what disposition of the black and white balls each deputy has made in the final analysis. This procedure is said to imply freedom of the lawmaker from subservience to groups; on the other hand, it also undercuts party discipline and the ability of the electorate to learn how individuals have voted on controversial issues. Finally, because the legislature enthrones and dethrones governments, elects the President of the Republic and a third of the membership of the Constitutional Court, and passes on important pieces of delegated legislation, groups seeking in a fundamental and long-term way to mold Italian political policy are strongly motivated to intervene there.

[13] See Adams and Barile, *op. cit.*, p. 67.
[14] Giovanni Sartori, "Parliamentarians in Italy," *International Social Science Journal*, 4 (October, 1961), pp. 596–97.

RULE APPLICATION

The day-to-day affairs of government are handled by the executive branch. This includes the President of the Republic, the Cabinet and its President (or Prime Minister), and the vast bureaucratic apparatus of the country. It is to these sectors that one would look for the formal activity of rule application. However, it is necessary to understand that, even with the formal framework established by the Constitution, the executive branch can and does have an important and direct bearing on rule-making. The President of the Republic, for example, has the constitutional power to designate the President of the Council of Ministers whenever that position becomes vacant for any reason. This power is not unlike that enjoyed by the King or Queen under the British parliamentary system. But, whereas the British monarch has had little choice except to designate the leader of the majority party in the House of Commons, the Italian President has been able to use greater discretion in view of the fact that no party enjoys such a monopoly of legislative seats and that, within the Christian Democratic Party, the choice of who should be the next Prime Minister is not always apparent. Thus ex-President Gronchi had—and he freely used—considerable influence over the determination of who would head Italian government. In making these choices, it is perfectly obvious that the President can have significant influence over the kind of rule-making activity that is likely to emerge in the legislature.

Whether the President of the Republic is supposed to be largely a figurehead, subservient to the Cabinet, or a person exercising substantive executive powers is a subject of considerable discussion and controversy in Italy. While, on the one hand, the Constitution grants the President a wide range of powers,[15] it requires, on the other hand, that all acts signed by him be countersigned by the minister (or ministers) proposing the act or who is responsible for

[15] See *Constitution*, Articles 59, 62, 72–75, 87, 88, 92, 132, 135, 138.

it.[16] Since the election to the Presidency of Giovanni Gronchi, a dynamic politician of the Catholic Left, the debate has been intensified. Gronchi did not hesitate to speak before the legislature, and in public, on fundamental matters of public policy. He made it plain, for example, that he favored active public intervention in the solution of many of Italy's basic social and economic problems. He was certainly also one of those Christian Democrats who favored having his party move away from dead Center in the direction of the Nenni Socialists on the Left. In this posture he reflected his long-term disagreement and discomfort with the centrist strategies devised by Alcide De Gasperi. If precedents set by Gronchi are institutionalized, it is evident that presidents of the Republic will play stronger roles in the furtherance of legislative and administrative policies than are usually associated with that office under parliamentary systems. In any event, it is significant that in Italy some secondary associations attempt to secure the good will and support of the President and that some political journals, such as *Incontri Mediterranei,* are widely understood to articulate the political policies, foreign and domestic, and interests for which the ex-President, himself, stands. Thus, while the President formally speaks only for himself, he is able to throw his considerable prestige behind one line of policy or another. Current evidence suggests that, if anything, Italy's contemporary President, Antonio Segni, is following along the lines of precedent established by Gronchi.

At the apex of the formal rule-application hierarchy stands the government, which consists of the Council of Ministers and its President. The Council President, or Prime Minister, is the head of government. From him is

[16] *Ibid.,* Article 89. For a discussion of presidential powers, see Paolo Barile, "I Poteri del presidente della repubblica," in *Comitato Nazionale per la Celebrazione* . . . , *op. cit.,* Vol. III, pp. 133–83; F. M. Dominedò, "Saggio sul potere presidenziale," *ibid.,* pp. 201–27; Mario Griscolia, "In tema di competenza amministrativa del presidente della repubblica," *Rivista trimestrale di diritto pubblico,* 10 (1960), pp. 70–141; Adams and Barile, *op. cit.,* pp. 75–83.

presumed to emanate the policy leadership exercised in the legislature. On him and his ministerial associates rests the ultimate responsibility for the administration of law. One serious limitation on the ability of the government to exercise leadership is brief tenure in office; between 1948 and 1962 there were fifteen governments in Italy, with tenure for anyone not exceeding twelve months by very much. Under the circumstances it is felt by some that the executive branch is characterized by serious lack of continuity. The facts, however, divulge much more continuity than one might imagine. During the same period there were four governments headed by Alcide De Gasperi; four, including one that lasted less than a month, by Amintore Fanfani; and two each by Adone Zoli and Antonio Segni. Moreover, Christian Democratic Cabinet reshuffles almost never involve a complete turnover of personnel; the same old faces keep reappearing in ministerial posts, even if the internal readjustments are occasionally striking. Thus, while the locus of power over government may shift right or left within the Christian Democratic Party, it is still that party which has been consistently dominant since 1948. The fact that it has exercised continuous political hegemony has had certain implications for interest group behavior that we shall examine in detail in later chapters.

The Cabinet usually consists of approximately twenty-five ministers. Roughly nineteen of these are men who govern the ministries into which public administration is divided.[17] Several other ministers serve without portfolio and are in charge of such matters as the development of southern Italy and the reform of the bureaucracy. The latter minister was initially appointed to effect bureaucratic changes that, among other things, might result in a

17 The ministries are: Foreign Affairs, Interior, Defense, Finance and Treasury, Budget, Labor and Social Security, Industry and Commerce, Agriculture and Forests, Public Instruction, Transportation, Postal and Telegraphic Services, Foreign Commerce, Merchant Marine, Health, State-Controlled Enterprises, and Entertainment and Tourism.

diminution of ministries. It is one of the typical ironies of Italian politics that the number of ministries subsequently increased, little change was effected in the bureaucracy, and the bureaucratic empire of the minister without portfolio grew considerably over the years.

It would be a mistake to view the Cabinet members as mere rule-applying instrumentalities. They are, to be sure, extremely important in the performance of that function, although, as we shall see, very limited in the degree of effective control they can maintain over the professional bureaucracy. However, there are several factors that make the Cabinet greatly significant as a rule-making instrument. In the first place, the Cabinet is usually chosen from the legislature and is expected under the Constitution to exercise legislative leadership. This means that the government regularly introduces important legislation, guides it through committees, fixes the conditions of debate that apply to it, and generally expects the majority it represents to support its proposals. Indeed, failure of the government to secure legislative concurrence concerning important legislation is generally viewed as an expression of nonconfidence that causes the government to fall. Nonconfidence can lead, first, to a new government; second, to a Cabinet reshuffling (*rimpasto*); and, third, to the calling of new elections. Such a vote has not been frequently taken since 1948. Rather, the evidence is clear that, once a government has been installed and has received an initial vote of confidence, it has pretty much its own way on legislative matters, at least for some months following installation.

In the second place, the government (and bureaucracy) derive considerable rule-making power from the relatively infrequent use of the legislative decree (*decreto legislativo*) and the much more frequent use of the "regulation" that is based on some law. The legislative decree is an administrative order passed in accordance with previous power-granting, enabling legislation. The enabling law defines the general purpose and limits for which subsequent legislative decrees may be issued. It also sets a time limit beyond which the government and administrative agencies may no longer issue decrees. Such enabling laws usually apply to highly complex legislative matters that would probably be beyond the average legislator's ken in any case. The "regulation," an administrative order not enacted by Parliament, is a device whereby the government can establish certain administrative "norms" without the covering blanket of delegated legislation. Its use is increasing, and the manner of its use suggests that one man's routine administrative matter may very well be another's legislative policy.

In the third place, the Cabinet is important in rule-making, for Italian political parties are generally disciplined parties. Party leaders, who inevitably gravitate to the legislature and occupy key positions there, expect their party colleagues to vote as the party leadership dictates. The party line is set with caucuses held by the parliamentary party groups. The rank-and-file are expected to follow it in committee sessions, legislative debate, and final voting on bills. As we have noted, the secret-ballot procedure on final votes gives the individual deputy an opportunity to defy party leadership. Some of this occurred on the final vote on the Merlin Bill abolishing legalized prostitution, with amusing attempts by journalists and others to analyze whether Communists or Christian Democrats had bolted. An even more dramatic example of deviation occurred in 1956, when Giovanni Gronchi was elected President, and in 1959 when the Second Fanfani government was toppled by the hidden Christian Democratic snipers. The very drama that surrounds such instances, however, is an indication of their rarity. By and large, the rank-and-file learn the party line and vote it.

Lastly, on the matter of effective executive rule-making power, we must note that the Italian legislature is simply not able meaningfully to assess and to cope with the increasing complexity of modern legislative matters. This phenomenon is certainly not unique to Italy but besets all contemporary democracies. It raises very serious questions about the contemporary applicability of classical democratic theory. If, as the Italian situation seems to demonstrate, the legislature is ill-equipped to deal with the onslaught of governmental and administrative expertise, we must question whether the necessary legislative equipment can be provided. If the answer is negative, it is probably time to rework the theory on which the idea of the legislature as the representative rule-making agency is based.

The Cabinet oversees the bureaucracy, the organizational apparatus that translates policies into actions that affect the individual in his daily existence. There are many facets to the bureaucracy. It includes the ministries, some of which, such as Foreign Affairs or the Budget, have little direct contact with citizens, while others, such as Agriculture and Forests, Industry and Commerce, spend most of their energies servicing and regulating the clienteles with which they are identified. It includes the regional administrative agencies that operate in semi-autonomous regions like Sicily and Sardinia, the agencies that operate within the 91 provinces and the nearly 8,000 communes. It also includes, in an indirect but important way, those public servants involved in the management of the vast network of state-controlled enterprises.

Each ministry is formally headed by a minister who generally brings with him a number of political appointments who constitute his "cabinet." His Chief of Cabinet is either an outsider or a high civil servant; in either case the chief is expected to be loyal to the minister and to see to it that the policies of the minister and the government are implemented within the ministry. The ministerial undersecretaries are normally members of the legislature, chosen for reasons of political patronage and for their compatibility with the policies of the ministers. One important level at which groups that seek to influence administrative policy intervene is with the minister, himself, or members of his cabinet. Favorable response at this level can mean that, at least as long as the minister and his personal entourage last, considerable impact over ministry policy can be achieved.

Below the Cabinet are the civil servants; about 250,000 career administrative employees of the regular ministries. The remaining public servants are teachers, members of the armed forces, employees of such government monopolies as tobacco, telephone and telegraph, state roads, and railways. In addition, if one were attempting a full count of public employees, those in provincial and local government as well as employees of state-owned economic enterprises would have to be included.

Within the ministries, career civil servants are divided into four services or "careers," namely the administrative class (*carriera direttiva*), executive class (*carriera di concetto*), clerical class (*carriera esecutiva*), and an auxiliary class (*carriera di personale ausiliario*) consisting primarily of ushers. Entrance into each of these classes is by competitive examination. Normally, a candidate for each class, respectively, must have completed university, upper secondary school, lower secondary school, or elementary education. In addition, members of the second and third classes can now aspire to be promoted, by examination, to the upper career services. This is a recent innovation, because until 1956 Italian public administration was governed by regulations enacted under Fascism in 1923.[18] Promotion is based on a combination of seniority and comparative merit. The latter criterion makes it possible to introduce considerations of merit—or of politics—in the matter of facilitating or inhibiting administrative careers. However, it is fair to say that those who can shoulder responsibility should get it sooner under the reorganized regulations governing careers.

[18] After several false starts, the government in 1957 finally passed the legislative decree on administrative reorganization that was authorized by the legislature in December, 1954. See Ignazio Scotto, "La Nuova disciplina del rapporto di pubblico impiego," in *Problemi della pubblica amministrazione* (Bologna, 1958), pp. 74–78.

Bureaucrats interviewed in this study belong exclusively to "Category A," the administrative class. There are normally seven grades in this class, beginning with three levels of councillors at the bottom and extending upward through section directors, division directors, inspector general, and director general. In most cases, the exalted position of *Direttore Generale* is the highest position reached by a career civil servant—and only after long years of service. It is for this reason that many of the men who currently occupy these posts began their careers under Fascism and often reflect both the innate conservatism and the disdain for the public that was so typical of the Fascist bureaucracy. The line units of the ministries are usually general directorates, divisions, or sections. There are also certain "services" that serve in a staff or auxiliary capacity for each agency.

Not all positions within the bureaucracy are based on competitive entrance, and not all promotion is by seniority and merit. On recommendation of the Council of Ministers, the President of the Republic, by decree, can name directors general, prefects, and councillors of state. Such appointments are clearly political, may be made from outside the bureaucracy, and are obviously frequently made either as matters of patronage or as a means of assuring that governmental policy will not be subject to bureaucratic inertia or sabotage.

Although some would say that the Italian public servant is poorly paid—average wage is about $100 per month —it is important to note that he receives all sorts of fringe benefits, such as pension funds, leaves with pay for assorted reasons, good vacation provisions, excellent severance pay based on seniority, free health care, indemnities for loss of health related to his job, and a thirteenth-month's salary each year.[19] In addition, in and through their ministries, civil servants can secure goods and services at greatly reduced cost, as well as various kinds of

19 *Ibid.*, pp. 89 ff.

subsidies that facilitate the construction and purchase of apartments. When one adds to this the good possibility that a higher civil servant may sit on special committees or economic enterprise managerial bodies that bring in additional income, the compensation picture is not nearly as bad as might appear at first blush.

Notwithstanding all of this, it is fair to say that bureaucratic morale is low, that waste and duplication of effort is endemic, that featherbedding and loose and undisciplined working conditions are rampant, and that the civil servant is not held in high esteem by the general public. It is significant, for example, that, as Italy expands economically, some bureaucratic positions requiring specialized skills and education are no longer easy to fill. If there is a choice for the urban northerner, at least, he tends to prefer private industry where wage and other incentives are higher. In spite of this, however, considerable numbers of Italy's security-minded youth look to government rather than to private enterprise as a preferable career.[20]

In general, Italian attitudes toward the bureaucracy combine disdain, hostility, frustration, and hopeless resignation.[21] To some extent, these are deeply engrained views born of centuries of arbitrary action from governments far removed from the people and scarcely in a position to understand their needs. For many Italians "il governo" tended to be the heavy-handed police,[22] the tax collector, and agents of the all-powerful prefect. Antagonistic atti-

[20] See Joseph LaPalombara and Jerry B. Waters, "Values, Expectations and Political Predispositions of Italian Youth," *Midwest Journal of Political Science*, 5 (February, 1961), pp. 43–46. For the Italian version of this study, see Joseph LaPalombara, "L'Orientamento politico della gioventù," in Alberto Spreafico and Joseph LaPalombara (eds.), *Elezioni e comportamento politico in Italia* (Milan, 1962), pp. 495–516.

[21] For a typical, even if somewhat exaggerated, view of the bureaucracy, see such works by Ernesto Rossi as *Lo Stato industriale* (Bari, 1953) and *Il Malgoverno* (Bari, 1955). Professor Rossi has fought an unending battle against bureaucratic excesses, inefficiency, and corruption.

[22] Italy continues to operate under many police laws and regulations enacted under Fascist dictatorship. For an examination of this important problem, see *Comitato Nazionale per la Celebrazione . . . , op. cit.*, Vol. V.

tudes directed at these administrators were, and are, extended to cover public administration in general. The public administrators, on the other hand, do very little to change this negative image. The Italian is bedeviled by myriad forms to be filled out and taxes to pay every time he turns around. When he has to report to some administrative agency, which is frequent, he learns the demeaning routine of the "antecamera"—i.e., waiting interminably to see an official, even when it is only a status consideration which "busies" the official. Even where the public servant wishes to accommodate the citizen, he, like his client, is a helpless captive of the administrative code, that morass of minutely specified procedure that is part of the legal academician's legacy to Italy. All the confusion creates the conviction that only particularistic considerations permit the citizen to survive. This leads to the widespread notion that administration is corrupt and that efficient and understanding service is rendered in direct relationship to the thickness of the money-laden envelope —*la bustarella,* as the more cynical Italians name it.

There is surely less corruption in the Italian bureaucracy than popular impressions would suggest. However, it is difficult to exaggerate the need for reform. In the complicated maze that currently characterizes public administration, there is a premium placed on the person who knows his way around and who can expedite the handling of problems which, in administrative parlance, are called *procure.* Much of the interaction between interest-group representatives and the bureaucracy involves nothing more than this. The interest group with real know-how is the one that has among its leaders those who can cut through administrative red tape when necessary—and who can use the administrative code and complex bureaucratic procedures to secure delay when such a strategy is desirable. It is fully apparent that, for many reasons, the structure of the bureaucracy offers great and attractive opportunities for those who seek to obtain leverage over the process of rule-application in Italy.

The public bureaucracy, in any complex society, is also a source of advice and information on the basis of which administrative decrees are issued and legislative proposals prepared. Insofar as the government and the legislature become dependent on the information that the bureaucracy husbands, organizes, and communicates, the bureaucrats become an intimate and important—sometimes dominant—factor in the rule-making process. The tendency of the observer is frequently to focus his attention on those legislative issues that create the greatest controversy and attract the greatest public attention. Regarding such issues, the bureaucrats may or may not play an important policy-making role. However, the great bulk of legislation is of the so-called routine, highly technical, and unspectacular variety. It is in this area that one can anticipate strong and often decisive bureaucratic influence over rule-making and rule-application. It is also in this area that organized groups will seek to enlist the support, collaboration, and understanding of the bureaucracy. One of the simple hypotheses of this study is that control of information is a key source of power over the functions of rule-making and rule-application. What we will note in later chapters is not merely that the legislature is dependent on the bureaucracy for information but that the bureaucracy in turn frequently looks to organized interest groups for its own information and for that which it passes on to Parliament.

The advisory function of the bureaucracy is strongly institutionalized in Italy. Within many of the ministries, special advisory bodies are set up by law. These include such varied agencies as the Supreme Council of Defense, the National Health Council, and the Council of Agriculture and Forests. It is the rare ministry that does not contain some sort of advisory council that reports directly to the minister. These councils combine civil servants and persons appointed from outside the government. In some cases, the councils must be consulted on administrative and legislative policy; in others consultation is optional.

While advice is in no instance binding, it is nevertheless an important means whereby decisions can be conditioned and hedged in.

Two such bodies, the Council of State and the National Council of Economics and Labor, have constitutional status. There are certain instances in which the government must consult the former on legislation. In other instances, the Council of State, as a whole or through one of its sections, advises the ministries. The National Council of Economics and Labor was finally established in 1957 after a long delay. It is authorized to give its opinion on legislation on the request of Parliament, the Council of Ministers, or the regional governments. It can also propose legislation on its own initiative, or make studies when it thinks appropriate or when requested to do so by Parliament or the Council of Ministers. The N.C.E.L. has 80 members who reflect a corporative system of representation. It is possible, although not yet probable, that it may become an important instrument for rule-making in the Italian system.[23]

Finally, in looking at the matter of rule-application, we should take note of the considerable extent of governmental involvement in economic enterprise. Beginning in the early years of the Great Depression, the Fascist government evolved the practice of bailing out sick industries by exchanging funds for stock. The stock, held by the *Istituto per la Ricostruzione Industriale* (I.R.I.), a vast holding company, was to have been returned to private investors as economic conditions improved. However, this did not happen; instead, I.R.I.'s holdings increased as the autarchic industrial practices of Fascism were stepped up. By the end of World War II, the Italian government controlled all or most of the enterprises in several important sectors, such as steel, communications, shipbuilding,

[23] See the interesting analysis and speculation concerning the Council by Giuseppe Chiarelli, *Il Consiglio Nazionale dell'economia e del lavoro* (Milan, 1957).

and the metal mechanical industries.[24] I.R.I. in turn formed a number of subsidiary holding companies, ostensibly to control and manage the state enterprises.[25] On all of these organizations, members of the public bureaucracy obtained highly remunerative positions as directors. The irony of it all is that, until recent years, direction was in no way intended to act as a yardstick over private enterprise. Rather, I.R.I. industries were notorious for their tendency to do whatever possible to keep the marginal producer in the field, even at a cost of continuous deficits to be covered by the public budget. One important change of policy occurred in 1958 when I.R.I. enterprises were removed from Confindustria control on trade union matters.[26] But, at this writing at least, the so-called reform of state-controlled enterprises had still not achieved the revolutionary changes that some Italians foresaw.

What we must stress here is that some of Italy's public servants are very much involved in industrial management. This is true not merely of I.R.I. enterprises but even more spectacularly of the *Ente Nazionale Idrocarburi* (E.N.I.), managed, until his untimely death in late 1962, by the enigmatic Christian Democratic "gray eminence," Enrico Mattei. Today, E.N.I. is the most dynamic instrument of industrial development in Italy. It is deeply involved in mining enterprises, the exploitation of gas and petroleum in Italy and abroad, the refining and retailing of petroleum products and fertilizers, chemicals, and a host of other manufacturing concerns.

E.N.I., like I.R.I., is more than an administrative agency. Because of their considerable interests in eco-

[24] For an indication of the extent of these holdings, see Ministero dell'Industria e del Commercio, *L'Istituto per la Ricostruzione Industriale* (Turin, 1955), Vol. I, pp. 3–88.

[25] For example, *Finsider* for steel, *Finmeccanica* for the engineering industries, *Finmare* for shipping companies, *Finelettrica* for electric power enterprises.

[26] See Confindustria, *Il Distacco delle aziende a prevalente partecipazione statale dalle organizzazioni degli altri datori di lavoro* (3 vols. Rome, 1958).

nomic enterprise, they are bureaucratic agencies that become important *institutional* interest groups. Like their competitors in the private sector, they have interests to articulate and they make demands on the rule-making and rule-applying institutions of government. More than any other sector of the bureaucracy, these economic giants are able to exercise enormous influence over political decisions in Italy. The extent of organizational freedom from parliamentary or other control is dramatically attested by the power that Enrico Mattei exercised in Italy—and by the fact that it is widely understood that *Il Giorno,* a leading Milan daily paper, is a creature of E.N.I. financial support.

RULE ADJUDICATION

Very little of what this study encompasses involves the Italian judicial system. Thus no effort will be made to describe the rule-adjudication function in detail. It is enough to point out that Italian judges, with few exceptions, are civil servants who are part of the Ministry of Justice. Only a national judicial system exists, and it is highly differentiated. Civil cases are differentiated from criminal, administrative cases from both. The Constitution is careful to specify that the magistracy is "autonomous and independent of every other power." [27] Judges are appointed on the basis of competitive examination, except in those cases where the Superior Council of the Judiciary calls distinguished law professors or lawyers to serve as judges. Judges serve for life on good behavior and may be removed only for cause. Everything possible is done to guarantee the independence of the judicial branch, although there are some scholars in Italy who want the judiciary completely separated from the Ministry of Justice. By and large, the image of the judicial system is positive, and, except in rare instances, the courts are viewed as reasonably objective arbiters of controversy.

[27] *Constitution,* Article 104. For other provisions on the judicial system, see Articles 101–13.

It is of some importance to note that, after years of delay, the Constitutional Court authorized by the Constitution was finally brought into existence in 1956. Among the important powers of the court is that of passing on the constitutionality of legislation and of administrative decrees enacted under enabling legislation.[28] The court is also authorized to judge controversies between the national state and the regions, and between or among regions.

The Constitutional Court has given every indication of its willingness to exercise the power of judicial review with vigor and determination. In its early years, the court has had the task of abrogating Fascist legislation and of having the Italian legal codes conform more meaningfully than they do to the principles of the 1948 Constitution.[29] In the exercise of this important function, the court has incurred the criticism and hostility of some Christian Democratic leaders. It seems reasonably apparent that, over the years, the Constitutional Court will become an important center of group interaction. Here is a place where defeated groups can go after they have been unsuccessful in their effort to influence the rule-making and rule-application processes. If the early years of the court are any indication, the predisposition will be that of strengthening and putting teeth into legislative and administrative practices that implement and safeguard the philosophy of liberal democracy that seems to underlie the Italian Constitution.

[28] See *ibid.*, Articles 134–37. Two interesting articles on the Constitutional Courts are Taylor Cole, "Three Constitutional Courts," *American Political Science Review,* 53 (December, 1959), pp. 963–84; John Clarke Adams and Paolo Barile, "The Italian Constitutional Court in Its First Two Years of Activity," *Buffalo Law Review,* 7 (1958), pp. 250–65.

[29] What the court has done to implement the Constitution is reported in detail in *Comitato per la Celebrazione* . . . , Vol. V, *op. cit.*

CHAPTER V · AN INTEREST
GROUP INVENTORY

IN a pluralistic democracy, voluntary associations have a vitally important role to play. They offer a means whereby those with similar interests can organize for the pursuit of those interests. They can provide an orderly, predictable means of transmitting demands to the authoritative structures. They also serve as significant instruments through which the authoritative structures communicate to the governed and reactions of the latter are fed back to the governors. It is difficult, indeed, to conceive of a modern, large-scale democratic system functioning adequately without a well-developed associational interest-group structure.

We have also observed how particular configurations of interest-group organization and behavior can act as disintegrative influences. Where associational groups organize within and reflect subcultures in conflict, they may exacerbate the inherent difficulties of governing a society democratically. Rather than provide a mechanism for effecting compromises among conflicting demands, many sectarian secondary associations crystallize and rigidify these demands and make compromise difficult or impossible to achieve. One is tempted to suggest that while a fair amount of differentiation of interest groups is a sign of political health and stability, the presence of extreme proliferation may be a short-hand way of predicting the existence or development of serious political instability.

In order to gain some insights into the degree and nature of Italy's associational interest-group differentiation, we conducted a general survey of voluntary associations that maintained either headquarters or branch offices at Rome. We wanted to know how many such associations existed, what their aims were, the nature of their membership, what characterized their internal organizations, what patterns of interaction they maintain with the various agencies of government, and what kinds of problems group leaders perceive as being particularly relevant to their organizations. Mailed questionnaires were sent to 129 associations selected from the universe described below. Replies were received from 68 groups. In most instances, the associations that replied also responded favorably to our request for copies of their constitutions, samples of proceedings from meetings, examples of their newspapers, magazines or other publications, and any other material they considered relevant. Coupling returned questionnaires with these other materials, we were able to obtain information concerning approximately ninety of the groups included in the original sample.

In addition, personal interviews, ranging in duration from one to three hours, were conducted with 81 group leaders. Twenty-four of these were representatives of Confindustria and twenty-three were leaders of Italian Catholic Action units. Their responses are dealt with primarily in later chapters. The remaining thirty-four interviews, however, were almost exclusively with leaders of associations that were included in the general survey. The purpose of the interviews was not merely to elaborate on questionnaire responses, but, more important, to delve into topics and problems that could not effectively be broached in a mailed questionnaire. Moreover, an overriding interest was also that of having group representatives tell how their organizations interacted with other groups and with the bureaucratic sector of government. In the present chapter, I shall report primarily the results of the general survey; in the following chapter I shall lay out what seems to be the general structure of interest-group communication and interaction.

KINDS OF GROUPS AND THEIR GOALS

It is probably impossible to know exactly how many organized interest groups of the associational type exist in Italy. In order to define some sort of universe from which

a sample might be selected, we [1] utilized a listing of associations in the *Guida Monaci,* a valuable guide prepared
by the Chamber of Commerce of the Province of Rome.[2]
From this source alone, we were able to count almost 2,400
associations. Assuming that the organizations omitted (e.g.
eleemosynary associations) and those not reported amount
to several hundred more, it seems reasonable to suggest
that in Rome alone there are probably 3,000 different voluntary associations that might possibly intervene in the
political process. Because the *Guida* itself frequently and
briefly describes the purposes of many of these associations, we were able to infer that for some political intervention is at most only intermittent. Particularly because
our sample was small, we did not select among the groups
randomly but by major category and with a view to maximizing the number of groups whose participation might
be more than intermittent. Nevertheless, a small number
of the presumably nonpolitical groups were also included.
We hoped to discover whether organizations such as
Lovers of Jesus and Mary, French Buildings in Rome and
Loreto, National Institute of Ancient Drama, National
Federation of Large Family Associations, the Italian
Basketball Federation, and the like do in fact intervene
politically. Unfortunately, we received almost no replies
from such groups, perhaps because the questionnaire did
not make very much sense from their own organizational
point of view.

The over-all panorama of associations can be suggested

---

[1] "We" here is recognition that in the survey and certain other phases
of the field research and data analysis, I profited from the valuable assistance of Dr. Gianfranco Poggi. Dr. Poggi's intensive study of Italian
Catholic Action was submitted as a dissertation to the Department of
Sociology at the University of California (Berkeley). It has been published
in Italy as *Il Clero di riserva* (Milan, 1964). The information on Catholic
Action in this study comes mainly from his initial analyses.

[2] Camera di Commercio del Comune e della Provincia di Roma, *Guida
Monaci: Annuario generale di Roma e provincia* (Rome, 1956). The organizations from which the survey sample were drawn are listed on pages
59–151.

if we pause for a moment to examine the various categories in which the *Guida Monaci* catalogues them. The first of these is "Catholic Confraternities," and 61 of them are listed. They include such names as Souls of Purgatory, Chains of St. Peter, Primary Pious Union of the Most Holy Sacrament, Our Lady of Lourdes, etc. Many of these associations are attached to churches and have both clerics and laymen listed as officers. We assume that most of them are largely inactive as far as the political process is concerned. On the other hand, we know that many of the organizations that fall under the "Diverse Catholic Associations, Circles, and Committees" are definitely interest groups. Here is where one finds Italian Catholic Action and its various branches catalogued. In addition, we find such politically suggestive organizations as Italian Catholic Junta for Emigration, Cardinal Mindszenty Association, Movement for a Better World, International Union for the Protection of Public Morality, Association of Catholic Doctors, and the openly political Pious Work of the Holiest Virgin of the Roads for Religious and Moral Assistance to Road Workers. There are seventy of these Catholic groups named.

Under the rubric "Administration of Foreign Buildings," six organizations are listed. These are followed by 29 associations grouped under the title "Associations, Centers, and Entities for International Relations." Among the latter are found such groups as the Italian Association for Public Relations, Italo-American Association, Italian Society for International Organization, and Catholic Union of Artists, all of which were included in our mailed survey.

Next follow such categories as "Diverse Cults," "Knightly Orders," and "Foreign and International Institutes." Within the last category, questionnaires were sent to (but not necessarily returned from) groups like the International Association of Mothers United for Peace, International Association for the Protection of Industrial Property, Lions Club, and the Order of Malta. In the field of science, comprising 35 catalogued groups, we sent questionnaires to the Italian Academy of Culture, the Italian Geological Society, and the Italian Hydrotechnical Association. Among the 212 groups classified as "Artistic Associations," we found such diverse-sounding names as Friends of Castel St. Angelo, Italian Association of Friends of Phonograph Records, Italian National Committee for the Scientific Organization of Work, Union of Italian Provinces, Catholic Union of Secondary Teachers, Friends of Organization Group, Union of Italian Catholic Jurists and the Young Men's Christian Association. This was a major category from which groups to be included in the general survey were selected.

Other categories (and numbers) of associations included fine arts and archeological (27), musical (18), mass media (38), tourist (20), commercial and industrial (65), employers syndical associations (285), trade unions (176), independent syndical associations (269), veterans organizations (56), political parties and movements (62), sports clubs and associations (over 500), philanthropic and humanitarian groups (161), and mutual aid societies (41). We oversampled employers syndical associations, independent syndical associations, and veterans groups.[3] Within the remaining categories, we selected units that seemed to be typical. What is generally impressive about the *Guida Monaci* is that every conceivable interest group, and many that seem inconceivable, are organized into secondary associations. In the field of sports alone, every possible type of athletic activity apparently has not merely its clubs but also circles, societies, associations, and federations of associations. The same thing, of course, is true of trade unions and employers associations, which are organized first by industrial category, then geographically, and finally in peak associations that comprise both the category and

[3] Only limited information was solicited from labor unions because the author had studied them intensively some years previously. See Joseph LaPalombara, *The Italian Labor Movement: Problems and Prospects* (Ithaca, 1957).

geographic units. In any event, if one is blind, or loves cats, or is a relative of someone wounded or killed in any one of several wars, or is a diabetic, or lives abroad, or is interested in heavy or light sports, or wants a united or federated Europe, or believes in peace, or is tenant or homeowner, Catholic or non-Catholic industrial manager, left-wing, right-wing, or Catholic woman voter, a manufacturer of Roman *pecorino* cheese, a producer of refrigerators or synthetic products, a lover of flowers, a Jew or a Baptist, a northerner or southerner, a woman or young lady, any imaginable kind of manufacturer or professional, public servant or small merchant, and so on through the full roll-call of human status or activity, at least one association is available at Rome for the articulation, protection, or furtherance of the interest involved.

In view of such a vast universe of associations, it seems excessive to try to generalize on the basis of a small sample. Yet our purpose was not to give a completely representative portrayal of all associations, but to provide some information concerning particular categories of groups, such as employers and industrial associations, professional groups, Catholic groups, and so on. It was also our view that any reasonable return from the mailed survey would permit at least a beginning description of interest-group organization in the country. Furthermore, it seemed of the utmost importance that we be able to compare against a somewhat broader background the more intensive data secured from interviews with representatives of Catholic Action and Confindustria. In no other way could we judge how typical or esoteric the patterns of organization and behavior evinced by these two prominent interest groups might be.

Questionnaires or other materials obtained from the various organizations are listed in Table 5. It should be noted that if the table were arranged ideologically, the associations could be ascribed in many instances to the Communist, Christian Democratic, Socialist, Liberal, or other parties. However, such a classification, except in

TABLE 5: Returns from Mail Survey, by Category
of Association

Category of Association	Type of Information Returned	
	Questionnaire	Documents
Employer and industrial	21	5
Professional	14	4
Trade union	4	2
Agricultural	4	1
Veterans	4	0
Catholic	4	2
Women	2	0
Other	15	4
Total	68	18

very obvious cases, is extremely difficult to make, because
often both the parties and the associations assiduously
deny any connection with each other. Further, it is apparent that the connections of the employer-industrial and
professional associations with political parties are sporadic
and indirect, not representing the degree of integration
that is true of trade unions, agricultural associations, veterans associations, and Catholic organizations.

Forty-eight of the questionnaires indicate that the associations were organized after World War II, twelve before
1922, four during the Fascist era. No response was obtained from the remaining four. These figures make sense
only if one is careful to distinguish between free, voluntary association, on the one hand, and controlled association, on the other. It is apparent, for example, that most
of the employer-industrial associations that give the years
following 1944 as their dates of origin are glossing over
the fact that they continued to exist, as units of Confindustria, throughout the Fascist era. Much more to the
point is the response of the Industrial Union of the Province of Turin that it was organized in 1906. It is significant that both Catholic Action and Confindustria enjoyed
continuous existence throughout the two decades of Fas-

cism. Continued existence, however, was not without its difficulties and organizational modifications. Catholic Action experienced periods of considerable tension with Mussolini and was forced to pull in its political fangs on more than one occasion. Confindustria was subjected to a high degree of Fascist bureaucratic inflation as it became one of the major instruments through which organized Italian industry achieved functional representation in the Corporative State. For some years the Confederation was hardly distinguishable from other agencies of public administration.

Nevertheless, there was both a resurgence and a considerable proliferation of groups after the collapse of Fascism. Organizations such as the trade unions that had been forced out of existence when the controls of dictatorship increased after 1925 were re-established. In addition, the war itself and postwar developments brought new and important associations into existence, as, for example, the auxiliary organizations of the political parties. The Italian Association for Public Relations (1954), the Association for the Industrial Development of Southern Italy (1946), the Italian Association for the Defense of Interests of Diabetics (1949), and the Italian Federation of Advertising (1947) are all manifestations of changing conditions that in the years since the war have led to greater associational activity. Of signal importance in this regard are some of the intellectual interest groups, organized around particular magazines or journals, that were mentioned in Chapter III. Equally significant are organizations such as the National Association of Italian Partisans (1944) and the Italian Federation of Volunteers of Liberty (1944), which emerged as a result of the heroic *Resistenza Armata* against Fascists and Nazis during the 1943-45 period of civil war and insurrection.

What of the purposes or goals of these organizations?

From constitutions and questionnaire responses it is not easy to identify goals that are obviously political. In many instances, the official documents are careful to point out that the organization is nonparty or nonpolitical.[4] What this means in most cases is that the association seeks to avoid being identified with any particular political party. In our interviews we frequently encountered the expression that the interest group involved was a moral association, completely divorced from any connections with the political or ideological forces of the society. Even in the most obvious cases of groups that are intimately a part of one of the political parties, this type of relationship is not openly divulged by either the constitutions or the responses to questionnaire items.

However, a careful reading even of official documents serves to alert one to the political involvement of the organization. Let us take as an example the very important Lombard Industrial Association—the *Assolombardo*—with headquarters at Milan. The *statuto* of that association defines its purpose as follows: "The Association has the aim of providing for the assistance and tutelage of industrial firms in all syndical, social, and economic problems that directly or indirectly regard them, favoring the development and progress of industry in the Lombard region." [5]

It is apparent from this and other sections of the organization's constitution that it will be primarily involved in labor relations, statistical services, and collective bargaining. It is also apparent, however, that the *Assolombardo* will, when necessary, represent the interests of its membership before public bodies. The apolitical nature of such an organization must not be seen, therefore, as nonintervention in the political process but merely as alleged nonassociation with political parties. Even when such absence of formal contact with the parties is denied,

---

[4] See, for example, Associazione Mineraria Italiana, *Statuto* (Rome, 1957), Art. 3; Associazione Nazionale dei Comuni Italiani, *Statuto* (Empoli, 1957), Art. 4; Associazione Nazionale Famiglie Caduti e Dispersi in Guerra, *Statuto* (Rome, 1955), Art. 4; Associazione della Stampa Romana, *Statuto* (Rome, 1957), Art. 3; Associazione Nazionale Combattenti e Reduci, *Statuto* (Rome, 1949), Art. 4; Confederazione Nazionale della Piccola Industria, *Statuto* (Rome, 1954), Art. 3.

[5] Associazione Industriale Lombardo, *Statuto* (Milan, 1945), Art. 2.

it is evident that contacts between association and political party leaders are frequent.

The industrial association at Bologna [6] is frank in specifying as one of its central purposes that it represents "the interests of members before State authorities." The National Hydrotechnical Association states as its purpose that of assisting members to understand and to deal with public administration,[7] no easy chore in Italian society. The National Association of Italian Communes, which asserts its nonparty character, goes on to point out that it represents its members before constitutional authorities, central administrative agencies and public bodies.[8] The General Confederation of Italian Agriculture (Confagricoltura), a major interest-group in this field, says nothing about its political coloration but does specify that it will represent its members before all public bodies and administrative agencies.[9]

Generally speaking, then, the constitutions define the purposes of these organizations in terms of protecting or furthering the interests and the objectives of the particular categories in which they belong. Confagricoltura seeks to defend its members' "general interests and advance Italian agriculture"; SVIMEZ (Association for the Industrial Development of Southern Italy) is organized to "promote . . . the study of economic conditions of Southern Italy to the end of proposing concrete action prgrams"; the Association of Italian Joint Stock Companies, among other things, works "for a progressive improvement of commercial, industrial, fiscal and administrative legislation, with particular regard to the discipline of joint stock companies"; the Roman Press Association purports to defend freedom of the press and the dignity of the profession of journalism, to protect the material, moral, and syndical

---

[6] Associazione degli Industriali della Provincia di Bologna, *Statuto* (Bologna, 1958), Art. 2.

[7] Associazione Idrotecnica Italiana, *Statuto* (Milan, 1946), Art. 2.

[8] Associazione Nazionale dei Comuni Italiani, *op. cit.*, Art. 5.

[9] Confederazione Generale dell'Agricoltura Italiana, *Statuto* (Rome, 1955), Art. 2.

interests of journalists, and engage in every activity that might contribute to the welfare of journalists and their families.[10]

Only rarely can one detect from official statements what may be the sectarian ideological character of an association. The National Confederation of Direct Cultivators, which is a major interest-group integrated with the Christian Democratic Party, is openly interested in encouraging the protection and extension of private property in agriculture, the guarantee of adequate agricultural income, the development of cooperatives, and the strengthening of the family-size farm.[11] Although the organization, dynamically led by Christian Democratic deputy Paolo Bonomi, fails to invoke the usual claim of being apart from party and politics, it does not state its obvious political goals or affiliation. The best clue to its orientation is the statement that the action of the Confederation "aspires to the principles of the Social-Christian School." [12] Similarly, the Christian Union of Directors and Managers, also closely tied to Christian Democracy, merely indicates officially that it "is constituted to promote the knowledge, diffusion, and actuation of the Christian Social doctrine." Members are expected to develop a Catholic professional morality and to apply the principles of Social Christianity in industrial and work situations.[13] It is perhaps indicative of some tension between this organization and D.C. that, in response to a questionnaire item, the organization identified as its major problem or difficulty that of "maintaining U.C.I.D. in its objective nonparty and nontrade union position."

10 Ibid.; Associazione per lo Sviluppo dell'Industria nel Mezzogiorno, Statuto (Rome, 1957), Art. 2; Associazione fra le Società Italiane per Azioni, Statuto (Rome, 1948), Art. 2; Associazione della Stampa Romana, Statuto (Rome, 1957), Art. 2.

11 Confederazione Nazionale Coltivatori Diretti, Statuto (Rome, 1956), Art. 3.

12 Ibid., Art. 1.

13 Unione Cristiana Imprenditori Dirigenti, Statuto (Rome, n.d.), Art. 1, 5.

The National Association of Partisans of Italy, widely believed to be dominated by the Communist Party, lists as one of its purposes that of making known the values, heroisms, and sacrifices of the Resistance "so that their teaching and their warning will always inspire the nation and free it of any survival or return of Fascism under whatever heavy-handed or disguised form." In addition, the organization aims at working for the defense and complete implementation of the Republican Constitution, for the recognition of patriotic traditions of the first and second Risorgimento, and for the great contribution against the Fascist traitors and Nazi invaders made by the men and women of the Armed Resistance. To this end it pledges cooperation with other groups, and particularly with other veterans associations.[14] This obviously political organization goes to some pains to profess its freedom from political contacts, responding in its returned questionnaire, for example, that it *never* has any contacts with political parties. Indeed, in response to the question regarding its major difficulty or problem, A.N.P.I. replied: "The major difficulties that A.N.P.I. must overcome lie in the preconceptions concerning its nature that exist in certain political places."

Another interest group that emerged from the Resistance is the Italian Federation of Volunteers of Liberty (F.I.V.L.). This is a peak association whose doors are ostensibly open to all legally constituted associations made up of partisans, patriots, and combatants of the war of liberation. F.I.V.L.'s constitution solemnly follows the ritual of stating that the Federation is apolitical and nonparty. It, too, wishes to safeguard the spirit of the Resistance and to keep faith with the ideals of liberty, democracy, justice, and civilization.[15] One might get the impression from all this that here, surely, is an association that

14 Associazione Nazionale Partigiani d'Italia, *Statuto* (Milan, 1956), Art. 3.
15 Federazione Italiana Volontari della Libertà, *Statuto* (Rome, 1955), Art. 2–4.

cuts at least partially across ideological lines for purposes of unifying the various political aggregations that were involved in the common experience of Italy's liberation. Yet, in answer to our question concerning the ends of the organization, F.I.V.L. replied, "the defense of democratic liberties against Fascist and Communist ideologies." The purpose enshrined in the constitution itself was not mentioned at all. Going to that document would be a certain way of overlooking the important fact that F.I.V.L. came into existence to provide competition for the left-wing A.N.P.I. Another index of this occurs in a later portion of the questionnaire, where the F.I.V.L. leader remarks: "Contemporary Italian society is always in greater degree becoming aware of its duties and its rights in the context of reconquered democratic liberties. The task of our organization is that of stimulating this awareness to the end of accelerating the process of democratic maturation, the *sine qua non* for the political defense of the country against the attacks of totalitarian ideologies."

If we transfer our attention from veterans to women, essentially the same difficulties are encountered. One of the most massive and impressive women's interest groups is the Italian Union of Women (U.D.I.). Its constitution states that it is "the Association of all women who, on the basis of the [Republican] Constitution, intend to work together for female emancipation." Emancipation is said to mean equal opportunities and treatment in work situations, re-evaluation of the moral, juridical, and economic position of women in the family, full participation by women in social, cultural, and political life, and (here is the ideological indicator) "the conquest of a true peace based on the friendship and collaboration of Italy with all of the other countries of the world." [16] The basic statute goes on to say that "all women, of whatever social class or ideological or religious belief," are eligible for membership.

16 Unione Donne Italiane, *Statuto* (Rome, 1956), Art. 2.

Although its constitution does not divulge it, U.D.I. is manifestly a Communist-front organization and generally recognized as such. Its top leadership has consistently been drawn from P.C.I.; its president, at the time of our survey, was Marisa Cinciari Rodano, a Communist member of Parliament. In response to questionnaire items, U.D.I. underlined the notion that the organization was open to all women "who accept the goals of the organization and the U.D.I. program, independently of race, social class, religion, political opinion, or membership in other organizations." Later in the questionnaire we are also told that "U.D.I. is the major *democratic, autonomous* women's association . . . the only women's mass organization that considers it possible to unite in common action all women, outside of any ideological consideration." When asked to discuss its major problem or difficulties, U.D.I. replied, in part: "The presence of profound division among political forces of the country; the integralist posture of the Catholic world which tends to subordinate the social actions of Catholics to ideological considerations, even in the feminine area . . . the more or less great lack of comprehension among almost all the social and political forces of the country of the problem of feminine emancipation, which all too often is seen in an instrumental or politically electoral way."

A careful reading of U.D.I.'s questionnaire responses, then, does divulge not merely its political intervention but its narrow and sectarian ideological base as well. Unstated is the assumption that only the parties of the Left have taken the needs of Italian women seriously into consideration. Quite openly stated is U.D.I.'s conflict with Catholic social and political forces. Papering over all of this, however, is the insistence that the organization is not oriented in a particular ideological, religious, or political direction.

Organized Catholicism's response to U.D.I. is the Italian Female Center (C.I.F.), founded at Rome in 1944, the same year that U.D.I. came into existence. The purposes, offered in the questionnaire, of the organization are "to educate women in a civic-social conscience; to promote social assistance activities; to represent the complex of Christian female forces before civil authorities and public institutions; and to collaborate with public offices and entities in every activity for the defense of the interests and rights of the family, women, and children." C.I.F. is said, further, to be based on the principles of "restoring public morality, social justice, and human solidarity." Full membership is open to Catholic women, or Catholic women's associations; supporting membership is open to women of "Christian sentiments." In contrast to U.D.I.'s claimed three million members, C.I.F. reports two million.

Unlike U.D.I., C.I.F. is openly oriented in a particular ideological direction. Curiously, whereas the former indicates that it maintains contacts with political parties "every once in a while," C.I.F. ingenuously claims that it never has any such relations. On the other hand, in response to a question concerning the nature of its relations with other associations, C.I.F. indicates close and intimate contact with the full array of other Catholic groups, particularly with Italian Catholic Action. In short, C.I.F. lists fully 22 Catholic groups, many of them obviously closely associated with the Christian Democratic Party, with which it maintains intimate relations. It is more than doubtful that a Catholic group claiming two million adherents would *never* have anything to do with any political party.

Turning to organizations of Italian university students, we note similar tendencies of ideological fragmentation. Within each university there is an elective organization representing the student body, and membership in and student financial support of these units is automatic, established by law. At the national level, there exists the Italian National University Representative Union (U.N.U.R.I.), a voluntary association that local university associations are free to join or not join as they choose. The peak association's constitution affirms that it has no power to represent its membership politically, ideologically, or confessionally, that it can neither interfere with nor control student associations, that it does not aspire to a political ideology, and that it cannot adhere to any political or confessional organization. Its functions are said to be those of representing students before public and private bodies, involving the students in the improvement of the university system, cooperating with professors to improve the content and conditions of education, and working for the implementation of those principles of the Republican Constitution concerning higher education.[17]

Like most associations, U.N.U.R.I. is at least somewhat involved in the political process, and its participation has increased in recent years. In the very nature of Italian higher education, controlled as it is by public authorities, any attempt to encourage reform necessitates intervention in both the legislative and the public administrative sectors. This kind of activity is severely complicated by the fact that, unlike many of the ideologically sectarian and cohesive associations, U.N.U.R.I. purports to cut across political party lines, uniting in a common cause student organizations of whatever ideological persuasion. For the truth is that each of the member units of U.N.U.R.I. is certain to be dominated by one of several other student organizations that compete electorally for control of the official units. The two most important of these are the *Unione Goliardica Italiana* (U.G.I.), which combines students who identify with the Liberal, Republican, Radical, Democratic Socialist, and Socialist parties—the laical forces —and the *Intesa,* which is the association of Catholic students. In addition, the Neo-Fascists, who are powerful in some universities, and the Monarchists have their particular associations. The Communists, who once had their own group, entered U.G.I. in the late 1950's for purposes of exercising dominant leadership there. But they are weak in university circles and have so far been effectively

<hr />

[17] Unione Nazionale Universitaria Rappresentativa Italiana, *Statuto* (Rome, 1957), Art. 1–6.

frozen out of leadership positions in both U.G.I. and U.N.U.R.I.

U.N.U.R.I. is thus internally something of a microcosm of the fragmented state of Italian politics and interest groups. In explaining this ideological differentiation among student groups, a U.N.U.R.I. leader pointed out that one reason for it is the historical conflict that developed over the very existence of the Italian liberal state. This division became even more marked after World War II with the advent of a strong Communist movement. "If the Communists had not existed in the universities," says this leader, "the Catholics might simply have accepted the liberal state without qualification. At least the Catholics in the universities would have. . . . It is particularly natural in this historical epoch that the university student organization should take on this ideological character and differentiation." The respondent goes on to remark laconically that, after all, group proliferation among university students is indistinguishable from the kind of group separation that occurs in every sector of Italian society.[18] It is apparent that, because of its extraordinary effort to bring ideologically disparate groups together under one roof, U.N.U.R.I.'s political intervention will be marked by considerable tension, even if cooperation between D.C. and P.S.I. in national politics should alleviate it somewhat.

Examples could be multiplied, illustrating how the practices reported in questionnaires and interviews do not square with the pious—really ritualistic—claims of organizational constitutions that the groups are nonpolitical, nonparty, or both.[19] As we shall note later, if the political process is broadly conceived to involve not merely political party or electoral affairs, almost every group we have surveyed is involved in the process more than intermit-

18 *Interview*, Number 35, Rome, February 11, 1958, p. 3.
19 It is, of course, possible that many of the groups surveyed entertain a very narrow definition of what is "political" and would therefore readily admit to involvement in the "political process" more broadly conceived.

tently. Indeed, the same constitutions that disclaim parties or politics frequently go on to identify as a central purpose of the organization that of representing members before all kinds of public authorities. It is perfectly apparent that one of the critical services that organizational leaders and bureaucrats provide for their followers is that of smoothing their relationships to agencies of government. Additionally, whenever it seems necessary, the group leaders will take the initiative in intervening in the political process in the interests of their organizations. Such intervention seems to run the whole spectrum of obvious access to decision-making; it therefore seems unlikely that, except in the rarest of cases, the group leaders would balk at making contacts with political party representatives. We can surely make this assumption safely about those associations whose very existence would seem to mirror the ideological sectors into which the political parties themselves fall.

In any event, the explicitly stated purposes of these associations constitute ample demonstration that they exist in part—often in whole—as instruments for relating their members to some branch of government. As I conceive of the term political involvement, therefore, most of the groups surveyed are an integral, vital part of the Italian political process.

GROUP MEMBERSHIP

Excluding Confindustria and Catholic Action, which are treated separately, the groups about which we have membership information cover a wide spectrum. In some cases, the membership consists of individuals who, at some level, must consciously affiliate—take out a *tessera* or membership card, as it were. In other instances, particularly where industrial unions or associations are concerned, membership is not by individual, but by plant or firm. The composite situation is in Table 6.

The smallest association recruiting individual members is the Friends of the Organization Group, which is in

TABLE 6: Membership Data for Groups Surveyed by Questionnaire or Interview

Claimed Membership	Number of Groups	Membership Range
Individual		
100–1,000	12	100–900
1,001–5,000	14	1,800–4,500
10,001–100,000	6	11,900–100,000
100,001–500,000	6	248,000–466,921
500,000 or over	9	1,474,000–3,000,000
Firm or Association		
0–100	14	23–89
101–500	8	105–200
501 or over	6	1,300–4,000

existence to diffuse the use of rational methods in the organization of work. The largest is the *Unione Donne Italiane,* which, as we have seen, works for the juridical, social, and economic equality of women. A special problem is presented by the very important *Confederazione Nazionale Coltivatori Diretti* (National Confederation of Direct Cultivators), the Catholic association that organizes a great many of Italy's small landowners. An official of this group claims that the membership is recruited into 13,556 sections, comprising 1,683,000 families. A total of 3,385,-000 active members is claimed, and it is added that, as an electoral force in the service of the Christian Democratic Party, the Coltivatori Diretti amount to approximately seven million persons. This latter figure seems somewhat exaggerated and, in any event, I have calculated effective membership in terms of the total number of families said to be members. If any of the other bases are taken, it would be necessary to conclude that this Confederation is the largest single interest group in Italy, exceeding in number even the combined forces of Italian Catholic Action.[20]

In identifying the Unione Donne Italiane as the largest

20 These are the 1957 figures for the organization. *Interview,* Number 96 (Rome, June 27, 1958), pp. 5–7.

group included in this survey, I have, perhaps, been unfair to C.G.I.L. (Italian General Confederation of Labor), the Communist-dominated labor organization that claims a total membership well in excess of three million. The fact is that accurate membership data are extremely difficult to come by, and the labor unions seem to have a special reason for making exaggerated claims in this area. Because I agree with the widespread perception in Italy that the labor unions have continually lost membership in recent years, I have not accorded C.G.I.L. the place of honor it might otherwise claim.[21]

The groups from which we obtained membership data claim to include in their ranks in excess of eighteen million persons. Were one to add the vaunted membership of Catholic Action, the figure would exceed twenty million persons, almost all of them adults. At first blush it appears highly improbable that so many Italians are affiliated with interest groups. One is led therefore to think of overlapping group membership and of the possibility that, say, about ten million Italians—one fifth of the total population—account for all associational membership. Interview data, for example, highlight the important pattern of militant Catholics joining more than one organization, militant Communists several organizations that are consonant with their ideological predispositions, and so on.[22] Yet it must be noted that our survey touches only a rela-

[21] The difficulties of estimating trade-union membership are examined in my *The Italian Labor Movement, op. cit.*, pp. 55–69. See also Giuseppe Tarozzi and Vittorio Emiliani, "La 'Grande Milano': La Crisi operaia," *Il Mondo*, 10 (December 30, 1958), pp. 3–4. Authors make the point that workers are tired of old-style trade unionism and are no longer renewing their memberships. C.G.I.L. is said to be a principal victim of the decrease in card-carrying members. This membership crisis was also verified by a national leader of C.G.I.L. *Interview*, Number 92 (Rome, June 28, 1958), pp. 2–4.

[22] Survey research data tends to challenge the view that Italians are joiners, particularly insofar as membership in political parties and trade unions is concerned. However, I believe the survey results would reveal a more pervasive pattern of interest-group affiliation if one were to include some of the less obviously political categories in the lists utilized in surveys.

145

tive handful of the groups listed in the *Guida Monaci,* even though several of the largest organizations in Italy are included. The truth seems to be that one's job or profession, the state of his health, his religious or political preference, his humanitarian or selfish instincts, his interest in recreation—any of a great variety of motivating factors—can logically lead him into some sort of associational life. That there nevertheless exist some absolute nonjoiners I have no doubt; that Italian society is one of flourishing and greatly proliferated voluntary associations relating to every conceivable phase of human social existence is equally not in doubt.

We are now compelled to speculate a bit about the meaning of organizational membership. Most of the organizational statutes at our disposal carefully specify qualifications and conditions of membership. In addition to laying out certain objective qualifications (based on sex, age, occupation, profession, religion, industrial activity, geographic region, etc.), the statutes also specify that members must be committed to the goals or purposes of the organization. The Catholic *Centro Italiano Femminile* expects its two million adherents to achieve and maintain certain moral standards; the National Association of Combatants and Survivors specifies that members may not join competing organizations; the Christian Union of Managers and Directors wants associates who will put into practice the Christian conception of work; the Italian Society of Parapsychology restricts its membership to those who "intend to participate seriously—through research and other work —in the social ends of the organization." Indeed, full membership in this group of 200 souls is restricted to the fifty (1957 figure) who have displayed "proven attitudes" toward the field. Thus each organizational statute also specifies the procedures whereby members may be expelled. This creates the presumption that, at least in formal terms, membership in good standing implies something more than the mere payment of dues.

Notwithstanding formal specifications concerning membership, it is obvious that motivations underlying organizational affiliation vary greatly and, in any case, should not be limited to the notion of strong ideological commitment to the goals of the groups. Persons may join something like the very old Italian Society of Surgery for reasons of professional prestige or convenience; others will affiliate with the Italian Association of Public Relations because the activity is relatively new in Italy and practitioners go in search of any means to make it visible and to promote its acceptance; women may join the *Unione Donne Italiane* or the *Centro Italiano Femminile* not because of commitment to the narrow goals or ideologies of these organizations, but because of the services they offer or the opportunity they provide to escape from boredom and drudgery. It is certainly not accidental, for example, that trade unions of whatever ideological coloration have long included a wide variety of recreational activity available to members. Such a pattern certainly implies in part that commitment to organizational goals is not enough and that other motivations for membership must consciously be created.[23]

One should understand, then, that in addition to ideological commitment as a factor motivating membership, there exist such other factors as convenience, satisfaction of personal needs, routine, and strong or mild forms of coercion. It can be a matter of considerable inconvenience for an industrial firm of some consequence to remain outside the provincial industrial union in its area; the other-directed personality may find associational life a significant means of satisfying this need to be with other people; a worker or farmer whose father and grandfather were members of syndical organizations may automatically fol-

[23] The provision of recreational activity is also a means of providing continual ideological indoctrination of members of mass organizations. This tactic, however, has tended to decline in importance as Italians have acquired television sets, automobiles, and other independent means of providing recreation. The traditional *camera del lavoro*—the union hall—seems clearly to be in serious decline in this regard.

low in their footsteps, even if the union satisfies very few needs and is not therefore a source of convenience.

The matter of coerced membership deserves a special word. One form of coercion—severe in the immediate postwar period but considerably abated recently—is that of the worker, sharecropper, or agricultural day laborer by his work peers. Pressure in the village or neighborhood from one's social peers can be quite intense. It is well known that this kind of pressure was consciously and systematically applied between 1945 and 1948, when almost all of Italy's trade unions were grouped in a single confederation. Where union affiliation was the norm, the nonjoiner risked a certain amount of social ostracism both on and off the job. The vast numbers of workers and farmers who disaffiliated as the labor unions broke up into warring ideological enclaves suggests that many of them were unwilling members who welcomed an opportunity to get out.

Some of this same kind of pressure is still applied, particularly in areas called *quartieri popolari,* which house many workers at close quarters. In addition, if we are to rely on the responses of several left-wing trade union leaders, those who seek employment in state-owned or state-controlled enterprises are frequently compelled to take out membership in the Christian Democratic Italian Confederation of Workers' Unions (C.I.S.L.).[24] The pressure may come from plant management, C.I.S.L. representatives, or members of the clergy. In one Montecatini plant, for example, the representatives of the C.G.I.L. and the democratic Italian Union of Labor (U.I.L.) are harassed from several quarters. At Isola della Scala, a priest is quoted as saying, "It pleases me that the workers should enroll in our union [C.I.S.L.] as the Pope would like." [25] Understandably, the leaders of C.G.I.L. and U.I.L. resent and protest such patterns, but the tactic itself is probably

24 *Interview,* Number 80 (Rome, May 9, 1958), pp. 5–7; *Interview,* Number 81 (Rome, May 9, 1958), p. 2; *Interview,* Number 94 (Rome, June 28, 1958), pp. 7–8.
25 *Interview,* Number 81, p. 3.

not different from what the disadvantaged unions have done or would do were they in a commanding position. The point is that, even where the union shop or closed shop do not officially exist, workers can be forced into trade-union associations.

Coerced membership is also true of the agricultural sector. When an association such as the Coltivatori Diretti establishes close ties with the government and is directly involved in the administration of certain social welfare activities through control of the *mutue* (social welfare agencies) and close ties with agencies of social insurance, the individual farmer refuses to join the organization at his great peril.[26] His needs for cheap fertilizer, cut-rate gasoline, extended credit, storage of his produce, and so on are not likely to be satisfied if he remains outside the massive confederation run by Paolo Bonomi. As one respondent put it, farmers who do not join the Coltivatori Diretti are likely to see their economic affairs mishandled, and they will therefore pay a material price for not becoming members of the syndical category.

It is difficult, of course, to know the proportion of interest-group membership that is a matter of subtle or overt compulsion rather than of conscious identification with organizational ideology, goals, and purposes. Unfortunately, survey research data are not very helpful on this score, because the proper kinds of questions have not been asked of samples of the national population. Yet compulsion as a significant means of motivating the act of membership emerges fairly clearly from a number of interviews. It is not easy, therefore, to escape the conclusion that many interest groups maximize membership because large numbers are in themselves impressive. The ability to refer to large numbers—and to threaten their

26 This was made quite clear to me not merely by a number of respondents who are openly hostile to the Coltivatori Diretti, but also by a responsible leader of the Confederation; *Interview*, Number 96, *op. cit.*, pp. 12–13. It was corroborated by one of Paolo Bonomi's close associates; *Interview*, Number 29 (Rome, January 29, 1958), pp. 2–4.

mobilization at the polls or elsewhere—is an important tactical attribute of many of the groups we have examined.

One generalization that can be drawn from an examination of questionnaire and interview materials is that the smaller the organization and the narrower or less diffuse its goals, the greater the demand for more than formalistic membership. Where the membership base is restricted, either for reasons of professional specialization or narrow specificity of organizational goals, membership tends to mean much more than holding a card, paying dues, and attending an occasional meeting. In such interest groups, full participation by members in the various activities of the group seems to be the norm. Failure to participate actively is quickly underscored; serious deviation from organization purpose is speedily noted. The frequency and quality of interaction is such as to maximize the value integration of members.

This is not to say that similar traits are totally absent in organizations that have mass memberships or whose interests are more diffuse. Interview data tell us that many of the largest organizations go to great pains to involve their members in organizational affairs. Local and provincial sections are created, meetings frequently called, a fair amount of communication from the center to the peripheral units occurs, yearly assemblies and elections are held, and, in general, much goes on that is designed to make the organization visible to its membership and to provide a sense of integration. Major Catholic and Communist groups, for example, appear to place relatively great demands for participation on their members. This is certainly true of such groups as the Coltivatori Diretti; the Italian Association of Christian Workers (A.C.L.I.); the National Association of Italian Partisans (A.N.P.I.); trade-union confederations such as C.I.S.L., U.I.L., and C.G.I.L.; the active feminine associations of C.I.F. and U.D.I.; Catholic Action and Confindustria. Yet even within these groups it seems essential to distinguish between the *militant* and the *casual* members. The casuals are there not because of strong and active commitment but for inertia, ritualism, or some of the other reasons mentioned above. They are not easy to mobilize—although, unlike the militants, they make the matter of governing associations oligarchically a relatively simple enterprise. Like boards of directors of joint stock companies in the United States, organizational leaders would probably be considerably upset if mass memberships began to take seriously and to act on constitutional and other inducements to participate in internal affairs.

If we remember to distinguish between militants and casuals and to note that there exists a broad scale of intensity of involvement and varying motivations for membership, we can more readily accept the allegations of widespread membership in secondary associations. The trade unionist who accepts a membership card and subsequently almost never pays any dues is patently different from another who regularly turns over a portion of his income to his labor organization. The first probably never attends any meeting and can only be persuaded to strike with some difficulty; the second is regularly and continually involved in trade-union affairs and contributes actively to the organization's life. A woman who on a single occasion signs a membership card in the *Unione Donne Italiane* is not the same kind of member as another who becomes deeply enmeshed in the myriad activities of the group. The first may do nothing more than read the weekly *Noi donne;* the second may attend meetings, serve on committees, be active in recruiting others to membership, and so on. Similar observations can be made for all the other mass associations. They are also true for professional and industrial associations in which membership occurs more or less routinely and automatically. The fact is, however, that group leaders do not distinguish among types or kinds of members; everyone is counted, even some, perhaps many, who have fallen into almost complete inactivity.

A central difficulty with sample surveys that seek to gauge the degree of Italian involvement in secondary associations is that they have not probed deeply enough into the intensity of group-membership identification.[27] Probes that do not go beyond a simple straightforward question are unlikely to uncover the full extent to which some sort of membership in interest groups, as they are defined in this volume, holds true for a great many Italians. Thus we conclude that, even after one has discounted an understandable tendency on the part of group leaders to puff their membership estimates, associational life in Italy is a distinctly important phenomenon—more important, no doubt, for the militants than for the casuals, but generally of considerable significance in the political process as a whole.

Our data show that group membership is more pervasive in the central and northern provinces than in the South, and that groups generally attract more men than women. With the exception of the Y.M.C.A., which recruits only five percent of its members in the North, individual group membership percentages for that part of the country range from 33 percent in the case of the Federazione Italiana Lavoratori Statali (a unit of C.I.S.L.) to 63 percent in the Associazione Nazionale Partigiani d'Italia (A.N.P.I.). In those instances where the member units are firms or associations rather than individuals, the relationship is even more pronounced. The range is from 36 percent in the North for S.V.I.M.E.Z. to 88 percent in the Associazione Italiana Industriali Risieri (Italian Association of Rice Industries). Even in the case of the National Association of Families of Fallen and Lost in War, which might logically recruit evenly throughout the peninsula, 41 percent of the members are located in

[27] Another difficulty is that surveys have often limited the respondent's choice to membership in political parties, trade unions, or sporting associations. Such queries have resulted in the impression that Italians are not joiners.

the North and only 33 percent in the South or on the Islands.

For some of the associations included in our survey, it is relatively easy to find an esoteric reason to explain the geographically uneven distribution of members. Some industries, such as rice and steel, either do not exist in the South or are in early stages of development. The armed Resistance was primarily a central and northern phenomenon, hardly visible in the South, with the possible exception of the "Quattro Giornate" of Naples in 1943. The potential memberships for partisan groups, such as A.N.P.I. and F.I.V.L., are therefore simply not to be found in many places south of Rome. However, even when one would expect the South to show greater membership proportion, this does not happen. Thus Confagricoltura reports that 65 percent of its members are in the Center and North, 23 percent in the South, and 12 percent on the Islands; the Italian General Confederation of Professionals and Artists specifies percentages of 60, 30, and 10; the Italian Federation of Advertising indicates that only 10 percent of its members are recruited south of Rome; even the *Unione Donne Italiane* specifies that most of its claimed three million adherents are found in central and northern areas and in the large rather than the smaller towns.

Although not all groups responded to the relevant questionnaire items, the evidence available is consistent and one-sided; the incidence of group membership in general increases progressively as one moves from south to north. Voluntary associations seem to be primarily a phenomenon that one would have to ascribe to the more urban and industrial areas of the country. This does not mean that agricultural regions are totally unorganized; the extensive development of cooperatives, Catholic organizations like the Coltivatori Diretti and Catholic Action itself, as well as agricultural trade unions would deny such an assertion. It does suggest, however, what is generally

153

sufficiently well known, namely that the more rural and tradition-oriented sectors of the society are least likely to crystallize human activity into a vast and overlapping network of secondary associations.

Not all of the voluntary associations that returned questionnaires provided a breakdown of the sex distribution of their memberships. From the data provided by the 30 groups that did do so, it is apparent that, with the obvious exception of groups that recruit only women, males far outnumber females. Highly technical associations like the Italian Hydrotechnical Association (900) and the Italian Mining Association (200) are made up exclusively of males. In the Italian Association for Public Relations, the male to female numerical relationship is 389 to 11; in the Italian Surgical Society there are 1,307 men and 2 women; in the Christian Union of Directors and Managers there are 1,650 males and 350 females; essentially the same ratio applies for the General Italian Confederation of Professionals and Artists, with its 9,600 male and 2,300 female members. In only one case—the Italian Association for the Defense of the Interests of Diabetics—was the ratio relatively balanced: 1,050 men and 750 women.

Unfortunately, none of the mass organizations reported membership by sex distribution. From several of the interviews we can infer that even in these instances members are drawn primarily from the male population. In part, this situation reflects the relatively large extent to which the Italian woman remains tied to the home and family. In addition, however, it is necessary to recognize that a definite majority of the associations included in our survey appeal primarily to men. This is certainly true of the industrial and agricultural trade unions, the professional associations, veterans groups, industrial organizations, and others. Where either the Catholics or the Communists set out deliberately to attract women, their claimed memberships suggest that they can be relatively quite successful in this quest.

To summarize, we might note, first, a great proliferation of secondary associations in Italian society. As we have tried to stress, the range of interests represented by these groups tends to cover most of the things about which the Italian is likely to have any serious concern. If the claims of leaders are to be given credence, it appears that a relatively small sample of groups (including, however, the presumably largest organizations) elicit some sort of membership allegiance from over twenty million Italians. Even after one discounts for overly enthusiastic membership claims and overlapping memberships, the total number who are likely to hold some sort of interest-group membership is striking. The phenomenon is even more impressive when one pauses to realize that there is a heavier concentration of membership in the central and northern provinces, that urban centers are more likely to attract group members than rural areas, and that, in general, more men than women find their way into secondary associations. If these findings and conjectures are accurate, it is apparent that more needs to be known about the nature and meaning of group affiliation in Italy. Only carefully planned and executed survey research, on special or cross-section samples of the population, is likely to produce more information regarding group memberships than is currently available.

GROUP LEADERSHIP

The interest groups we have studied generally include two kinds of leaders. The first are the elected leaders, the presidents and vice-presidents of national confederations or federations, provincial associations, zonal, communal, or sectional units of interest groups, and so on. Also included in this category are the elected members of general councils, executive juntas, and boards of directors or executive committees of the organizations at the various geographic levels. These men and women may be viewed as the *political* leaders. In one way or another, usually formally specified by group constitutions, they are expected both to make policy and to oversee its execution. All who hold such positions of political (or policy) leadership are generally held to be responsible to the total membership which, through various forms of organizational participation, enjoys the sovereign right of setting organizational goals.

Questionnaire responses show a wide variation in the number of elected leaders existing at the national and local levels of the organizations. At the national level, the number ranges from zero (which seems unlikely) in the case of the Friends of Organization Group (*Gruppo Amici dell'Organizzazione*), to 169 in the General Italian Confederation of Artisans. Where local geographic organizational units exist and data concerning them were reported, elected officials varied between four for U.C.I.D. and a fantastic 12,710 in the National Association of Families of Fallen and Lost in War. The typical case for the groups surveyed involves about 25 elected leaders at the national level and approximately 400 who function at the regional, provincial, and local levels.

In all cases save one, the elected officials serve without stipend, except for expenses that may be covered in connection with attendance at meetings or the execution of other organizational responsibilities. Those who serve in this capacity are not considered employees of the group but simply people doing other things primarily but who give some of their time to the management of organizational affairs. The important exception to this kind of arrangement occurs when a full- or part-time functionary, who may be an association's leader, is elected rather than appointed. Such a person is generally paid a stipend. Typical of this type of leader would be the responsible (general) secretary of a trade union, an industrial association, or similar group. It is safe to say that, as a rule, the elected leaders serve without pay.

Not so, however, those leaders who are appointed and who constitute the permanent bureaucracy of the association. These functionaries—or *bureaucratic leaders*—include everyone from a secretary-general to a lowly clerk. They are appointed—usually by the president or executive committee—not to make policy but to handle the technical, day-to-day details of group policy execution and implementation. They are usually full-time paid employees who often make a career of working for voluntary associations. As we shall later note, these men and women, particularly when they reach important executive levels, do in fact have policy ideas of their own, attempt to give strong direction to the associations, frequently develop antagonisms and hostility toward the elective (and presumably temporary) political leaders, and sometimes succeed in exerting considerable impact on the organization itself. To be sure, when those who occupy the top bureaucratic positions are appointed, the step is taken with a view not merely to professional competence but also to the degree of a person's commitment to the goals and purposes of the organization. But, within any large association, these goals and purposes are not monolithic, they change over time, and the bureaucratic leaders become intimately involved in steering them in one direction or another.

Of the 42 groups that provided information concerning bureaucratic leadership, all but eight indicated that the appointed functionaries work for salaries provided either by the national or the peripheral offices of the group. Those groups that say they do not pay their employees are such varied ones as the Italian Hydrotechnical Association, the Italian Mining Association, the Italian Center of Administrative Studies, and the Italian Federation of Volunteers of Liberty. Gratis labor, however, is definitely exceptional; those who are expected to spend most or all of their working time carrying on organizational affairs—and even many who work on a part-time basis—expect to be compensated.

The number of appointed and salaried organizational officials and employees varies considerably. The Industrial Union of the Province of Turin, with 3,107 reported member firms, employs 110 functionaries; the National Association of Families of Fallen and Lost in War, with 466,921 members, gets along with 25 at the center and 192 in local branches. The Italian Federation of Public Employees (F.I.L.S.), encompassing a membership of 72,000, claims to get along with a single functionary at the center. This suggests either that the report is inaccurate or that the Federation receives considerable administrative assistance from C.I.S.L., the parent association. As one would expect, Confagricoltura reports 101 at the center and at least 1,000 employees manning the Confederation's field units.

Although the number of functionaries is not strictly related to membership size, the more important mass associations seem to have evolved the most extensive bureaucratic leadership structure. For all of the groups surveyed, the typical situation involves about 16 officials and employees at the center.[28] Organizations with 50,000 or fewer individual members appear to get along with an average of five functionaries. The average number of bureaucratic officials and employees doubles with memberships of from 50,000 to 250,000 members, and doubles again with memberships of from 250,000 to 500,000. The important exception to this pattern involves the industrial unions and associations, which generally retain a high number of paid employees, regardless of size. This suggests that the incidence of bureaucratic leadership is also a function of the economic wealth of the particular interest group.

Although the questionnaires did not elicit background information regarding organizational leaders, our interviews with group leaders do permit some tentative generalizations. Group leaders seem to be quite young. Age estimates for 40 of them break down as shown in the following table.

[28] Questionnaire data are too sketchy to permit even an educated guess about the number of field officials and employees. Too many groups either did not respond or included the notation "many."

Age	Number
25–39	14
40–49	12
50–59	10
60 or over	4

The average age seems to be about 43 years. Most of those interviewed had been with their groups for some years, many of them since the reorganizations or initial organizational activity that occurred after the war. In only rare instances did a leader manifest less than complete knowledge concerning his group or less than strong devotion to its goals and purposes.

All but three of those in our sample were college graduates. Thirteen identified themselves as lawyers, although we assume that the number of those graduated in jurisprudence is even higher. There is a sprinkling of journalists and economists among them, but the technical fields such as engineering are almost totally lacking. Approximately half of these men would qualify as serious intellectuals—that is, more than merely bureaucrats holding down sinecures. Several of them have written for technical and other journals; several are involved in political party matters; most of them bring to bear on their work a considerable capacity for relating the problems of their organizations to broader issues of public policy confronting Italian society.

I do not mean to suggest here that Italian group leaders are by and large active intellectuals. Those who were interviewed represented for the most part the top-echelon political or bureaucratic leaders at the center. It may well be that the pattern changes as one moves down the organizational hierarchy, or as one might go from headquarters at Rome to field offices in the provinces. Nevertheless, it is noteworthy that so many of those interviewed were university graduates, that they gave strong evidence of being broadly educated, and that they were able to be intellectually articulate about their own organizations and the way these latter relate to other groups, the political process, and Italian society in general.

One clue to the possibility that those interviewed might be somewhat unrepresentative of group leaders might be garnered from responses to a questionnaire item having to do with the perceived importance of the interest group in Italian society. However, very few of these responses were not intellectual, at least in part. To be sure, some of them were narrowly interest-oriented and several were clearly ideological. The most narrow responses were provided by industrial associations. One such frankly stated that the importance of the association lies in its intention "to guard and protect the interests of private enterprise and entrepreneurial freedom." Another, in seeking to underline its importance, said: "We govern a sector that deals with a product worth 200 billion lire a year, that exports annually 15 billion lire worth of material and imports 13 billion lire." The Italian Association of Public Relations provided this response: "We have created in Italy an understanding of the utility of public relations for both private and public firms. We have succeeded in three years in creating a sense of professionalism and in creating a concrete interest in the disciplining of the category. We are trying to create a new profession and to develop a particular orientation among the executive class favorable to the principles of collaboration with and sympathy toward the community."

Although this reply is largely personal-interest-oriented, the concluding sentence suggests the type of articulation of interest we encountered in many of the interviews. The point is that one can detect, from both the interviews and the questionnaire responses, some effort to relate organizational interest to the broader national interest. Thus another professional group makes the point that "our associational movement could be validated if greater value were placed in our national life on cultural movements consisting of citizens in general, without regard to their political origin." Another questionnaire contains the remark that "Each productive sector [agriculture in this case] must possess an organizational means of interacting with other groups and with legislative and administrative authorities. Organization is needed to handle this continuously and efficaciously." The General Confederation of Professionals and Artists spoke as follows about its importance: "The Confederation has much importance in contemporary Italian society, since it includes categories that represent the aristocracy of thought in every field. It can exercise the function of providing an orientation on many of the problems of national life."

While both organizational constitutions or questionnaire responses may state quite narrowly the purposes or ends of interest groups, group leaders seem to be able to think and to articulate considerably beyond such restricted goals. It may well be that such articulation represents something of a gloss for basic interests. This is certainly the case when representatives of extreme ideological groups begin speaking of things like "democratic maturation," "the creation of the civic person," or "the inculcation of a sense of patriotism." Nevertheless, it is a datum of some importance that group leaders—of both the political and bureaucratic variety—feel some compulsion to relate their groups to the society and their organizational goals and welfare to the broader needs of the collectivity. Insofar as this may become a generalized phenomenon in Italy, it may serve as a factor mitigating the extreme fragmentation and isolation of interest groups that is so typical of the general situation.

ORGANIZATIONAL PATTERNS

It will not be necessary to try to specify the ways in which the groups surveyed differ in their formal organizational structures. Such differences often appear to be slight and of no apparent importance. Moreover, neither the official constitutions nor the questionnaire responses afford sufficient information to permit analytical observations regarding the degree of power concentration in central organs, the amount of freedom of action permitted group leaders, or how much *actual* and *meaningful* membership participation in organizational affairs occurs. Only with regard to Confindustria and Catholic Action, concerning which we have some information in depth, can we generalize with confidence about matters and problems of internal organization.

On the other hand, a composite picture of formal structure can be laid out, particularly because Italian interest groups display striking similarities in their major organizational outlines. As we have already observed, group membership is usually free and voluntary; it is open to anyone (or any firm or association) who meets generalized qualifications and who subscribes to the stated purpose of the group. Once a member is accepted and remains in good standing, he (or it) may be expelled only for cause, and then only after carefully specified procedures have been followed. Membership carries with it various kinds of opportunities to participate in the life and affairs of the group. These, too, are painstakingly enumerated and described in organizational constitutions.

The first thing to note about associational interest groups is that membership may be direct or indirect, or that a single association may make membership available to individuals, to other groups or associations, or to both. A category trade union, for example, representing a particular industry or classification of workers, will generally recruit individual members. The broader national confederation of which the category union—or national federation—is a part will consist not of individual members but of these specialized associational units. Similarly, in the agricultural field, the National Confederation of Direct Cultivators consists of provincial federations of direct cultivators that in turn recruit small agricultural proprietors as individual members. In the field of industrial management, an association like the Italian Confederation of Plant Directors is made up of the National Federation of Industrial Plant Managers and of national associations that take their individual members from among commercial, insurance, and banking managers. Most of the associations included in our survey display the indirect or "secondary" membership characteristic. The important exceptions consist of relatively small groups—such as the Y.M.C.A., the Italian Hydrotechnical Association, the Italian Association for the Defense of Interests of Diabetics, the Italian Association of Public Relations, the Economic Center for Reconstruction, the Italian Center for Administrative Studies, and the Italian Society of Parapsychology—that recruit their members directly on a national basis. Whenever a particular interest segment becomes large enough—and this holds true for veterans, laborers, farmers, artisans, professional persons, university students, etc.—there quickly emerges a tendency either to articulate organization at a local and provincial level or to create a peak association that brings other organizational units together under one roof. An exceptional pattern is seen in the case of SVIMEZ, which opens its doors to societies, associations, single enterprises, and individual persons.

In the sector of industrial organization, the group members are either individual firms or category associations of such firms. The Italian Mining Association, for example, may be joined by any individual enterprise engaged in mining activity. The same is true of associations created to reflect the interests of the dairy, wool, rice, cotton, and other industries. Thus the National Association of Merchants of Agricultural Products consists of individual firms in this field; the Petroleum Union consists of firms involved in the production, manufacture, import, and distribution of petroleum and petroleum derivative products. There are some instances in which individual industrial sectors are combined into a national confederation, such as the General Confederation of Traffic and Transport, but this is rare. As we shall see later in greater detail, the individual category associations generally tend to be integrated into Confindustria both through territorial industrial unions and through direct national membership in the peak association.

A second point to note is that the major interest groups are generally articulated at various territorial levels. Single-category associations will frequently develop provincial and local units. National confederations—peak associations—that bring together several national category associations will often do the same thing in the regions, provinces, cities, and even zones. Let us use an individual metal worker to illustrate this.

Such a person is free to join a local or provincial unit of any one of several ideologically defined metalworkers' unions. He may elect membership in a local unit of the left-wing Italian Federation of Metalmechanical Workers (F.I.O.M.) His union will then be a member of a Chamber of Labor (in the city or province) that groups together several other unions operating in the same area. The union will also be a local unit of the national federation. Then, both the national F.I.O.M. and the Chamber of Labor will hold membership and be separately represented in the Italian General Confederation of Labor (C.G.I.L.). Thus this individual C.G.I.L. member, as the Italians put it, is *vertically* represented in the Confederation through his direct membership in F.I.O.M. and *horizontally* represented through his indirect membership in the municipal or provincial Chamber of Labor.

The same pattern is repeated for the individual firm or industrialist. British Petroleum or Shell Italiana, for example, are members of the Petroleum Union, a national association which is also a member of Confindustria. Individual B.P. or Shell plants, however, wherever they are located are also likely to be members of municipal or provincial industrial unions, such as the Lombard Industrial Association (Assolombardo) or the Industrial Union of the Province of Turin. Again, the plants find vertical membership in the category association and horizontal membership in the territorial group. The vertical memberships represent very specific and narrow interests; the horizontal memberships are more diffused to reflect the desires of an entire class rather than any specific category.

As a rule, then, group members (whether firms or individuals) are several steps removed from the national associations and federations or the peak associations that presumably represent their interests. The very existence of such a complex structure means that all the national organizations are intimately involved in the function of interest aggregation. Where only a single, national category with essentially narrow and specific interests is involved, the differences of opinion regarding policy articulated by territorial units must somehow be reconciled before a cohesive national policy can emerge. To return to our metalworker example, it is resoundingly clear that workers in this category located in such diverse places as, say, Catania, Bari, Naples, Bologna, and Turin do not think alike, are treated differently as to wages and working conditions, and have conflicting notions regarding the direction and content that industry-wide policies should take. A crucial function of the national leadership of F.I.O.M. (and of any other national association) is that of reconciling the differences in views that emerge from membership groups and units around the country.

The task is even more demanding for those who govern national confederations (peak associations), or the territorial, horizontal microcosms of these organizations. Here it is necessary to weave together the diverse interests of large and small industries, of metalworkers and public employees, of the wool and cotton or steel and automobile industries, of lawyers and doctors, television and motion picture actors and producers, men and women, youth and the aged, and so on, through an inexhaustible list of groups in conflict. To be sure, there are important factors, such as social class, ideology, religion, and education, which serve to balance centrifugal with centripetal momentum. Nevertheless, our interview data show that it is the rarest of groups that does not manifest these internal tensions. Not even Catholic Action, for all of the homogeneity of policy that the clergy seek to impose, is free of this problem.

The most typical way of coping with the matter of diverse geographic, particularistic interests is that of affording representation in the deliberative and executive organs of an association. In all cases where local units of the groups exist, several representative structures exist. These generally include an annual assembly in which the membership is invited to participate, a local council which is chosen by the assembly, and a local president (and vice-presidents) or responsible secretary (and vice-secretaries) who are chosen either by the assembly or by the council.

At the national level, a similar organizational pattern is generally followed. In the case of single-category associations or federations, each geographic unit is entitled to send delegates to a General Assembly that ordinarily meets annually. Where a peak association is involved, there are usually two classes of delegates, one representing the category associations and federations, the other representing regional, provincial, and local units of the peak association itself. Delegates are voting members of the general assembly, and the strength of their ballots is normally tied to some relative quantitative factor, such as the number of individual members represented by the delegates, the proportion of dues or finances provided by the units represented, and so on. In every case that we have examined, the principle of differential voting power applies to some extent. Although this suggests relatively strong attachment to the principle of democratic majoritarianism, it also means, in some cases, that a concentration of economic power within an interest group is translated into the domination of the general assembly.

Normally, a series of local and provincial assembly meetings precedes the holding of the annual general assembly. The local groups, through this mechanism, often take stands on issues confronting the national organization and instruct their delegates on the formal posture to assume when the national general assembly convenes. However, it is the latter organ that is usually assumed to be the supreme policy-making unit for the group, and the subsequent activities of all other divisions of the association are expected to conform to the policy guidelines set by the General Assembly.

Beyond setting general policies, the General Assembly will often engage in such activities as (1) effecting modifications in the constitution, usually by greater than majority votes; (2) setting and approving the operating budget of the organization; (3) creating or abolishing local units or divisions; (4) hearing appeals from decisions to expel or to discipline members; (5) setting basic procedures and regulations; and (6) electing other representative and directive bodies, frequently from among its own membership. Regarding these latter, a typical structure may be outlined as follows:

1. In about one-half the cases, the General Assembly names a National or General Council that is expected to function between meetings of the Assembly. In the other half of the cases we have examined, the Councils are made up of officials and delegates who directly represent member units or associations.[29] Where this latter procedure is followed, we have examples of greater recognition in decision-making afforded the category groups that make up associations. These particular interests apparently demand *assured* representation, preferring not to leave such an important matter to chance factors that might operate in a General Assembly. It should be noted that, since General Assembly votes are normally based on relative membership or relative financial contributions to the association, this second method of constituting Council membership is essentially the more democratic one, assuring as it usually does equal representation and voting strength to the small minority units.

---

[29] In the case of some peak associations, the National Councils are made up both of members elected by the General Assembly and by presidents of member associations who sit on the Council as a matter of right.

The Council typically meets every three or four months. Like the General Assembly, it may be convened in extraordinary or special session by the President or Executive Committee. The Council is supposed to oversee the proper execution of policies set by the General Assembly. Moreover, it is usually authorized to set policies for situations not anticipated by the General Assembly. In this sense, the Council stands in place of the latter; its decisions—even when they must subsequently be ratified by the General Assembly—are binding on the organization.

2. Forty-two of the groups we surveyed empower their General or National Councils to select (usually from among their own memberships) the members of an Executive Committee or Junta. In twelve cases, on the other hand, even this organ's membership is named by the units of the association acting independently. In twelve more instances, the Committee or Junta is staffed by vote of the General Assembly. Ten of the second group are also ones that do not permit the General Assembly to name Council membership. We may reasonably infer that these are organizations in which the drive to assure representation of internal sectarian interest is very pronounced.[30] However, there is no evident pattern that would permit us to identify one type of selection of organizational executives with a particular category of interest group.

In some instances, the Executive Committee will contain both elected members and others (representing regions, provinces, or member groups) who sit by right and who either have full voting rights or only a consultative or advisory voice. As a rule, these committees or juntas are much smaller than the councils, ranging in size in our survey from three to thirty-eight members. The typical membership is about fifteen, which means, among other things, that this group is less unwieldy than either

[30] Included in this category are Confagricoltura, *Assolombardo*, General Confederation of Traffic and Transport, and Italian General Confederation of Artisans, all of which encompass many diverse categories.

of the other two organs discussed previously. The Executive Committee meets more frequently than the National Council. Where fixed meeting intervals are specified by constitutions, every three or four months is a typical provision. Over half the constitutions, however, leave the calling of meetings to the discretion of the president or of a percentage of the committee's membership. Presumably, this can occur just as often as there is need of a decision or other action by this body.

The Executive Committee is required to assure that decisions of both the General Assembly and the National Council are followed: It is also expected to cope with any urgent business that may be brought before it by the president or other officers. However, the Committee is normally defined as the maximum executive organ of the association, which suggests that its formal authority to innovate policy is limited and that it is expected to deal primarily with new policy issues that do not involve a long-term commitment by the association.

3. Executive officers of associations consist of the president, one or more vice-presidents, a secretary-general (often also vice-secretaries), a group of auditors (*sindaci* or *revisori dei conti*), and a group of judges or arbitrators (*probiviri*). Judges and auditors are almost always elected by the general assemblies. The function of the auditors is self-evident; that of the judges includes appeals from decisions to expel members, decisions regarding constitutional questions, or opinions concerning problems submitted to them by officials of the organization. Both groups exercise a watchdog function and for this reason are made responsible to the most representative organ of the general membership. In many instances, neither the auditors nor the judges need be members of the interest group itself, it being felt that objective impartiality is reasonably assured when such officers are drawn from the outside.

In thirty cases, the presidents of the groups we surveyed are elected by the General Assembly; in thirty-two cases they are chosen by the National Council. Frequently, when the former procedure is followed, the National Council is authorized to select the one or more vice-presidents who are permitted by the Constitution. Once again, the apparently more democratic procedure of having the top political officer chosen by the General Assembly is not narrowly restricted to one classification of interest groups. However, industrial territorial associations are strongly represented in this category. Also included are the important Coltivatori Diretti, Confagricoltura, and Confcommercio. In no case was a group included from extreme left or that represented veterans organizations. The same thing is true of the Catholic groups. It seems reasonable to suppose that, where tight control over membership is a central motivation, national councils will emerge from general assemblies, executive committees or juntas from the latter, and presidents and vice-presidents either from the juntas or from the national councils. To leave the matter of top leadership selection to processes of large and unwieldy assemblies is extremely risky business except in those cases where assembly membership itself is very carefully rigged.

The day-to-day affairs of the typical association are normally in the hands of the Secretary-General and his staff. In very rare cases (the National Association of Italian Communes is an example) this top-level administrative officer is elected by the General Assembly. Much more common is the hiring of this bureaucratic official and his assistants by the Executive Committee (in some cases by the National Council) on recommendation of the President. The Secretary-General reports to the President, and one of the former's major responsibilities is to assist the latter in the preparation of the report on organization affairs—the *relazione*—that is presented to the General Assembly whenever it convenes.[31] These *relazioni* are

---

[31] It should be noted that the labor unions normally do not have a president but only an elective Secretary-General, who manages the affairs of the federation or confederation. This person is both the top political and the top bureaucratic leader of his organization.

often elaborate documents that examine organizational problems in detail and therefore provide some important information regarding the degree of success that has accompanied attempts of the group to influence the legislative or bureaucratic process. The Secretary-General is presumably the key person who develops a long-term career identification with the interest group. When he is an able person, he soon develops the kind of control over information and technical expertise that makes the political leadership—including the President—considerably dependent on him. As we shall later note, this continuity of bureaucratic leadership implies both strength and weakness for any interest group. It is obviously a matter of strength that elected leaders do not have to begin from scratch every two years, which is the most frequent tenure specified by group constitutions. It is a matter of weakness, however, when newly elected leaders, bent on effecting major changes in organizational policies and strategies, encounter the conservative "let's-do-it-as-we-always-have" views of the typical organizational bureaucrat.

What we have outlined here for Italian interest-group organization depicts a formal structure that certainly does not do violence to the tenets of democracy. Yet it is obvious from the behavior of many groups and the internal tensions that characterize others that policies, strategies, and tactics are not matters that flow up from the bottom of the organizational pyramid. Interest-group members, like members of most complex organizations, are not leaders but are led. Often, beyond being led, they are manipulated. Yet the test of democratic organization would seem to lie not in the existence of oligarchical control, which is inevitable, but in the degree to which formal processes permit the general members to voice their views and to elect those who accept them and remove others who do not. For many—indeed most—of the interest groups we have examined, these formal procedures are available. That they are not more frequently used is probably an index either of satisfaction with leadership or of apathy concerning the affairs of the association. Concerning any of the groups included in our survey, much more detailed information would have to be gathered before the groups themselves could be arranged along a continuum of democratic-authoritarian leadership or decision-making.

What is impressive about formal organization is its extensive and detailed articulation for most associations. It is fairly obvious that Italian society has had considerable experience with secondary associations, experience which was, if anything, intensified rather than diminished during the Fascist era. Interest-group constitutions are often gems of legal expertise: vital procedures are laid out in detail and with great care; the rights and obligations of membership are painstakingly enumerated; the formal authority and power to be exercised by each organ and unit of the association are made a matter of written record and not left to chance; the formula for expanding or contracting the scope of the association's membership and activities is there for all to read and understand. In short, a very well-developed framework for the organization and articulation of interest is clearly in existence and, unless our membership figures are grossly in error, manages to attract some attention from a significant portion of the Italian population. How that articulation is translated into patterns of intervention in the political system is a matter to which we can now turn our attention.

CHAPTER VI · PATTERNS OF GROUP COMMUNICATIONS AND INTERACTION

A GREAT many of the interest groups we have examined are continually and often deeply involved in the Italian political process. There are, of course, differing kinds of involvement and various indices of patterns of political intervention. One important means of political action lies in the communications activities of organized interest. A group that develops an interest—what we have previously defined as a desire to have public policy move in a particular direction—must be able to communicate this interest both internally to its leaders and members and externally to the general public, to other groups, and to formal structures of government. So-called "latent interest" may also characterize most groups, but I do not see that such "interest" is very meaningful for the political process; even in those instances where policy-makers are presumed to be responding to some sort of "latent" interest, my surmise would be that the interest has somehow been communicated to them.

GROUP PUBLICATIONS

Even in an isolative culture such as Italy's, interest groups do not function in mutually exclusive compartments; in general, they go to great pains to communicate their fears, desires, and expectations. Fifty-eight of the sixty-eight groups that returned questionnaires indicate they turn out at least one publication, excluding the annual report provided by all groups in one form or another.[1] The most common publication is the monthly

[1] Only one group, the Italian Center of Administrative Studies, indicated no publications, and nine other groups did not respond to the question.

magazine, which is directed primarily to members. Circulation ranges from 500 in cases of groups like the Italian Association of Public Relations and the National Association of Rubber Industries to from 10,000 to 15,000 in the case of the Italian Female Center's *Cronache* and the Italian Federation of Public Employee's *Il Libero statale*. For the 46 groups reporting circulation figures, the average for monthly publications is 4,800 copies.

Ten of the groups say they publish weekly newspapers and an additional fourteen turn out bi-weekly papers. Circulation varies between 1,500 for the *Natiziario industriale* of the Industrial Association of the Province of Bologna and a claimed 250,000 for the fancy *Noi donne* produced by the Italian Union of Women. More typical are circulations ranging from 15,000 to 25,000 copies, belonging to the National Association of Partisans of Italy with 300,000 members, Confagricoltura with 248,000 members, the General Confederation of Professionals and Artists with 11,900 members, and so on.

Publications examined vary considerably in quality, substance, explicitness of political content, and the breadth of population to which directed. *Noi donne,* for example, is a relatively elegant rotogravure in color that covers with both text and illustrations political affairs, motion pictures and theater, short stories, economic and social problems affecting women, sports, fashions, adult and children's literature, the rearing of children, radio and television programs, and many others. It is clearly a publication intended for mass circulation (it is sold in the kiosks) rather than for purely internal consumption. Its political content is seldom blatant or obviously sectarian; its intention is to recruit broad public support for the political demands of the extreme left.

The inclusion of sections that may satiate the thirst of all sorts of people is also true of some group publications intended largely for organization members. This is certainly the case for C.G.I.L.'s *Il Lavoro italiano* and C.I.S.L.'s *Conquiste del lavoro*. Such papers differ from

Noi donne, however, in the sense that the political content is more blatant and manifest and the sectarian viewpoint more openly and aggressively stated. Indeed, whenever a group publication is internally directed, one can
expect to find frank statements of the group's interest as
well as intense—sometimes vicious—attacks on government and, more often, on other groups in the society
identified as enemies.

The most elegant publications, rarely intended for mass
or public circulation, are the monthly magazines of industrial associations. Typical of these would be *Progresso
agricolo* (National Association of Merchants of Products
for Agriculture), *Ospitalità e alberghi* (Federation of
Italian Hotel and Tourist Associations), *L'industria dei
farmaci* (National Association of Industrialists of Chemi-
cal-Pharmaceutical Products), and *Laniera* (Association of
the Italian Woolen Industry). There are invariably slick-
paper magazines, with fancy covers, obviously deriving
their affluenec from the considerable institutional advertising that they contain. As a general rule, these magazines
give a great deal of attention to matters of technological
development in the industry. They also report on industrial congresses and conventions, and devote some space
to the analysis of technological, legislative, economic, or
political problems that are of importance to the membership. In recent years, as one would expect, a great
many articles have been devoted to the problems and
prospects for Italian industry incipient in or emerging out
of the development of the European Common Market.
These industrial association magazines are not usually as
openly political as the labor union publications, and they
rarely engage in the kind of intergroup polemics characteristic of them.

It is important to recognize that most of the larger (or
more affluent) groups will turn out several publications,
some intended for general consumption, others directed
at group members, and still others intended to be read
by leaders at various levels. Even where a group does not

possess the economic means to permit a large-scale, highly differentiated publication program, mimeographing and other cheap means of reproduction are utilized to assure that the group's interests and strategy reach various audiences or targets, in one form or another. The point is that the amount of internal and external communication is immense, and that the communication mechanism is the chief means of securing group integration and of carrying on group interaction with other associations, with government, and with the public at large.

While monthly magazines and annual reports afford some flavor of the nature of Italian interest groups, a full picture of the demands and access to government emerges only in their newspaper publications. These are usually four-page, not very attractive publications which attempt to keep the membership up to date regarding what the political and bureaucratic leaders are doing and what events in the political sphere seem to affect the group adversely or otherwise. One often finds in such newspapers running commentaries on legislative proposals, legislation and administrative regulations affecting the group. Great attention is paid to stating the group's position on issues of public policy of concern to it. If there existed no other means of gauging the deep-seated way in which Italian secondary, so-called apolitical, associations are involved in the political process, even a casual reading of these publications would suffice.

Let us look briefly at the issue of March 1, 1958, of *Corriere della attività mediatorie,* biweekly organ of the National Federation of Business Brokers. The headline reads: "The Approval of the Law for 330,000 Brokers Crowns the Hard Work of President Renato Cini." The legislation was requested by the Association and manifestly represents an attempt to determine the way in which the public authorities would regulate entrance into the profession as well as the ethical conduct of those who are its practitioners. One would infer from the write-up that the Association has not always been successful in its legislative intervention. In the lead article, the editor writes: "It does not seem possible! One of our bills passed! Just as the faint-hearted colleagues despaired over the improbability that, in the legislature's last days, among thousands of bills to be examined, exactly the one close to our hearts might be inserted among the eleventh-hour privileged ones, the miracle happened." [2]

The article goes on to describe the intensive lobbying efforts that underlie the passage of the bill. The group's president is described as following the bill "from desk to desk, from office to office, committee to committee" throughout the interminable parliamentary procedure. Although the bill that emerged is described as not the original one submitted, it is accepted as something the group can live with. Then the paper goes on to give thanks where they are evidently due. The language is fascinating as well as somewhat ingenuous: "Thanks above all, and not only thanks, to those elite parliamentarians who understood our feelings and who became generous interpreters of them. We will remember their names."

The same front page contains an article on the national electoral campaign which was then in progress. Evidently the Association had sought, without success, to get its president, Baron Renato Cini, named as a legislative candidate of the Christian Democratic Party. The newspaper laments this failure, but turns again to expressing its pleasure over the passage of the bill it had sponsored. Reflecting on the successful campaign, the article comments: "However, we cannot but turn a thought of thanks to all the deputies who supported our bill. Brokers know how to exchange the 'note' that falls due on May 25, and in anticipation of the electoral climate that is slowly pervading the entire peninsula, we can only remind all brokers of their duty, reminding everyone that *promissio boni viri est obligatio*." [3]

2 *Corriere delle attività mediatorie* (March 1, 1958), p. 1.
3 *Ibid.*

Remaining portions of this issue deal with internal organizational as well as political affairs. There is nothing atypical about the content of the paper, except, perhaps, that it makes more explicit than usual the intimate way in which the association intervenes in the legislative process. Other interest-group news organs randomly brought to our attention display essentially the same pattern. Thus the April 25, 1957, issue of the weekly newspaper published by the building construction industry indicates that a piece of legislation dealing with the regulation of bidding for construction projects was drafted in 1951 by the Minister of Public Works *at the request* of the National Association of Building Constructors (A.N.C.E.). This bill was subsequently opposed by the Minister of Justice, who questioned its constitutionality. The newspaper applauds a decision of a high court that supports the A.N.C.E. and Ministry of Public Works position as against that of the Ministry of Justice. The accounts of this complex problem contained in a single issue of the newspaper eloquently portray the exquisitely political function of this important interest group.[4]

To select a third and last example of the point I am making, we might examine the October 25, 1957, issue of *Fertilmacchine,* the official organ of the National Association of Merchants of Products for Agriculture. The lead article deals with the deliberation and vote of a Senate committee considering a tax bill on fertilizer that the Association had helped to draft. The article contains a carefully reasoned, particularistic rationale for the legislation, as well as a description of the Association's role in guiding the bill through Parliament.[5] Other portions of the issue are devoted to an attack on the Ministry of Finance for allegedly unfair regulations affecting the

[4] *Il Corriere dei costruttori* (April 25, 1957), p. 1. For an index of the group's concern with and attention to Italian public administration, see the articles "Il Motivato parere del Consiglio di Stato," and "Nomine e destinazioni al Ministero dei LL.PP."

[5] *Fertilmacchine* (October 25, 1957), p. 1.

group, a suggestion to the Ministry of Agriculture concerning the specific regulations to apply in the sale of fertilizers, and several discussions of the steps taken by the association to intervene in the public administrative sector on behalf of the interests of the membership. Among other things, it is apparent that this association is in conflict with the Coltivatori Diretti and is bent on preventing the law from being administered in a manner that gives an advantage to the latter and damages the former. Succinctly put, almost the entire content of this particular issue deals with matters political and with association behavior that places it directly in the main stream of the Italian political process.

INTERNAL COMMUNICATIONS

Publication of house organs or of magazines or newspapers destined for a larger audience is clearly not the only means of communication adopted by the groups we have studied. The associations surveyed by questionnaire were asked, for example, what kinds of contact were maintained between group headquarters and their memberships, and with what frequency. The leaders were asked to specify, in addition, whether the contact (excluding newspaper and magazines) was direct or through other organizational units. Table 7 is a summary of the responses to this question:

TABLE 7: Frequency of Contact between Leaders and Members, by Nature of the Contact

Nature of Contact	Frequent	Once in a While	Rarely	Never	NR
Direct	37	12	—	—	19
Indirect					
Regional units	16	7	2	2	19
Provincial units	22	4	4	—	19
Local units	19	5	—	—	19

Six of the groups indicated only direct contact between headquarters and memberships. They are the relatively small Italian Society of Surgery (1,309 members), the Italian Society of Parapsychology (200), the Friends of Organization Group (100), the National Association of Italian Communes (4,000), the National Association of Rubber, Electric Cables, and Related Industries (172 firms), and the Hemp Association (105 firms). In one case—that of the General Confederation of Italian Artisans—it was specified that direct contact is rare and that communication takes place almost exclusively through provincial units of the organization.

Where the membership is small, it is understandable that intermediate channels of communication are not essential. But when the membership grows in size, there emerges both a need and a tendency to add regional, provincial, or local units to the organizational and communications network. For the large-scale peak associations, one finds a great river of communication between leaders and members. The main flow of this process involves not a single channel but a vast and often complicated system of tributaries. This has reference not merely to the various geographic levels at which the interest group may be articulated but also to the degree of bureaucratic differentiation that a given group may have evolved. Once again, of course, it is the larger or more affluent groups that create many specialized bureaucratic subdivisions each of which may become a generator of both internal and external communications. When asked by questionnaire to specify the extent of this differentiation in the national headquarters, the groups responded as in Table 8.

It is significant for our purposes that, where specialized divisions exist, that of press and propaganda (with organizational affairs) heads the list in Table 8. To be sure, there are sixteen groups, representing over a fourth of those that responded, that have not created such an administrative subdivision. In almost all cases they are the smaller groups. The Italian Hydrotechnical Association,

TABLE 8: Degree of Bureaucratic Differentiation, by Type of Division or Office

Type of Division	Exists		Does Not Exist		
	No.	Percent	No.	Percent	NR
Organizational affairs	40	71	16	29	12
Press-propaganda	40	71	16	29	12
Finance	28	50	28	50	12
Research	28	50	28	50	12
International affairs	28	50	28	50	12
Legislative affairs	25	45	31	55	12
Economic	21	37	35	63	12
Trade union affairs	18	32	38	68	12
Coordination	18	32	38	68	12
Leadership	11	20	45	80	12
Other	18	32	38	68	12

for example, with a claimed membership of 900 individuals and 400 groups indicates no administrative subdivision at all. The same is true of the Association of Industrialists of the Province of Bologna which claims to utilize the specialized services of the Confindustria, and of the small Italian Federation of Advertising which points out that member units take care of various specialized administrative tasks. All of the mass associations that reported, except one, include a press and propaganda office in their national headquarters. The exception is a curious one, involving as it does the highly political National Association of Partisans of Italy whose claimed membership exceeds a quarter of a million persons.

I am assuming here that Table 8 is at least a broad index of the relative importance the groups place on various kinds of activities. That nearly three-quarters of those that provided the information include a specialized division dealing with press and propaganda affairs underscores the importance of communicating to the outside world. It is true that these divisions are generally responsible for producing and supervising the distribution of publications destined primarily for internal membership consumption. But such activity is quickly routinized and handled on a highly stable and regularized basis. The basically important, highly volatile and demanding responsibility involves the production of news releases, special reports and similar items that are designed for circulation externally. To some extent, this external circulation is handled by the group's own organization and the utilization of its own resources.

OTHER COMMUNICATIONS MEDIA

On the other hand, a great many of the groups are increasingly aware of the necessity of utilizing all possible means in their campaigns to get their messages across to both members and others. In this regard, the surveyed groups were asked whether, beyond the publication of their own news organs, they utilized other means or devices aimed at informing or influencing the formation of public opinion. Thirty groups responded affirmatively, twelve negatively, and twenty-six did not reply. Among those that replied, the graduated list of Table 9 emerged.

TABLE 9: Use of Other Means of Communication,
by Types of Means

Types of Communication	Number of Groups
Newspapers	30
Conferences	18
Radio	14
Special courses	11
Television	7
Periodicals	5

All of the groups responding to this item claim to utilize newspapers other than their own, underscoring this outlet as a critical means of providing information and disseminating propaganda. However, it is important to understand a number of things about the relationship between groups and Italian newspapers. In the first place, it is the rare group that is likely to get broad newspaper coverage for its press releases. By and large, Italian papers tend to feature only the releases of groups with which they are identified ideologically or with whose general policies the newspapers are basically in agreement. When there occurs a deviation from this pattern, it usually involves an attack by the newspapers on the policies or behavior of groups toward which they are antagonistic. Thus the so-called independent press is likely to be quite harsh concerning the demands of the trade unions, particularly those of the Left. Even some of the political party press, such as the Christian Democratic *Il Popolo,* may treat a Christian Democratic trade union confederation like C.I.S.L. negatively when the union's policies run counter to the more conservative views of the segment of the party that controls the newspaper. C.I.S.L. leaders have complained bitterly about this in the past, particularly when the union was attempting very earnestly to differentiate its organizational strategy and tactics from those of competing union confederations. In general, and for varying reasons, it is difficult for the trade unions to get much widespread national newspaper publicity for their viewpoints.

There are, of course, exceptions to what has been said. When, for example, the unions, alone or in concert, succeed in paralyzing a sector of industry, agriculture, or transportation through a strike, most newspapers will carry items concerning it—even if only to refute the union's claims of the extent to which the strike is successful in halting the work activity involved. Or, to cite another example, when ceremonies to celebrate the anniversary of the Armed Resistance are first impeded by public officials and then turned into riots involving ex-Partisans, Neo-Fascists, and the police, these activities are treated quite prominently by the bulk of the nation's press. One of the most dramatic and successful efforts of left-wing groups to find the broadest national coverage for their point of view occurred in 1954 in connection with the execution of the Rosenbergs. Here, a campaign which began slowly and quietly built up momentum until it was shrilly treated in the left-wing press. Before it terminated, however, the Rosenberg case had become a national issue in Italy, receiving saturation coverage in the daily newspapers and periodicals. Even the conservative *Osservatore romano,* the Vatican's official news organ, was eventually compelled—really goaded—into treating prominently Pope Pius' appeal to President Eisenhower for clemency toward the Rosenbergs. The point is that certain events are intrinsically newsworthy in Western countries where there exists press competition, and as a result some of the events in which interest groups become involved automatically appear in the newspapers and magazines.

A second point to make about interest groups and newspapers is that some papers are so closely tied to particular groups as to constitute official or quasi-official organs. A good example of this would be the coverage of C.G.I.L. affairs given by the Communist daily *L'Unità* and the Socialist daily *Avanti!* Significant segments of these papers are regularly devoted to the affairs of the labor confederation. While the coverage rarely includes many of the highly technical matters that the confederation must communicate to its members, most of the positions or strategies of political import assumed by the labor organization are given prominent coverage. To a more limited extent, *Il Popolo* in recent years provides the same service for C.I.S.L. In the field of organized Catholicism, it is well known that *Il Quotidiano* speaks for Catholic Action. Even an important, ostensibly independent daily such as Milan's *Il Giorno* is widely understood to be financed by the public corporation—*Ente Nazionale Idrocarburi* (E.N.I.) and to operate as E.N.I.'s mouthpiece. When we turn to organized business, we find major newspapers like *La Stampa* (Turin) identified with Fiat, *Corriere della Sera* (Milan) reflecting the cotton and other interests of the Crespi family, *Resto del carlino* (Bologna) and *La Nazione* (Florence) to some extent expressions of the powerful sugar interests. Beyond the favorable reception that industrial interest groups are likely to get in such places, it is estimated that there are over twenty newspapers in Italy that are semi-official outlets for the viewpoint of Confindustria. These are smaller papers to which a press agency (A.G.A.) controlled by Confindustria provides boilerplate and other press materials free of charge.[6] Needless to say, groups that maintain such a close relationship with one or more newspapers outside their own organizations have a considerable advantage on other groups not so well endowed.

INTELLECTUAL GROUPS

A third observation concerning newspapers is that in some instances they constitute the major instrument whereby an interest group will seek to mold public opinion and influence public policy. A prime example of this kind of publication is the prestigious *Il Mondo* published at Rome. The *Mondo* group was born in 1949 shortly after the 1948 elections, in which the Christian Democratic Party received an absolute majority in the legislature. One of the group's major spokesmen says that the principal architects of the *Mondo* group were the same persons who during the Resistance reorganized the Liberal Party but who subsequently bolted the Party because it retained "too conservative a position regarding both political and economic issues." The group, under the urging of Bruno Villabruna, returned to the Liberals for a brief period but left it again when, according to my respondent, "Malagodi and Confindustria gained control of the Party." Because of this, the *Mondo* leader stresses that their influence in Italian society is more the influence

---

6 See Ignazio Weiss, "Proprietà e finanziamento della stampa quotidiana italiana," *Tempi Moderni*, 3 (July, 1960), pp. 8–9. This article is worth consulting for more detail on the general point I am making here.

of the newspaper itself than of any kind of organized pressure or association with a political party.[7]

The intellectual leaders of the *Mondo* group are convinced that, despite their small size, they pack a fairly potent punch in Italy in terms of influencing a very important segment of public opinion. The newspaper is certainly not intended for mass consumption and is geared instead to tastes of the intellectual elite. Its content is generally of very high quality, and articles that examine political, social, and economic problems are written in depth—almost never superficially. Even when the paper enters openly into polemical debates with other groups or segments of government, its authors seek to bring to bear on the argument the full force of logical and intellectual persuasion.

It is difficult to know exactly how much influence is exerted by *Il Mondo* as such. The group admittedly includes some formidable intellectuals. One of them, Professor Ernesto Rossi, has written voluminously on the alleged corruption, inefficiencies, and political particularism of the Italian bureaucracy. Others of equal or greater intellectual merit have carefully examined and attacked the most nagging problems confronting the Italian political system. There is little question that, for those in Italy who consider themselves members of the group, the distinguished newspaper is an important, perhaps vital, means of group integration. Whether its influence extends much beyond the group itself is problematical. It is true, as its leaders claim, that Thursdays find all sorts of reasonably well educated Italians, in all sectors, reading the newspaper. I was able to see this at first hand in the offices of Catholic Action, Confindustria, and the public bureaucracy. There does seem to be some compulsion on the part of even *Il Mondo's* greatest detractors to find out what the newspaper is saying and what battles

7 *Interview*, Number 27 (Rome, February 21, 1958), pp. 1–2. It should be noted that, following the elections of 1953, the *Mondo* group was strongly involved in the creation of the Radical Party.

it is fighting from week to week. The *Mondo* leaders point to this avid readership as an index of its importance in Italian society. This may be so, but if electoral results constitute one crude measure of an interest-group's impact, the 1958 election would suggest that the group has failed clamorously. The Radical Party, with which *Il Mondo* identified, suffered an extraordinary electoral disaster. Moreover, the intensive anticlerical campaign conducted by *Il Mondo,* as well-founded as it may have been given the facts of life in Italy, clearly failed to appeal to many Italians and, according to some observers, actually backfired.

My intention here, however, is not to provide a definitive analysis of the degree of *Il Mondo's* success or failure as an interest group. It is rather to underline the existence in Italy of several such groups that use the publication of a newspaper, magazine, or journal as their most important means of intervening in the political process. *Nord e sud,* published at Naples, and *Il Mulino,* produced at Bologna, are additional examples of the same phenomenon. One leader of the latter publication frankly admitted that those who identify with the journal and publish in it constitute an interest group in every sense of the word. He indicates that they consciously try to conduct studies and publish results on special problems with a view toward influencing governmental decisions. Unlike the activities engaged in by other interest groups such as the trade unions, the action of *Il Mulino,* in the words of the respondent, "is of an intellectual variety. *Il Mulino* does not have a mass membership, nor does it attempt to develop one. But it does have a significant impact on the formation of the views of that fairly important segment of the Italian public that regularly reads the review. . . . Our task is that of molding the views of certain elites in Italian society and not necessarily that of organizing mass demonstrations or engaging in other actions that are characteristic of trade unions, political parties, agricultural associations, and like organizations." [8]

Obviously groups organized around newspapers or magazines are not so aloof from the political process as to avoid intervening directly. Direct contacts with some members of the legislature are reported by all interviewed representatives of the groups mentioned above. In some instances, specific legislators are actually members of the groups, themselves, and quite assiduous in pushing the group view or demands in the legislative chambers. On one occasion, for example, the *Nord e sud* group was directly responsible for introducing an important amendment to a law governing the economic development of southern Italy. The *Nord e sud* representatives felt that state agencies should be compelled to spend a percentage of *all* (not merely *new*) investments in the South. In this effort, the *Nord e sud* leader claims that they were able to split the ranks of Confindustria, which opposed the amendment. The industrial associations of the South, particularly those of Sicily, were most interested in maximizing the amount of public money spent in the South for new plants and equipment as well as for repairs and modernization.[9] Before this campaign was successfully concluded,[10] the respondent and his associates were able to recruit the support of *Il Mulino* and other similar groups in the country.

[8] *Interview,* Number 19 (Bologna, March 8, 1958), pp. 1–2. Essentially the same rationale and description of his group was provided by a leader of *Nord e Sud. Interview,* Number 69 (Rome, June 1, 1958), pp. 1–2.

[9] *Interview,* Number 69, *op. cit.,* pp. 2–3. This respondent adds that at the beginning of this campaign, *Il Mondo* and its allied newspaper *Espresso* were opposed to the amendment. This led to some polemical exchange among the journals which, according to the respondent, "eventually led to the education of our friends on these two news organs."

[10] The respondent wisely points out that the campaign did not end with the passage of the amendment in 1957. It would subsequently be necessary to assure that the law, as amended, would actually be implemented. This would require, among other things, pressure on E.N.I., which wants no interference from any quarter concerning its developmental activities. According to the respondents, the plan will also eventually call for the nationalization of electricity, the gigantic *Italcementi,* and the equally large Montecatini Chemical Company.

Thus the activities of these publication-centered groups often lead to some form of direct intervention. A *Mondo* leader stresses that his group almost never seeks to intervene in the bureaucratic sphere because of the negative reception that will be accorded it by public administrators. Because of many written attacks on the bureaucracy, "it is fairly obvious that a well-known member of the Radical Party (*Mondo* group) is not likely to receive a very welcome hearing in the public administration. Many of the top-level administrators of Italy are of the view that the Radicals have been much too unkind in the public comments they have made about the patterns of administration that prevail in Italian society."[11]

This last comment signals an attitude toward government widely manifest by those associated with the publications we have mentioned. *Mondo* leaders are disdainful and suspicious of public administration and openly view it as shot through with corruption and particularism; *Nord e sud* supporters, with some justification, see government in general as still essentially in the hands of northern industrial interests and southern notables who manage public affairs to the decided disadvantage of the South; a chief leader of *Il Mulino* frankly describes the typical legislator as an ignorant oaf, incapable of behaving rationally, tied too closely to his political party and generally representing, in the words of this respondent, "only highly limited interests in the society rather than the general interest."[12] This man added: "Because of these deficiencies, they [the lawmakers] either speak ridiculous banalities or become the captives or mouthpieces of those particular interests that seek selfishly to favor their own narrow goals rather than to encourage in Italian society the kind of legislation that would be generally helpful of the nation as a whole."[13]

We have here typical expressions of the serious conflict

---

11 *Interview,* Number 27, *op. cit.,* p. 3.
12 *Interview,* Number 19, *op. cit.,* p. 2.
13 *Ibid.,* pp. 2–3.

in Italy between the intellectuals and the politicians. To some extent, this is a conflict between secular, laical forces, on the one hand, and organized Catholicism, on the other. But this does not account sufficiently for the phenomenon, particularly when one notes that there are active Catholics identified with all of these publications and that the *Il Mulino* group, once much more independent, is now generally considered to have some ties with Christian Democracy.[14] For a great many of the postwar years, the intellectuals viewed themselves as essentially alienated from the Italian political system. Those on the extreme Left have been outside the decision-making system since 1947; those representing the "liberal Left" or center have had to endure all sorts of temporizing with basic problems in the interest of having some sort of coalition government maintained; those within Christian Democracy have been essentially ineffective, because of the conservative nature of the Party's center of gravity until very recently.

It may be that a shift to the Left politically may give these groups greater voice in the evolution of public policy. To some extent this would serve to reduce the sense of alienation which can be corrosive in a democratic system. However, in the best of circumstances, the groups are likely to experience continued frustration as their well-made formulas and prescriptions meet the fate of political compromise. For this reason, it would be healthier if those who identify with *Il Mondo, Nord e sud, Il Mulino,* and similar newspaper and magazine groups recognized that they, too, represent particular interests in Italian society. Interview responses suggest that this sort

[14] I do not wish here to take sides in the polemic regarding whether *Il Mulino* is or is not an instrument of the sugar interests or an organization abjectly dependent on Christian Democracy. I personally feel that, over the years, the orientation of the group has changed, but this may possibly be ascribed to the fact that its members have become older and less uncompromising in their views. The point here is that, regardless of its particular ideological coloration, *Il Mulino* partakes of the antagonism between intellectual and politician.

of cold-blooded self-appraisal has not been achieved. Like most interest-group leaders in the society, they see Italy organized into the "good" and the "evil" groups, the "selfish" and the "altruistic." From the responses of one of *Il Mondo's* major exponents, one can detect a self-righteous and zealous missionary spirit that identifies the welfare of the whole with the views expressed in the newspaper. There is both paternalism and disdain expressed toward the public—toward Italians who "really haven't learned to think for themselves yet and who are therefore still susceptible to the inducements of a dictatorial regime." [15] Another leader—of the *Mulino* group this time—denies that he and his associates have a particularistic interest and says that, in this sense, it must be distinguished from Confindustria. To hammer home this point, he says: "We look objectively at certain major problems of Italian society, such as, for example, the school-reform issue. We have nothing to gain by our studies or by the recommendation made to the legislature and to members of the administration. We believe in a free democratic society and are opposed to totalitarian tendencies in any form. We are in favor of a liberal approach to social reform." [16]

It is this inability to see oneself as only one among many competing groups, and to recognize that one's own formulas do not possess a special status, that aids and abets the sense of alienation and frustration that intellectual interest groups manifest.[17] It is no doubt true that a group organized around a central publication and seeking to exert its impact primarily through the instrumentality

[15] *Interview*, Number 27, *op. cit.*, p. 4.

[16] *Interview*, Number 19, *op. cit.*, p. 3.

[17] On the other hand, it must be admitted that the intellectual is paid scant attention by the typical Italian politician. Our Christian Democratic Party leader frankly said that the intellectual generalist, the person who is not an expert in any particular aspect of the socio-economic system, is simply not listened to by the ruling (Christian Democratic) political group in Italian society. *Interview*, Number 40, Rome (February 6, 1958), p. 6.

of the written word has reason to differentiate itself from other interest aggregates that have mass memberships or that, in any case, regularly intervene in every conceivable aspect and sector of the political process. Nevertheless, it is curious that the very groups that now purport to study (and to expose) the machinations of organized interest in Italy fail to place themselves meaningfully into the total context.

OTHER MEANS OF INTERACTION

As our tables suggest, newspapers and other such publications are not the only way in which the groups communicate either externally or internally. Each of the organizational divisions depicted in Table 8 is a continuous source of communication, although many of them are primarily involved in the internal process. Moreover, there is a great need in many organizations to keep the membership and field leaders informed of technical information that concerns them. Offices of international affairs, ubiquitous in industrial associations and trade-union confederations, keep up with what transpires technologically or in collective bargaining in other countries; trade-union divisions deal with the complicated minutiae of labor contracts and social welfare regulations; legislative divisions keep track of what is transpiring in the Legislature as well as of administrative regulations affecting the group.

The pressure to circulate messages is also evidenced in the frequent use of conferences depicted in Table 9. These affairs are often held at a very high intellectual level; they are designed not only to educate the leaders and members of groups but also as a means of lending greater authority and respectability to the demands of the groups as they are transmitted to government. Conferences sponsored by such intellectual groups as *Il Mondo*, *Il Mulino*, and *Nord e sud* frequently eventuate in solid books; other major affairs sponsored by the trade unions almost always are followed by formal publications and suggested legislation. The conference is seen as an additional important means of crystallizing public opinion and of transmitting demands to various branches of government.

The relatively less frequent use of radio and television as means of communication and propaganda may be ascribed in part to the retarded evolution of Italian interest groups. It may also be attributed in some measure to the fact that both radio and television are controlled by the government and are not freely available to all groups that might have the financial means of handling such activity. It is significant, I think, that among those groups that did indicate a use of either of these media, the industrial associations were most prominent. In no instance was there included an association identified with the extreme political Left or Right. In six of the seven instances where television was mentioned, the groups involved also use radio.

In order to obtain something of an over-all view of the degree of group communication and interaction with the outside world and with government, our questionnaire included an item asking respondents to specify with what frequency a variety of activities are carried on. The responses to the question, depicted in Table 10, give a very interesting composite picture.

Table 10 clearly depicts the relative importance placed on various kinds of interaction. What we have noted about the use of conferences is amply confirmed by the data. All of the groups responding utilize national meetings at some time or other, and almost 85 percent of them bring together their members and others in local gatherings as well. Industrial associations in no case say that they hold national conferences often. On the other hand, trade unions, women's groups, Catholic and Communist organizations, and professional groups claim in general to hold both national and local conferences a great deal. Although it is not possible to be precise about this phenomenon, it is apparent that leaders of industrial

TABLE 10: Frequency of Group Interaction, by Type of Contact (N = 58)

Frequency

Type of Contact	Often		Once in a While		Rarely		Never		NR	
	No.	Per-cent	No.	Per-cent	No.	Per-cent	No.	Per-cent	No.	Per-cent
Other organizations	36	62	16	28	4	7	—		2	3
Political parties	11	19	7	12	4	7	19	33	7	29
National conferences	20	35	36	62	2	4	—		—	—
Local conferences	23	40	20	35	2	4	—		13	21
Organs of public opinion	28	48	14	24	9	16	—		7	12
Parliamentary	29	50	6	11	9	15	5	8	9	16
Propaganda and pub-licity action	35	61	6	11	4	7	3	5	10	16
Public administration	39	67	11	19	5	9	1	1	2	4
Local public bodies	32	54	11	19	6	11	—		9	16

associations see their organizations as bringing leaders, members, and others together only once in a while. Leaders of remaining groups, on the other hand, tend to emphasize more frequent encounters and, therefore, a greater intensity of organizational activity in this area.

Regarding contacts with other organizations, the questionnaire contained a subsequent item designed to probe the nature and scope of intergroup relations. The 52 groups responding to this item indicated that contacts are (1) maintained primarily through the exchange of letters and memoranda, and (2) concentrated with groups that are similar professionally or ideologically. Forty-six of the groups say that they correspond with other groups, twenty-three of them designate direct meetings as a means of interaction, and twenty-one point to conferences and work sessions as a means of dealing with other organizations. As one would expect, there are some groups that engage in all three of these activities. However, it is noteworthy that fifteen groups specify only correspondence as the means used to maintain contact with other organizations.

It is also significant that only rarely did groups identify hostile or competing groups as units with which relations are maintained. Of all of the groups responding, only Confagricoltura and the General Italian Confederation of Artisans specified that they maintained contacts with the trade unions. As a rule, industrial associations see themselves as interacting primarily with other national and international organizations, hospital doctors and surgeons say they maintain relations with other medical associations, unions remark that they relate to other unions, professionals and artists to other cultural groups, left-wing veterans and partisan associations to similar organized aggregates, the Lions Club to the Rotary and other service clubs, Italian communes to groups organizing the mountain or coastal communes, and so on. In the case of the Catholic Female Center, over twenty groups with which C.I.F. maintains contacts were specified—all of them Catholic.[18] Now it is perfectly apparent that many of the groups included in the survey could not function very well unless they did come into relatively frequent contact with other interest groups. The important phenomenon to note is that when the groups were asked, "Does the organization normally maintain relations with other *similar* or *diverse* organizations?" almost all of them were moved to ignore the "diverse" groups. This manner of responding may well be an indication of the sense of differentiation and isolation from other aggregates that the Italian groups feel. At least as far as re-

[18] Some of the groups with which C.I.F. maintains frequent contact are: the Feminine Movement of the A.C.L.I., the Italian Catholic Union of Obstetrics, the Association of Italian Catholic Doctors, the Union of Italian Catholic Jurists, the Feminine Youth of Catholic Action, the Italian Association of Catholic Teachers, the National Feminine Movement of Artisans, the Teachers Movement of Catholic Action, the Union of Italian Catholic Pharmacists, the College Graduates of Catholic Action, and the Union of Italian Catholic Artists. A similar ideological concentration is noted for the groups with which the Communist-dominated U.D.I. maintains relations.

sponses to the questionnaire item are concerned, there is little evidence that the broad kind of intergroup relationship is viewed as important or very meaningful. The group clusters that can be perceived are those involving allies—other groups that share one's interests and from which one may expect to obtain support and cooperation regarding demands.

Of particular interest to us here are the patterns of response involving interest-group contacts with the obviously political sectors of Italian society. It is noteworthy that at the head of this list we find public administration, with which over two-thirds of the groups report the most frequent contact. This is followed by contacts with local public bodies, the Parliament, and the political parties. Fully one-third of the responding groups claim never to have any contacts at all with the latter, and in this we have a good indication of the narrow meaning that must be ascribed to the term "apolitical" when it is used, by group leaders or others, to describe the nature of Italian interest groups. It seems reasonably apparent from Table 10 that when the political process is broadly conceived, from three-fifths to over four-fifths of the groups are politically active at least once in a while and from one-half to two-thirds of them often.

That as many as one-third of the groups were led to disclaim any interaction at all with political parties and that almost as many simply refused to respond to this item are matters of considerable interest. For example, an examination of the questionnaires fails to identify any group category as more prone than others to assume such a posture. Among those claiming no contacts at all, there occur four industrial associations, one women's organization, two trade unions, two service clubs, four professional associations, and one veterans association. Those that did not answer the item involve six industrial associations, two medical associations, one veterans association, and two professional associations. One fragmentary inference that may be drawn is that Catholic and Communist associations do not attempt to mask their party contacts, although this is contradicted by the claim of both C.I.F. and A.N.P.I. that they have no party contacts. In each of these instances, one can be certain that the response is misleading. Whether the same judgment can be made of all other groups is problematical, however. Perhaps the most candid comment concerning the industrial group category was offered by the Association of Industrialists of the Province of Bologna, which typed "not officially" next to the item concerning interaction with political parties. In any event, it is unclear why, say, the Italian Association of Rice Industrialists should be involved with the political parties often and the other associations not at all, or why Confagricoltura should maintain frequent contact and the confederation representing the artisans meet with party officials only rarely.

The temptation is strong, therefore, to view responses to the political party item as not accurately reflecting the real situation. It may well be—indeed I assume—that group contacts with the bureaucracy and the legislature far exceed those that occur with the parties. Nevertheless, it is doubtful that only 30 percent of the groups ever interact with the latter; the divergence between this and other kinds of political intervention highlighted by Table 10 seems too great.

No attempt was made in our general survey of groups to gather data in depth regarding the interaction between interest groups and political parties. That for some groups, such as the trade unions, such relationships are intensive and intimate, I have demonstrated elsewhere,[19] and there is no reason for supposing that the pattern has changed in recent years. That major groups like Catholic Action and Confindustria are also intimately associated with the parties will be shown in detail later in this volume. It is my primary intention to spell out the type of interaction that occurs between interest groups and the

[19] Joseph LaPalombara, "The Political Role of Organized Labor in Western Europe," *Journal of Politics*, 17 (February, 1955), pp. 59–81.

Italian bureaucracy. Before doing so, however, it will be useful to note some of the general patterns of intervention that characterize the groups as they seek to intervene in the legislative process on which the bureaucracy is very much dependent and concerning which the bureaucrats play quite important roles.

CHAPTER VII · LEGISLATIVE
INTERACTION

THE USE OF CONFERENCES

INTEREST groups may relate to the legislative process
in a number of ways that vary in nature and intensity.
As we noted earlier, intervention may take place at
some distance from the legislature itself; groups may
simply articulate their desires in print and hope that their
views will come to the attention of lawmakers. When the
published desires are supposed to convey the weight of
rational and objective consideration, or of technical authority, they may emanate from special congresses or conventions called to consider a particular problem. If the
groups sponsoring such meetings wish to assure that the
demands reach the proper persons, ministers, members of
Parliament, or other public officials may be invited to
participate. Thus, when the Unione Goliardica Italiana
once sought to emphasize the inter-ideological character
of one of its important political proposals, the Christian
Democratic mayor of Florence, Giorgio La Pira, was invited as a main speaker. This event was subsequently
played up by newspapers favorable to the U.G.I. initiative.[1] Or, when Dirstat, an interest group representing
Italy's top-level bureaucrats, felt the need of adding the
weight of numbers and of objective considerations to its
views concerning the reform of the bureaucracy, a special
congress was called for this purpose. Out of this meeting
came a list of proposals and the specification of the sort
of legislative action which Dirstat supported or opposed.[2]
Or, when the Italian Union of Labor sought to gain support for its views concerning the role of the trade union

[1] See Paolo Pavolini, "Gioventù senza uniforme," *Il Mondo*, 4 (October
11, 1952), p. 1.
[2] The meeting and its outcome is carefully reported by Paolo G.
Glorioso, "Il Burocrate aggiornato," *Il Mondo*, 5 (April 4, 1953), p. 3.

in the economic and social development of southern Italy, a special convention was called for this purpose, and it was favorably reviewed by one of Italy's major spokesmen for sound public policy toward *Il Mezzogiorno*.[3]

Perhaps the most systematic use of the congress as a means of interest articulation was developed by the Italian branch of the European Federalist Movement. An official of that group remarks that, for several years, the Movement concentrated its attention on Alcide De Gasperi and Count Carlo Sforza, both of whom were viewed as favorable to European federalism. Given the positions which de Gasperi held in the country (i.e. simultaneously Secretary of the Christian Democratic Party, President of the Council of Ministers, and Minister of Foreign Affairs), it was felt that reaching him was the most effective way of trying to implement the single-purpose goal of the organization. The respondent indicates that de Gasperi was generally very responsive to their suggestions and demands and that he did much to further their cause.

When de Gasperi died and the European Defense community failed, the Federalist Movement in Italy, as in all of Europe, entered a serious crisis. It was then felt that it would be necessary in Italy to broaden the approach to government if the group was to survive. Some in the Movement would have turned it into a political party; others, who prevailed, were strongly opposed to this step, holding that the group's effectiveness was largely tied to its ability to avoid identification with any of the contending sectarian ideologies in the country. The solution to the need for a broader approach at interest articulation was found in the holding of private primary elections in Italy's major cities. In these elections, delegates would be chosen to attend a national congress. The congress, in turn, would pass major resolutions in favor of federalism, which would then theoretically be the expression of the

---

[3] Francesco Compagna, "Una 'terza sigla' sindacale nel sud," *Mondo Economico*, 13 (June 22, 1957), pp. 12–13.

desires of a majority of people in the country's major population centers. The resolutions of the congress would be communicated to the press, produced in brochures and manifestoes to be distributed throughout the country, and communicated to members of the Italian legislature.[4]

Examples such as these could be repeated for most of the groups of any importance that exist in Italy. Where the groups are either very large or represent significant sectors of the economy, they can almost certainly count on obtaining the formal adherence of at least some lawmakers—and possibly Cabinet members—at their proceedings. This kind of interest articulation emphasizes a moderate and rational flow of demands from groups to government. On its face, it does not imply that the interest groups will do more than make their wishes known. Indeed, the central purpose of holding the meeting at all is to demonstrate that not a sectarian interest but the whole national interest would be furthered through the evolution of policies that conform to or reflect conference deliberations and recommendations.

PROVISION OF INFORMATION

Closely related to the practice of holding objective and scientific conferences is the providing of information on which the legislature will in part rely in reaching its decisions. As one member of the Chamber of Deputies points out, the study office or reference service available to the national legislature is primitive and therefore not of genuine utility in the gathering of necessary, detailed information concerning legislative problems. For this reason, individual deputies—and particularly the *relatore,* who is responsible for researching proposals referred to committees—tend to go outside the legislature for both research and secretarial assistance. They usually turn to the organized groups, and those latter so privileged as to be frequently consulted are in a strategic position to

[4] *Interview,* Number 5 (Rome, December 11, 1957), pp. 1–2.

influence at least the frame of reference within which committee or parliamentary debate evolves.[5]

Both legislators and group leaders point out that this type of interaction occurs with considerable frequency and is of great importance in understanding the extent to which some of the associations are intimately tied into the legislative process. A Communist senator, for example, emphasizes that, on many occasions, he and his colleagues turn to the research office of the Italian General Confederation of Labor (C.G.I.L.) for vital technical information and studies concerning proposed legislation. Socialist Party deputies are free to utilize the same services, and do so regularly. The key justification for this is that the legislative minority must seek to overcome its disadvantage of lacking opportunity for recourse to the technical facilities of outside groups—an opportunity which the government parties have.[6]

A representative of the Italian Association of Automotive Industries (A.N.F.I.I.A.), in describing the organizational structure of his group, underlined the importance of its research or study office. This unit gathers data and prepares technical releases not merely for the consumption of the Italian press but also for use by members of the Association who maintain contacts with legislators. However, the respondent also points out that members of the legislature often approach his association on their own initiative, asking it to take a position regarding a proposed law or administrative regulation. At this point, A.N.F.I.I.A. proceeds to conduct its own research for purposes of presenting the lawmakers involved with a "highly technical and very competent point of view." Reflecting on the Association's capability in this general area, the respondent remarks that "it does not often happen that the association is unable to provide legislators or administrators with a great deal of technical information

5 *Interview*, Number 36 (Rome, January 31, 1958), p. 2.
6 *Interview*, Number 31 (Rome, February 1, 1958), p. 3.

which can ease their task and without which their activities would be somewhat less than acceptable, at least as far as this association and the industries we represent are concerned." [7]

A.N.F.I.I.A.'s leader, like many other group representatives in Italy, holds the average lawmaker in low esteem. The deputy is viewed as a sectarian politician who tends to be completely uninformed regarding the very matters with which he purports to deal intelligently. With this as the basic group assumption, it is easy to reach the conclusion that the assistance provided by the groups is a noteworthy public service. Thus a leading official of the Italian Banking Association prides himself with the knowledge that his group is frequently consulted regarding legislative matters. He asserts that, notwithstanding its involvement, the association avoids political entanglements and cannot permit itself the luxury of sabotaging a particular piece of legislation. It is presumably this very posture of removed objectivity that permits the Association to be regularly consulted by both the legislative and administrative branches of government.[8] However, the respondent also indicates that the services of his association are not available to deputies across the ideological spectrum but are provided almost exclusively to representatives of the Center and Right. Furthermore, something more than altruistic public service is suggested by the comment of another official of the Banking Association, who remarks that the group is able to increase its impact on the legislature precisely because a certain number of deputies regularly come to it for assistance. "In return," he says, "the association can expect that these same individuals will turn a sympathetic ear toward proposals which the association may have to make from time to time." [9]

[7] *Interview*, Number 1 (Rome, November 28, 1957), pp. 1–3.
[8] *Interview*, Number 63 (Rome, January 16, 1958), pp. 1–2.
[9] *Interview*, Number 48 (Rome, December 18, 1957), p. 8.

One of the most respected technical groups, to which other interest groups as well as legislators and ministers go for assistance, is the Association of Italian Joint Stock Companies. The group, which has very close ties with Confindustria, dates from 1910. It was created by a few industrialists and bankers, and, according to one of its present leaders, it was endowed with a vast scope of activities. One of its earliest endeavors was a special study of the Italian tariff structure, a task subsequently taken over by a Royal Commission composed almost wholly of members of the association. From the very beginning, then, and throughout its history, the association has maintained strong ties with government. Today, its expertise in the economic field and particularly in the area of fiscal problems is widely recognized. The leader interviewed stresses that the Italian government *always* gives particular attention to the positions assumed by the association regarding certain problems because the latter "is widely recognized for its special competence and its unquestioned objectivity." [10]

One would certainly have little reason to doubt the technical competence of the Association of Italian Joint Stock Companies. Among its seventy employees are found a score of professional experts in such fields as local taxation and finance, indirect and direct taxation, and general economic analysis. Most of these individuals are continuously involved in research activities. Reflecting this, the association produces the respected bimonthly journal *Rassegna economica,* widely circulated in Italy. An English-language summary version of the journal, *Italian Economic Survey,* is distributed in the United States and England. Other important publications include *Note di economia aziendale,* a monthly that analyzes foreign and economic and fiscal situations; *Rassegna della stampa,* another monthly that reviews books and articles on fiscal subjects published throughout the world; and *Giurispru-*

10 *Interview,* Number 95 (Rome, June 24, 1958), pp. 1, 5.

denza delle imposte, an important review that appears twice each year. Thus the surface image of the association is definitely one to suggest that a data-starved legislature is completely justified in relying on this voluntary association for information.

However, it is necessary for the legislature to understand that even a prestigious, seemingly unbiased group such as this will take a number of preconceptions to the problems it analyzes. The identification of the association with the industrial class and its close historical and present ties with Confindustria cannot be doubted. Thus, when an Association leader was asked whether it had taken a stand on a controversial law to compel the public listing of all stock exchange transactions (known in Italy as the Article 17 issue), the leader first replied that Article 17 was obviously somewhat beyond the competence of the Association. However, on probing, it became apparent that the Association did take a position that reflected essentially the views of Confindustria and the industrialists. The respondent then went on to say that the parties supporting the legislation did so for purely demagogic reasons, that the law would be a failure, that it had reduced stock transactions perilously, and that, therefore, the association had made its negative opinion regarding the law known to various members of the government and the legislature.[11]

Article 17 was immensely controversial; it involved strong ideological conflict among political parties, legislators and major interest groups. The fact that the Association of Italian Joint Stock Companies did enter the fray, even if discreetly, establishes that, for all of its unquestioned competence, its approach to research problems is less objective than would be that of a research service of equally high quality maintained directly by the legislature. In theory at least, the latter kind of agency would be politically neutral and its services would be equally

[11] *Ibid.,* pp. 6–7.

available to all rather than just to a particuar segment of the rule-making body.

If we are to lend credence to the interview responses of several legislators, it would appear that the aid provided lawmakers by groups sometimes extends beyond simply research assistance. One Socialist deputy, for example, flatly asserts that Confindustria provides free secretarial services for selected legislators as well as the cost of transportation between Rome and their constituencies.[12] Another party official, a Social Democrat in this case, claims that the *Federconsorzi,* a private association with many quasi-public functions in the field of agriculture, regularly sends gift boxes valued at over $300 to selected deputies at Christmas and Easter. This man adds that he himself regularly received such favors as long as he held office in his party or committee assignments in the Chamber of Deputies.[13] An outside observer and careful student of the Italian political process asserts that a fair number of legislators, particularly among the lawyers, are in the employ of interest groups. Reflecting that such relationships do not necessarily imply corruption, he says: "They are paid a certain sum each year for acting as discreet consultants to the groups. In some cases, the lawmakers may actually perform a substantial service. In others the arrangement may be essentially phony and simply a means, therefore, of providing for an exchange of funds between the group and the legislator who supports the group position in Parliament." [14]

Needless to say, it is extremely difficult to provide acceptable documentation for allegations such as those few cited above. One can speculate about legislators the world over and conjecture that some instances of covert relations between lawmakers and groups would be true of any society. One might also reflect on the relatively low salary paid the Italian legislator and on the striking paucity of

---

12 *Interview,* Number 13 (Rome, December 19, 1957), p. 2.
13 *Interview,* Number 62 (Rome, January 16, 1958), p. 3.
14 *Interview,* Number 17 (Rome, February 19, 1958), p. 5.

secretarial and other services available to him—and suggest that conditions such as these might well cause some to find added goods and services elsewhere. But our data simply do not permit us to say anything persuasive about the incidence of cases in which Italian legislators are financially obligated to interest groups.

The data do suggest, however, that there is in Italy more than what one might call a reasonable amount of reliance of the legislature on the technical information services of certain voluntary associations. To the extent that this is true, the rule-making structures of government are less free to be removed and objective than a model of the democratic system would imply. Furthermore, it appears fairly obvious that the ability to provide information is, other factors being equal, a significant variable affecting the degree of influence that competing groups can hope to exert. Therefore, those 50 percent of the organized groups that do not maintain research units are at something of a disadvantage vis-à-vis competitors. So much is this the perceived situation that even where formal research units do not exist, the groups will go to some pains to provide lawmakers with draft bills and "studies" in the areas of legislation in which they are presumed to possess particular interest and competence.

CAMPAIGN ASSISTANCE

A particular kind of assistance that may establish a strong obligation on the part of the legislator toward an interest group is financial or other kinds of help offered during an electoral campaign. By and large, as one would anticipate, group leaders who speak quite openly about research aid are less candid when this particular type of group-legislator nexus is broached. Yet we do have some information which suggests that, at least as far as the major groups are concerned, this type of support is fairly common—and generally accepted as a legitimate aspect of the political process. Once more it may be noted that, other variables being equal, a group is likely to be given an advantage if it can provide campaign money, campaign workers, or masses of electors who will cast appropriate ballots and, better still, selected preferential votes on election day. One member of Parliament, in speaking about this matter, reflects that one of the critical ways of affecting legislative decisions "is that of providing a certain amount of financing for political parties and political candidates. The groups expect that, in return for the outlay, those elected will not then proceed in the legislature to favor legislation not wanted by the group. This is not always the way things work out in reality, but it happens often enough to warrant the continuation of this kind of financial support." [15]

It is widely understood among group leaders, members of the legislature, political observers—almost anyone with a sharp political nose—that single industries and industrial associations make financial contributions to the electoral campaigns of candidates they favor. One man who was for years deeply involved with the affairs of the Liberal Party puts it this way: "The industrialist who says he is uninterested in politics will very often be the same one who contributes a considerable sum of money to guarantee that there will be in the legislature a minimum number of representatives who will support the business of the industrialist groups of the country." [16]

Some aspects of this type of financing are completely above board and create no analytical difficulties. Thus, when under the leadership and impetus of de Micheli, Confindustria decided in 1956 to organize the *Confintesa* for the express purpose of electing deputies favorable to the interests of the owning classes, there could be no doubt that tens of millions of lire, emanating from industrial sources, were being spent in the electoral campaigns of that and subsequent years. However, *Confintesa*, as we shall later note in detail, represented a radical departure from the postwar posture of Confindustria. Much more

---

[15] *Interview*, Number 62, p. 3.
[16] *Interview*, Number 109 (Rome, July, 1958), p. 2.

difficult to document is the widely held view that the typical mode of industrial intervention is to provide funds for the campaigns of Christian Democratic, Liberal, Monarchist, and Neo-Fascist candidates.

A much-repeated version of Confindustria's electoral posture is that, under De Gasperi as Prime Minister of Italy and Angelo Costa as President of Confindustria, the latter preferred to avoid open intervention in politics, exchanging campaign funds for a basically reasonable, nonthreatening legislative attitude toward industrial interests. A radical change is supposed to have begun in 1953 when Confindustria is alleged to have withheld campaign funds promised the D.C. because of the party's failure to elect Confindustria-supported candidates. The upshot of this allegedly involved a shift to the left in Christian Democratic party power (represented by the advent of Amintore Fanfani), a campaign of harassment against industrial and land-owning interests (e.g., Article 17, Sganciamento, Patti Agrari),[17] and a reaction to this threat in the form of *Confintesa*.

That Confindustria does finance candidates of the political parties singled out above is claimed by a leader of the confederation itself, an official of Christian Democracy, a leader of the Liberal party, and many interest group leaders and lawmakers who presumably are not the beneficiaries of such largess.[18] On occasion, Confindustria's intervention in the legislative electoral struggle has been the subject of public criticism. Responding to this—and giving us some insight into the validity of the allegations discussed above—is the following comment by the confederation's official organ, *L'organizzazione industriale:*

---

[17] Article 17 is mentioned above, pp. 205–206; *sganciamento* and *patti agrari* are discussed below, pp. 233, 324, 401.

[18] *Interviews,* Number 27, *op. cit.,* p. 5; Number 40, *op. cit.,* p. 5; Number 62, *op. cit.,* p. 4; Number 109, *loc. cit.;* Number 95, *op. cit.,* p. 8. See also Anonymous, "I conti della Confindustria," *Dibattito Politico,* 2 (July 9, 1956), p. 14, which reports on the electoral action of Confindustria during the Confintesa phase.

"Some perhaps tend to forget that the employers category consists of citizens who have full political rights and
that they intend to exercise those rights just as does any
citizen in the realm of the State. To create an artificial
division between employers and citizens, or to consider
that employers . . . must remain outside political life,
or that in political life they must be only objects toward
which there should be created a ring of diffidence is ab-
surd. . . . Employers . . . have and intend to have, fully
and entirely, all of the rights of citizens, and they will not
permit particular limitations to be imposed on or suggested or counseled them." [19]

The article goes on to say that, for many reasons, the
employers must be involved in influencing the votes that
would be cast in the forthcoming national elections—they
must confront the necessity of having the nation feel the
weight of their experience and their attitudes toward political policies. The intervention of employers is said to
be completely purposeful, an expression of the will never
to be excluded from the political life of the country, or
maintained in a position of inferiority regarding it.[20]

If one is to judge by the legislative events of the years
since 1953, it is apparent that Italy's industrialists have
fallen considerably short of their goal. The industrial and
land-owning groups have been on the defensive; they have
experienced limited attacks and serious onslaughts not
merely from the extreme Left but from the Center-Left
as well. The "Opening to the Left" which brings the
Socialist Party closer to the reform-minded leaders of
Christian Democracy is viewed by Confindustria as impending disaster. Those in Italy who blandly speak or
write about the overbearing political power of the industrial confederation are well advised to examine in detail
the outcome of elections as well as of the major pieces
of legislation on which Confindustria assumed a strong
position.

[19] *L'Organizzazione industriale*, 8 (June 4, 1953), p. 1.
[20] *Ibid.*

I do not mean to depict Confindustria as a helpless infant in a carnivorous jungle. I do mean to emphasize, however, that when one is attempting to assess the relative *legislative* power of an interest group, it is vital to steer clear of the facile generalization that money equals power. For it is resoundingly apparent that industrial money has been unable to stem the legislative shift to the Left that has been under way since 1953. In the determination of who does or does not sit in the Italian legislature, the groups with mass followings, which can deliver large numbers of votes, have been much more successful than the groups with merely money at their disposal. These groups include the trade unions, the Direct Cultivators, the Christian Association of Italian Workers (A.C.L.I.), the Italian Female Center, the Italian Union of Women, some of the veterans associations, and, above all, Italian Catholic Action.

This simple but painful fact is generally well perceived by Confindustria's leaders. Indeed, it is basic to the rationale that the Confederation should become much more massively and openly involved in electoral campaigns. Many of these same men, however, have little confidence in the ability of strategies such as the *Confintesa* to bring the industrialists dramatically favorable outcomes. As a leader of the Association of Italian Joint Stock Companies articulates the problem, the Italian masses have always been anti-industrialist, and the current mass mentality is violently so. He says: "Whoever in Italy represents himself as the spokesman for the industrial class earns at least the diffidence if not the open and organized hostility of the Italian masses. These latter refuse to accept the idea that the industrialist can possibly promote the general interest as well as the special interest in politics." [21]

These sentiments are echoed by an official of the Italian Banking Association who remarks that, even when there is a member of Parliament who identifies with the interests of the business community, he does not and cannot openly

[21] *Interview*, Number 95, *op. cit.*, pp. 7–8.

support it. Asked why this should be so, the respondent replies that it is strictly a question of varying numbers. Those deputies and senators who represent or identify with the masses feel less inhibition when they rise to speak in the legislative halls. On the other hand: "Those members of Parliament who do understand the needs of the business community and who are capable from time to time of advocating and supporting, to a degree, plans and proposals fostered by business groups must do so much more cautiously. This creates the impression that members of the legislature favorable to business are attempting to function in an underhanded way. On the other hand, were these individuals to stand up openly in the chambers to declare that they are attempting to present a point of view of the industrial class, a great furor would break out in the country, insisting that this is basically an undemocratic position to assume and that the deputies involved are without doubt attempting to do the nation damage." [22]

The banking association leader goes on to lament that the newspapers—even those owned by major industrial groups or families—give aid and comfort to those who trade on this negative image of the industrial class. The papers give space to demagogic and irresponsible attacks and maneuvers by mass groups because they consider such things newsworthy. The result of this is that the industrial class as a group intervenes in the legislative process under serious handicaps. For this reason, the respondent reflects with considerable nostalgia on the time in Italy when members of the Senate were appointed by the King, and the Senate became a chamber in which certain interests—not identified with or supported by mass groups—could find representation.[23]

LOBBYING

Despite handicaps such as these, nothing prevents business groups, or any other group, from engaging in lobby-

[22] *Interview*, Number 63, *op. cit.*, p. 4.
[23] *Ibid.*, pp. 3-4.

ing activities as another means of interaction with the legislative process. By lobbying is meant informal or formal contacts with members of the legislature designed to elicit their cooperation in support of or in opposition to a particular legislative proposal. The essence of lobbying as I am using the term is contact, direct or indirect, with a lawmaker in order to persuade him to act in a particular way in regard to a legislative issue. What the legislator is asked to do might include introducing a bill or offering amendments, talking to colleagues, making speeches in legislative committees or party or parliamentary group caucuses, presenting evidence for or against a proposal, engaging in dilatory or delaying tactics, making public pronouncements concerning an issue, coordinating support for or opposition to a bill, voting for or against a bill, or abstaining from voting. This listing does not exhaust what a lawmaker may be asked to do for a group, but it covers the major actions that might be taken. Representations of group leaders to the legislators may range all the way from abject pleas to threats of sanctions; inducements, explicit or implied, may vary between the expressed gratitude of the group to promises of economic and electoral support. It is important to understand that the act of lobbying involves a two-sided relationship between, on the one hand, an interest group that makes demands, and, on the other hand, a legislator who is formally in a position to satisfy the demands that are communicated.

A great many respondents comment on the pervasiveness of lobbying activity in Italy, and data from interviews suggest that this represents the most frequent type of interaction between groups and lawmakers. One member of Parliament comments that one should not be misled by the widespread belief that the United States experiences more lobbying than does Italy. He notes that the arm-chair scholars often assume that the combination of centralized legislative control under a parliamentary system and the existence of highly disciplined parties reduces the efficacy and attractiveness of legislative lobbying. This is largely myth, says the respondent. He adds that there are probably as many interest groups in Italy as in any country in the world and that many of them are continually in touch with the lawmakers. As far as trying to maximize the effectiveness one can have in the legislature is concerned, our respondent remarks: "Obviously, if the pressure group leaders can reach the party leadership, so much the better. But this does not mean that the groups ignore the individual deputy. In fact, pressure groups often send whole delegations to talk with various members of Parliament for purposes not necessarily of influencing a single vote but of encouraging the single deputy to represent the position of the pressure group in the meetings of the parliamentary group." [24]

Speaking to the same general point, a Communist lawmaker emphasizes that, notwithstanding the existence of some highly disciplined parties in the legislature, it behooves the interest group to devote its energies not only to legislative leaders but to single deputies as well. These individuals, even within the Communist party, may be persuaded to make the group's case before the party leadership. In his words:

"When you consider the political party as a whole (that is, not merely its deputies and senators), then for any political party the deputies and senators are the very vertex of leadership that we have in mind; they are the ones on whom the groups attempt to bring the most pressure. . . . Not even the Communist deputies and senators are excluded from the attention of many groups about which one might assume that they can expect to obtain very little from the left. . . . Furthermore, it is important to remember that the final votes on legislation in Italy, unlike the American situation, are by secret ballot. It would be extremely interesting to discover the way in which many deputies, including members of my own party, vote once they are protected by the secrecy of the ballot. An example of this difference between open and secret voting was seen

[24] *Interview*, Number 2 (Rome, November 28, 1957), p. 3.

in the final vote on the Merlin Law,[25] where a fairly large number of votes shifted to the opposition once the open teller vote gave way to the secret ballot used for the final disposition of the law." [26]

If, as certainly seems to be the case, Italian deputies can deviate from the party line in the legislature to some degree, and if they can represent the views of groups to their party leaders, it is obvious that interest-group approaches to them can pay some rewards. However, it is also necessary to understand that not all points of access in the legislature are of equal attraction to groups seeking to articulate interest. As we noted earlier, the European Federalist Movement found it convenient to concentrate its earlier activities on De Gasperi, who was at the apex both of his party and of the legislature. Representatives of *Il Mulino* and other such groups also indicate that they attempt where possible to gain the attention and support not of the average legislator but of someone—in the majority or minority—who is viewed as holding more than average power. Thus, for example, a leader of the *Il Mondo* group says that they rely heavily on Ugo La Malfa, long a prestigious, brilliant, and articulate Republican leader who entered the Fanfani government as Minister of the Budget in 1962.[27] Confindustria, Catholic Action, and other conservative groups tend to rely very heavily on someone like Giulio Andreotti, a Christian Democratic

[25] The Merlin Law, sponsored by a spinster Socialist senator, Angelina Merlin, was approved in 1958 after almost a decade of knocking about in Parliament. It brought an end to legalized prostitution in Italy. One would have assumed from the parliamentary debate that the law would pass overwhelmingly. However, the final vote was close, leading to widespread speculations concerning which deputies voted contrary to the stated positions of their parties. Also noteworthy is the fact that serious consideration of the Merlin Law brought into existence and very much into the open the Italian Association of Owners and Managers of Houses of Prostitution. This association lobbied avidly and carried on an intensive campaign in favor of preserving the legality in Italy of one of the world's oldest professions.

[26] *Interview*, Number 31, *op. cit.*, pp. 1–2, 4.

[27] *Interview*, Number 27, *op. cit.*, p. 2. La Malfa has also served in previous governments.

notable with an immense electoral following at Rome who has held ministerial positions in several governments. It is fairly obvious, to single out one example to which we have already alluded, that on the controversial issue of Article 17 (concerning making stock transactions a matter of public record), the Italian Stockbrokers Association managed to elicit his active support.[28]

Similarly, we are told by a leader of the Italian Banking Association that a complete hierarchy of relationships prevails between the group, on the one hand, and the legislature, on the other. At the top level, there are maintained contacts between the top leadership of the association and the top leaders of the government. When matters not of crucial import may be at issue, lesser association leaders will contact individual numbers of Parliament. In the words of the A.B.I. respondent: "A very important aspect of our work might be described as that of maintaining both formal and informal contacts with members of the government and other public entities. One of the obligations of the president and the director general of the association is that of establishing very close contacts with the Council of Ministers, single ministers and the President of the Council of Ministers. . . . Other members of the staff seek to establish contacts with single members of the legislature and within the agencies of public administration." [29]

Not all groups, however, are able so readily to choose the points at which legislative intervention will occur. For clearly depicted in our interviews is the existence of the fragmented and isolative nature of group-governmen-

---

[28] For a documentation of this, see *Giornale d'Italia* (December 12, 1957), p. 2; *Il Globo* (November 16, 1957), p. 1. More important than Andreotti's posture were the tactics employed on behalf of the association by the Christian Democratic senator and former banker, Teresio Guglielmone. According to a leader of the Stockbrokers' Association, this man succeeded single-handedly in having the issue of Article 17 referred back to committee twenty-nine times! *Interview*, Number 82 (Rome, May 29, 1958), p. 7. Cf. *Avanti!* (January 17, 1958), p. 1; *Il Globo* (January 16, 1958), p. 1.

[29] *Interview*, Number 28 (Rome, February 8, 1958), p. 7.

tal relationships that we noted in an earlier chapter. The Italian Association of Building Constructors (A.N.C.E.) tells us that it must rely primarily on Giovanni Malagodi (P.L.I.), Giovanni Spagnolli (D.C.), and Mario Dosi (D.C.), "who are good friends and very reliable." [30] The Italian Banking Association deliberately singles out the bankers in the legislature because "The association feels that it can approach these individuals and in most instances obtain a sympathetic hearing for a proposal that the association wishes to make." [31] The Italian Stockbrokers Association had a stalwart supporter in Senator Teresio Guglielmone (D.C.).[32] The Italian Union of Labor, largely because it is considerably handicapped in the public administrative arena, concentrates its efforts in the legislature and relies on the sympathetic attitudes of Ugo La Malfa (P.R.I.), Guido Ceccherini (P.S.D.I.), and Cino Macrelli (P.R.I. Mixed).[33] The Italian Confederation of Professionals and Artists, which strongly eschews political involvement, tends to restrict its legislative contacts to deputies and senators of the political right because of the particular ideological coloration of one of its top leaders.[34] As far as industrial groups in general go, one political party leader put it this way: "All major industries have their hand-picked deputies. These deputies are rewarded

[30] *Interview,* Number 9 (Rome, December 11, 1957), p. 9.

[31] *Interview,* Number 48, *op. cit.,* p. 8.

[32] See note 28, above.

[33] *Interview,* Number 80 (Rome, May 9, 1958), p. 4; *Interview,* Number 30 (Rome, May 10, 1958), p. 8. It should be noted that U.I.L. leaders unanimously speak of discrimination against the union in public administrative circles in favor of C.I.S.L. or other labor groups associated with Christian Democracy. It is this failure to find adequate access in the administrative sphere that disposes the group to concentrate its energies in the legislature.

[34] *Interview,* Number 93 (Rome, June 27, 1958), p. 9. This respondent insists that his group is the only syndical organization in Italy that is truly independent of all political parties, and notes that this is attested by the presence in the Confederation of Christian Democrats, Communists, Socialists, Monarchists, Republicans, and Fascists. The respondent identifies himself as a "nostalgic Fascist" who has many personal friends among lawmakers of the extreme right.

either by consultantships or by patronage in the sense that the deputy is given an opportunity to reward his electoral helpers by finding them jobs in the industries with which they are identified." [35]

Only two of the group leaders interviewed made a point of stressing that they attempt to lobby with lawmakers of decidedly different ideological leanings. One of these represents *Confapi* (National Confederation of Small Industries), which is in open competition with Confindustria for the membership allegiance of small and medium-size business firms. The organization, which claims to include 15,000 of such industries in its ranks, deals with their trade-union, economic, personnel, credit, fiscal, and other problems. In so doing, and notwithstanding its avowed apolitical nature, the *Confapi* often drafts legislative proposals and attempts to have them introduced in Parliament. A leader of the confederation stresses that it seeks the widest possible political support and, for this reason, attempts to maintain contacts with legislators representing widely different political parties.[36]

The other group that maintains a relatively broad approach to the legislature is the Italian General Association of Entertainment (A.G.I.S.), a federation encompassing a number of other associations organized at both the national and the local levels. The Association itself cuts across ideological lines, including in its midst the Catholic Association of Motion Picture Distributors. A central function of the group is that of safeguarding in every way possible the common interest of theater owners, motion picture distributors, comedians, circus owners, impresarios, and others who make up its membership. In so doing, this apolitical group nevertheless finds it necessary frequently to intervene in the legislature and, at the time of the interview, in the Undersecretariat for Entertainment, which was then located in the Office of

---

[35] *Interview*, Number 65 (Rome, January 23, 1958), p. 2.
[36] *Interview*, Number 104 (Rome, July 2, 1958), pp. 2, 5–6.

the Presidency of the Council of Ministers.[37] As far as the legislature itself is concerned, there has apparently existed for some years a parliamentary "center for entertainment," with which the association maintains close relations. Although the strongest support for A.G.I.S. is said to come primarily from Socialist and Neo-Fascist deputies, the "center" includes deputies from many parties. Among those specifically named by our respondent were Giulio Andreotti (D.C.), Iaures Busoni (P.S.I.), Giuseppe Clabrò (M.S.I.), Bruno Corbi (P.C.I.), Giuseppe Brusasca (D.C.), Guido Mazzoli (P.S.I.), and Luciana Viviani (P.C.I.).[38] Needless to say, basic legislative support for an interest group including such disparate ideological positions as these deputies represent is most unusual. It is largely a function of the mixed ideological character of A.G.I.S. and of the fact that the association is not likely to raise issues of major national import.

Where the area of interest of a group is closely linked to major social, political, and economic policies, and where interest groups themselves fall into different ideological categories, the groups tend to find in the legislature supporters who share their values and who can give aid that is consistent with their own ideologies. Although this pattern is probably true to some degree whenever there are groups and lawmakers interacting, it seems to be true on a much larger scale in an isolative culture such as Italy's. Where the rigid conflicts and antagonisms that characterize the groups are transferred in turn into the legislature, it makes much more difficult for that body the task of fulfilling its function as an interest-aggregating mechanism.

I am noting here exclusively a form of contact—lobbying—which may be viewed as *external* to the legislature. That is, this process involves the establishment of a particular kind of rapport between a group seeking access and one or more members of the legislature who have no open

---

[37] In 1962 the Undersecretariat for Entertainment was upgraded and reorganized as a full-blown Ministry of Entertainment and Tourism.

[38] *Interview*, Number 18, Rome (December 12, 1957), pp. 2–3, 9, 14.

or official connection with the group itself as leaders, members, employees, consultants, and the like. As we shall note in the next section, there also exists in Italy an *internal* form of access of certain groups to the legislative process, and this fact quite radically changes the groups' prospects of influencing the making of public policy. Before we turn to this matter, however, we should say something more about a critical point of access, namely the specialized committees of the Italian legislature.

Several of our respondents volunteer the observation that the group that wants to maximize its impact must seek to effect strong connections with the committees of each chamber—and quite obviously with those committees that handle legislative matters of concern to the group. One of the major points made is that the committees are authorized to function in *sede deliberante*,[39] as we noted in Chapter IV. This procedure, in which the committee, by majority vote, can actually enact legislation, applies to all laws except those concerning treaties, taxes, the budget, public expenditures, and elections. Theoretically, sessions of the committee acting in *sede deliberante* are open to the public, because the committee is assumed to be acting for the whole legislature; but according to one respondent, the public rarely attends. On the other hand, because of the great power in the committee's hands, many groups are well advised to intervene with committee members, and do so with considerable frequency.[40]

Attitudes regarding the importance of the *sede deliberante* are mixed. On the one hand it is asserted that a small number of deputies can compel a proposal to be submitted to the whole legislature for disposition. Moreover, says one legislator, the truly important bills and the

[39] This is sometimes called *sede legislativa*. Both *sede deliberante* and *sede legislativa* are to be distinguished from *sede referente*, in which a committee simply considers a legislative proposal with the intention eventually of referring it back to the whole chamber for debate and disposition.

[40] *Interview*, Number 36, *op. cit.*, pp. 2–3.

great issues of abstract public policy are not decided in this way. In short, if the proposal is important enough, it is not likely to be decided by a few men in a legislative committee.[41] On the other hand, another deputy stresses that the so-called less important or technical bills that are enacted in this way often reflect large interests that are at stake: export and import regulations, rules and procedures concerning state-owned industries, matters affecting the tariff, and so on. Thus what may appear superficially to be nothing more than a highly technical and terribly complicated matter is frequently all of that and more. To assume that the *sede deliberante* does not offer extraordinary opportunities to those groups that are interested in technicalities is to ignore a vital aspect of the legislative process.[42]

There does exist general agreement, however, that intervention in the committees is an important aspect of the lobbying process. A major leader of Confindustria singles out this activity as of considerable import for that Organization.[43] A leader of the Italian Banking Association frankly comments that banking problems receive better treatment in committee than in the legislature as a whole. This is the stage and sector in the legislative process where the A.B.I. can make its weight felt. "Committees," says our respondent, "do not operate in the limelight and therefore do not become the subject matter for sensational treatment by the press. As a result of the committee's relative removal from public view, even those committee members who may be opposed to the ends or goals of the association do not very often make sensational or demagogic statements to the press concerning the discussion or debate that takes place within the committee." [44]

[41] *Interview,* Number 31, *op. cit.,* p. 3.

[42] *Interview,* Number 36, *op. cit.,* p. 3.

[43] *Interview,* Number 85 (Rome, May 22, 1958), p. 17. But see below for this respondent's lament concerning the general difficulties Confindustria encounters with legislative committees.

[44] *Interview,* Number 63, *op. cit.,* p. 6.

Beyond sending materials to committees and meeting informally with committee members, a prime objective of the interest group is to influence the appointment of the *relatore*. As we have noted above, the *relatore* has the major responsibility for gathering technical information concerning a proposal and is free to choose the outside groups and sources from which the information will be elicited. In the conduct of his investigations, he is in a position to hurry along or delay the proposals for which he is responsible. Furthermore, the *relatore* is the person who will make the major speech concerning a bill that is reported. The speech itself, together with other documentation, can have a major bearing on whether and how the chamber involved responds to the proposal. Thus, to cite one example that was offered, on a bill concerning the way in which electric companies make their financial operations public, the industries are alleged to have succeeded in getting Noverino Faletti (D.C.), a man identified as a friend of Confindustria, appointed as *relatore*. What he produced is viewed by those who sought tight regulation of the industry as a masterpiece of confusion and technical objections to the proposal.[45] At worst, the result of such a stratagem is to delay legislation; at best it can be permanently defeated.

DIRECT REPRESENTATION

To some degree, as far as the legislative rule-making arena is concerned, all of the various kinds of *external* intervention pale alongside the tendency of some major groups to achieve direct *internal* access to the Parliament. There are some interest groups that succeed in electing their own leaders to the legislature and, in some instances, these lawmakers openly organize as a parliamentary group demanding formal recognition. For obvious reasons, this

[45] *Interview*, Number 36, *op. cit.*, pp. 3–4. One should add here that the victory described was temporary, even if important. Italy's electrical industries came under severe attack by the political elements that support Amintore Fanfani, and were nationalized in 1962.

strategy or style of intervention seems to be available primarily to the larger groups with mass followings. When such groups achieve this degree of participation in the legislative process, to continue, as some do, to call themselves "apolitical" implies either extraordinary ingenuousness or self-delusion of striking magnitude.

In order to achieve direct representation, the interest group is compelled to effect very close ties with one of the established political parties—or to establish its own party. An interesting example of the latter type occurred in 1958 when the *Comunità* groups, associated with and headed by the now deceased Adriano Olivetti, organized as a political party. The result of this effort was disappointing; only Adriano Olivetti, a brilliant and humane person with strong misgivings about personal involvement in the legislature, was elected. Many leaders of the *Comunità* movement, skeptical about the strategy from the beginning, would rather not repeat the experience and would return instead to the kinds of interaction with government that prevailed prior to Olivetti's daring attempt at a quantum political jump.[46]

The major interest groups with direct representation are Italian Catholic Action, the Direct Cultivators, some of the auxiliary political party organizations, the Christian Association of Italian Workers (A.C.L.I.), and the Christian Democratic (C.I.S.L) and Communist-Socialist (C.G.I.L.) trade-union confederations. Because of some overlapping, it is difficult to know exactly how many Catholic Action leaders are in the legislature. For the moment, it will suffice to observe that the number is considerable and that Catholic Action has tried deliberately to place them where they are. Nor is Catholic Action the only agency through which organized Catholicism finds representation in the legislature. If one wanted to, of

---

[46] Another small group with limited direct representation is the Italian Confederation of Plant Managers (C.I.D.A.), whose leader, Giuseppe Togni, is a leading Christian Democrat as well as a person identified with the Montecatini chemical enterprises. *Interview*, Number 94, *op. cit.*, p. 1.

course, the entire Christian Democratic contingent might be viewed in this way. Such a characterization, while it makes sense at a very broad level of abstraction, is both excessive and possibly misleading when one stops to consider the many ideological faces of organized Catholicism as well as the fact that Christian Democracy itself is a brokerage party consisting of a number of groups that are in conflict with each other.

THE CHRISTIAN ASSOCIATION OF ITALIAN WORKERS

One of the significant Christian Democratic groups is the A.C.L.I. It came into existence at war's end when it was apparent that the Italian workers would probably be engulfed by a single, unitary, labor confederation that cut almost completely across ideological lines. In the face of this pressure for labor unity, one of two alternatives were available to the Catholics. The first would have required the creation of a clear-cut Catholic or "white" trade union organization similar to what one finds in a country like France. The second alternative would involve going along with trade-union unity but, in order to immunize and otherwise protect the Catholic worker against the wrong kind of class-oriented ideology, creating a special organization whose purpose would be "the education of Christian workers for responsible participation in the trade union life of the country." [47]

From the very beginning, the A.C.L.I. has been deeply involved in trade-union affairs. One of its leaders asserts, for example, that it was this organization that decided, in 1948, to bring an end to labor unity and to create a new confederation to which Catholic and other workers could repair. However, with the birth of C.I.S.L., the Christian Democratic Confederation, the A.C.L.I. did not go out of existence, because, as the respondent says, there had to be kept in reserve the nucleus of a trade-union organization that could absorb Catholic workers—even from C.I.S.L. if that need should ever arise. In addition,

---

[47] *Interview,* Number 34 (Rome, February 6, 1958), p. 2.

the A.C.L.I. must remain in existence, he says, because it manages a great many social welfare activities for its members and because the organization is a critically important political force on the side of the D.C. The nearly one-million members who are militant Catholics help to keep C.I.S.L. on the right track and constitute a significant Christian Democratic electoral reservoir.[48]

A.C.L.I.'s presence in the labor field is the source of considerable tension between it and C.I.S.L. For example, the A.C.L.I. leader asserts that C.I.S.L. would like to absorb the social welfare (*patronato*) activities administered by the A.C.L.I. However, it is apparent that the latter is not willingly going out of business, that it will probably continue to provide some competition for C.I.S.L., and that it does remain the Vatican's threat of giving Italy unequivocal "white" trade unionism if C.I.S.L. strays too far from official Catholic doctrine. The respondent attempts to minimize this conflict by viewing C.I.S.L. as a narrow collective-bargaining agency and his own organization as a broader social movement. Reflecting this, he says: "We prefer to think of the A.C.L.I. as a large-scale social movement which does not limit itself to day-to-day collective bargaining problems that are properly the affairs of the trade unions. Instead, the A.C.L.I. is interested in the workers and peasants of Italy as Catholics, as people needing Christian training, as people who must be prepared to carry on responsible roles as Catholics and Christians within the labor organizations that they join." [49]

The A.C.L.I. leaders, all of whom have come out of the various branches of Catholic Action, are said to maintain very close ties with the latter organization. Like the units of Catholic Action, the A.C.L.I. units retain "ecclesiastical assistants," although in the latter organization their powers are said to be purely advisory. The A.C.L.I. is said to possess greater autonomy than Catholic Action, in that its work is not apostolic. Nevertheless, A.C.L.I. is a

48 *Ibid.*, pp. 2–4.
49 *Ibid.*, p. 7.

Catholic organization and it is expected to conform to the Catholic-Christian principles sought by the Vatican, which, after all, was responsible for bringing it into existence.

In the furtherance of its interests and the articulation of its demands, the A.C.L.I. leadership has brought the Association directly into the Christian Democratic Party and the Italian legislature. At least 12 of the 144 members of the D.C. National Council of 1961 emanate from the A.C.L.I.[50] Not all of these can be considered abject instruments of the A.C.L.I., particularly when one stops to consider that the list includes Giulio Pastore, who was the first Secretary General of C.I.S.L. On the other hand, A.C.L.I. makes its presence felt in party circles, develops its own programs, and makes demands on the party to have its program incorporated into what the Party stands for.

Even more important, according to the A.C.L.I. leadership, is the contingent of A.C.L.I. leaders who have entered the legislature as Christian Democrats. He names fourteen deputies and one senator[51] who are identified as strictly A.C.L.I. men. In addition, there are said to be five or six strong supporters (e.g., Amatucci, Micheli) on whom the A.C.L.I. can regularly rely for support. The group is evidently well satisfied with its parliamentary representation. As the A.C.L.I. leader articulates it, "No item which is of major interest to the A.C.L.I. will fail to be introduced in some manner into the legislature. Furthermore, the basic group of fifteen deputies can be counted on to give tenacious battle in favor of A.C.L.I.

[50] They are Badaloni, Berloffa, Borrini, Cangialosi, Ciccardini, Curti, Gasparo, Hazon, Pastore, Penazzato, Rumor, and Valsecchi. See Giovanni di Capua, "Il Consiglio nazionale della DC," *Tempi Moderni*, 4 (July, 1961), pp. 81–100.

[51] Only twelve of the fourteen named could be found in *I Deputati e senatori del secondo parlamento repubblicano* (Rome: La Navicella, 1955). They are: Bersani, Butté, Cibotto, Delle Fave, Gatto, Merenda, Penazzato, Rapelli, Repossi, Rubinacci, Rumor, and Sabatini. Two others named were Fasina and Viasutti. The single senator is Lorenzi.

programs and against those programs, either of the Christian Democratic Party or from the outside, to which the A.C.L.I. is opposed.[52]

THE TRADE UNIONS

The advantages stemming from built-in legislative representation are also shared by some of the trade-union confederations. Following the elections of 1953, C.I.S.L. managed to place twenty-three deputies and one senator in the national legislature.[53] Five years later, the Confederation succeeded in naming almost one hundred of its leaders as candidates on Christian Democratic or Social Democratic electoral lists. As a result, over thirty C.I.S.L.-D.C. candidates and one C.I.S.L.-P.S.D.I. candidate were elected, increasing the union's parliamentary contingent by at least fifty percent. More dramatically put, this feat meant that more than ten percent of the current D.C. parliamentary contingent owed their elections to the places of leadership they occupied not within the Party but within the union.

For the Communist-Socialist dominated C.G.I.L. the situation is somewhat similar. Within the P.S.I., at least ten of the eighty persons elected to the Party's Executive Committee at the Thirty-Fourth Congress are leaders of the C.G.I.L.[54] For the Communist Party we have data from the Ninth Congress (1960), indicating that among the delegates were included fourteen national C.G.I.L. leaders, 125 provincial leaders, and 59 local union leaders.[55] In 1953, fifty deputies—almost ten percent of the legislature—represented C.G.I.L., thirty-five of them with

[52] *Interview,* Number 34, *op. cit.,* pp. 9–10.

[53] See Joseph LaPalombara, "The Political Role of Organized Labor in Western Europe," *Journal of Politics,* 17 (February, 1955), pp. 75–76.

[54] They are: Boni, Brodolini, Colombo, Di Pol, Foa, Giovannini, Lizzadri, Mosca, Santi, and Vergelli. See Antonio Landolfi, "Partito Socialista Italiano: Struttura, organi dirigenti, correnti," *Tempi Moderni,* 5 (January, 1962), pp. 54–60.

[55] Cited in Anonymous, "Modificazioni strutturali e politiche del Partito Comunista Italiano al suo 9° congresso," *Tempi Moderni,* 1 (April, 1960), p. 16.

P.C.I. credentials, fifteen carrying the P.S.I. label.[56] There is some evidence that by 1958 Palmiro Togliatti was seeking to downgrade union leaders by reducing their representation in the Party and the legislature. Thus one leader of C.G.I.L. sardonically points out that while C.I.S.L., which stresses its apolitical nature, was boasting of its increased parliamentary representation, Togliatti, for internal political reasons, was compelling C.G.I.L. provincial union secretaries to choose between being deputies or trade-union leaders.[57] Notwithstanding this pressure, however, a leading Communist leader of C.G.I.L. asserts that the Confederation's representation in Parliament actually increased in 1958.[58] Whatever the statistical niceties of this situation, it is certain that the C.G.I.L. represents strong parliamentary contingents in both the P.C.I. and P.S.I. legislative delegations and that, even within the highly centralized and disciplined framework of the Communist Party, the union leaders attempt to articulate the narrower interests of the sectors they represent.

Even the Italian Union of Labor—some of whose leaders eschew parliamentary representation and claim (falsely) [59] that U.I.L. ran no candidates in 1958—is not free of this urge to find a formal place in the legislature. Among the candidates of the Democratic Socialist

[56] LaPalombara, op. cit., p. 71.

[57] Interview, Number 106 (Rome, July 15, 1958), p. 1. This respondent confides that Palmiro Togliatti was trying to increase the Party bureaucracy's control over the organization and that, to do so, he felt it necessary to reduce C.G.I.L.'s voice in the Party. Thus, if C.G.I.L. provincial secretaries who became deputies should be forced to choose between assignments, a separate base of financial and electoral power would be removed from C.G.I.L. deputies.

[58] Interview, Number 94, op. cit., pp. 6–7.

[59] In view of the data that are in my possession, it is curious that a major leader of U.I.L. should have asserted (Interview, Number 80, op. cit., p. 2) that not a single U.I.L. leader was a candidate for the national legislature in 1958. Perhaps the reference was strictly to the small group of national leaders at Rome. However, even at that level there was the candidacy of Leo Solari, a member of the U.I.L. National Directive Committee. In 1963, Italo Viglianesi, Secretary General of U.I.L., was elected to the Italian Senate.

(P.S.D.I.) and Radical-Republican parties, in excess of seventy U.I.L. leaders, most of them organizers and provincial secretaries, were included. The failure of every one of these to win enough votes to be elected does not mean that U.I.L. would renounce direct, internal access to the legislature if it could be made available.

The experience of the unions offers an excellent illustration that direct representation on political party organs and in the national legislature is definitely a two-edged weapon, in one sense cutting for the unions, in another cutting against them. Integration into the party—and into the party's legislative contingent—carries with it the implied obligation of adhering to party discipline. Thus, in exchange for greater direct access to the legislative decisional machinery, the groups involved tacitly agree to circumscribe the freedom of action they might otherwise exercise.

The dilemma I am outlining is certainly well known to Italy's trade-union leaders and has been debated for some years. A leader of U.I.L., who consistently refuses to accept political candidacy, holds that C.I.S.L. and C.G.I.L.—and the working class—are put to a serious disadvantage by the presence of so many of their leaders in the legislature. Unlike these confederations, he claims, U.I.L. has greater genuine freedom and is not compelled to make serious compromises with the parties in favor of political expediency. For the union leaders who do get to Parliament, remaining there tends to become more important than protecting and defending the interests of their union members. Thus, while the unions should certainly be deeply interested and active in political party affairs, they should not accept responsibilities that clearly imply greater self-restraint.[60]

C.G.I.L. leaders provide a perfectly straight-forward rationale for their direct representation. One of them puts the matter like this: "The problem is: how can workers

[60] *Ibid.*

participate in political and economic life? We hold that the workers must be accorded a quota of power. This leads us to follow traditional trade-union tactics and to enter directly into the legislative process. When one considers the kinds of problems that confront the workers, the unions must be heavily committed to legislative activity." [61]

The C.G.I.L. view, articulated for many years and now generally accepted in many trade-union circles, is that since most of what is of interest to the working class has political implications, the unions isolate themselves from the affairs of parties and politics only at their great disadvantage. Indeed, if one fully understands the mission of the parties of the Left, it is obvious that the unions have a major role to play in helping to effect revolutionary or peaceful change. As our C.G.I.L. leader says, "The ends of the Social State and of the trade unions are identical. The trade union is entitled *directly* to ask the state that its legislation does not exclude the ends which are close to the hearts of the unions. . . . If in Parliament they never discussed laws of interest to labor, there would be no need of a trade-union representation in the legislature." [62]

Views such as this, while they provide a rationale for direct representation, also lead to the conclusion that the unions should be instrumental for the broader goals of the party. Thus another leader of C.G.I.L., who opposes Togliatti's efforts to reduce the power of the union in the party and the legislature, echoes the tenets of democratic centralism. He points out that in the interest of the working class the unions have every right to make their presence felt in all political spheres, including the legislature. However, once such representation is achieved, the union must necessarily be conditioned by party discipline. As party and legislative leaders, the union leaders can ask that questions be raised in which they have an interest.

[61] *Interview*, Number 116 (Rome, July 3, 1958), p. 1.
[62] *Ibid.*, pp. 2, 3.

But once this is accomplished, he says, "Trade unionists cannot be so sectarian as to jeopardize the unity of the party in the legislature. If this were permitted, the result would be chaos." [63]

A man who spent most of his adult years as a Communist Party leader takes strong issue with the position of his former C.G.I.L. colleagues. He says that, with few exceptions, the C.G.I.L. members of Parliament within the Communist Party have been abjectly docile in the face of party discipline. Rather than represent the interests and the needs of the working class, they became, as Lenin intended, nothing more than "transmission belts" for the views and commands of the political leadership of the Party. As an example of this, the respondent points to the internal party activities of Giuseppe di Vittorio, the then Secretary-General of C.G.I.L., at the time of the Hungarian Rebellion. Evidently di Vittorio saw the uprising as a working-class phenomenon and not, as the U.S.S.R. claimed, as a Fascist-inspired counterrevolutionary plot. Di Vittorio is said to have tried to have the P.C.I. identify with the Hungarian workers but that he, too, failed and was compelled by the "hards" within P.C.I. to bow to the official line. In short, the unions are said to pay a heavy price for their integration into the P.C.I. and Parliament.[64]

In contrast to this view is another expressed by a Socialist Party leader who describes an internal situation which is much less centralized. He holds that the P.S.I. is to a considerable, even a remarkable, extent nothing more than a confederation of warring ideological, geographic, and functional groups. The ideological differences among, say, the "Morandiani," "Autonomisti," "Bassiani," and other segments is obvious to anyone who reads the Socialist press and follows the proceedings of Socialist congresses. The same kind of sectarianism can be detected if one notes the conflicting positions of several of the

[63] *Interview*, Number 106, *loc. cit.*
[64] *Interview*, Number 21 (Florence, December 17, 1957), p. 7.

Party's leading regional federations. Additionally, there can be no questioning the presence in the Party—and in the Party's legislative contingent—of a strong and articulate trade-union faction that does not automatically adhere to the views or directives that the Party's leadership may proclaim. Men like Vittorio Foa, Fernando Santi, and Oreste Lizzadri are singled out as Socialists, to be sure, but also as individuals with a profound understanding of the more limited interest they represent both in the Party and in the legislature.[65] However much abstract validity there might be in such a posture, my own interviews with several of the people named definitely suggests the pervasiveness of the conflict between one's position as an interest-group leader and his role as a lawmaker representing a party that feels a strong need and expects to present a united front in the Chamber of Deputies or the Senate.

The labor confederation in which the matter of direct parliamentary representation has caused the greatest debate, as well as the most elaborate kinds of rationalizations for it, is C.I.S.L. The Confederation's major difficulty arises in part out of the claim, adamantly made over several years, that C.I.S.L. is apolitical in the sense of being free from any subservience to the Christian Democratic Party. Theoretically, C.I.S.L. representatives in the legislature must be there because other labor groups such as C.G.I.L. are also represented. Moreover, it is alleged that the C.I.S.L. deputies are essentially free agents, who can choose whether to vote on the basis of the union's particular interest or on the interests expressed by the controlling group in the D.C. Over the years, the C.I.S.L. leaders have been able to cite a few instances where at least a portion of their contingent in the Chamber of Deputies did not follow party dictates.

Among the more interesting arguments presented by the C.I.S.L. leaders is that when trade-union leaders enter

[65] *Interview*, Number 13, *op. cit.*, p. 5.

Parliament, they do so as Christian Democrats and not as representatives of the Confederation. If this view is accepted, it is impossible to argue that the union loses any of its autonomy as a result of this step.[66] Thus, as one of C.I.S.L.'s foremost exponents puts it, direct representation in no way jeopardizes the integrity of the Confederation. When asked to comment on the fact that in 1958 Giulio Pastore, the then Secretary-General of C.I.S.L., had, as a minister, entered not only parliament but the government, the respondent replied: "With Pastore the world of labor enters the government for the first time. But this does not mean that C.I.S.L. is entering the government; this does not mean that the organized trade union is entering the government. The C.I.S.L. as such will never enter the government." [67]

This same respondent emphasizes that the D.C. has not carried party discipline to the extreme and that C.I.S.L. deputies have been able to disagree without being expelled from the Party. As an example, he cited those C.I.S.L. legislative leaders who deviated from the majority vote of the Christian Democrats on the controversial *patti agrari* question.[68] However, another C.I.S.L. leader who opposes any kind of parliamentary representation comments bitterly that the *patti agrari* issue clearly illustrates that unions that obtain direct representation mortgage their freedom. For in the final vote on the measure, C.I.S.L.'s vaunted 22 legislators diminished to a mere 9; the remainder preferred not to risk party censure by voting for the union's position. In the words of the respondent: "Of the 22 men elected under C.I.S.L. sponsorship, not more than 9 were willing to challenge the power of the bishops and of the direct cultivators. They did not

---

[66] *Interview*, Number 107 (Rome, July 8, 1958), p. 1.

[67] *Interview*, Number 114 (Rome, July 7, 1958), p. 1.

[68] The *patti agrari* issue involved an attempt to regulate contracts between landowners and tenants in a way that the landowners considered damaging. C.I.S.L.'s Secretary-General, Giulio Pastore, was a strong exponent of the legislation, the unsatisfactory disposition of which helped to topple the government of Antonio Segni in 1956.

want to run the risk of not being re-elected." [69] Put into axiomatic form, another C.I.S.L. leader remarked: "One cannot enter Parliament on a Christian Democratic list without having heavily compromised and conditioned oneself and one's values." [70]

Even some of those C.I.S.L. leaders who support current direct intervention have mixed feelings about it. One of them remarks: "But attachment to a political party, of whatever coloration, is too compromising for union leaders. . . . When the unions achieve power, they become the State and are no longer the unions. Trade-union leaders who share power can no longer view themselves as trade unionists. I do not want the union as such in power, because this would then clearly curtail the union's activities on behalf of the membership. Such a situation raises the greatest difficulties for the unions, because it raises theoretical contradictions and limits liberty of action." [71]

Another C.I.S.L. official frankly admits to the internal debate that raged in 1958 over the matter of parliamentary representation—and which led some of the more sanguine young leaders to conclude that the legislative contingent would actually be reduced in the elections of that year. This man stresses that 90 percent of C.I.S.L.'s leaders agree that, sooner or later, the Confederation must renounce its parliamentary representation, but they also understand that this cannot be done as long as there are problems of unemployment and economic development of the country which the trade union cannot easily resolve through the normal kind of union activities. [72]

One is tempted to remark that the problems cited are likely to plague Italy for many decades and that it is reasonable to expect that C.I.S.L., which has continuously increased its parliamentary representation since 1948, is

[69] *Interview*, Number 6 (Rome, November 29, 1957), p. 6.
[70] *Interview*, Number 51 (Rome, January 16, 1958), p. 3.
[71] *Interview*, Number 107, *op. cit.*, p. 2.
[72] *Interview*, Number 114, *loc. cit.*

not likely deliberately to reverse this trend soon. Never-theless, some of the "theoretical contradictions" alluded to above are dramatically out in the open now that there has been a formal "Opening to the Left" which promises to involve the unions in the rule-making and rule-application functions, as they have not been in the past. Amintore Fanfani made it clear that he expected the unions to participate in the evolution of certain reforms, and that the unions, in order to fulfill this role, would have to be "responsible" and exercise considerable states-manship and self-restraint. In short, a union that genu-inely wishes to share power must not expect to behave like a union not so endowed. In response, the secretaries-general of C.I.S.L. and C.G.I.L., Bruno Storti and Ago-stino Novella, express concern lest the unions be turned into nothing more than instrumentalities of the Center-Left policies. While Fernando Santi, a Socialist leader of C.G.I.L., eschews maximalist union policies and urges collaboration, the confederations themselves begin to un-derstand that, in the future, the articulation of interest may have to evolve within a general context that is less rigid, isolative, and sectarian, or more conducive to bar-gaining and compromise. Far from constituting a settled matter, this is exactly the question that remains largely unresolved.[73]

THE DIRECT CULTIVATORS

One important factor compelling the trade unions to hang on to direct representation in the legislature is the presence there of other groups with which they compete for influence. We have already noted the presence of A.C.L.I. Even more apparent are those who emanate from the various units of Catholic Action. But one of the most powerful groups in Italy, one often at odds with the unions and massively present in the legislature, is the

[73] See the interesting letter by Fidia Sassano, "Sindacati e centro-sinistra," *Tempi Moderni*, 5 (April, 1962), pp. 77–79. Cf. the lead article in *Unità* (March 22, 1962), p. 1.

Coltivatori Diretti, led by the Honorable Paolo Bonomi. Because of the frequency with which the group is mentioned in interview responses, some note should be taken of it here.

The Coltivatori Diretti is a massive interest group representing Italy's small and medium landowners and farmers. The relatively disadvantageous economic position of its members makes it more analogous to the American Farmers Union or the National Grange, rather than to the Farm Bureau Federation, whose Italian Counterpart is the Confagricoltura. However, the analogy is necessarily of extremely limited value: by every conceivable test the Coltivatori Diretti represents a much more formidable group than American agriculture was able to muster, except, perhaps, in the heyday of the Farm Bloc. It is not merely the result of chance that many of Italy's group leaders, legislators, and bureaucrats cite the Coltivatori Diretti when they are asked to identify the most powerful association operating on the Italian political scene.

In order fully to understand the power wielded by the Coltivatori Diretti it is necessary to look briefly at the structure of agriculture. In most rural areas there exist agricultural consortiums (*consorzi*) which, while essentially private, are endowed with a number of quasi-public functions. Basically, the *consorzi* function as field agencies for certain of the national ministries at Rome, and particularly for the Ministry of Agriculture. The consortiums are able to provide gasoline, fertilizer, and other agricultural raw materials at cut-rate prices; they have special arrangements for the sale and distribution of farm machinery; they can facilitate the obtaining of credit; they arrange to have crops stored, and so on through a fairly long list of activities that are of immediate economic importance to the farmers within a particular district who are its members. In each of Italy's 92 provinces there is a *Federconsorzi* which unites all the local units and generally sets policies and provides other administrative services for them. The general tendency is for the various competing ideological groups in the country to seek control of both the local and the provincial consortiums.

During the Fascist era some effort was made to reorganize the small landowners' movement, which had existed in Italy from the late 19th century. An organization that might meaningfully relate to the consortiums was created, but, like most such units, it fell into a crisis of chaos and disorientation when the Fascist regime collapsed. Into this vacuum, according to one of his collaborators, stepped Paolo Bonomi and a small group of associates. It was Bonomi's intention not merely to revitalize the consortiums but also to provide a kind of parallel interest-group structure that would permit him to control the former. Then, in 1944, the National Confederation of Direct Cultivators came into existence. One measure of its success, according to our respondent, is that, by 1958, it controlled 65 of the 92 provincial consortiums, the remaining ones resting in the hands of Confagricoltura. In no case, then, are the *Federconsorzi* in the hands of the extreme Left's agricultural-interest groups.[74] Thus, when one thinks of this occupational-economic category as a source of interest articulation, it is necessary to understand that its demands are translated primarily through Paolo Bonomi's confederation.[75]

In 1944, the Coltivatori Diretti included 349 local sections, 70,925 families, 106,388 workers, and a total of 220,742 persons represented.[76] By 1958, the association claimed 13,556 local sections, encompassing 1,683,141 families and 3,385,571 workers and representing a total of 7,768,100 persons.[77] Such impressive—even fantastic—

---

[74] It should be noted, however, that the Left groups are strong in the organization of the sharecroppers (*mezzadri*) and agricultural day laborers (*braccianti*).

[75] *Interview,* Number 37 (Rome, January 29, 1958), p. 2.

[76] Confederazione Nazionale Coltivatori Diretti, *Relazione del presidente al VII congresso nazionale* (Rome, 1953), p. 6.

[77] Confederazione Nazionale Coltivatori Diretti, *Relazione del presidente al XII congresso nazionale* (Rome, 1958), pp. 4–9. Also, *Interview,* Number 96 (Rome, June 27, 1958), p. 5.

growth results in part from the charismatic personality and brilliant organizational and political skills of Paolo Bonomi, but in part also to two other factors: the association provides its members with a wide spectrum of services, and it has managed to win many important legislative concessions for the membership. Additionally, it must be stressed that the Communists and Socialists were at the beginning antagonistic to the small landowners, opposed concessions in their favor, and entered the organizational struggle for their allegiance long after Bonomi had established hegemony over the economic group.

Services performed for members touch on every conceivable interest. At the local level, special units organize youth and women; where land reform has resulted in the assignment of land to peasants, special divisions are created to help the new proprietors confront their many new problems; at the provincial level there are special units that offer the landowner assistance regarding social insurance, trade-union matters, fiscal problems, developments in technology, and so on; throughout the organization there are educational units that not only aim at raising the level of literacy but also examine the myriad problems that confront the farmer in an era of changing technology and rapid urbanization. At all levels, from the local commune, through zones and provinces, and until the national level is reached, members are encouraged to participate in organizational affairs and in the election of those who represent the membership on policy-making and executive organs of the confederation.[78]

At Rome, the Coltivatori Diretti headquarters is located in a sumptuous, well-guarded palace. I was warned that I would not be permitted to interview anyone in the organization until a security check (which included an inquiry to the U.S. Embassy regarding my ideological reliability) had been completed. The central offices are divided into a number of administrative divisions, all of

[78] *Interview*, Number 78 (Rome, June 4, 1958), *op. cit.*, pp. 6–7.

them well staffed, including organization and general affairs, fiscal assistance, technical-economic assistance, legal-legislative assistance, trade-union affairs, administration, archives, ecclesiastical counselors, and press and propaganda. Each of these offices is said to have a provincial counterpart. In addition there exists a national secretariat as well as special national offices dealing with social insurance, small peasant proprietorship, sheep herders, and problems of land reform. All of this activity requires the services at Rome of 110 professionals, not counting clerks, secretaries, ushers, and lesser personnel.[79]

As one might expect, the press-propaganda office turns out an avalanche of publications, some of them geared to the leaders, others to members, and others still to the general public.[80] The existence of an ecclesiastical office, which supervises the work of 273 ecclesiastical counselors, reveals the strong tie between the Confederation and organized Catholicism. Although the units of the Organization are not required to install any of the clergy, the bishops of Italy will appoint one on request. According to one of the group's leaders, the counselors are needed to look after the spiritual problems of the members and to guarantee that they are exposed to the proper religious values.

In addition to services of various kinds, the organization also produces for its members a pattern of legislation that responds to the articulated demands of the group. Between 1953 and 1958, the Confederation lists 101 laws and ministerial decrees passed in response to the needs of Italian agriculture. These include legislation dealing with agricultural credit, aid to distressed areas, regulations concerning the planting, storage, and transportation of agricultural products, subsidies to encourage the development of the family-size farm, legislation protecting the purity

[79] *Ibid.,* pp. 7–8.

[80] Publications and some problems surrounding them are discussed by Paolo Bonomi in Confederazione Nazionale Coltivatori Diretti, *Relazione del presidente al XI congresso nazionale* (Rome, 1957), pp. 15–19.

of certain products, norms to be applied in zones of land reform and reclamation, prohibitions against higher taxes on livestock, and so on through a long list of legislative enactments that clearly benefit the particular group that Bonomi and others represent. It is this impressive legislative record, as well as organizational service, that must account in large measure for the enormous inflation of membership that the confederation has experienced since 1944.[81]

Obviously not all the laws listed were enacted at the behest of the Direct Cultivators; nor should the legislation be seen as a precise index of the group's power. It is certainly well enough known that Italian agriculture has had to confront a number of crises since the War, and only a government bent on suicide or the fomenting of revolution would have ignored these. But the Direct Cultivators have made a significant difference and at least some of the favorable legislation might not have materialized were they not in existence or were they an interest group dominated by the political Left.

To illustrate this point we might consider one piece of legislation that served simultaneously to improve the condition of Italy's direct cultivators and greatly to increase the power of the confederation. In 1948, Paolo Bonomi and associates introduced in the Chamber of Deputies a bill designed to extend to direct cultivators the provisions of Italy's compulsory insurance against sickness and disease. Not until 1952 was the group able to push the bill along to the point where the Committee on Labor and Social Security took it up in *sede deliberante*. The committee seemed on the verge of approving it when the Left began a major campaign against it, during which they compelled the proposal to be placed on the chamber calendar for full debate. Not until the spring of 1953 did the bill come up for debate. Although it was approved by the lower chamber, the dissolution of Parliament in an-

[81] For a complete listing of this legislation, see *Coltivatori Diretti*, 2 (May, 1958), pp. 349–63.

ticipation of the elections of that year prevented its passage in the Senate. The bill was reintroduced in October, 1953, after Bonomi secured strong support for it from a caucus of the Christian Democratic Party. At the same time, the Communists and Socialists, who had voted against the bill previously, introduced their own bill to deal with the problem. Evidently, they understood too late that their failure to support the direct cultivators might cost them potential electoral support.

By the middle of November, 1954, the bill had passed both chambers of the legislature.[82] One of its provisions required that there be established to administer the law *Casse Mutue* (Mutual Funds) in all areas where direct cultivators exist. The *Casse* would in turn be run by boards of directors that would be directly elected by those direct cultivators who were covered by the district involved. Needless to say, as with the case of the *consorzi,* control of the *Casse* would constitute a source of considerable power and prestige in the countryside. The funds, to which both cultivators and government make contributions, provide a wide range of medical assistance for the persons involved.[83]

The first elections to the *Casse* took place in March, 1955. Elections were held in 7,608 communes, and the two main competitors for representation were the Coltivatori Diretti, led by Bonomi, and Federterra, representing the extreme Left. The results, as the Confederation frankly points out, clearly demonstrated the overwhelming power of the former. The Direct Cultivators gained control of 7,416, or 97.5 percent, of all of the *Casse.* Three and six years later, although the percentages are not so high, the Confederation remained absolutely dominant in the field. In 1958, among 7,599 communes in which

[82] See Law of November 22, 1954, No. 1136. Printed in *Gazzetta Ufficiale,* No. 285, December 12, 1954.

[83] For a review of the medical services provided during the first three years of the Law's administration, see *Coltivatori Diretti, op. cit.,* pp. 93–116.

elections were held, the Coltivatori Diretti won control of 7,466 and attracted a total of 1,047,749 votes. The Left succeeded in attracting only 104,947 voters and gaining control of only 106 *Casse,* mostly in Piedmont, Lombardy, and Emilia Romagna.[84] By 1961, the Peasant Alliance of the Left had suffered a further decline. In that year they won in only 68 of the 7,297 communes in which elections were held. The Coltivatori Diretti gained control of 7,209, and the remaining 20 went to other groups. In the voting, the Peasant Alliance attracted 90,399 votes (7.5 percent) against 1,096,021 (91.4 percent) for the Confederation.[85]

Commenting on these smashing victories, one journal observes: "The explanation of this phenomenon, which is unparalleled in the political composition of the peasant electorate, must be attributed in part to the irregularities committed by the Bonomi leaders who dominate these organizations. These irregularities were denounced by the Peasant Alliance and recognized by the Minister of Labor in a speech before the Chamber on March 24. The Honorable Sullo declared that the limited intervention of the Ministry has revealed situations that imply the annulment of elections." [86]

Anyone acquained with Bonomi's electoral methods will appreciate that accusations such as this are not manufactured of whole cloth. One member of Parliament asserts that the Bonomi henchmen exercise very careful control over the way in which Direct Cultivators cast ballots, not merely in *Casse Mutue* elections but in national political contests as well. Peasant farmers in each district are told what combination of preference-vote numbers to cast. While this method does not completely destroy secrecy of the ballot, it does give the leadership an opportunity to gauge how closely each district adheres to the line established by the leaders. Where deviation is too pronounced, retaliatory measures can be taken. In summary, he says:

[84] The statistical details are reported *ibid.,* 2 (April, 1958), pp. 239–42.
[85] See *Tempi Moderni,* 4 (July, 1961), p. 143.
[86] *Ibid.*

"Mr. Bonomi has brought into existence one of the truly powerful groups that operate within the D.C. and that is in a position to determine the line which the Party follows on agricultural policies. This group is similar to the Farm Bloc, with the important qualification that Bonomi has definitely taken over every facet of the Direct Cultivators and is able rigidly to determine the manner in which the Organization will move and the kinds of decisions it takes. Unlike the American Farm Bloc, we have here an organization rigidly led and maneuvered by one man and by those whom he pleases to name as his trusted clique." [87]

A Communist leader ascribes the organization's power to the control exercised over the Federconsorzi, which in turn have the power of economic life and death over the small landowner. It is alleged, for example, that although Bonomi (who once led Federconsorzi) is no longer formally affiliated with the group, he is the president of F.A.T.A.—*Fondo Assicurativo Tra Agricoltori,* a private insurance firm that began in 1953 with capital of 2,500,-000 lire and five years later publicly divulged capital of 750,000,000 lire. While there is no interlocking directorate between Coltivatori Diretti and Federconsorzi, leaders of both are said to sit on the directive organs of F.A.T.A., a convenient arrangement if true.[88]

Top leaders of the Bonomi organization will not openly discuss F.A.T.A. One of them, when asked directly to comment on the nature of the organization replies that the only relationship he can possibly think of is that Bonomi, who heads the Direct Cultivators, also happens to be president of the insurance firm. F.A.T.A., however, is said to have no other connection with the confederation, representing as it does merely one of the private enterprises in which Bonomi is engaged.[89] Another close friend and associate of Bonomi claims to know very little

[87] *Interview,* Number 62, *op. cit.,* pp. 7–8.
[88] *Interview,* Number 53 (Rome, January 21, 1958), pp. 3–4.
[89] *Interview,* Number 96, *op. cit.,* pp. 9–10.

about F.A.T.A. but freely adds that, notwithstanding Bonomi's absence from any formal leadership role in the Federconsorzi, he still has much to say about the people who are chosen to head those organizations.[90]

Whatever may be the real sources of appeal that Bonomi and associates have for the Italian peasantry,[91] it is dramatically apparent that they are able to transfer it into considerable political power. As we have noted, this power is grudgingly conceded by group leaders and lawmakers who oppose Bonomi. It is implicitly recognized when, on the occasion of the Confederation's Twelfth Congress, Pope Pius XII sends a lengthy message in which he implies that the organization has played a significant role in the Italian ideological struggle, and when, in addition, personal messages to the delegates are voiced by Secretary of the D.C., Amintore Fanfani, Minister of Labor and Social Security, Gui, and Minister of Finance, Andreotti.[92]

Coltivatori Diretti leaders do not hesitate to speak of their political purposes and the manner in which they go about trying to make them prevail. Discounting the obvious drive for power that is typical of Bonomi and others in the confederation, the Coltivatori Diretti have a broad program of particularistic demands. In 1958, for example, they worked out and campaigned for an agricultural legislative program that encompassed cheap credit, reduction of prices on agricultural machinery and fertilizer, greater technical and educational assistance to farmers, protec-

[90] *Interview*, Number 37, *op. cit.*, p. 37.

[91] Bonomi's detractors speak of corruption and electoral irregularities. They also insist that the 1954 law on the *Casse Mutue* is gimmicked against the minority because of its majoritarian principle, the limited time permitted for the compilation and public dissemination of electoral lists, and, above all, because of its authorization of proxy votes. However this may be, it is also apparent that the political Left has simply been most inept in appealing to the small landowners, and that this has caused some contrast between the Communists and the Socialists. See *Tempi Moderni*, 4 (July, 1961), p. 144.

[92] For all these messages, and particularly the significant one of the Pope, see *Coltivatori Diretti*, 2 (May, 1958), pp. 309-38.

tion of prices, removal of taxes on livestock, abolition of inheritance taxes for certain aspects of agricultural patrimony, agricultural labor contracts that reflect the varied kinds of land holdings, representation of farmers in public bodies concerned with land reform and reclamation, extension of certain additional kinds of social insurance to direct cultivators, and greater financial outlays for electrification and rural housing.[93]

In order to press for these measures, Bonomi's organization has successfully found direct representation in the ruling organs of the D.C. and in rule-making bodies at all levels of government. Within the National Council of the D.C. there sit at least seven leaders of the Coltivatori Diretti.[94] Regarding representation on legislative bodies, we can best paraphrase the proud claims of a national leader of the Confederation. This man claims that, as of 1958, there were 23,000 direct cultivator members and leaders sitting on the communal councils of the country. All of these are Christian Democrats and must be seen as a very heavy proportion of the total of 53,000 Christian Democrats who hold such offices. In addition, there were 37 deputies in the Chamber who are identified as either local or provincial leaders of the confederation. Beyond this, the respondent asserts that there are at least 13 other deputies "who are very close to us" and who are members of the Coltivatori Diretti parliamentary group. If one were to give the broadest definition to this latter group, as many as 66 deputies are in the camp of the confederation. When one adds an estimated forty senators, the total legislative contingent exceeds 100.[95]

Our respondent tells us that all of these Christian Democrats, who owe their elections to the confederation's capabilities for preference-vote delivering, will naturally do the bidding of Bonomi on most legislative issues.

[93] *Ibid.*, 2 (April, 1958), pp. 231–32.

[94] They are: Bruni, Ducci, Fanton, Forlani, Gui, Salizzoni, and Vetrone. See Giovanni di Capua, *loc. cit.*

[95] *Interview*, Number 96, *op. cit.*, pp. 9–10.

"These individuals," confides our respondent, "are our men. They are in the legislature because of the kinds of activities carried on by the local and provincial units of the Confederation." [96]

While the Coltivatori Diretti runs neither the D.C. nor the legislature, its 100 legislators, 23,000 communal councilors, and over 200,000 volunteer electoral activists cannot be easily ignored. Not only does Bonomi get out the vote, but members are very carefully indoctrinated and instructed regarding precisely *how* to cast their Christian Democratic ballot. As outspoken opponents not merely of Communism but also of Socialism in any of its manifestations, the Confederation has won the support of the Vatican. Those within the D.C. who may be bent on large-scale socio-economic reform, cooperation with the P.S.I., and the extension of party control over the groups that constitute it will find a formidable opponent in Paolo Bonomi who, according to one of his own lieutenants, prefers to "extend his hand" to the monarchists and Neo-Fascists on the Right rather than to any of the political factions on the Left.

SUMMARY OBSERVATIONS

Aside from the very obvious conclusion that many of Italy's interest groups interact with the national legislature in one way or another, a number of generalizations suggest themselves at this point.

First, it seems apparent that, although the mere holding of "scientific conferences" may have limited utility by itself as a means of influencing legislation, it is a useful device when it is coupled with lobbying activities as

[96] *Ibid.* This claim is confirmed by a leader of C.I.S.L. (*Interview, Number 6, op. cit.,* p. 4); a P.S.I. leader (*Interview, Number 13, loc. cit.*); a Republican Party provincial leader (*Interview, Number 22, Bologna, March 8, 1958, p. 4); a Communist senator (*Interview, Number 31, op. cit.,* p. 5); an industrial executive (*Interview, Number 45, Rome, January 14, 1958, p. 2); an ex-minister (*Interview, Number 58, Rome, January 22, 1958, pp. 3-4); a leader of C.G.I.L. (*Interview, Number 53, op. cit.,* p. 3); and an associate of Paolo Bonomi (*Interview, Number 37, op. cit.,* pp. 2-3).

lobbying is commonly understood. Respondents who focused on the utility of conferences emphasize the need for appearing rational and objective, for playing down the particularistic nature of a group's demands, and for trying to cloak one's policy desires with the mantle of the public or general interest. Reading between the lines of interview responses, one is impressed by the likelihood that some of Italy's lawmakers are inclined to what Giovanni Sartori calls the roles of *resistor* to group demands or an *outsider* in the sense of being outside the group process.[97] Where this type of legislator is encountered, the need for articulating interest in terms that take the general welfare into consideration is rather compelling. Moreover, in order to conform to the general expectation of the political system itself, it is probably essential that most of the groups that approach the legislature from the outside couch their demands in the same kind of objective framework. The mere fact that pressures in this direction exist tends to force at least some of the groups into a pattern of communicating demands that is not so raw and uncompromising as might otherwise be the case.

Second, if we are to draw the normal conclusion from our data, it would appear necessary for the legislature to develop a better system of providing its members with more adequate secretarial and research assistance. Although voluntary associations will always play an important role in providing lawmakers and legislative committees with useful data, the latter cannot perform their functions to best advantage from a democratic standpoint if group-furnished information and studies constitute the most significant source of data. Nor, as we shall see in the two chapters that follow, is it sufficient to remark that the ministries will provide information to offset possible group biases. The truth is, from this standpoint the bureaucracy is as impoverished as the legislature. On the basis of what we have learned, it is possible to conclude

that, other things being equal, the groups that can produce reports and studies are in a most advantageous position vis-à-vis groups that do not have similar resources.
The flow of a constant stream of information from group
to legislature, even where the information as such is
basically unreliable, would seem to create a presumption
that the legislature will take seriously into account the
views of the group involved in this stream of communication.

Third, if the recent history of Confindustria is any test,
money would seem to be less potent than numbers as a
device for maximizing legislative influence. Money may,
of course, buy a certain amount of campaign support and
is not to be wholly discounted. Moreover, it may play a
much more critical role—as Confindustria funds probably
did—at a time when the political party involved has not
yet succeeded in establishing other sources of monetary
supply. But after almost fifteen years of unchallenged control of the apparatus of government, the D.C., as one of
its leaders confides, has found other sources of funds and
no longer has a desperate need for the financial aid that
industrial organizations can provide. Theoretically, the
situation would be radically different if the control of
government changed frequently and there were less of
what the Italians ominously call *sottogoverno*. Where
there is unchallenged control of the multifarious sources
of political patronage, it is probably the ability to deliver
votes that primarily qualifies an interest group to lay
strong claims on the direction of public policy.

I am fully aware that there are many in Italy who will
challenge this observation. The accepted stereotype, not
merely on the Left but also among Center supporters, is
that the country is an impotent victim in the claws of
monopoly capitalism. My view is that the picture is exaggerated, particularly because Christian Democracy is able
to tap sources of electoral financing and campaigning that
to some extent free it from abject dependence on Fiat,
Montecatini, Italcementi, Pirelli, and other industrial

giants of the country. Thus, although as we shall see, the industrial sector is not without its sources of influence, it is essentially on the defensive—particularly in the legislature, where nothing seems to count so much as the ability to deliver the required number of preference votes. In this particular game, organized industry takes a back seat to its friendly or antagonistic counterparts among the trade unions, Catholic Action, Coltivatori Diretti, and the other mass organizations.

Fourth, discernable patterns of lobbying fortify our earlier assumption that Italy's interest groups are isolative and essentially nonbargaining. Antagonistic groups that rarely communicate with each other and go in search of legislators of like ideological predispositions are ill-equipped to bargain democratically. The basic divisions that permeate the society are not aggregated but actually exacerbated by the pattern of group interaction with political parties and the legislature. It is difficult to prescribe a solution for this problem, especially because the fragmented groups find their equivalents in some of the political parties. Indeed, the latter, in order to assure themselves a portion of those who are potential group members, will often contribute directly to the fractionalization of interests. A vicious structure is thereby created, wherein one can detect mutually exclusive ideological aggregations that funnel demands through interest groups and the political parties into segmented portions of the legislature. The deep, basic conflicts of the social system are therefore reproduced intact in the legislature and, incidentally, are manifested in the surprisingly violent behavior that often breaks out in the latter body.

Fifth, one of our findings, concerning the *sede deliberante*, clearly points to the importance of formal institutional arrangements as a factor affecting the pattern of interest-group behavior. For all the safeguards available to the minority (note the behavior of the Left on Bonomi's *Casse Mutue* law), many highly technical laws are actually enacted by small groups of committee members. Groups whose day-to-day interests involve primarily the technicalities of noncontroversial legislation can develop a quiet but important impact on what emerges from the legislature. It seems rather apparent that this segment of the legislative process deserves a closer look than anyone has accorded it thus far.

Last, I would suggest that, in spite of the problems it creates for the groups involved, there is no substitute for direct representation in the legislature. Some of the groups examined, such as U.I.L. and C.G.I.L., feel compelled to be represented, because, they say, they fail for narrow political reasons to gain adequate access to the agencies of public administration. Whatever the motivation for moving in this direction, the creation of a legislative bloc definitely means that the group will have more leverage over rule-making than would otherwise be available. To be sure, leverage is maximized for groups like Coltivatori Diretti, C.I.S.L., and Catholic Action, whose legislators are members of the party that controls government. But by comparison with the *external* groups, it is immensely valuable for opposition groups as well, and frankly recognized as such by minority group leaders.

Confindustria, largely unrepresented, is desperately aware of the need to be able to compete with the unions on equal terms in this sphere. One of the Confederation's most respected leaders laments that not a single Confindustria representative sits on the labor committees of the Chamber and Senate, where a great many bills of interest to industrialists are handled in both *sede referente* and *sede deliberante*. Confindustria, he says, which is viewed as immensely powerful, is in a striking position of inferiority when its proposals emanating from the ministries can be sabotaged in committee and when it can turn to almost no one in the legislature to champion openly its point of view.[98]

I fully recognize that direct representation creates for

---

[98] *Interview,* Number 85, *op. cit.,* p. 16.

the deputies and senators involved a serious and interesting conflict of roles. In Sartori's terms, these men are particularly torn among their roles as parliamentarians, representatives, and clientele exponents. Differently stated, they must try to adjust their legislative behavior to the demands of their parties, their electorates and the interest groups they represent. If we are to judge merely from the casting of final votes, it is far from certain that group representatives are primarily oriented to the role of facilitors of the interests of clientelistic groups. But in order to fully assess their actual roles, we would have to watch these special pleaders at work in party caucuses, legislative committees, and informal contacts with Cabinet members and the bureaucracy. In any event, if we begin simply to take a nose count of the number of deputies who are more or less the direct exponents of the various groups we have examined in this chapter, we are led to question the validity of Sartori's observation that most of Italy's lawmakers are "outsiders," in the sense of being relatively ignorant of the group process.[99] Groups seem to be omnipresent at Montecitorio and Palazzo Madama. When they are not intervening there, they can usually be found in the bureaucracy, to which we now turn our attention.

[99] See pp. 107–108, above.

CHAPTER VIII · BUREAUCRATIC INTERVENTION: CLIENTELA

INTRODUCTION

AS we noted earlier, the greatest degree of acknowledged interaction between interest groups and government seems to involve the sector of public administration. This is certainly not to say that in a parliamentary system contacts between groups, on the one hand, and political parties and legislatures, on the other, are relatively insignificant. The previous chapter highlights the various patterns whereby interest groups intervene in the legislature—externally or through one of the established parties; the following chapter will demonstrate how critical may be the political party even for those groups that seek to concentrate their attention on the administrative sphere.

Given the classical model of democratic government, one might logically conclude that it ill behooves the interest group—as defined in this study—to spend any of its time in the public administrative arena. For the classical democratic model ascribes to the bureaucracy a number of attributes that derive in part from Max Weber, in part from the normative orientation of democratic philosophy. The Weberian view of a legal-rational bureaucratic system specifies the existence of specialized, highly differentiated administrative roles; recruitment on the basis of achievement (measured by examination) rather than ascription; placement, transfer, and promotion on the basis of universalistic rather than particularistic criteria; administrators who are salaried professionals and who view their work as a career; and administrative decision-making within a rational and readily understood context of *hierarchy, responsibility,* and *discipline.* According to this rosy and simplistic view, what the bureaucracy ideally does is influenced by neither traditional (family, feudal) nor transitional (charismatic) considerations; rational and enlightened man in the public administrative sector proceeds by the same laws that impel and govern him in the economic sector.

The classical view of democracy incorporates the Weberian description of rational-legal bureaucracy, makes the conceptualization normative, and buttresses it (hedges it about) with a series of additional norms. The first and most important of these norms is that the bureaucracy will be instrumental for the various political institutions of the society—the chief executives, legislatures, councils, cabinets, and assemblies. Policy-making institutions are expected to be strong enough to limit the bureaucracy to its instrumental role, even if it is conceded that a strict and thorough separation of rule-making and rule-application can never be fully achieved. The political system is assumed to have evolved a degree of structural differentiation and specialization to the point that one can associate the authoritative functions of government with *specific* and essentially *separate* concrete structures, or institutions.

Other normative assumptions can be cited.[1] Public administrators, for purposes of implementing or applying rules, are expected to interact on a free and open basis with a plurality of voluntary associations; privileged access or dominance over administrative decision-making by special interests is supposed to be avoided, and, where it exists, is to be made the subject of strong criticism and remedial action; administrators are expected to recognize the sovereignty of the electorate and to do everything possible to give operating expression to the will of the people as expressed by the legislature and other rule-making bodies; those in public administration are supposed to be free of corruption in the exercise of their functions; and,

[1] The problem I am developing only briefly here is treated in greater detail in my "Bureaucracy and Political Development: Notes, Queries and Dilemmas," in Joseph LaPalombara, ed., *Bureaucracy and Political Development* (Princeton, 1963), pp. 34–61.

finally, public administrators are required to accept and to be loyal to the political system of which they constitute an integral part. Overarching all these norms and expectations is the notion that, in its general organizational and behavioral patterns, the bureaucracy will tend to support and reinforce, rather than sabotage or undermine, the Weberian-democratic model.[2]

Even a most cursory look at any existing bureaucracy will show that systems of public administration are, at best, faint approximations of the ideal type that is outlined above. What one discovers empirically is essentially a transitional or dual [3] situation involving an admixture and juxtaposition of the particular and universal, the sacral and secular, ascription and achievement, functional diffuseness and specificity—in short, of the traditional and the modern. In such a transitional setting, the requisites of Weber's legal-rational model are only imperfectly met, even if the formal structure of the bureaucracy is close to Weberian requisites. Recruitment, placement, transfer, and promotion on the basis of merit will to some unspecified degree be limited by particularistic considerations of family, geographic region, religious or other attributes, ideological orientation, and so on. To some extent, bureaucratic roles will be assigned on the basis of ascriptive rather than achievement criteria; sacral rather than secular, irrational rather than rational considerations will underlie some administrative decisions; the degree of

[2] A bureaucracy that does conform to this model—even if it exercises certain important rule-making functions—has been called by Fritz Morstein Marx a "merit bureaucracy," as distinguished from "caste," "patronage," and "guardian" bureaucracies. See his *The Administrative State* (Chicago, 1957), Ch. 4.

[3] Fred Riggs is not happy with the concepts generally used to describe this phenomenon and has therefore suggested new terminology deriving from optics and other sources. See his "Prismatic Society and Financial Administration," *Administrative Science Quarterly*, 5 (June, 1960), pp. 1–46. Cf. his very illuminating "Agraria and Industria; Toward a Typology of Comparative Administration," in W. J. Siffin, ed., *Toward the Comparative Study of Public Administration* (Bloomington, Indiana, 1957), pp. 23–116.

professionalism, hierarchy, responsibility, and discipline registered will vary widely from one bureaucratic system to another and within various sectors of a single system.

Exactly the same obvious observations can be made for the empirical application of democratic norms concerning the bureaucracy. It seems unnecessary to stress that the dichotomy between "policy" and "administration" is empirically untenable, that voluntary associations are often not voluntary at all but governmentally created and manipulated, that interest groups rarely enjoy free and equal access to key points in the bureaucratic power structure, or that the bureaucracy is not always free from corruption and from tendencies to become an intimate part of the political struggle over public policy.

Thus one very important reason why Italian interest groups should seek to intervene in the bureaucratic sphere is that the bureaucracy definitely makes rules in a number of ways ranging from the interpretation of minute legislative and administrative regulations to the drafting of bills and lobbying for them in the legislature. It may be that the Italian bureaucracy has not evinced as much rule-making autonomy as has been suggested regarding the French counterpart under the Fourth Republic,[4] but its scope of effective power in this area is broad enough to make group intervention worth while. The high interaction that does take place, as we noted in our survey of groups, is one reason for suggesting this generalization; it is unlikely that Italian interest groups would continue to intervene in public administration as much as they do were they finding such activity largely unproductive or unrewarding.

A second and related reason for group attention to the bureaucratic sphere is that the increasing complexity of public policies and the regulations concerning them have served to give the executive-administrative branch a greater rule-making role than was true of earlier eras, in

[4] Henry W. Ehrmann, "French Bureaucracy and Organized Interests," *Administrative Science Quarterly*, 5 (March, 1961), pp. 534-36.

which the legislative "generalists" might reasonably cope intelligently with public issues. Where rules cannot be made except within a context of amassed statistical and other technical information, the administrative specialists who are presumed to be in control of the facts naturally achieve a degree of *de facto* rule-making power that is certainly not anticipated in the classical democratic model. This shift in actual decisional power is a topic of concern to many students and others who are troubled by the decreasing ability of lawmakers to control administrators which is so typical of the twentieth century.[5] It is perhaps regrettable that, as often as not, the *de facto* power of the bureaucracy is simply attacked and criticized (and the loss of effective power by the legislature lamented) with little that is practicable suggested to remedy the situation.

The growth of the positive state, carrying with it a great proliferation of welfare activities by government as well as increased intervention in the technical economic sphere is a third reason often cited to explain heavy interaction between interest groups and public administration. As Samuel Beer formulates this generalization: ". . . the structure of the welfare state and the controlled economy associates pressure groups more closely with the administration and makes pressure groups more concerned with the decisions made at the administrative level." [6] There is some merit to this observation. This shift of group attention from one sector of government to another, however, should not be thought of as strictly a recent phenomenon. It must be associated historically with the growth of delegated legislation wherein it is apparent to any alert

[5] See the excellent survey by Henry W. Ehrmann, "Les Groupes d'intérêt et la bureaucratie dans les démocraties occidentales," *Revue Française de Science Politique,* 11 (September, 1961), pp. 541–68. Ehrmann points out: "Pressed to take multiple decisions of all sorts, for which they are badly equipped, Parliament and frequently also the executive power have recourse to the bureaucrats as possessors of the knowledge necessary to obtain the desired political results" (p. 542).

[6] Samuel Beer, "Pressure Groups and Parties in Britain," *American Political Science Review,* 50 (March, 1956), p. 15.

group leader that administrators have considerable discretion over the making of policy, no matter what may be the contrary observation of the ivory-tower juridical scholars.

It should also be noted that, as the bureaucracy becomes something more than the custodian of law and order, as its activities begin to focus more and more on regulatory and developmental activities, its members feel a great need to communicate and to interact with relevant segments of the population in an orderly way. Interest groups afford a most convenient means for the bureaucracy to affect stable and profitable relationships with relevant publics. Moreover, the publics themselves, particularly when they are organized into secondary associations, offer the bureaucracy a potentially important basis of support for both the expediency and the principled or program interests of the bureaucrats themselves. It is largely for this reason that some observers correctly note the tendency on the part of bureaucrats to create their own interest-group structure when it does not already exist.[7]

All these forces, then—growth of executive power, *de facto* rule-making power in the bureaucracy, growing complexity of rule-making, the emergence of delegated legislation, the burgeoning of welfare state activity, the needs of regulatory and developmental bureaucratic agencies, and the most imperfect empirical application of the Weberian model or democratic bureaucratic norms—all help us to understand why a bureaucracy cannot be adequately understood unless we take careful account of the role of interest groups in the bureaucratic process. Summarizing what he assumes to be true of bureaucracies everywhere, an outstanding scholar tells us: "A structure of interests friendly or hostile, vague and general or compact and well defined, encloses each significant center of administrative discretion. This structure is an important determinant of the scope of possible action. As a source

---

[7] See, for example, H. Simon, D. Smithburg, and V. Thompson, *Public Administration* (New York, 1950), pp. 461–65; and H. Simon, *Administrative Behavior* (New York, 1947), Ch. 10.

of power and authority it is a competitor of the formal hierarchy." [8]

My purpose in this and the next chapter is to examine aspects of the structure of interest-group interaction with the national bureaucracy in Italy. Just as we noted regarding legislative intervention, the process whereby Italian groups relate to the bureaucracy is not open and fluid. Rather, one can detect that the situation is highly structured and somewhat rigid, and that within it one can discern certain broad types of access and influence, at least as these types are perceived and articulated by bureaucrats, group leaders, and others who have some knowledge of the administrative process. I have called the first of these types *clientela*, referring to a clientelistic relationship between groups and the bureaucracy. The second relationship is called *parentela* and implies a process of group interaction with the bureaucracy which is essentially based on political kinship. Although no group will manifest exclusively one of these types in pure, unblemished form, they are analytically separable and will be treated separately. The analysis itself should also lead to some observations and insights regarding how far Italy's bureaucracy deviates from Weberian requisites or democratic norms, or, to put it in terms of the basic conceptualization worked out earlier, how "traditional," "transitional," or "modern" this particular aspect of Italy's political system might be.

THE MEANING OF CLIENTELA

The process whereby groups exert influence over organs of the state is *structured* rather than *fluid*. It is necessary to emphasize the point, in order to avoid the perilous naïvete about the political process that tends to grow up in democratic countries—or that is held by some advocates of the democratic process. The notion of structured in-

[8] Norton Long, "Power and Administration," *Public Administration Review*, 9 (Autumn, 1949), pp. 257–58. This article is a classic, full of extraordinary insights into the complex processes of public administration.

fluence is an overriding generalization. It is meant to suggest, among other things, that the existence of the structured pattern itself will make it both easier to understand the interest group phenomenon and more difficult to manipulate or modify (or restructure) the patterns of access and influence. This is not to imply a static social mechanism; it means that formulas that aim to change the nature of group interaction with government will have to take account of the degree to which the patterns themselves have become institutionalized.

As this matter is articulated by one of our respondents, a Socialist deputy, the Italian political and social systems must be seen as inhibiting certain interest groups from gaining meaningful access to the legislature, the executive, and public administration. As an illustration of this, he asserts that left-wing groups often find it extremely arduous and sometimes impossible to make even formal appearances before ministers, representatives of the Cabinet, and public administrative officials for purposes of communicating demands or attempting to influence the direction of policy. Reflecting his own ideological bias, the respondent attributes this unequal access—this lack of freedom of opportunity—to social patterns that are essentially Fascistic in meaning and origin. The respondent's complaint is that the inequity is allowed to continue, that little is done to make the social and political systems conform more exactly to an implicit democratic model.[9]

A distinguished and scholarly member of the Italian Communist Party takes a somewhat similar view. After stressing that Catholic Action is among Italy's most powerful groups and that this is so in part because the Catholics were able to perfect and solidify their organizational apparatus during the Fascist era, he cautions against the facile generalization that the balance among interest groups can be redressed merely by improving the organizational structure, resources, and capacities of the inter-

[9] *Interview,* Number 46 (Rome and Florence, January–March, 1958), p. 2.

est groups themselves. As he sees it, there are historical-structural reasons that account for the evolution of Italian administrative methods and for the relative access of groups to the public administrative sector. One should therefore be sensitive to the ways in which the juridical structure of the state (i.e., the authoritative structures) favors certain kinds of groups that exist in the society.

Thus, proceeds this respondent, it is both unnecessary and misleading to assume either the possibility or the existence in the Western world of a bureaucracy that is instrumental for the legislature. Even in the Soviet Union it is probable that the bureaucracy responds not so much to the legislature as to the major and dominant groups and subgroups of the society. In any event, the bureaucratic system is likely to reflect the relationship among social classes in a system; it is this dependence on, say, interclass relations that suggests why there will occur built-in advantages for certain but not all groups as they try to impinge on the process of making decisions—in the bureaucracy or in other governmental spheres.

Turning concretely to the Italian case, the respondent claims that the present structured differential access and influence of groups can be clearly traced back to feudal times. The contemporary feudal power in Italy is represented by the industrialist class, and particularly by monopoly capitalism. The very groups, such as industrial associations, that claim not to be involved in political affairs are in fact deeply immersed in politics. If this participation is not as visible as one might expect, it is to some extent the result of the dominant groups having succeeded in weaving their values and desires into the very fabric of the social and political systems. The fact is that the contemporary dominant groups have succeeded in having medieval corporative values widely accepted by vast sectors of Italian society—even by those groups that ostensibly are opposed to corporativism and its attendant paternalism. Thus one would expect to find in Italy that the actual configuration and patterns of group behavior are simply manifestations of much more general and basic phenomena of the social system. It is because an intricate relationship between social structure and the political system prevails that one can assert that the present institutional arrangements favor employer groups, high finance, and monopoly capitalism. This same structure, as empirical evidence should show, tends to work to the disadvantage of the trade unions, the cooperatives, and political parties and groups whose intention it is to effect basic changes in the social structure itself. Until such essential changes are made, it is important to recognize, as viable Marxist organizations must, that under the prevailing institutional arrangement the disadvantaged groups can extract not much more than fleeting and ephemeral concessions. This will remain the case until the basic infrastructure of the society is subjected to fairly radical evolution.[10]

Our respondent feels that this bit of Marxist analysis is so obvious as to be a truism. He does not mean to state it so rigidly as to compel the judgment that the non-dominant groups are completely powerless. Were this the case, he is convinced that the Italian Republic would never have come into existence or that, by this time, it would have been rendered an empty shell. However, the fact that one can point to small victories, that one can show some representation of and response to the interests of the have-not groups, does not remove what is the respondent's, and my, first point—namely, that the process of interest articulation and aggregation are not free floating but anchored to some degree. Drift may bring some unanticipated advantage to some groups but will be no indication of a totally unrestrained system.

If the notion of structured access and influence makes good sense, it is necessary to bear in mind that by looking at the activities of secondary associations we see only one facet of the way in which interests are articulated and

[10] *Interview,* Number 23 (Bologna, March 9, 1958), pp. 3–6.

aggregated. What often pass for the basic rules of the game of politics are in fact the values that are strongly held by only a sector of the society—the sector with access. Laws of property and contract are typical manifestations of this. But so are the formal and informal institutionalized patterns of government. It is perfectly obvious, as we shall see in detail as we proceed, that those groups in Italian society which aim, as our respondent notes, at the basic transformation of the society (and, incidentally, which do not play by the rules) are to a considerable degree disadvantaged. This would be so if the advantaged groups were able to claim no more than that particular interest-group tactics tend to undermine the basic stability of the system.

What I call the *clientela* relationship between interest groups and the bureaucracy illustrates and helps us to understand the notion of structured access. Briefly put, the *clientela* relationship exists when an interest group, for whatever reasons, succeeds in becoming, in the eyes of a given administrative agency, the natural expression and representative of a given social sector which, in turn, constitutes the natural target or reference point for the activity of the administrative agency.[11] Before I turn to an examination of the variables that govern this phenomenon, it will be useful to summarize the frequency with which those interviewed allude to its existence.

A noted intellectual with close ties to the Liberal Party points out that the administrative agencies dealing with economic affairs maintain natural-logical relationships with economic and industrial groups of the country. These groups tend to provide the ministries with special studies, memoranda, a mass of data which is useful, even essential, in the making of administrative policy. A good example, cutting across several agencies, would be the

[11] An early statement of remaining portions of this and the following chapter appears in Joseph LaPalombara and Gianfranco Poggi, "I Gruppi di pressione e la burocrazia italiana," *Rassegna italiana di sociologia*, 1 (October–December, 1960), pp. 31–55.

C.I.P.—the Interministerial Committee on Prices on which several economic groups are formally represented. This Committee, which fixes prices on everything from newspapers to fuel and power, must necessarily maintain on-going contacts with the very groups that are likely to be the objects of its regulative activities. It would not be conceivable that the Committee could long operate with any effectiveness if this intimate nexus were nonexistent.[12]

A Cabinet member with a great deal of direct experience with this phenomenon emphasizes the importance of understanding that, to some extent, the power relations among groups will be rather firmly fixed in the initial selection of the political appointees who manage the various ministries. Hence various influential groups tend to concentrate much of their energies on the task of assuring that those who reach the top levels of the ministries with which they have many relationships will be sympathetic to, or will identify with, the goals of these groups. Expanding this point, he says: "Thus, one might possibly view the various branches of Italian public administration as the feudal holdings of the various major groups of the society. The administrators, in each of these feudal sectors, tend to be about as rigid in their attitudes as the groups of which they are the expression and representatives. This may also be true of the ministers themselves, and, to the extent that it is, the possibilities of the Cabinet serving to counteract this advantage are thereby and to that degree limited." [13]

This respondent cautions that his spoken views on the matter would be considered unorthodox within the Christian Democratic Party of which he is a prominent leader. He insists that it is important to the future of the country that responsible administrative and political officials be completely candid about recognizing the problem of interest-group influence within the sphere of public administration. He notes that most of the top-level directors

---

12 *Interview*, Number 54 (Rome, January 17, 1958), pp. 2–3.
13 *Interview*, Number 28 (Rome, February 8, 1958), pp. 4–5.

general, who were trained and received their basic administrative experience under Fascism, tend to be overly suspicious of anyone who seeks a close look at the administrative process. They tend to be mightily opposed to any effort to modify the nature of that process; and in the exercise of their considerable power they are frequently nothing more than the mouthpieces of the dominant organized groups in the society.

Our experience proves, however, that many of Italy's higher administrators are perfectly willing to talk about the *clientela* relationship. One such person in the Ministry of Industry and Commerce frankly admits that the Ministry views industrialists and associations that represent them as its most significant and important clientele. Because the ministry provides services for industry, regulates industrial activities and relies on information that the industries and their associations provide, it is natural that a very close system of day-to-day contacts should be maintained. Were this not the case, the work of the ministry itself would be considerably more complicated and abstract.[14]

Under probing, this respondent makes several qualifying observations. The first of these is that, given the extreme centralization of administrative authority in the Italian bureaucracy, groups seeking bureaucratic access are well advised to seek contacts with the directors-general. The fact is that attempts at administrative reform, which included decisional decentralization under the so-called Lucifredi decrees, have not been successful. This comes about, in part, because of administrative inertia, in part because of the great jealousy with which directors-general seek to guard their authority and prerogatives. The total impact is the persistence of extreme hierarchy and centralization in which the powers of the directors-general, considerable under formal allocation, are greatly magnified as a matter of actual practice. While

---

[14] *Interview,* Number 83 (Rome, May 17, 1958), pp. 4–5.

this does not mean that bureaucrats below that level are useless to clientele groups, it does suggest the place in the hierarchy where attention must be concentrated.

Second, the respondent emphasizes that the Ministry of Industry and Commerce does not limit its contacts to groups that are a part of its clientele. In his words:

"The ministry always establishes contacts with agricultural and other organizations such as the trade unions whenever the problem involved affects more than the industrial groups. That is, whenever the problem extends beyond the narrow range of Italian industry, the ministry feels an obligation to consult not only with other ministries but also with groups or associations that are not those with which there is constant liaison. . . . Various groups that are not a part of the ministry's clientele often send delegations or representatives to the ministry in order to intervene in some administrative matter. Normally, the ministry is always open to such approaches. I know of no policy within the ministry that says that there are certain groups in Italian society whose representatives will not be at least received. It is true that once this has been done we will assign different importance or give varying weight to the proposals made by such groups, but they are free to approach us. This is the essence of the administrative process, and we are unfortunately often embarrassed by alluding to it because those who ask us questions always seem to suggest that our decisions are not reached according to the juridical assumptions of the good professors of administrative law. As soon as we admit that we maintain close relations with certain associations, people quickly conclude that the associations and not the functionaries are disposing of administrative matters. Yet, this is what the public administration is all about, and I do not know of any ministry at Rome, including the Ministries of Foreign Commerce, Agriculture, and Labor and Social Security, that does not do the same thing." [15]

As we shall note below, the respondent's view that the *clientela* relationship is not a narrow and essentially exclusive one is untypical of the attitudes of his administrative colleagues and of many interest group leaders. Here,

[15] *Ibid.*, pp. 8–9.

I wish to cite the view of a highly placed Treasury official who emphasizes that there are internal motivations that impel the ministries to establish strong clientelistic relationships. Those motivations stemming from the regulatory nature of a ministry's activity have already been touched on. The Treasury respondent recognizes these drives, and, like most of his colleagues, he views such contacts as a normal part of the administrative agency's behavior. Not so normal, in his view, but equally pervasive are motivations based on the ministries' desire to use the clientele groups to further interests of expediency. According to this view, each administrative agency, in its efforts to survive and to expand in the struggle with other administrative units, will seek to develop a very close and intimate *clientela* relationship for purposes of having the group or groups apply pressure on government on the *agency's* behalf. Typical of such pressures are those applied in the *sottogoverno* on the Bureau of the Budget, with which the respondent is identified. Thus, he points out, it is not unusual for Confindustria, say, to make an approach to the Budget Bureau on behalf of the Ministry of Industry and Commerce or, more typically, on behalf of some specific directorate-general within the ministry. The same thing, to a lesser extent, is true of trade unions that intervene on behalf of some segment of the Ministry of Labor and Social Security, or the Direct Cultivators who front for the Ministry of Agriculture.[16] The point to bear in mind is that the *clientela* relationship is established and thrives because *both* sides to the relationship can and do derive certain clear-cut advantages from it.

As far as clientelistic relationships go, the one about which we have the most information involves Confindustria and the Ministry of Industry and Commerce. This information was consciously and specifically sought. Similar, if less dramatic examples could undoubtedly be dis-

---

[16] *Interview*, Number 79 (Rome, May 27, 1958), pp. 9–10.

covered in other sectors of Italian public administration.

It is widely perceived and understood both inside and outside the bureaucracy that Confindustria has for several decades maintained a clientelistic relationship to the Ministry of Industry and Commerce. One leader of the Confederation speaks of the many friends it has in the Ministry and points out that over the years the latter has come to understand how fully it is dependent on the good will and the cooperation of the Confederation. The Ministry as a matter of practice prefers to deal with it. So much is this the case that whenever a member association or an individual firm makes a direct approach to the Ministry, the latter will immediately contact Confindustria in order to assure itself that the Confederation is aware of and has no objection to what might otherwise be interpreted as an attempt to intervene in the administrative process over the head of the peak association. Confindustria's leader remarks: "From these friends we can expect a loyal attempt to keep the Confederation completely informed regarding attempts on the part of single member associations or individual plants to engage in the kind of activity with the public administration that might be damaging to the industrial sector as a whole. . . . A combination of the personal friendships we have plus the inevitable dependence of the ministry on our facilities means that, over a period of time, our relations with the Ministry have been more than cordial. We continue to maintain extremely cordial relations with these people." [17]

I wondered whether the happy situation this respondent describes reflects some specific and limited contacts within the Ministry or whether the *clientela* relationship amounts to a generalized phenomenon. The Confindustria leader is careful to note that the latter situation is true. He indicates that it is not valid to say that only one of the directors-general (a man frankly and openly identified

[17] *Interview*, Number 91 (Rome, June 28, 1958), p. 11.

with Confindustria) is a close friend of the Confederation. Rather, Confindustria is said to maintain strong and continual contacts with all the directors and inspectors-general within the Ministry. Most of these people are identified as personal friends—often of long standing—of functionaries within the Confederation and of some of Italy's leading industrialists. Because of this, at least as long as the then prevailing relationship persists, the Confederation does not feel that it has any serious problems concerning its ability to interact fruitfully with this particular branch of the national administrative system.[18]

The strong *clientela* pattern is invariably confirmed by bureaucrats in the Ministry. A leading director-general frankly sees as the central mission of the Ministry that of providing services to and otherwise aiding the Italian industrialist. This man is openly hostile to state-owned or state-managed economic enterprise; he wants the Italian economy managed and developed by the private sector, and he therefore sees his ministry, and government in general, as an instrument for facilitating private enterprise. In order to fulfill its mission, the ministry through its leading functionaries would have to maintain continuous contacts with the nation's industrial leaders and with the organizations that represent them. In the respondent's view, the basic reason for the Ministry's existence would disappear if these intimate contacts are not maintained, if the bureaucrats do not respond to industrial exigencies, if they do not turn to Confindustria for advice whenever administrative or legislative problems concerning the industrial life and economic expansion of Italy are brought into question, and if the Ministry itself "does not consist of a notable number of bureaucrats and technicians who are capable of understanding and therefore of sympathetically responding to the major needs of the Italian industrialists." [19]

It is unnecessary to cite all the administrative views that

18 *Ibid.*, pp. 16–17.
19 *Interview*, Number 38 (Rome, February 15, 1958), pp. 7–8.

confirm the privileged place that Confindustria has achieved in the Ministry of Industry and Commerce. It is interesting, however, to note that the bureaucrats in no way perceive the various interest groups as enjoying equal access to or influence on the Ministry. One such administrator flatly asserts that Confindustria is clearly and without any doubt the dominant group in the Ministry. The reason for this, according to the respondent, is that Confindustria represents the largest industries in Italy and, therefore, an enormous source of wealth. The Ministry of Industry and Commerce, because it operates in an area of prime interest to Confindustria and its members, cannot afford to ignore this fact or refuse to grant the Confederation a strong voice in ministerial affairs. As he points out: "Administrative decrees and the legislation handled by this Ministry affect more directly the firms represented in Confindustria. It is natural to expect that these organizations will have a vital interest in our activities. It is true that our actions affect other groups as well, but not as often or as intensively or directly as they do the industrialists. One would then naturally expect that between the leaders of Confindustria and the directors of the Ministry there will be a strong bond and understanding." [20]

Another administrative leader, an inspector-general in this case, flatly states that other kinds of groups, such as the trade unions, simply do not enjoy the kind of rapport with the Ministry that the industrial associations have established. In his own work, for example, he *never* has met with trade-union representatives but limits his contacts to certain individual industrial associations and, more frequently, to Confindustria.[21] Once again, the nature of this man's rationale for the pattern outlined emphasizes the *natural* tendency on the part of the Ministry's personnel to effect contacts with the agency's normal clientele. Thus, while it is acknowledged by some of the bureaucrats that other groups are able to gain

20 *Interview*, Number 8 (Rome, December 11, 1957), pp. 2–3.
21 *Interview*, Number 102 (Rome, July 3, 1958), p. 7.

access, it is also apparent that they are not received with as much sympathetic understanding or predisposition to be accommodating as is accorded the representatives of Confindustria and its member associations.

We saw above how, in the *clientela* relationship, the interest groups are sometimes used to press the interests of particular ministries or agencies in other administrative sectors (and, presumably, before the legislature as well). It must be noted that this service is often reciprocal in the sense that the Ministry may and usually does press the interests of its clientele groups in both the rule-making and rule-applying spheres of the political system. To some extent, then, the situation we are describing implies that an interest group tends to become the clientele of a single ministry and does not distribute its energies throughout the hierarchy of the public administration. This is evidently true of Confindustria, one of whose leaders points out that although the Confederation *sometimes* approaches, say, the Ministry of Labor and Social Security, this method is an exception rather than the rule. Speaking of this latter agency, he remarks: "When we go to the ministry we expect to be treated as equals. However, the ministry with which we have the best rapport is not the Ministry of Labor but the Ministry of Industry. Whenever we are trying to advance a point in the labor field, we inform the Ministry of Industry and Commerce, the Ministry of Finance, and the Presidency of the Council of Ministers." [22]

Thus, although Confindustria will interact, even on a daily basis, with several or many of the ministries and other administrative agencies, its first and basic contact is with the Ministry of Industry and Commerce, which is viewed as an advocate of the Confederation's demands. To a much more limited degree, it may be that similar advocacy, as two of our bureaucrats claim,[23] is manifested

---

[22] *Interview*, Number 85, *op. cit.*, pp. 13–14.

[23] *Interview*, Number 8, *op. cit.*, p. 4; *Interview*, Number 28, *op. cit.*, p. 2. The latter, a Cabinet minister, remarks: "It is natural that those

by the Ministry of Labor and Social Security on behalf of (some of) the trade unions. However, for historical as well as for some of the sociological reasons outlined earlier in this chapter, no other interest group in Italy appears to have been as successful as Confindustria in establishing a *clientela* relationship. This leads us to specify the *conditions* or *variables* that seem to affect whether, and to what extent, such a relationship can be established.

CLIENTELA VARIABLES

Two classes of variables are related to the *clientela* relationship, one class pertaining to the administrative agency, the other to the groups.[24] In the first of these categories we can list the following:

1. *Vertical nature of the administrative agency.* By the vertical—or functionally specialized—nature of the agency, I mean that ordinarily the private objects of the agency's action constitute a specific, even if vast, social category. Henry Ehrmann, who also uses this concept of verticality,[25] seems to apply it not merely to a "specialized public" but also to agencies that are concerned with a single if sometimes composite interest. What I consider critically important is not the specialized nature of the agency or of the groups that constitute its clientele, but rather primary interaction, even across a wide band of interests, with a composite or cohesive social category. Indeed, as one of our respondents from the controller's office points out, the highly specialized nature of the bureaucratic agency may actually serve to limit both the access and effectiveness of

within the Ministry of Labor and Social Security who are specialists regarding the problems of labor and of the trade-union movement should feel much more close to the unions than they do to Confindustria. On the other hand, the bureaucrats within the Ministry of Industry and Commerce develop much closer ties with their counterparts in Confindustria than they do with those who represent the trade unions of the country."

24 It should be understood that for some of the following variables the crucial consideration is not *objective existence* but *perceived existence* on the part of the bureaucrats.

25 Ehrmann, "French Bureaucracy," *op. cit.*, pp. 538–39.

the groups that attempt to reach it. Thus what makes an agency vertical, and susceptible of entering into a *clientela* relationship, is that most of its activity, no matter how varied in nature, is within a limited social sector—and not the fact that the agency's activity may be homogeneous. The case of the Ministry of Industry and Commerce and the business-industrial community is a prime example of what I am driving at.

2. *Regulatory activity as modal.* As one of the leaders of the Ministry of Industry and Commerce puts it, most of what the Ministry does affects the industrial firms represented by Confindustria. It is natural to expect that these firms and their representative associations will be vitally interested in what the Ministry does—in the decisions it reaches, the regulations it promulgates, the interpretations it places on legislation, the way in which it allocates public resources, etc. Or, as a top leader of Confindustria phrases it, the very nature of social legislation in Italy compels continuous contact between the Confederation and the bureaucracy. In the words of a man who once managed the whole ministry: ". . . continuous contact is maintained between branches of the Ministry and representatives of Italian industrial organizations primarily because of the enormous amount of legislation and administrative regulation which has a quite definite impact on the economic future and freedom of activity of industrial organizations in the society." [26]

In order that regulatory conditions be fulfilled, two other related conditions must obtain. First, the objects of administrative activity—the addressee category—must be receptive to the regulatory activity. If this is not the case, some regulation can probably be effected but not on the basis of a *clientela* relationship. In a very loose sense, one might call the underworld a cohesive social sector that constitutes the clientele group for a nation's police administrators. However, the clients here do not want to be

26 *Interview*, Number 28, *op. cit.*, pp. 2-3.

regulated and do what they can to make administration difficult. Widespread opposition to regulation on the part of the regulated group would certainly tend to make the implementation of regulations very costly, and sometime prohibitively so.

By receptivity, I do not mean to suggest that the end-objects of regulations are pleased to have administrative intervention. It is reasonably clear, for example, that the interest of many of Italy's industrialists is to minimize the degree of governmental-administrative interference with their freedom of action. It is equally obvious, however, that many of the demands made by industrial and other interest groups is for greater rather than less governmental intervention. Typical of this would be, to cite just two examples, demands by organized grocers for regulations that would in fact hamper the development of supermarkets, or demands by organized dentists to severely restrict the activities of dental technicians. While these examples may be trivial compared to demands having to do with tariffs, transportation regulations, and the allocation of scarce industrial resources, they suggest that legislative and administrative rules themselves emerge from the very process of the group-governmental interaction we are analyzing. Furthermore, it goes without saying that the *bureaucratic* (as opposed to the *political*) leaders of the interest groups quickly develop rather strong desires to see a great proliferation of complicated laws and administrative decrees. It is on their ability to operate within such a morass of rules that they thrive. Reflecting this very attitude, one leader of the Italian Banking Association suggests: "It is the business of this office [or group] to make the relationship between the member banks . . . and the public administrator less frustrating and complicated than it would otherwise be if a specialized organization such as our own did not exist." [27]

A second condition relating to regulatory activity is that

[27] *Interview,* Number 48, *op. cit.,* p. 5.

the administrative agency involved must be continuously and effectively informed of the real nature of the interests affected by its activity. Even under the best of circumstances, the administrative agency, which is always in need of data on which to base its decisions, will have to rely to some extent on the information provided by the groups regulated. As we shall note below, this matter takes on pathological significance in Italy because many of the administrative agencies lack their own independent data-gathering divisions and tend to become abjectly dependent on the "data" provided by the clientele groups. In any event, it is impossible to conceive of the regulatory process between administrative rule-maker and rule-applier and group client evolving very effectively except on the basis of a well-developed two-way channel of communication, with exchange of information. Where the channel does not exist, or where it becomes overloaded or unbalanced by an uneven control of informational data, regulation is not likely to be very effective and its consequences will often be precisely those that are not anticipated or desired by the rule-makers.

3. *Administration perceived as serving interests regulated.* This variable is critical and implies that in the *clientela* relationship something more is at work than merely the desire or intention to regulate. The policeman, as I have said, wants to regulate but has no wish to promote the interests of his clientele. The Ministry of Industry and Commerce, on the other hand, came into existence and continues to function today to promote the interests of the industrial class. The same thing may be said to characterize the origins and on-going activity of the Ministry of Agriculture.

On the other hand, the *clientela* relationship may not be nearly as strong between the trade unions and the Ministry of Labor and Social Security. For the Ministry confronts an ideologically and organizationally fragmented clientele. In addition, unlike the industrial ministry, the labor ministry did not come into existence with an explicit mission to protect the interests of organized labor. To some extent, then, the underlying historical rationale for creating a particular administrative agency should tell us something about the extent to which the condition I am specifying here is met. The striking thing about bureaucratic attitudes in the Ministry of Industry and Commerce is that they reflect the mission of service to a particular socio-economic group. This perception, I would suggest, is widely shared in Italian society. A somewhat different perception—involving the administration of social welfare laws and the regulation of labor conditions and activities—operates, in and out of the bureaucracy, as far as the realm of organized labor is concerned. If this is true, then it will be easier for Confindustria than for the unions to achieve a strong *clientela* relationship with the ministries to which it primarily relates.

4. *An administrative agency needs more than its own initiative to regulate.* This condition is implied in our previous discussion. If it is possible to conceive of regulation that does not require some cooperation and participation by the objects of regulation, then a form of non-clientelistic regulation can evolve. Police administration is one such example. So is the collection of taxes, although widespread evasion in Italy suggests that there is an implicit *clientela* problem here which has not been fully recognized or examined. The more typical regulatory situation will clearly be one in which cooperative interaction of considerable magnitude is required of administration and the regulated groups.

5. *An administrative agency does not have full control over information.* This condition, too, is implied above. Again if one can visualize an agency that is able to rely for its regulations exclusively on the data it is able to gather independently, then no *clientela* relationship is likely to come into existence. Ideally, there should be some balance between the control over information supply and dependence on one another that the groups and the agencies manifest. One of the great problems of

Italian public administration is that such balance is rarely found to exist in practice. As a consequence, we find essentially the same pattern of unequal group access and influence that we detected for the legislature in Chapter VII.

There are several dimensions to this problem. One of them simply involves the obvious inability of the single ministry to secure all of the information it needs in order to produce rational policies and regulations. It is this thirst for information beyond what it can find internally that sends the agency in search of groups that can assist. Thus a Cabinet member points out that there is nothing surprising about the tendency of bureaucrats in the Ministry of Industry and Commerce to turn to industrialists and industrial associations for information which the Ministry itself does not have readily at its disposal. He points out that the bureaucrats quickly learn that groups such as Confindustria employ a large number of experts who continually do research involving legislative proposals, administrative regulations, or certain general or specific problems that are germane to the activities of industrial groups. When the Ministry is confronted with any problem concerning which its internal supply of data is felt to be inadequate, it will naturally turn to the other source in the society that can furnish them.[28]

This view is echoed by another administrator who believes that in the United States public administrative agencies do not go outside for data as often as they do in Italy. He stresses that it is typical of Italy that groups do not come to the bureaucracy for information but the bureaucrats turn to the groups. It is true, in his view, that the ministries are able to obtain a certain amount of global and aggregate information from the Central Institute of Statistics, but the narrower, more minute kinds of data are generally secured from the associations with which the ministries interact.

[28] *Interview*, Number 28, *op. cit.*, p. 3.

Curiously, this respondent is uncomfortable about their interactive process in part because, after the collapse of Fascism, secondary associations were no longer accorded juridical recognition. Thus, under the Italian system of public law, the state does not formally recognize the existence of Confindustria or of most other interest groups.[29] This situation differs markedly from that which prevailed under Fascism when the secondary associations that survived dictatorship were accorded juridical recognition and were functionally integrated into the corporative state. In any event, bureaucrats such as the one we are citing are somewhat uncomfortable when they deal with *de facto* entities and would much prefer to interact with units that enjoy *de jure* status. The respondent emphasizes that, so long as the associations have no formal juridical status in public law, the bureaucrats must deal with them cautiously.[30]

A second dimension of this problem extends considerably beyond the fairly routine pattern of bureaucrats turning to groups for information that is unavailable internally. I refer to the widely held view that the Italian bureaucracy possesses extremely primitive and underdeveloped means of producing its own data. It is impossible to cite here all the bureaucrats and interest-group leaders who refer to this situation. An interest-group leader casually comments that short-handed ministries regularly turn over to his organization major problems that require solution and recommendations. He frankly acknowledges that in this sense the ministries became strongly dependent on the kind of expertise that the association recruits and willingly places at the disposal of the bureaucracy.[31] An experienced bureaucrat in the Ministry of Industry and

---

[29] There are exceptions to this. For example, a number of secondary associations are constituted or recognized by legislative decree. See, for example, Federazione Italiana Volontari della Libertà, *Statuto* (Rome, 1955); Ministero dell'Agricoltura e delle Foreste, *Ordinamento dei consorzi agrari e della Federazione Italiana dei Consorzi Agrari* (Rome, 1948).

[30] *Interview,* Number 102, *op. cit.,* p. 5.

[31] *Interview,* Number 1, *op. cit.,* p. 5.

Commerce describes his agency as woefully lacking in technicians. As a consequence, the ministry is compelled to rely for technical information on the very groups and associations it is supposed to regulate. His words are interesting:

"An association like Confindustria is rich in technicians who often present the bureaucrats with massive studies to support their own ideas regarding the action which the ministry should take. The bureaucrat then is in a very weak position if he seeks to oppose Confindustria, particularly when the latter says, 'you must do the following regarding this industrial sector or you will cause crisis, bankruptcy, and unemployment.' The fact is that there is not a single ministry that has at its disposal the number of technicians and research facilities that Confindustria has organized in this postwar period." [32]

The bureaucrat goes on to cite the frequency with which the ministry turns to Confindustria for technical information. Once this step has been taken and the data—and recommendations—submitted, the ministry is unable really to evaluate their objectivity. As a result, the decision, while formally made by the bureaucracy (or the legislature), may in fact be the decision of the industrial confederation. According to the respondent, this influence is excessive and might be markedly reduced if the ministry could rely more directly on its own research facilities.[33]

The failure of Italian public administration to provide itself with adequate data-gathering facilities is a result of both history and psychology. Historically, when the Italian State first came into existence, having inherited its formal bureaucratic structure from Piedmont, the need

[32] *Interview*, Number 8, *op. cit.*, p. 6.
[33] *Ibid.*, p. 7. This view of Confindustria and other clientele groups is strongly substantiated by high-level bureaucrats in the Ministry of the Treasury (*Interview*, Number 16, Rome, April 9–11, 1958, p. 8) and the Ministry of Finance (*Interview*, Number 17, *op. cit.*, pp. 8–9). One of Confindustria's major directors agrees that the lack of facilities in the bureaucracy is of considerable advantage to the Confederation (*Interview*, Number 91, *op. cit.*, p. 11).

for highly specialized administrators and technical administrative facilities was not as great. Field administration was largely in the hands of the omnipotent prefect, who represented the authority of Rome. He governed locally, relatively free of any serious restraints. The emphasis on administrative generalists, which the early system typified, was strongly reinforced by the educational preparation of the administrative class, which reflected almost exclusively the field of law and jurisprudence. Then, as the state began to be involved in more complex and technical fields, public administration lagged behind, in that it failed to recruit the technicians and specialists that the newer rule-making and rule-applying areas required. Such specialists as were trained by the universities were concentrated in the central and northern provinces and were quickly absorbed by industry, where the technicians were in scarce supply and attracted by greater economic rewards.

The upshot of this kind of historical evolution is that some of the secondary associations that came into existence as a result of economic and social modernization developed better technical facilities than the government itself. Although the initial reason for such development may have had nothing to do with the exercise of power over government, the development of the latter was and clearly remains at least an unanticipated consequence. If the development of a particular economic sector requires those involved to gather much data both internally and internationally, it is natural that the groups or associations that can do this should enjoy a position of considerable superiority over a public bureaucracy that cannot.

There are members of the bureaucracy who cite the need for better fact-gathering capacity as the prime target of long-neglected administrative reform. Yet the more perceptive among them point out that some of Italy's interest groups have absolutely no stake at all in encouraging such change. They much prefer a continuation of the existing pattern, whereby the lopsided control over information and the capacity to gather it are strong weapons in the hands of certain organized groups like Confindustria. Given existing circumstances, one bureaucrat concludes: "Even in the best of all possible worlds, one cannot expect an interested group to present a public administrative agency with completely objective information regarding a problem. However, because the groups enjoy this advantage, any effort to create in a particular ministry a high degree of independence of these groups is likely to involve an uphill battle." [34]

A second impediment to change here is psychological. As perceptive administrators themselves acknowledge, the typical public servant is disdainful of specialists and tends to downgrade highly technical administrative work. To a considerable degree this posture is fortified by the dominant position of Southerners in public administration. Men who emerge from a traditional-ascriptive culture, trained as "gentlemen" in the abstract field of jurisprudence, are likely to take poorly to the kind of administrative work that is considered menial and unbecoming the status of a university graduate and public servant.

The same pressures within the bureaucracy that impede administrative reform, that make decentralization decrees merely pious paper expressions, that generate scorn and hostility toward specialized divisions for organization and management, serve to make the development of research divisions arduous if not unlikely enterprises. For example, those few administrators who were subjected to the administrative training experience sponsored at the University of Bologna, with financing from the United States government and the Ford Foundation, have tragicomical experiences to report after their return to bureaucratic assignment. Many of these men, who are supposed to have a new commitment to modern administrative methods (not always the case in fact), are subjected to ridicule and harassment by their superiors and colleagues. They are

[34] *Interview,* Number 8, *loc. cit.*

often given extraheavy work loads, presented with trivial organizational problems to solve, and, having been given new titles, hidden away in some obscure sector of the ministries where they can do the least damage. Worst still, as one of the best of this "new breed" puts it, on their return from Bologna (and, perhaps, the University of California), they are treated no differently than when they return from a trip to the men's room: they are utterly ignored.

Only a strong commitment to bureaucratic reform, plus radical reorganization of the preservice training experiences available to public servants, is likely to change this situation. Thus far, so-called attempts to reform have been laughable. Decrees pointing to decisional decentralization have simply not been implemented. When asked about this, administrators reply in part that status-conscious directors-general, nurtured under Fascist authoritarianism, are unwilling to delegate responsibility. On the other hand, there is also hesitancy through the hierarchy to accept greater responsibility. Insecure and inadequately trained bureaucrats who view their positions as sinecures strongly prefer to have final responsibility for action rest at the pyramidal apex. Given their particular brand of psychology, it is no wonder that for most administrators there is nothing objectionable about having to depend on clientele groups for the technical and other information on which decisions will be based. Thus deeply institutionalized social and psychological factors serve to perpetuate a structure of privileged access and unbalanced control over administrative decisions.

The picture I am painting is admittedly stark. On closer examination a number of things are fairly obvious, and they are carefully summarized by a leading inspector-general in the Ministry of Industry and Commerce.[35] First, it is important to recognize that few groups are as technically well equipped as in Confindustria. Many second-

---

[35] *Interview*, Number 83, *op. cit.*, pp. 13–15.

ary associations manifest the same disdainful attitudes toward research and fact-gathering as do the bureaucrats themselves. Where this happens, our respondent asserts that it is the groups that approach the ministries for data and not vice versa.[36] Secondly, it is emphasized that administrators are perfectly aware that group studies are rarely objective and generally represent an aspect of special pleading. While the recognition of this fact does not in itself solve the information problem, it does alert the administrator to the need for using such studies cautiously and for seeking other data elsewhere. Moreover, because he is not narrowly involved in the pursuit of a limited interest, the administrator's view and disposition of a problem will reflect the broader picture. This wider vista, it is claimed, will somehow temper any single group's ability to dictate bureaucratic decisions. Lastly, the typical administrative agency does have some data sources that are not group-dominated, to which it can repair. The Central Institute of Statistics, which gathers a wide variety of statistical information, is one of these. Additionally, a ministry that wishes to can turn to other branches of the bureaucracy for information, even where there do not exist easily accessible intrabureaucratic channels for such exchange. It might be added that, even where a ministry retains a close working relationship with a single group, that group's opponents, on major issues of policy, will literally compel the bureaucracy to receive its data and studies as well.

In short, there are some bureaucrats who recoil from the inference that they are helpless slaves at the mercy of interest-group taskmasters. This view would be more reassuring were it not for the fact that the same inspector-general, later in the interview, makes three observations. He says, first of all, that when the groups communicate qualitative as well as statistical information, there is a

---

[36] Nevertheless, it is noteworthy how many of the groups included in our surveys *do* contain research divisions and how often group leaders indicate that they furnish technical data to the ministries and other agencies.

strong predisposition on the part of the ministry to accept those views that are articulated by the groups with which a *clientela* relationship is maintained. Group leaders and the bureaucrats in these situations simply think alike. In the second place, top-level bureaucrats in the ministry are almost always opposed to reforms that would improve data-gathering services. Thus, within the Ministry of Industry and Commerce, most directors-general are opposed to an effort to create an Industrial Inspectorate that would make unnecessary any reliance on those who are regulated in order to obtain reports concerning the implementation of administrative regulations. Finally, almost by way of a bitter afterthought, when the formal interview had been concluded, the respondent remarked, "Every time we need a single datum, we have to turn to Confindustria or the other professional associations. We are completely dependent on them and literally at their mercy." [37]

To return to the point made at the beginning of this section, a *clientela* relationship is not possible if the administrative agency has complete control over the information it needs. The Italian milieu, on this dimension, not only encourages *clientela* but manifests a degree of information imbalance which suggests that certain clientele groups, other factors being equal, can in fact become the very centers of administrative decisions—or, differently put, that the regulated succeed in establishing the terms of regulation itself. The consequences are too many to elaborate; the one that suggests itself within our frame of reference is extremely inadequate boundary maintenance between the polity and the society. Our model of a bureaucracy as essentially a rule-applying structure is considerably marred by the facts that (1) bureaucracy *makes* rules, as against the legislature, and (2) bureaucratic rules are frequently the direct, unaggregated expression of narrow, organized interest. If this is the case, one can under-

---

[37] *Interview,* Number 83, *op. cit.,* pp. 16–17.

stand why some of Italy's interest groups feel that they are kept completely at the periphery or outside of the political system itself.

6. *The administrative-group relationship must be reciprocal.* This final administrative condition for a *clientela* relationship is clearly implied from what has been said above. Basically, the flow of communication must be in two directions. The administrative agency must find it necessary and useful to receive signals from its clientele; the latter must derive certain satisfactions from signals transmitted from the bureaucracy. We have considerable evidence that this mutuality is implicitly or explicitly understood by bureaucrats and group leaders. When a bureaucrat speaks of not wanting to be too far removed from the realities of society, or a group leader emphasizes that the group's membership must be kept continuously informed of legislative and administrative decrees affecting the organized category, the two-way relationship I am specifying is clearly implied. As we shall note subsequently, there are times when this need is so strongly felt that certain interest groups are accorded formal representation on some advisory and consultative administrative bodies. For our present purposes, it is sufficient merely to note the importance of mutuality in the *clientela* relationship.

To review what has been said, we have noted several variables—pertaining primarily to the administrative agency—which must be present in some degree before a *clientela* relationship is viable. These include a *technical* need for information; a *political* need to domesticate to some extent the object of administrative regulation; a *value orientation* implying that the administrative agency exists in part to help or assist the objects regulated; some *structural deficiencies* in the administrative agency that make it impossible or unlikely that it can secure information on its own initiative and from its own resources; and, finally, the *sociopsychological* need of maintaining an orderly and reasonably predictive relationship between the agency and the groups affected by its actions.

The last need implies that the clientele groups must also satisfy certain conditions. What is the nature of these variable conditions?

1. *Representativeness of the group.* There is some evidence in our interviews that public administrators prefer to deal with group clients that are reasonably representative of the category organized. This tendency is easy enough to understand, given the general mission of many administrative agencies, which is that of both making and applying rules that affect important segments of the society. Thus one director-general in the Ministry of Industry and Commerce says that Confindustria is not a syndical organization representing the interests of a majority of its members, but a tightly controlled unit which, in effect, is a political operation in the hands of a few businessmen." [38]

Even if this is interpreted as a tongue-in-cheek remark, it implies that the matter of representativeness is seen as important. Within Confindustria itself, both historically and at present, a great deal of attention is paid to the necessity of presenting the Confederation to the public and to government as the group that encompasses the interests of Italian industry. Thus some of Confindustria's leaders lament the tendency on the part of single giant firms like Fiat to intervene directly in the political process; other confederal leaders go to great pains to stress that the Italian Confederation of Small Industries (Confapi) is a minuscule organization recruiting only the insignificant fringe of industrial firms; a major leader of the Confederation strongly spells out "the continuous need to remind the industrialists of the common denominator and a need for presenting a united front toward labor and other groups in Italian society through the agency of the Confederation." [39]

[38] *Interview,* Number 38, *op. cit.,* p. 4.
[39] *Interview,* Number 85, *op. cit.,* pp. 7–8.

The drive toward representativeness is felt, then, by both bureaucrats and group leaders. One way to understand its meaning is to consider a group's ratio of effective to potential membership. As Robert Merton points out, "The relative standing of a group in the community, for example, may be affected (though not necessarily in linear fashion) by the extent to which it approaches completeness, as distinct from its relative or absolute size." [40] In many instances, of course, potential size is extremely difficult to define. The Society of Italian Surgeons, with just over 1,300 members, probably recruits a fair proportion of the practicing surgeons in the country, and on some matters will enjoy considerable prestige by reason of this fact. Confindustria, with a membership that exceeds 80,000 firms, might be said not to recruit a high proportion of Italy's estimated 680,000 firms, but the picture changes considerably if the potential membership is limited to industrial enterprises that employ twenty or more persons. Within this latter category, the Confederation may be viewed as including the overwhelming number of potential members and is generally accorded deferential recognition by bureaucrats partially for this reason. When we turn to the trade unions, on the other hand, it is apparent that all of the confederations taken together encompass as members a relatively small proportion of a labor force that exceeds twenty million persons. While the proportion is obviously higher when industrial workers in plants of, say, one hundred or more employees are considered, neither the fragmented nature of trade-union organization nor the proportional decline in membership in recent years has gone unnoticed in the society and, presumably, within the bureaucracy.

When thinking about the matter of representativeness, it is necessary to consider absolute and relative size, as

[40] For some illuminating general remarks on this subject, see Robert K. Merton, "Continuities in the Theory of Reference Groups and Social Structure," in his *Social Theory and Social Structure* (rev. ed., Glencoe, Illinois, 1957), pp. 310–26. The passage quoted is at page 314.

well as the effective-to-potential membership ratio. Thus, even if the ratio is low, neither the society nor the bureaucracy can afford to ignore interest groups that recruit several million members. Catholic Action clearly contains a small proportion of all Catholics, but its phalanx of over four million members cannot but be impressive simply because of its numbers. The same thing is true of such other mass organizations as the Italian Union of Women and the Italian Female Center. In terms of absolute numbers, even the larger trade-union confederation will have an impact.

However, in terms of bureaucratic-group relationships, the relative size of the group must also be considered. In the first place, if there are several groups operating in the same field (e.g., veterans associations, trade unions, women's associations), the bureaucrat, as well as other group leaders, will wonder immediately just how representative is a given group of a particular category (i.e., what is its relative size). Where a group that seeks to effect a strong *clientela* relationship is confronted by the competition of another group, a challenge to its representative character is definitely implied. For example, a leader of Confapi strongly urges that Confindustria represents primarily the large industrial enterprises and that the small firms either are not members of the latter confederation or are badly represented. This man says: "The small industries within Confindustria are dominated by the industrial giants. How can small industries there possibly seek decent electric power rates when the electric monopolies control the Confederation. . . . Confindustria does not accord the small industries the same treatment it gives Falck, Edison, Fiat, and Montecatini. . . . We are thus greatly disturbed that Confindustria succeeds in keeping Confapi off all administrative committees, including the National Economic and Labor Council, despite the fact that we include 15,000 small and medium industries in the country. Confindustria even refuses to enter into the negotiation of agreements if we are present." [41]

This respondent goes on to assert that at least one-half of the small industries in Italy are unorganized and that, of those which are, Confindustria and Confapi recruit them in essentially equal numbers. For this reason, he resents Confindustria's reporting of membership data as if it enjoyed the exclusive representation of this particular category. He adds that he can understand Confindustria's hostility in view of Confapi's demands for credit and fiscal reforms, and the extension of social legislation, all of which are designed to injure financially the larger industrial enterprises.

When asked about Confapi, one of Confindustria's leaders tries to write it off as a laughable organization that recruits very few members, that denies the commonality of interest of the industrial class, and that injures collective bargaining by insisting that small industries need not adhere to contracts entered into between Confindustria and the trade unions. Because of the latter tendency, Confindustria favors the *erga omnes* type of contract which, through the legal sanction of the state, would make labor contracts binding on every unit in the category, regardless of whether they are members of the contracting associations. In the respondent's view, Confapi will disappear from the scene as soon as the *erga omnes* legislation is enacted. In the meantime, Confindustria plays down the significance of Confapi. According to the respondent, the small industry confederation "does not include more than three or four thousand plants. These are the extremists and malcontents; they are likely to be individuals in the industrial world who genuinely hate Confindustria." [42]

It is apparent that neither the bureaucrats nor the competing interest groups in the industrial and trade-union sphere accord Confapi serious attention. In the words of

[41] *Interview*, Number 104, *op. cit.*, pp. 2-3.
[42] *Interview*, Number 91, *op. cit.*, pp. 14-15.

the Confapi leader himself: "We really encounter almost insuperable difficulties in the various ministries. Confindustria exercises full control over the Ministry of Industry and Commerce. Even those functionaries who wish to help my organization or small industry in Italy are afraid to do so because of the reprisal activities in which Confindustria (and even the trade unions) can engage. One director-general was actually removed from his job because he sided with Confapi. As a result, the bureaucrats are unwilling to deal even at arm's length with my association." [43]

A second and final point to make regarding this variable is that the presence of many groups of relatively equal size will greatly hinder the establishment of a single *clientela* relationship. Groups that are equally powerful in numbers clamor equally for access to the bureaucracy. If access, for whatever reason, is accorded to only one group, the unrepresented groups are strongly critical and the bureaucrats themselves are uncomfortable in the relationship. For many reasons, not the least important of which are the previous variables enumerated, the bureaucrats would prefer to interact with a single association with a high effective-to-potential membership ratio. One obvious reason for the powerful *clientela* relationship that Confindustria has maintained with the Ministry of Industry and Commerce is the near perfect satisfaction of this desideratum.

2. *Respectability of the group.* The lack of perceived representativeness of an interest group is not the only reason why a *clientela* relationship might be impeded. Another very important influence is exerted by what, for want of a better term, I call the group's respectability. There is both a negative and positive aspect to this concept. Negatively, the group's total configuration must be such as not to embarrass the administrative agency with which it wishes to establish a *clientela* relationship. Positively, contacts with the group must in some sense be

[43] *Interview*, Number 104, *op. cit.*, p. 6.

rewarding for the agency or, more precisely, for the agency's functionaries. Thus, if for any of a number of reasons (e.g., its style, tactics, the nature of its leadership, its ideological coloration) a group is seen by the bureaucrats as not being respectable, it is for that reason partially or wholly disqualified from establishing a strong pattern of interaction with the bureaucracy.

Evidence that this variable is important can be discerned from the interview responses of both bureaucrats and group leaders. In the Ministry of Industry and Commerce, one highly placed inspector-general frankly admits that "public administrators make an effort to assess the ideological character of groups." Once this is done, two conclusions, which may or may not be similar, help to dictate the bureaucrat's response. First, the group is considerably advantaged if it is identified ideologically with the political dominant party.[44] This advantage may have absolutely nothing to do with the bureaucrat's ideology but be a function of administrative expediency or opportunism. Second, there are also advantages that accrue when there is detected an ideological communion between the bureaucrats and the group leaders. One bureaucrat whom we have already cited in this chapter frankly admits that his ministry lends greater weight to the views of its clientele groups than to the others. He goes on to specify that weight will vary with the *political* nature of the groups, the importance they seem to have in Italian society, and the influence they appear to exert on government in general.[45]

In the Ministry of the Treasury we find a similar articulation of this phenomenon. Thus an administrator expects that any one of his colleagues who is closely attached to the Christian Democratic Party or to a Catholic organization would naturally tend to favor those groups identified with the party or the Catholic world. As an

---

[44] This phenomenon refers to the *parentela* relationship, which is analyzed in Chapter IX.

[45] *Interview*, Number 83, *op. cit.*, pp. 8, 12.

example of this, he suggests that administrators within the Ministry of Labor and Social Security are much more inclined to see the "reasonableness" in the arguments of a Catholic-oriented trade union than they are to appreciate the "rationality" or the "reasonableness" of demands of a Communist-oriented or Socialist-oriented union. There is nothing particularly vicious about such tendencies; they must be viewed as the way public administration is likely to function anywhere.[46]

Although this phenomenon is probably universal, it seems to me that it operates much more intensively in a society of great and deep ideological fragmentation. In such a setting, ideological differentiation is much more clear-cut and severe. In addition, when one is disposed to wonder about a particular group's ideological credentials, identification is specific; it is associated with a complete aggregation of interest groups, political parties, parliamentary groups, public spokesmen, programs of public policy, and demands on the authoritative structures of government. Roughly comparable voluntary associations in the United States might be the Ku Klux Klan, the John Birch Society, the N.A.A.C.P., or the C.I.O. However, such groups, even though individually discernable as organizations, tend to be seen against a less stark background of an interclassist political party system that serves to integrate or at least to dampen demands. This is simply not the case in Italy for most of the major voluntary associations.

Needless to say, the Italian groups that fail to achieve respectability in the eyes of the bureaucrats bitterly complain about it. One of the Italian Union of Labor's more articulate leaders expatiates at great length on how both his organization and C.G.I.L. are grossly underrepresented on the National Economic and Labor Council because C.I.S.L., as an ideologically more acceptable union, is given many more seats than its relative membership strength would warrant. As far as public administration

[46] *Interview*, Number 3 (Rome, November 28, 1957), pp. 4–5.

in general is concerned, the bureaucrats, from the minister on down, are said to favor C.I.S.L. Cooperation involves a high degree of collusion, which makes it appear that C.I.S.L. demands are accepted when in fact the Christian Democratic labor confederation has been alerted to demand no more than the bureaucracy and the government are prepared to concede. Even in those instances where the bureaucracy, essentially, accedes to demands made by U.I.L., it is deliberately made to appear that the demands were C.I.S.L.'s, which lends respectability to the demands and unearned prestige to C.I.S.L. The respondent concludes for all of this that his organization is completely impotent in the realm of public administration, not only in ministries selected at random but also and particularly in the Ministry of Labor and Social Security, where the unions might be presumed to exercise considerable influence vis-à-vis other associations in the society.[47]

The same refrain is voiced by a C.G.I.L. leader: "We are systematically discriminated against in all of those public administrative bodies on which the trade unions are supposed to have some representation. This includes the National Economic and Labor Council, where, notwithstanding that we are larger than C.I.S.L., we were initially accorded a smaller representation on the Council than they. And, even after we conducted a very big battle, we were simply given equal representation to that of C.I.S.L." [48]

This leader goes on to specify other administrative bodies on which his organization finds it impossible to break the domination or monopoly of representation held by C.I.S.L. By and large, the bureaucrats are not favorably disposed to C.G.I.L.; even where some representation is achieved, the Confederation is described as never attaining the dominant or controlling voice. Because of this inability to gain access to the bureaucracy, the Con-

---

[47] *Interview*, Number 30, *op. cit.*, pp. 6–7.
[48] *Interview*, Number 94, *op. cit.*, p. 9.

federation has been compelled to focus greater attention on the legislature (and on direct representation there) than might be the case if the bureaucratic milieu were less hostile.

The tendency of administrators to respond more readily to the *respectable* interest groups is also recognized by lawmakers. One of the latter notes that, at the upper levels, bureaucrats are likely to be pliable by the political party in power. This has a direct consequence for the relative ability of associations to make their needs felt in the bureaucracy.[49] Another deputy notes that, under the present distribution of political power in Italy, left-wing groups often find it impossible to make appearances before ministers, Cabinet members, and public administrative officials for purposes of trying to determine the direction that policy might take.[50] The unstated but often implied conclusion is simply that, in the context of the Italian political system, some groups are grossly unrepresented in bureaucratic interaction, which in part illustrates why the group leaders say that they are kept "outside the game."

A last point concerning the variable of respectability is that the bureaucrats should find a *clientela* relationship rewarding. This would require, among other things, that the interest group possess its own basis of wealth and prestige—that is, that it not be directly dependent on the bureaucracy itself for its existence. Thus, in this formulation, Italy's school teachers' associations are not in a *clientela* relationship with the Ministry of Public Instruction, because the teachers cannot *step back;* they are in fact dependent on the Ministry, which is actually their employer. The claim of teachers to a special relationship to the Ministry of Public Instruction is not based on, say, a bargaining relationship between two independent entities but on the fact that the teachers are organically tied to the ministry. Thus, while the teachers can and certainly

49 *Interview,* Number 49 (Rome, January 15, 1958), p. 5.
50 *Interview,* Number 54, *op. cit.,* p. 6.

do operate as an interest group in Italian society, their organizational configuration is more that of an institutional than an associational type.

When bureaucrats speak of genuine *clientela* groups, they almost always refer to both independence of the bureaucracy and sources of wealth and power. Thus Confindustria is viewed as representing the vast sector of industry which is also an enormous source of wealth. The Coltivatori Diretti is identified as a massive organization whose economic base and impressive electoral prowess are said to account for the respectable attention it is able to command. Another bureaucrat, as we noted above, alerts us to the tendency of bureaucrats to assess the *weight* which an interest group has in Italian society.

What about the rewards that groups can provide for the bureaucrats? We have dealt at some length with a critical one, namely the ability of certain groups to provide data and information on the basis of which administrative decisions can be facilitated and rationalized. Although public administrators who condone the information-dependence pattern do not speak of rewards as such, it is apparent that clientele groups that are able to turn out the technical memoranda and studies are greatly appreciated. Indeed, such groups—and Confindustria is a prime example of these—win the grudging respect even of those administrators who might wish to see the bureaucracy freed of too much reliance on the groups for data.

Other examples of rewards might be cited. It is evidently satisfying, for example, for administrators to be able to interact with group leaders who are publicly recognized specialists in a particular field. The experts that can be mustered by the Italian Banking Association, the National Association of Automotive Industries, or the Association of Italian Joint Stock Companies enjoy considerable prestige in the bureaucracy. As another example, the bureaucrats themselves have their status needs satisfied when they are invited to participate as experts in the conferences and conventions organized by the interest groups. These conferences—including the speeches and observations of bureaucrats—are reported at least in the interest-group publications and often in the national press. It would be the extraordinary bureaucrat who failed to derive psychological gratification from such activities, particularly if the group involved met the other criteria of representativeness and respectability. Lesser kinds of rewards might be invitations (with pay) to certain bureaucrats to contribute articles to the journals published by the interest groups. In short, motivations based on an anticipated *quid pro quo* are not wanting.

For many in Italy who are critical of the bureaucracy, the crucially important rewards are said to be the corrupt and illegal ones—graft or, as the Italians quaintly put it, the *bustarella* (little envelope). Needless to say, there is no way of demonstrating how much of this kind of thing actually takes place in the Italian bureaucracy. As far as some of the upper-level bureaucrats are concerned, there is undoubtedly a certain amount of "legal graft," as when they are assigned to serve as directors of state-owned industries. Such assignments usually enable a public administrator to add substantially to his basic income. Insofar as some of the interest groups can influence this form of what is essentially political patronage, we might say that they are able to reward bureaucratic friends and advocates in an extraordinary and basically fruitful way. However, achieving this kind of influence over bureaucratic appointments will almost certainly involve a pattern that is more closely involved in the *parentela* relationship, which I take up in the following chapter.

As far as the actual transfer of money for favors is concerned, it is referred to by only two of our respondents, and neither is able to produce any concrete evidence to sustain the charge. On the other hand, there are many more respondents who caution that claims of the extent of this kind of corrupt practice are generally irresponsibly made and enormously exaggerated. Among these latter are included not merely the bureaucrats, who might be viewed as defensively cautious, but also a Communist senator, a Liberal scholar, a Republican deputy, and a leading industrialist. That some specific instances of corruption might be detected is conceded; that the scope of such activity is sufficiently widespread to warrant its inclusion as an important kind of reward leading to respectability and *clientela* is too hazardous a conclusion to detain us here.

3. *Functionality of the group*. This variable simply means that the interest group in question is actually capable of behaving as an effective instrument of contact between its membership and the bureaucracy. To the extent that a group is not respectable it will also not be functional, but for reasons that have nothing to do with its internal organizational characteristics. What I intend to suggest here is that a group may be well or badly equipped organizationally to act as an efficient intermediate agency between individual members and bureaucrats, both of whom have needs that must be satisfied. Thus a leader of the Italian Banking Association divulges that most of its interaction with the bureaucracy grows out of requests to the association that emanate from its membership. He sees his organization as vitally involved in making the interrelationship as smooth as possible. Similarly, a large number of group leaders emphasize the importance of their research divisions and activities, whereby the demands of members are in fact transmitted to the bureaucracy in a rational, systematic way.

One observer, commenting on the strong *clientela* relationship that the A.C.L.I. has established with various sectors of the bureaucracy, says: "A.C.L.I. has some topnotch economists on its research staff. The fact that they are adequately prepared in this area gives them an opportunity to deal realistically and effectively with Confindustria." [50]

Presumably the same characteristics that equip a group to deal effectively with a formidable organization like

Confindustria will serve it well in dealings with the bureaucracy. It is apparent, too, that bureaucrats tend to downgrade groups that are not well endowed in this regard and that tend to become abjectly dependent on the bureaucracy. Where, as one man asserts, the data provided by groups are actually faked—unabashedly false—the group's utility to both the bureaucracy and its own membership is considerably undermined. In other words, there appear to be both organizational and leadership characteristics of the interest groups that are important determinants of their functionality as far as the *clientela* relationship is concerned. Relating this variable to a previous one, we can say that functionality generally matches the administrative agency's need for information.

4. *Authoritativeness of the group.* This variable or condition complements the need of the administrative agency to have compliance with its regulations somehow guaranteed. There is no doubting the great interest of the bureaucrats in this particular group characteristic. Some of them, in referring to it, do so with nostalgia, rather clearly revealing a preference for the kinds of corporative bureaucracy—secondary association relationship that existed under Fascism.

For a peak association like Confindustria, the matter of maintaining its authoritativeness is a critical need as well as a perplexing problem. Basically, the Confederation is confronted by a tendency on the part of some of its largest members to intervene directly in the political process—outside the framework provided by Confindustria. On occasion such intervention may imply a break in industry's united front, causing considerable consternation among the confederation's bureaucratic leaders. As one industrialist spells this out, giant firms like Fiat and Montecatini tend to use Confindustria only when it suits their interest and convenience to do so. When it does not, they incline to direct intervention. For the particular firms named, as well as others, the tendency to break ranks is also frequently dictated by the fact that the confederation is usually in the hands of the more conservative—even reactionary—of Italy's industrial enterprises.

A director-general in the Ministry of Industry and Commerce tellingly laments Confindustria's lack of complete authoritativeness. He suggests that Italy's medium and smaller industrialists have not yet learned the necessity of being more political than they are. According to him, "They sit back and deal strictly with business affairs while the monopolists, both public and private, are permitted to own deputies, newspapers, and other means of consolidating their position in Italian society. The medium-size industries could exert more influence inside Confindustria than they presently do, but they are not sufficiently well organized. Confindustria is thus not really a syndical organization representing the interests of a majority of its members." [51]

Another of Italy's bureaucrats, an official of the I.R.I. (Institute for Industrial Reconstruction), stresses that although colleagues in the Ministry of Industry and Commerce might well be viewed as the mouthpieces of Confindustria, they are not necessarily tied to the ideologies or the tactics of the country's largest industries. He points out that, because their activities often threaten the authoritativeness with which the Confederation can approach the bureaucracy and the legislature, enterprises such as Fiat and Montecatini are considered to be the black sheep within Confindustria. Whenever these firms find the Confederation pressing a particular line that they will not or cannot support, they do exactly as they please, blatantly ignoring the responsibilities and obligations of organizational membership. In his words, "Large industries can and do get along without the support of Confindustria because they have been able to establish their

---

[51] *Interview*, Number 38, *op. cit.*, p. 4. The reluctance of Italy's industrialists to be more openly political is examined in detail in Chapter XI, below. See also Joseph LaPalombara, "La Confindustria e la politica in Italia," *Tempi Moderni*, 4 (October, 1961), pp. 3–16.

own direct relations with governments and because, in many instances, the trade associations within Confindustria are much more important pressure groups than Confindustria itself." [52]

This tendency is supported by a leader of the Industrial Union of Lazio (Rome) who takes the view that, although it is vital for Confindustria to maintain a united front, it is not always possible to achieve this goal in practice. He remarks: "In actuality, this united front is not maintained. The few large industries that exist in Italy have extraordinary prestige and are all national in nature. It is natural that these industries should feel that they have the right to deal directly with the ministries, rather than always channeling their activities through the local industrial unions or the national confederation." [53]

According to this regional Confindustria leader, the confederation expects a certain amount of such direct interaction. Furthermore, he says that firms employing such tactics often inform Confindustria in advance of the steps they are about to take in administrative agencies and generally wait until they learn what the Confederation's official position may be before taking action. At the very least, the firms generally keep Confindustria completely informed concerning their bureaucratic interventions. Equally important is the certainty that, when individual industries seek to lend greater prestige and authority to their demands, they will seek to operate not outside their industrial organizations but through them. In any event, the respondent cautions against the judgment either that Confindustria is putty in the hands of the giant firms or that these firms casually violate the policy directives that emanate from regional industrial unions or from Confindustria itself. [54]

The matter of the prestige of the Confederation is not lightly to be discounted. Confindustria leaders argue that

---

[52] *Interview*, Number 89 (Rome, May 27, 1958), p. 6.
[53] *Interview*, Number 98 (Rome, June 28, 1958), p. 2
[54] *Ibid.*, p. 3.

this factor is so important with the bureaucracy that, in general, the latter will avoid taking decisions simply on the strength of a demand by a single firm or by a single trade association. Reflecting exactly this point of view, an inspector-general in the Ministry of Industry and Commerce stresses that the bureaucracy sees Confindustria as an instrument for mediating the conflicting demands of its member associations. In the interaction between organized industry and the bureaucracy, the fact that the national Confederation presents a united front means that certain problems of internal conflict have already been resolved. So important is this posture of authoritativeness on the part of the clientele group that the bureaucrats will go some distance to support and reinforce it. Thus, says the respondent: "Whenever a single association seeks to gain a particular concession or to influence a particular policy, the functionaries with whom association representatives are in contact will almost immediately get on the telephone and call someone in Confindustria in order to hear the opinion of the Confederation. . . . Thus, in addition to the temporizing influence generated by different inspectorates-general of the ministry, the Confindustria greatly helps in the resolution of many problems." [55]

Other group leaders stress that a major function of peak associations is that of bringing some policy order out of the confusion and chaos that would emerge if each member unit were to approach agencies of government entirely on its own initiative. It is apparent, for example, that the national organs of labor confederations such as C.I.S.L., C.G.I.L., and U.I.L. pay considerable attention to the need for keeping the individual category federations in tune with overriding national organizational policies that cut across more particularistic interests.

[55] *Interview,* Number 87 (Rome, May 26, 1958), p. 9. The same point concerning the bureaucracy's tendency to reinforce the Confederation's authoritativeness is made by one of Confindustria's leaders whose special concern is the small and medium industrial sector. *Interview,* Number 91, *op. cit.,* p. 11.

Whereas the national confederations are supposed to provide technical and other assistance to member units as they make demands on government, great energies are expended on the business of guaranteeing that single organizational interests do not seriously conflict with or contradict the national policy line. When member units seriously deviate, the acts of indiscipline—or "sectarianism" or "egoism"—are certain to meet with internal reprimands and may be publicly exposed at annual congresses of the peak confederations. To put this within the frame of reference of the trade unions, we might simply observe that there is considerable pressure on the economically privileged workers of Turin to exercise self-restraint in favor of the collectivity, or not to articulate demands that would dramatically increase the differences in pay, status, and other perquisites of the high- and low-skilled labor categories.

But although each labor confederation certainly engages in some aggregation of internal interest similar to that engaged in by Confindustria, it is fairly clear that each single confederation falls short of achieving the degree of authoritativeness that characterizes Confindustria. With the relatively unimportant exception of Confapi, Confindustria does confront the bureaucracy monolithically. Even when one can point to instances of individual firm or associational intervention in the bureaucratic process, it is reasonably apparent that Confindustria, particularly on the major issues, speaks authoritatively for the private sector of industrial enterprise. The same is not true of C.I.S.L., C.G.I.L., and U I.L., each of which clearly represents and communicates the ideological fragmentation of the labor movement. Were one of these confederations to recruit a substantial majority of Italy's organized workers, its authoritativeness would be greatly enhanced. The fact that this is not the case—and, indeed, that C.I.S.L., which is smaller than C.G.I.L., is close to the party in power—creates considerable confusion and discomfiture in bureaucratic circles.

A working *clientela* relationship between bureaucracy and organized labor is clearly impeded because the condition or variable we have been discussing here is imperfectly realized.

5. *Proximity of the group.* The last organizational variable affecting the *clientela* relationship I call "proximity." This means that, in order to function well as a clientele, the group involved must be physically close to the locus of administrative decision-making, and will to some extent articulate its organizational structure to facilitate interaction with the bureaucracy, or administrative agencies with which the *clientela* relationship is maintained. Thus, in explaining why the North-centered automotive association maintains an office at Rome, a leader of A.N.F.I.I.A. frankly asserts that "the office is primarily a public relations endeavor, aimed at having the various initiatives of the association in matters of tariffs, legislation, and administrative regulation reach the attention of the public powers." [56] It is also relevant in this connection that Confindustria maintains its headquarters at Rome, industrially a rather underdeveloped area, and has about 350 employees there, while in Milan, the country's industrial nerve center, there is only a regional office with approximately twenty employees. Bureaucrats themselves remark that the presence of the confederation at Rome makes it much easier for the bureaucracy to deal with organized industry The same factor presumably holds for the many other interest groups that have established either headquarters or important branch offices in the nation's political capital.

Equally important to the concept of proximity is the discernible tendency of interest groups to develop counterpart positions, specialists or divisions that correspond to the administrative subdivisions of ministries with which they are in close and continual contact. In the case

[56] *Interview,* Number 1, *op. cit.,* p. 2.

of the National Association of Building Constructors (A.N.C.E.) an official remarks that a basic reorganization of his Association came about as a result of a specific request on the part of the Ministry of Industry and Commerce. Evidently, the Ministry felt that over a period of time it could work much more efficiently and effectively with the Association if it were articulated into the kinds of administrative subdivision that corresponded to some of the branches of the ministry itself.[57]

I do not imply here that the organizational format of clientele groups will invariably be dictated by the bureaucracy. But some pressure, implicit or overt, does exist in this direction. It is perfectly apparent that both group leaders and bureaucrats involved in a *clientela* relationship tend to search out those arrangements and patterns that will facilitate the evolution and maintenance of the relationship itself. Whether by organizational structure or the designation of specific individuals and titles, clientele groups try hard to establish within their midst counterparts to the significant bureaucrats with whom interactions are maintained. Thus, as we noted in previous pages, the Italian Banking Association seems to have worked out a careful set of hierarchical relationships whereby the group's top leaders deal with Cabinet ministers, functionaries lower down the hierarchy relate to top-level bureaucrats, lesser group leaders with lesser bureaucrats, and so on. As this aspect of proximity is described by a leader of the Italian General Association of Entertainment (A.G.I.S.), "even the single functionaries of the Association talk from time to time with their counterparts in the agencies of public administration." [58] This appears, then, as a strong factor conditioning the intensity and equilibrium that will characterize a specific *clientela* relationship.

[57] *Interview,* Number 9, *op. cit.,* p. 2.
[58] *Interview,* Number 18, *op. cit.,* p. 10.

CONCLUSION

We have set forth a number of variables or conditions that relate to the establishment of a working *clientela* nexus between interest groups and the bureaucracy. It should be apparent that these are ideal conditions, that in practice no empirical relationship manifests all of them in perfect balance, and that weakness in one variable may be canceled out by strength in another. Although some of these variables may have been posited theoretically for any political system, it is important to recall that they emerge as significant from the field investigation itself. It is conceivable that, in another society, the full range of these conditions would not be critical to the establishment of *clientela* between interest groups and bureaucracy. In Italy at least, the interest-group leaders and the bureaucrats who talk about the interaction between groups and bureaucracy say the kinds of things that suggest the particular analytical situation I have expounded. Seen in terms of the variables enumerated, the Italian situation would seem to offer a model against which relationships in other societies might be compared.

It is also fairly obvious that few groups in Italy manage to approach the ideal *clientela* relationship. A strong factor inhibiting this has to do not so much with the bureaucrats as with the group variables we have discussed. Few groups in a highly fragmented society can lay firm claim to the characteristics of representativeness, respectability, functionality, authoritativeness, and proximity. The labor unions are badly split; veterans' associations run the spectrum of political ideology from extreme left to extreme right; professionals often affiliate not on the basis of a common economic or professional interest but rather as Catholics, Communists, Socialists, Liberals, or laics; student groups also reflect ideological divergencies; women's organizations are fragmented; even the field of agriculture, where the Coltivatori Diretti can claim to recruit the vast majority of the particular category it encompasses, is anything but cohesive in terms of the interest groups emanating from that sector.

In this kind of setting, Confindustria looms as the most perfect example of a clientele group. The same thing is true of many of its member associations. Under the circumstances, one might expect that, within the bureaucracy, it exercises overwhelming influence as against its competitors. Indeed, as far as the Ministry of Industry and Commerce is concerned, there are many in Italy who will argue that this is precisely the case. The facts reveal that such a view of the Confederation's prowess is somewhat exaggerated. The reason is that alongside *clientela* there functions within the bureaucratic sphere the *parentela* relationship. It is to this phenomenon that we must now turn our attention.

CHAPTER IX · BUREAUCRATIC INTERVENTION: PARENTELA

INTRODUCTION

A*parentela* relationship is the second major pattern of interest-group intervention in the bureaucracy. In its strict Italian sense, *parentela* means consanguinity, lineage, or kinship. A *parente* is a member of one's family and in Italian culture is entitled thereby to special consideration. In the traditional South, whence most of Italy's bureaucrats are recruited, ties of *parentela* are particularly strong, implying the kinds of rights and obligations that are generally associated with pre-industrial societies.

As used here, *parentela* involves a relatively close and integral relationship between certain associational interest groups, on the one hand, and the politically dominant Christian Democratic Party (D.C.), on the other. It is this relationship between group and party—and not strictly between group and bureaucracy—which is of interest to us. The generalized proposition we shall explore is that where *parentela* exists, and where certain other related conditions are met, interest groups that enjoy the relationship can exercise considerable influence over a bureaucracy quite apart from any consideration of *clientela*.

At first glance it may appear truistic to suggest that interest groups can have an impact on the bureaucratic process as a result of the intimate relationship the groups may enjoy with the party or parties in power. However, the phenomenon is much more complex than may appear at first. How pervasive and intensive may be the impact of any particular group on public administration will depend on a number of *parentela* conditions or variables that are discussed below. Moreover, it must be remembered that, according to the strictures of the classical democratic model, the administrative sector of government is supposed to represent an instrumental meritocracy, unblemished by patronage, and the party or parties in power presumably are there to guarantee that the access of organized groups to the points of decision and policy is not too badly unbalanced.

Obviously the groups that intervene in the bureaucracy do not do so exclusively on the basis of *clientela,* on the one hand, or *parentela,* on the other. Very frequently, aspects of both relationships are present. However, a central tendency can usually be isolated for any of the major groups and the nature of that central tendency, in the Italian setting, will tell us a great deal about group style as well as the relative influence—in both the short and the long run—that the group involved can expect to exercise over public administration. For these as well as other reasons that might be adduced, the analytical differentiation I am suggesting appears to be of considerable interest and importance.

ASSERTIONS OF PARENTELA

That *parentela* is a significant phenomenon affecting interest group influence on the bureaucracy—and limiting the bureaucracy's freedom of action to some degree—is widely asserted or acknowledged by group leaders, political leaders, and bureaucrats who were interviewed. Some of these assertions are *positive* in the sense of recognizing that a given group's relationship to the D.C. does make a difference in the bureaucracy. Other assertions are *negative* in that they involve comments regarding the disadvantages experienced by some groups precisely because they do not enjoy a *parentela* relationship with the dominant Catholic Party.

In the first category we can include the comments of an inspector-general in the Ministry of Industry and Commerce who tells us that the bureaucrats are perfectly aware of the ideological coloration and affiliations of organized groups and that public administrators almost inevitably tend to be more receptive to the demands of groups that are closely allied with the party in power. Even when the bureaucrats, as is often the case, are interested in maximizing their freedom of action against interference from political parties and affiliated groups, the existence of an overwhelmingly dominant political party makes such freedom difficult to achieve and in many instances actually impossible.[1]

Another respondent stresses that, when viewing the pressure activities of a group like Catholic Action, it is necessary to recognize that its mode of intervention—its style—will differ qualitatively from that manifested by Confindustria or other groups that we would depict as enjoying primarily a *clientela* relationship. This respondent speaks of Catholic Action as a mass movement, displaying immense electoral prowess and generally inclined to approach policy-makers in the name of goodness and morality, rather than openly on behalf of the interests of its membership. Moving from that premise, he cautions:

"This difference in approach should not lead to the conclusion that Catholic Action or any organization is less influential in public administration than is the case, let us say, with a trade union confederation or Confindustria. The nature of Catholic Action, and the manner in which it has succeeded in injecting itself into the political process, are such that one might say at this stage that Catholic Action can and does determine who will be the higher civil servants in many of the ministries. It may also be in a position to determine to some extent which members of the Christian democratic party are chosen as ministers and as undersecretaries in certain ministries. The ability to achieve this degree of influence obviously illustrates the enormous power in Italy that Catholicism can and probably does exercise."[2]

The respondent, a keen observer of the administrative process, stresses the necessity of keeping the basic nature

[1] *Interview*, Number 83, *op. cit.*, pp. 12–13.
[2] *Interview*, Number 54, *op. cit.*, pp. 8–9.

of interest groups as well as their patterns of political action analytically separated. As we shall note more than once in the pages that follow, only this kind of separation will permit us fully to understand the essential differences (as interest groups) between Catholic Action and Confindustria. That the distinction we are making has more than merely analytical meaning is persuasively demonstrated by the varying ways in which bureaucrats respond when they discuss *clientela* groups like Confindustria or *parentela* groups like Catholic Action.

Thus one of the top career officials in the Ministry of the Treasury flatly—even if somewhat simplistically—asserts that "the only groups that count in Italian public administration, as long as the Christian Democrats hold governmental power, are the Catholic groups. The Catholics, because they have direct access to the ministers, are likely to get anything they wish from the ministries. Other groups, such as the left-wing parties and trade unions, are not as fortunate. They are compelled to come to the ministry hat in hand. They are not in a position to make telephone calls to the ministers. They are not in a position to have administrative decisions made in their favor as a result of political interference from the apex of the administrative organization." [3]

Essentially the same general point is made by one of Italy's major writers, who has also been deeply and intimately involved in the politics of the country. His words are worth quoting at some length:

"After ten years of the same party in power, there remain very few facets of Italian life which are not governed by the D.C.—and therefore by the major groups that the party itself represents. This, then, is why a pressure group which operates inside the Christian Democratic Party has an enormous advantage over those groups in Italy that do not have this kind of entree and that are consequently compelled to operate outside the party apparatus. . . . It is not an exaggeration to argue that today in Italy very few jobs are awarded and very few

[3] *Interview,* Number 3, *op. cit.,* p. 3.

careers are made if the individuals who are hoping to get the jobs or make the careers find themselves clearly at odds with the Italian clergy. The power of the clergy is pervasive; it has been extended enormously in the past few years, and the extension itself has been made possible as a result of the dominance of political power exercised by the Christian Democrats essentially since 1947." [4]

Catholic Action is not the only group concerning which *parentela* assertions are made. Others include the Coltivatori Diretti and the Italian Confederation of Workers Unions (C.I.S.L.), which also enjoy positions of considerable, even if limited, prominence within the D.C. Regarding the latter organization, leaders of the Italian Union of Labor (U.I.L) and the Italian General Confederation of Workers (C.G.I.L.) are quick to point to the advantages in bureaucratic interaction that C.I.S.L. enjoys because of its involvement with the D.C. [5] A particularly vital source of disgruntlement, which we have previously noted, concerns the appointment of trade-union representatives to ministerial advisory committees, to important groups such as the National Council of Economics and Labor, and to such international bodies as the International Labor Organization. The evidence is uncontestable that the Christian Democratic government favors C.I.S.L. in such appointments. Where the other labor confederation at issue is the Social-Democratic-Republican U.I.L., greater representation for C.I.S.L. can be justified on the simple criterion of numerical differences in membership; by any test, C.I.S.L. is several times the size of U.I.L. But if the same criterion is generally applied to all trade unions, it is difficult to understand why C.G.I.L., still the largest single Confederation, should often receive less representation than U.I.L. or be excluded completely. In these instances, it is obvious that ideological considerations are

---

[4] *Interview*, Number 33 (Rome, February 7, 1958), p. 8.

[5] *Interview*, Number 30, *op. cit.*, pp. 6–7; *Interview*, Number 80, *op. cit.*, p. 5; *Interview*, Number 94, *op. cit.*, p. 9; *Interview*, Number 81, *op. cit.*, p. 2.

at work and that C.I.S.L. receives preferential treatment as a direct result of its *parentela* relationship to the D.C. The fact that, were the Communists and Socialists to achieve political power, they would engage in the same kind of favoritism toward C.G.I.L. is of more than polemical interest; it suggests that the *parentela* relationship arises out of deep-seated pressures in a society that is as fragmental and noncompromising as Italy has been since the fall of Fascism—and really throughout her history as a nation. When leaders of C.G.I.L. and U.I.L. evoke abstract principles of democracy and fair play to justify their complaints concerning the effects of *parentela*, they appeal to a set of values which has never sunk roots in Italian society and which they themselves would probably not apply were they to develop a strong *parentela* relationship to the party in power.

The benefits deriving to C.I.S.L. from its *parentela* relationship are also mentioned by leaders of Confindustria. One of them says that "the industrialists are outraged over the power of the Christian Democratic trade unions to compel agencies of public administration to behave in a certain way." As an example, he cites the case of the National Productivity Committee which, according to the respondent, told all of those Italian industrial plants asking for productivity subsidies that no money would be forthcoming unless the shop committees [which have important labor representation functions] in their plants were staffed with a majority of C.I.S.L. members and unless the industrialists, in addition, refused to deal at all with C.G.I.L.[6]

This kind of denunciation is what one has come to expect from the political left and from groups with which Christian Democratic organizations such as C.I.S.L. are in acknowledged conflict. Greater credence must be lent to the claim, however, when the information is offered by an industrial leader who is at odds with all of the unions

6 *Interview*, Number 98, *op. cit.*, p. 7.

and who cannot be supposed to want to increase the power in industrial firms of the Socialists or Communists. The point underlined by our respondent is really that the industrialists detect a pattern of cooperation—even collusion —between Christian Democratic interest groups and the Italian bureaucracy which the industrialists might find extremely damaging in the long run. In terms of the conceptualization I have been developing, it is apparent that some of Confindustria's leaders—indeed, most of them— understand that the *clientela* relationship they have established with the bureaucracy is severely challenged, possibly basically jeopardized, by the *parentela* relationship that C.I.S.L. and other Catholic groups have cemented with the Christian Democratic Party.

We need not be detained here by an exhaustive enumeration of positive assertions of the *parentela* relationship's existence. It is noteworthy, however, that members of the disadvantaged groups often complain bitterly about the consequences of their exclusion from the Christian Democratic family. U.I.L. and C.G.I.L. leaders speak of the difficulties implicit in attempting to obtain fair hearings from the bureaucracy. One such leader speaks of U.I.L. as being essentially impotent in the public administrative arena. He points out that Italy does not manifest a pattern of public administration that would be considered typical of a democratic pluralistic society. The notion of a loyal opposition to those in power is utterly lacking. Thus: ". . . those in power—even if they get there by a legal vote—once in power consider themselves to be the exclusive owners of government. They consider government as an instrument of sheer power rather than an instrument of public administration. . . . Those in political power view all of the other groups with which they compete as enemies. . . . The bureaucrats and functionaries tend to obey the minister and the political party he represents, and they at the same time tend to ignore those parties and those associations that are not instruments of or representatives of the parties in power. The functionaries think that this is a natural thing for them to do." [7]

It is striking to follow some of the consequences that this respondent identifies as flowing from the armed-camp, exclusivistic atmosphere of the Italian political system. Where the existence of a loyal opposition is not conceded, and where outside parties and groups are viewed as enemies to be utterly deprived of power, the political system merely serves to intensify the divisions of the society. One important manifestation of this is the conviction of minority parties and groups that they must fight and oppose rather than cooperate with the majority in any meaningful way. Parliamentary behavior then becomes obstructionist, essentially destructive in character, and adds to the forces that make for legislative immobilism. This basic orientation toward political power can probably be traced far back into the history of Italy, certainly to the era of rigid, uncompromising politics that characterized the Guelphs and Ghibelines. Its dogged persistence over time right into and through the recent history of the country suggests that any effort to create workable pluralistic democracy will have formidable obstacles to overcome. Thus, according to our respondent, to ascribe the current behavior of the party in power simply to the existence in Italy of a strong, destructive Communist Party is to ignore profound historical conditions out of which present patterns emerge. [8]

Interestingly, comments concerning interest groups that are discriminated against extend beyond those of the political Left. Confindustria is often included in the category of organizations that suffer adverse consequences because of the lack of a *parentela* relationship to the D.C. Thus, in comparing Confindustria to Catholic Action, one Socialist deputy observes: "There is an analytical difference to be drawn between an organization such as Catholic Action, which has managed to become the heart and

---

[7] *Interview,* Number 30, *op. cit.,* p. 2.
[8] *Ibid.*

soul of Christian Democracy, and an organization such as Confindustria, which, while it may have greater power than some of the left-wing groups, is nevertheless compelled on occasion to go hat in hand to Christian Democratic politicians before it can have the kind of influence it would like." [9]

The fact that Confindustria does not yet enjoy a *parentela* relationship to the D.C. leads others to comment on this factor as a sign of some organizational weakness. To be sure, there are individual firms that are able to overcome this handicap. It is remarked, for example, that prestigious industrial representatives like Valletta (automobiles), Faina (chemicals), and Marzotto (textiles) have direct access to leading members of the D.C. and of government and therefore continue to exercise power quite apart from what may be the relationship of Confindustria to the ruling party. Indeed, it is possible to take the position, as some in Italy do, that despite formal structures that suggest democracy, Italy is nothing more than a feudal holding in the hands of leading industrial families, top-level public administrators, some university professors, and journalists. This view leads to an analysis of economic holdings, of family genealogies, and argues a thesis that I am unwilling to accept, namely that regardless of what may be the political issues involved, decisions in Italy are taken by a firmly fixed economic elite. Everything in society—legislature, public administration, the banks, Confindustria, political parties, the economy, etc.—is seen as helplessly in the hands of a small ruling clique. The major actors in this devil's theory of government and politics then become such persons as the Pirelli and Agnelli families, Giuseppe Cenzato, Donato Menichella, Francesco Giordani, Attilio Pacces, the Crespi family, and a host of other leading families. [10]

[9] *Interview,* Number 46, *op. cit.,* p. 6.

[10] For a typical and very interesting polemical work that takes this particular approach to the Italian political process, see Enrico Nobis, *Il Governo invisibile* (Rome, 1955). Although a great deal of the informa-

No one will doubt that leading families and large economic concentrations exercise some, even considerable, influence over the legislative and administrative processes in Italy. But as one of our trade-union respondents observes, it is critical to recognize that economic power is now divided between the traditional Liberals and a segment of Christian Democracy. As we shall note later, it is far from clear that these two groups are in collusion. Indeed, events of recent years, including a monumental 1962 decision to nationalize the powerful electric power industry, suggest that leaders of Confindustria are perfectly right in viewing at least the left-wing of Christian Democracy as a serious threat. Recognizing that Confindustria has been subjected to political adversity since 1953, one of our respondents aptly remarks: ". . . groups such as Confindustria and other associations which had previously been able to operate effectively outside Christian Democracy are today required, if they are to have any weight at all in the making of governmental policy, to insert themselves in some way inside the D.C. and to achieve some control over the making of laws and their application through the agency of the dominant party." [11]

This argument suggests that if Confindustria wishes to continue to maximize its political effectiveness, it must achieve a *parentela* relationship to the Christian Democratic Party as well as a *clientela* relationship to the bureaucracy. For many reasons which will be noted later, movement in this direction is fraught with all sorts of difficulties, both external and internal to Confindustria. In any event, under the most favorable of circumstances,

---

tion adduced by the author is of immense interest, his rigidly Marxist assumptions and conclusions appear extreme. In looking at Italian society, he makes the same errors of conceptualization and judgment that are typical of the work of C. Wright Mills and Floyd Hunter concerning the United States. In short, the process of reaching decisions is not as simple as Nobis' analysis would suggest. On this point, see my "Le Manchevolezze concettuali ed operative del modello della élite politica," in *Les Elites politiche* (Bari, 1961), pp. 75–79.

[11] *Interview*, Number 46, *op. cit.*, pp. 10–11.

it is most unlikely that Confindustria, in the foreseeable future, will be able to effect the type of *parentela* to the D.C., and consequent impact on the bureaucracy, that is true of C.I.S.L., the Coltivatori Diretti, and Catholic Action.

What, then, are the conditions or variables on which successful *parentela* is based?

1. *The Hegemonic quality of the party*. This is the key variable affecting *parentela*, and it has two dimensions —spatial and temporal. Spatially, the hegemonic party is overwhelmingly dominant; its bases of support outweigh by far those of all others; other parties with which it might collaborate in the business of governing do so not so much because of intrinsic power qualities but because they are essentially *guests in power*. In short, this dimension of hegemony is not present where there exists any uncertainty regarding which of the several parties that may be competing is the dominant one. Thus, despite the omnipresence of the French Radical Party in succeeding governments through the years of the Third and Fourth Republics, it did not possess this quality of hegemony. On the other hand, Adenauer's Christian Democratic Union has manifested this quality at the national level ever since the birth of the Bonn Republic. Similarly, the Italian Christian Democrats, first under De Gasperi and now under Fanfani and Moro, are clearly the hegemonic party as far as the spatial dimension is concerned.

Christian Democratic leaders frankly recognize that they enjoy this privileged status. They speak of the "governmental vocation" of the D.C., of the fact that there would occur a very serious power void in Italy should the party step out of government. One of the leaders whom I interviewed candidly says: "Christian Democracy is the party of government, and as such it exercises a clear monopoly of power, of the opportunities for acquiring and exercising it, and, more important, of its distribution in Italian society." [12]

[12] *Interview*, Number 40, *op. cit.*, p. 4.

This respondent goes on to point out that this favored position regarding political power is critical to an understanding of why and how the D.C. can bring together under one roof a number of contrasting groups and a number of political leaders whose views are far from compatible with each other. Concerning the attractive quality of political hegemony, he says: "It may well be that every group or individual within the party cannot enjoy the same opportunities for the control or exercise of power. But at least they have no intention of cutting themselves out of the power game—that is, they would not cut themselves out of the major instrument through which power can be secured, exercised, and generally controlled." [13]

The D.C. is then described as an organization with which two kinds of groups are associated. First, there are the *internal* groups (i.e., those that enjoy *parentela*), which seek to condition the Party from the inside. Although it is true that these groups are often in conflict, it is not accurate to conclude, as many in Italy do, that the issues that divide them are irreconcilable. For example, differences between Giulio Pastore, Paolo Bonomi, and Giuseppe Togni—all of whom lead different *parentela* groups—are not as acute as may appear in the national press or in the parliamentary debates. These men are all Christian Democrats—Catholics who share not merely an urge to exercise power but also the methodology of moderation and compromise that is implicit in Catholicism itself. Even when the internal groups genuinely differ, they do so within narrow parameters; revolution or radical, intemperate proposals are not likely to emerge from any of them.

The D.C. is also seen as having to cope with groups that are *external* to it. These groups do not share a *parentela* relationship but, to some extent, they seek to make their influence felt through the agency of the dominant party. Confindustria is seen in this light. Whereas it once enjoyed a very close and tight external relationship

13 *Ibid.*

to the D.C., largely as the result of personal friendship and understanding between Alcide De Gasperi and Angelo Costa (the then president of Confindustria), the situation has now changed. The present relationship is not only loose but essentially antagonistic. According to many respondents, including Christian Democratic leaders, Confindustria no longer supplies the D.C. with the financial aid that was provided a few years ago. To a considerable degree, the industrial Confederation has become an outsider as far as the D.C. is concerned, scarcely different in its party influence from some of the left-wing groups and obviously the victim in administrative circles of power thrusts that are based on a *parentela* relationship. It may well be that Confindustria is now trying to re-establish the relationship to the D.C. that existed under the Costa presidency. The current and critical difference is that the D.C. no longer needs Confindustria funds.

The spatial quality of *parentela* we are discussing is not only understood by Christian Democratic leaders but also and necessarily by the bureaucrats as well. Thus, an official of the Ministry of Foreign Affairs states that while his ministry tends to ignore interventions of single deputies or senators on behalf of interest groups, there are important mitigating circumstances to this practice. According to this respondent, an M.P. who represents the party in power is always accorded more respectful attention than any other. If the M.P. is also the chairman of a parliamentary committee, he will receive still more attention. If, to add to his qualifications, the lawmaker is on the Cabinet or close to the Cabinet, or if he is viewed as a potential Cabinet member, even greater attention will be accorded his requests. In short, public administrators are capable of making careful and rational calculations regarding exactly how much influence on behalf of a group an individual legislator is potentially entitled to exert on the machinery of public administration. Reflecting exactly such a calculation, as well as the spatial dimension of party hegemony, the respondent observes:

"As far as the political party affiliation of the deputy is concerned, the only party that counts at the moment in public administration is Christian Democracy. We find little need to pay attention to the demands or the threats of the other political parties, or their representatives, or their deputies, or their senators. The political parties are certainly aware of this game and they understand that things would change to some extent if the D.C. were no longer in power." [14]

If the dominance of the D.C. were absolutely, unqualifiedly unchallenged, we might suppose that certain of Italy's interest groups would be totally excluded from the policy process. Such a consequence would logically follow from the extreme nature of intergroup antagonism and from the discernible widespread tendency of group leaders to assume that to share political power means to keep the "enemy" completely bereft of it. But the fondest hopes of many of the more ardent D.C. Catholics have been somewhat dashed by the electoral results of 1953, 1958 and 1963 which compel the dominant party to rely on the collaboration of the minor Center parties, and in 1964 of the P.S.I. A result of this is the according of some influence to groups that are not in a *parentela* relationship to the D.C. but which may have such a relationship with one of the minor parties in a governmental coalition. The Italian Union of Labor is one of these, and one of its leaders, in explaining why his organization is not completely impotent in administrative circles, says: "The reason for this is that the D.C. does not yet have an absolute majority in the parliament and therefore really has need of its allies, particularly among the Social Democrats." [15] The point is, however, that even when such a pattern exists, it is made possible not because of any intrinsic strength of the minor party involved but really because of its more or less temporary relationship to the dominant, hegemonic party. In short, minor parties and

[14] *Interview,* Number 7 (Rome, December 11, 1957), p. 7.
[15] *Interview,* Number 80, *op. cit.,* p. 5.

the groups they encompass may be guests in power and share in the feast of influence which is everyday fare for the *parentela* groups.

The temporal dimension of party hegemony involves the perception of the party's dominant position as being stable over time and not transitory. The interviews evince a great deal of attention to this particular dimension of hegemony, as they naturally would. An official in the Ministry of the Treasury stresses, when discussing the impact of groups on the administrative process, that "the situation for the Italian bureaucrat has become aggravated by the continuous presence over a period of a decade of a single party in power in Italy." [16] A leader of the Italian Union of Labor, attempting to analyze the patterns of bureaucratic response to group demands, says, "Much depends on the kind of judgment that the bureaucrat can make regarding the permanency of the party involved in the government coalition. . . . The bureaucrats are likely to pay much less heed to a minister who represents a party about whose future in government the bureaucrats . . . have very serious doubts." [17]

A member of the Senate whose perceptions regarding public administration are very acute treats the matter of permanency in office as a significant variable. He points out that, to some extent, the pressure that can be exerted on the bureaucracy is in part a function of the character of the bureaucracy itself. To put this matter simply, bureaucrats will differ in both their capacity and their willingness to resist attempts to dictate administrative decisions on the basis of *parentela* considerations. However, even when bureaucratic characteristics are held constant, it is apparent that a group's relationship to a party long in power will make a significant difference to its influence potential in bureaucratic circles. The increasing incidence of *parentela*-dictated administrative decisions, in the view of our respondent: ". . . is due primarily to the fact that

16 *Interview*, Number 3, *loc. cit.*
17 *Interview*, Number 30, *op. cit.*, p. 3.

the same party has been in power for ten years. If there had been more frequent changes in the Parliament, then this might very well have worked to the advantage of the bureaucracy itself. But when, year after year, the same men are in power, it is inevitable that the bureaucracy will begin to take on a political coloration that does not conflict with that of the majority party. This is instrumentalization of the bureaucracy with a vengeance. I feel that this tendency would be true of whichever dominant party were in a position to appoint the superior bureaucrats." [18]

Echoing essentially the same viewpoint, an official in the Ministry of Industry and Commerce observes that: ". . . one cannot escape the fact that the Christian Democrats have been in power for some years, that they are likely to be the party in power for some years to come, and that they have the means for taking certain kinds of reprisals against those elements of the public administration who create difficulties either for the Party or for groups created by the Party or otherwise identified with it." [19]

The presence of hegemony as it has been defined here deserves a great deal of additional research attention. As the senator cited above suggests, the absence of long-term rule by the same party would tend to provide the bureaucracy itself with greater freedom of action. Regarding France, this matter has been explored by Henry Ehrmann, who points out that "in twentieth-century France the bureaucracy has enjoyed an unusual degree of autonomy because of the absence of a stable political leadership and the ineffectiveness of parliament and political parties as a voice and molder of public opinion." [20] At another place,

18 *Interview*, Number 31, *op. cit.*, p. 9.
19 *Interview*, Number 83, *op. cit.*, p. 12.
20 Henry W. Ehrmann, "French Bureaucracy and Organized Interests," *Administrative Science Quarterly*, 5 (March, 1961), p. 535. Cf. the important supporting evidence presented by Alfred Diamant, "The French Administrative System—The Republic Passes but the Administration Remains," in W. J. Siffin, ed., *Toward the Comparative Study of Public Administration* (Bloomington, Indiana, 1957), pp. 182–218.

the same author tells us that "many French functionaries maintain that, under the Fourth Republic, they were perfectly able to defend themselves against parliamentary pressures transmitting requests of interest groups." [21] This is precisely because there did not exist a strong party system capable of aggregating interests and exercising control over the bureaucratic apparatus. Under these conditions, the bureaucrats could comply with or ignore group requests almost at will.

Parentela would not be possible under the conditions that Ehrmann describes for France. In Italy, on the other hand, the postwar situation has been dramatically different. Beginning as early as 1946, the D.C. has been a major factor in politics; from 1948 to 1953 it enjoyed absolute majorities in both branches of the legislature; and from 1953 to the present it has been the unchallenged dominant political party. Its leaders have acquired considerable skill in dealing with power centers such as the bureaucracy, and, if our respondents are to be believed, they have not hesitated to use their considerable power to bring the bureaucracy into line when such a move was felt to be important. For these reasons it would indeed be very surprising if groups sharing a *parentela* relationship to the D.C. did not derive a certain advantage from the Party's hegemony.

2. *Willingness of party to intervene.* But hegemony is not alone sufficient to create the *parentela* pattern I am describing. A second condition requires that the bureaucrats perceive the dominant party as willing to intervene in the administrative process on behalf of its own narrow interests, or those of groups affiliated with the party. The D.C.'s "will to power" is so often uttered by the Party's leaders and so widely understood in Italian society as to require little documentation here. Public administrators, interest-group leaders, and political officials are almost

21 Henry W. Ehrmann, "Les Groupes d'intérêt et la bureaucratie dans les démocraties occidentales," *Revue Française de Science Politique,* 11 (September, 1961), pp. 555.

unanimous in viewing the dominant party as perfectly willing to go to considerable lengths to impose its will on the country. The increasing talk of the "under-government" (*sottogoverno*) that has characterized the country in recent years reflects not only this widely held perception but also the conviction that the Party will not be hobbled or restrained by genteel considerations of legality or democratic propriety.

It should be noted, however, that the perceived "will to power" does not necessarily imply massive intervention in favor of implementing a coherent and cohesive political program. The same party that is seen as having created a vast and complicated labyrinth of *sottogoverno* is generally criticized for offering the country little by way of an integrated program, for temporizing with many of the basic problems that cry out for attention, and for reflecting in its behavior the disparate groups, interests, and orientations that make up the Party itself. Thus, when speaking of the Party's willingness to intervene in the bureaucracy, U.I.L. and C.G.I.L. leaders remark that it does so in favor of C.I.S.L.; leaders of, say, the Italian General Association of Entertainment claim that intervention occurs on behalf of Catholic Action, Confindustria representatives see the intervention as designed to favor E.N.I. and other state-owned economic enterprises; Confagricoltura officials worry that the Party may be favoring Paolo Bonomi's Coltivatori Diretti; U.N.U.R.I.'s young Christian Democrats assert that the Party interposes its will on the bureaucracy in favor of the Old Guard or party notables; E.N.I. directors see their own party as aiding and abetting the interests of Confindustria; and so on.

Given the nature of the D.C., it is probably reasonable to suppose that, depending on the issue and the occasion, intervention in the bureaucracy may occur for any one of the particular and sometimes antagonistic groups that make up the party. As we have noted in an earlier chapter, the D.C. is perhaps the only political party in Italy that substantially encompasses groups of somewhat varied ideological and programmatic persuasion, and it would therefore be surprising if the Party did not perform a relatively important role as both interest articulator and interest aggregator. If every issue that involved the bureaucracy succeeded in mobilizing at opposed points all of the major groups that enjoy a *parentela* relationship to the D.C., the Party would very quickly break to pieces. Even under existing circumstances, where major groups might be defined as interested in particular policy spheres, there is overlapping of interests that causes considerable strain within the Party. For example, C.I.S.L. and the Coltivatori Diretti are certainly not of a single mind on the issue of the *patti agrari* (agricultural contracts); E.N.I. and the Christian Democrats in the Institute for Industrial Reconstruction (I.R.I.) are scarcely in agreement regarding the role to be played by state-owned economic enterprises; the Party was clearly split on the issue of Article 17 regarding the publication of transactions on the stock exchange; and, to cite perhaps the most dramatic recent example, groups within the Party have radically different orientations toward the "Opening to the Left" which brings the Socialist Party of Pietro Nenni closer to the locus of power than has been the case for fifteen years. It is not merely a matter of childish petulance, in short, that leads Catholic Action to lament and fear the consequences of a shift in internal party power from the Old Guard to the Fanfani and Moro groups.

But from the vantage point of the public administrators, the critical consideration is not so much the nature of the *parentela* groups on behalf of which the D.C. is willing to act as it is the knowledge that the Party is willing to intervene at all. To be sure, it may be that members of the Ministry of Industry and Commerce would prefer to have the Party approach the bureaucracy to further Confindustria's rather than organized labor's interests. Or, to put this obvious surmise differently, the bureaucrats would welcome political interference in favor of decisional directions in which the bureaucrats were moving in any case. When this is not the case, the demand of a *parentela* group, or of the party on behalf of such a group, clearly raises for the bureaucrat the question of how far the Party is willing to go in having a particular interest prevail.

Bureaucrats who respond to the stimulus of *parentela,* and few of them do not, even though they may claim immunity, are prone to take certain presumed rewards and punishments into consideration. The most apparent of these involves the Party's perceived willingness and ability to have an impact on bureaucratic careers. Bureaucrats who candidly speak of this matter insist that most sensible public administrators will not react to *parentela* group demands in a manner that will in some way jeopardize professional mobility. It may be, as some of our bureaucratic respondents suggest, that fewer of them will deliberately work out a pattern of behavior designed to encourage promotion on the basis of political considerations; but the absence of initiative to use the dominant party opportunistically does not imply that the bureaucrat who is under pressure will also be tenacious in resisting that pressure. That some opportunities to resist are at work in Italy will become evident in the next chapter. It is far from my intention, therefore, to suggest that the Italian bureaucracy is a limp instrument to be used by the D.C. and its *parentela* groups exactly as they desire. I do mean to say, however, that bureaucrats believe that the Party can and does interfere in the careers of public administrators and that the presence of this fear is an important reason why the *parentela* pattern is possible at all.

Commenting on this aspect of the phenomenon, one of our respondents claims that, in the years since the war, an increasing premium within the bureaucracy is placed on the matter of affiliation with the Christian Democratic Party. Christian Democrats, he says, are given the better assignments, they are promoted faster, they enjoy greater prestige. The situation is now described as being worse than it was under Fascism, when all bureaucrats had to be or become Fascists and where, therefore, except for the relatively small number of *Ventottisti,* no special premium attached to dominant-party membership. Thus, those who are not in the D.C., or firmly cooperating with the Party or its dominant groups, are said to be somewhat—even considerably—handicapped in the development of an administrative career. "The Christian Democratic Party," says our respondent, "is in a very strong position to corrupt the bureaucracy, because those bureaucrats who do not cooperate with the party—and therefore with the groups that have power within it—have little hope in general of making a career." [22]

A highly placed official in the General Accounting Office corroborates what is said above. He describes his office as one of the most powerful in the Italian bureaucracy. Whoever wants money, credit, or any other kind of significant administrative concession must sooner or later deal and come to terms with the General Accounting Office. In the final analysis, the powerful Minister of the Treasury must ask the State Accounting Officer whether there are funds available for something the Minister wishes to do. If he wants to do so, the latter is in a strategic position to make life difficult and uncomfortable for anyone in the bureaucracy. Because of the strategic nature of this position, the respondent says that no one who is in any way unacceptable to the dominant party is ever likely to be appointed to it. [23]

One can certainly understand why a dominant party would intervene to assure that critically important bureaucratic posts do not fall into the hands of those who would hobble or sabotage the party's program. Very little by way of productive governmental output would be forthcoming in the Italian context if the party or parties in power did not control the commanding heights of the public administrative arena. If the strategy of party inter-

[22] *Interview,* Number 31, *op. cit.,* pp. 9–10.
[23] *Interview,* Number 79, *op. cit.,* p. 5.

vention were limited to such key positions, the point I am making here would be superfluous.

But the impact of Christian Democracy and its *parentela* groups on bureaucratic recruitment, placement, and promotion evidently extends considerably beyond commanding heights and involves levels that, in theory at least, are supposed to be staffed strictly on the basis of merit and seniority. Among the groups most frequently mentioned as active in interfering with bureaucratic careers is Catholic Action. A left-wing legislator, who may be assumed to be somewhat biased in his views of and reactions to Catholic power, suggests that Catholic Action can do a number of things regarding Italian bureaucrats. These include: (1) having an uncooperative bureaucrat removed from a responsible position; (2) having bureaucrats transferred to attractive or unattractive places or positions, depending on how Catholic Action feels about the man; and (3) having uncooperative bureaucrats passed over for promotions to higher levels.[24] Another observer who emphasizes the *parentela* variable cautions against the assumption that the *parentela* relationship may be weaker than *clientela* as a mode of intervening in the bureaucracy. He says that "The nature of Catholic Action and the way in which it has succeeded in injecting itself into the political process are such that one might say at this stage that Catholic Action can and does determine who will be the higher civil servants in many of the ministries." [25]

Returning to our representative from the General Accounting Office, we find a lengthy specification of exactly this kind of influence. His own words make the point as well as anyone can:

"Although I do not like to have to admit it, the truth is that there are some groups that are increasingly active in the determination of promotions. Two or three recently created inspectors-general in the Ministry of the Treasury are indi-

24 *Interview*, Number 31, *op. cit.*, p. 9.
25 *Interview*, Number 54, *op. cit.*, p. 9.

viduals strongly supported by Catholic Action. This is not
unusual; it has been done with growing frequency since the
War. As a matter of fact, I personally know a significant
number of persons within the ministry who have in recent
years joined the D.C. for purely opportunistic considerations.
Often these same individuals thoroughly detest the party, but
they nevertheless understand that possibly the only way of
making a career in public administration today is to achieve
this kind of rapport with the party in power.

"The moral consequences of this kind of system are very
bad, even if those who get promoted are able men. That is,
I am not saying that those who receive promotions as a result
of pressures applied by Catholic Action are incompetents. But
promotion on this basis makes a mockery of the criterion of
comparative merit. It introduces a new criterion, with which
most of the bureaucrats who are at all perceptive become very
quickly acquainted.

"In my own case, I experience a great amount of pressure
from my wife, who insists that I should stop being so ideal-
istic and join the D.C. Up to the present, I have been able to
resist this, but I cannot guarantee what my action may be in
the future. I frankly want to be promoted, to make a good
career, and I fully understand that this kind of mobility is
fully closed to those who do not have the support of the D.C.
or of Catholic groups. But I have made reasonable progress
so far without joining these groups as a matter of opportunism. I will bide my time and wait to see what may be the
personal consequences of not joining the parade of those who
become supporters of the D.C. as the best means of acquiring
professional mobility." [26]

Additional statements of this nature from other bureaucrats can be adduced. An official of the Ministry of the
Treasury, detailing his criticisms of the farcical consequences of establishing a Ministry for Bureaucratic Reform, alleges that the Ministry provided an excuse for reshuffling seniority and promotion lists. Almost overnight,
as if by magic, all sorts of individuals, fairly far down in
the Ministry of the Treasury, were catapulted upward to
important managerial positions. It became apparent to

[26] *Interview*, Number 79, *op. cit.*, pp. 8–9.

even the densest observer that those whose careers were aggrandized by the new ministry's creation were persons whose political and religious papers were in good order. The respondent claims to be able to cite dozens of cases involving the promotion of bureaucrats who had either failed competitive examinations or who had performed very badly on them. He says that this kind of behavior, from a ministry ostensibly created to *reform* the bureaucracy, seriously demoralized many who looked to it to implement the desperately needed changes in the Italian bureaucracy.[27] Exactly the same criticism is offered by an official of the *Commando Generale* of the Ministry of Finance. He scores the Ministry for Bureaucratic Reform as a center of political patronage, inefficiency, and particularistic staffing, and a striking example of the very patterns of public administration that the Ministry's creation was expected to drive out of existence. He says: "In my opinion, one of the most damaging actions in which the Ministry has thus far been engaged is that of reshuffling the seniority lists and the merit lists for promotion on the basis of vague and undefined criteria. Such behavior on the part of the Ministry shortly after its creation is largely responsible for its now being seen by many within public administration as a political instrument designed to further the careers of those who, under previous arrangements, were not moving along as rapidly as they would have liked." [28]

Other comments from bureaucrats regarding the willingness of D.C. to interfere in bureaucratic careers are more soft-spoken than those we have cited, but they make the same general point. When asked about these allegations, a leader of the Christian Democratic Party cautions against deriving inflexible generalizations from them. He acknowledges that the bureaucracy is likely to be very sensitive to the needs of the ruling party, that the party itself will attempt to some extent to bend the bu-

27 *Interview,* Number 16, *op. cit.,* p. 3.
28 *Interview,* Number 17, *op. cit.,* p. 7.

reaucracy to its will, that powerful *parentela* groups such as Catholic Action can often dictate bureaucratic interference of one kind or other, and that there are undoubtedly instances in which bureaucratic careers have been either facilitated or hampered for purely arbitrary political reasons. To illustrate this last point, he flatly states that a high school teacher who is a Communist will never become a superintendent, and therefore never an inspector-general or director-general in the Ministry of Public Instruction. Similar statements could be made about career chances and patterns in other sectors of the bureaucracy.

On the other hand, the respondent reminds us that the top-level bureaucrats are generally hostile to all politicians and that if they really oppose what the dominant party wishes to do, they have all sorts of weapons at their disposal. The very complex machinery of bureaucratic organization and procedure can be used to frustrate efforts of the D.C. or its member groups to dictate what decisions are made in the realm of public administration. Moreover, as far as careers are concerned, the top-level administrators are said to have as much influence over them as can be exercised by Catholic Action or other groups affiliated with Christian Democracy. In this respondent's view, the bureaucracy is still influenced by patterns that developed under Fascism, is still strongly tied to the values of Freemasonry and the Liberal Party, and "it continues to maintain a fair amount of independence both from Christian Democratic leaders and from members of the clergy who are probably interested in remaking public administration to conform to the desires of the Catholic world." [29]

Even if all of this were true, it is apparent that the view is not widely shared by the bureaucrats themselves. For these latter, it is the perception of what is real or probable that counts when a *parentela* group seeks to extract

[29] *Interview*, Number 40, *op. cit.*, pp. 13, 15, 16.

concessions from the bureaucracy. Furthermore, our Christian Democratic leader himself acknowledges that Catholic Action and the clergy do intervene in the bureaucracy, that bishops are respectfully listened to by public administrators, and that, even if the upper reaches of the bureaucracy have some defenses to erect against political interference, this protection does not extend to the lower levels of the administrative hierarchy, where "positions are awarded or promotions to them are affected on the basis of the kinds of recommendations that the bureaucrats involved can secure either from D.C. leaders or from influential members of Catholic groups or members of the clergy." [30] In short, both the perceptions of the bureaucrats and the realities of Italian politics seem to fortify the assumption that the dimension of *parentela* we examine here is an important one.

3. *Group capacity to condition the party.* Obviously not all interest groups in Italy are in a *parentela* relationship to the D.C., and, among those that are, not all represent for the bureaucracy equally powerful aggregations. We can begin by observing that *parentela* requires that a group succeed in finding a place *inside* the Christian Democratic Party. For most of the groups that fall into this category, a basic commitment to Catholicism seems to be important, although not absolutely essential. For example, in the days when Angelo Costa was president of Confindustria, the Confederation was to some degree a *parentela* group—not as closely related, perhaps, as Catholic Action or the Coltivatori Diretti, but a *parentela* group nevertheless. Whatever else might be said about Confindustria, it would certainly be far-fetched to maintain that, as an organization, it is committed to the goal of aggrandizing Catholic power in the society. Even though, in terms of reactions to such problems as economic planning and industrial nationalization, Confindustria and Catholic Action often appear on the same

30 *Ibid.*, pp. 13–14.

side, the leaders of both organizations agree that the industrial Confederation is strongly opposed to the integralistic tendencies that many Catholic groups manifest. Indeed, when speaking of their own political goals, Catholic Action leaders are almost certain to observe that they wish to reduce the degree of influence that the Freemasons and Liberals in Confindustria have long been able to exercise over the social, economic, and political systems. When leaders of left-wing or laical groups indiscriminately couple Confindustria and Catholic Action politically, they not ony obscure the difference between *clientela* and *parentela* but slide over the very real points of conflict that exist in the interaction between these two associations.

It is also obvious that D.C. groups such as C.I.S.L., on the one hand, and A.C.L.I., on the other, differ considerably in the extent of their commitment and devotion to the aims of organized Catholicism. For all of their having to adhere to the general policy orientations of the D.C., it is obvious that C.I.S.L. leaders are often restive in this role, that they are strongly cross-pressured by basic trade-union needs, on one side, and the requirements and demands of Catholicism, on the other. The fact is that even if non-Christian Democrats constitute a very minute proportion of C.I.S.L.'s total membership, the Confederation does purport to recruit from various political groups and is also adamant in proclaiming its nonconfessional nature. No such considerations characterize or inhibit the A.C.L.I. It is openly a Catholic organization, intervening in the labor sphere specifically for the purpose of counteracting among Italian workers what it (and organized Catholicism in general) considers the nefarious consequences of Marxist, materialist, and laical ideas.

Thus, in thinking of *parentela* groups within the D.C., it is of importance not to assume that they are all equally confessional. While it may be true that a basic confessional thread is what holds the many varied D.C. units together in the Party, it is manifestly too simplistic to assume that what the group leaders share in common is a firm devotion to Catholic philosophy and a commitment to increasing Catholic power. To some extent—and it is now clear to me that Catholic Action leaders recognize this—Italians have joined Catholic groups for purely opportunistic reasons. In a country where the Catholic Party has enjoyed unchallenged political hegemony for fifteen years, those who experience strong drives toward the exercise of political power see the *parentela* groups as channels of political mobility. In any event, the fact that most such groups seem to have some fairly strong relationship to Catholicism should not lead to the conclusion that this commitment is the central condition on which *parentela* status can be achieved. To cite the one most dramatic exception, it is apparent that, at least in the years before the D.C. had established its own strong bases of patronage and financing, Confindustria managed to develop reasonably strong *parentela* simply by providing the Party with badly needed campaign funds.

As far as the relative *parentela* strength that a group can achieve is concerned, the critical factor seems to be how many votes the group controls and can deliver to the party. One member of the Chamber of Deputies comments that an important reason why Catholic Action has strength in D.C. is that it is strongly and directly represented on party councils and in the legislature. Men who entered politics after long years of activity in Catholic Action or who, even after entering politics, retain positions of leadership in Catholic Action units can be counted on to articulate the interests of the latter organization. However, he goes on to stress that direct representation and the voicing of Catholic Action views is in turn related to a much more significant phenomenon. He says:

". . . even those Christian Democratic deputies who have never had any formal affiliation with the Catholic world will pay great attention to the positions assumed by the Catholics. The major reason is that Catholic organizations are in key positions to influence the outcome of elections. For example, a Christian Democratic deputy who clearly runs into the

opposition of the civic committees runs the risk of being sur-
passed [in number of preferential votes] by those other Christian Democrats, in good standing with Catholic Action and its
civic committees, for whom the greatest amount of campaign
activity will be exerted. The electoral power of Catholic
Action is one of the major weapons it uses in disciplining
even those deputies who are not members of Catholic Action
or of other Catholic organizations." [31]

Although there is evidence that organizations such as
C.I.S.L., Coltivatori Diretti, A.C.L.I., and E.N.I. derive
benefits from the *parentela* relationship, the organization
most often cited as the most powerful in this regard is
Catholic Action In a somewhat exaggerated form, we have
the assertion of a Socialist deputy that Catholic Action can
name ministers and prime ministers, and that "nothing
much happens within the Christian Democratic Party
that Catholic Action really and actively opposes. . . .
Catholic Action has the political fate of D.C. in its
hands." [32] A member of P.S.I.'s executive committee
shares the view that no group in Italy is as powerful as
Catholic Action. According to his image of the situation
—also somewhat distorted—"most of the major policies
that have evolved in this postwar period have been either
policies favored by the Catholic hierarchy or at least policies that did not run strongly counter to the values of
Catholicism. . . . The balance was tipped in favor of
Catholic Action in 1948 when the Vatican decided to approve the Catholic Action effort to create the civic committees. These committees were obviously responsible
for the amazing victory registered by the D.C. in the elections of April 18 [1948]. Without the aid of this kind of
capillary organization, the left might very well have come
out of those elections if not with majorities in the legislature at least as the most powerful political force in Italy.
. . . The committees should have been disbanded. They
were not, and they have become the real Catholic politi-

31 *Interview*, Number 2, *op. cit.*, p. 2.
32 *Interview*, Number 36, *op. cit.*, pp. 4–5.

cal party in this country. . . . Because the Catholics have
these committees, their bargaining power in the D.C. is
tremendous. . . . The committees can defeat Christian
Democrats who do not cooperate or, at the very least, they
can make the re-election of these individuals extremely
difficult." [33]

An editor of one of Italy's slightly left of center political
weeklies takes essentially the same position, identifying
Catholic Action as the most important subgroup making
up the D.C. His point is that Fanfani and other D.C.
leaders who would wish to restrict the impact of Catholic
Action are hamstrung by a critical fact, namely that at
least seven of the twelve million votes that the D.C. is
able to attract come from women, and that the control
over women exercised by Catholic Action is truly extraordinary. Catholic Action—through its civic committees
controls these female votes and delivers them to the
party.[34]

There are one or two observations to make at this point
that will help to place statements such as these in a more
balanced context. First, it is apparent that the leaders of
Catholic Action—like those of every *parentela* group—
have a tendency to exaggerate their ability to deliver votes
to the D.C. C.I.S.L. officials claim that the organization's
presence prevents hundreds of thousands of votes from
going over to the political parties with which C.G.I.L.
and U.I.L. are closely associated; leaders of the A.C.L.I.
assert that without the vital Christian preparation that
the organization provides for workers and farmers, many
of them would not have the proper philosophical standards on the basis of which to reject the political forces of
Marxism and materialism. Catholic Action leaders do not
differ in this regard; they see the vast organizational apparatus of Catholic Action as designed in important measure to instill the kinds of religious and civic values that
would immunize the Italian voter against the virulent dis-

[33] *Interview*, Number 46, *op. cit.*, p. 3.
[34] *Interview*, Number 59 (Rome, January 9, 1958), p. 9.

ease transmitted by all of the laical parties, and particularly those of the extreme Left.

It is apparent, however, that education and indoctrination do not exhaust the politically related activities of Catholic Action. Official disclaimers of Catholic Action leaders notwithstanding, it is more than dimly apparent that the civic committees are in fact a Catholic Action electoral instrument. This is conceded by a major leader of the National Civic Committee—the parent organization—who confides that the civic committees have no constitution in order to permit Catholic Action to avoid any embarrassment under the provisions of the 1929 Concordat (recognized by the present Republican Constitution), which requires that Catholic Action stay out of direct participation in politics. According to this leader, the civic committees are organized throughout Italy, they were specifically authorized by the Vatican as a means of influencing electoral outcomes, they have continually functioned to coordinate the electoral activities of Catholic groups, and they are responsible for delivering the largest single bloc of votes—several million—to the D.C. on election day.[35]

Without suggesting that the civic committees are unimportant it is possible to surmise that their leaders tend to puff up their importance, both within the D.C. and in their communications to the populace at large.

The second point to make is that the overwhelming power of Catholic Action is the source of considerable tension within the Christian Democratic Party itself. Leaders of C.I.S.L.—some of the younger ones in any case —are quick to decry the extraordinary power that Catholic Action is able to wield both within the Party and, as a result of this, in the legislative and public administrative sectors. Several respondents, both within the D.C. and outside, say that one of Amintore Fanfani's major campaigns has been to reduce Catholic Action's power. Thus

[35] *Interview*, Number 20 (Rome, December 13, 1957), pp. 1–4.

Fanfani, over several years, has tried to strengthen the party apparatus, hoping in this way to weld a relatively independent electoral machine that would make the D.C. less dependent than in the past on the vote-delivering prowess of Catholic Action. A journalist who is very close to Christian Democracy asserts that, regardless of what his personal motivations might be, Fanfani has been fairly successful in cutting back the power of Catholic Action and the civic committees.[36] A Christian Democratic leader, who has sided with Fanfani in this effort, points out that in 1958 the latter took various steps designed to reduce Catholic Action's control over Christian Democratic nominations. Among other things, Catholic Action representation on provincial list-forming (nominating) committees was reduced, and Fanfani has sought to induce Catholic Action exponents to enter the D.C. as bona fide leaders. Moreover, even if one is greatly impressed by the four million D.C. votes that Catholic Action is generally conceded to control, it is of some significance to remember that in the final analysis the D.C. is the only party to which Catholic Action can logically direct its captive voters.[37]

Needless to say, there are those in Italy—and several among our respondents—who are far from convinced that, in the face of a real showdown, Catholic Action and the civic committees would balk at supporting the extreme Right. This suggests that its independent power position is formidable. However, our purpose at this point is simply to underscore the fact that no one *parentela* group rigidly controls the D.C. and that, as a matter of political practice, the *parentela* groups within the party vie with

[36] *Interview*, Number 90 (Rome, June 21, 1958), p. 2.
[37] *Interview*, Number 40, *op. cit.*, pp. 7–8. The same point is made by another D.C. leader, who argues that the civic committees have no alternatives except to support D.C. candidates. However, he concedes that the committees might support only the more conservative D.C. candidates, although the local bishops would presumably resist an effort by the National Civic Committee to dictate which D.C. candidates were to be supported in each diocese. *Interview*, Number 29, *op. cit.*, pp. 8–9.

one another for the amount of political influence they can exert.

As far as the bureaucracy is concerned, it is fairly apparent that the *parentela* groups that loom as the most formidable are generally the ones with the greatest vote-getting strength. Catholic Action is seen as enormously powerful in this regard and quite able and willing to do whatever is necessary to have its views accorded a very respectful hearing in bureaucratic circles. Bureaucrats who mumble about priests and bishops who scurry about ministerial corridors in search of concessions tend to associate this activity with Catholic Action, even when the connection between the clergy's personal intervention and the massive Catholic holding company is anything but clear. Depending on the ministry involved, the other *parentela* groups of the D.C. are identified as deserving of special consideration because of the mass basis of their memberships and the presumed ability of group leaders to use them to elect Christian Democrats in general and group leaders in particular. The one important exception to this generalization is E.N.I., which does not have a mass membership base. In its case, however, bureaucrats, like Confindustria's and those of other groups, are convinced that E.N.I.'s advantaged position grows out of its unchallenged ability to use funds to aid in the election of some legislative candidates and the defeat of others.

We can conclude discussion of the electoral source of a group's ability to achieve a *parentela* nexus to the dominant party by quoting the perceptive remark of a Christian Democratic leader of U.N.U.R.I., the inter-ideological national association of university students. Speaking of U.N.U.R.I.'s decision not to provide electoral support for any of the competing political parties, he says: ". . . it is both an advantage and a weakness. It is an advantage in the sense that the organization does not become too closely identified with any party or with any candidate. It is a disadvantage in the sense that when the organization goes to the political parties in search for support of its programs, it does not have the ability to exchange, perhaps, what the political parties themselves find the most important weapon that a group might have—that is, the ability to assure a number of votes in political elections." [38]

4. *Characteristics of the bureaucracy.* As we noted briefly earlier, the ability of a *parentela* group to utilize the dominant party to make its influence felt in the bureaucracy will also depend on certain salient structural characteristics of the latter. When attempting to understand the impact of this variable, we are led to ask such questions as: How much centralization of decisional authority does the bureaucracy manifest? Regardless of the requirements of formal authority, how much decentralized decisional power exists in fact? Is there a merit system and, if so, how far up the public administrative hierarchy does it extend? What are the norms that are in fact applied in matters of personnel, such as recruitment, placement, transfer, and promotion? Are there particular types of agencies that seem to be more or less susceptible to the application of *parentela* pressure?

The Italian bureaucracy has been characterized by extreme centralization of authority, both geographical and functional. Internally, the directors-general are at the apex of the structure of authority. Presumably nothing of any consequence can occur within their directorates for which they fail to affix their formal approval. A complaint frequently voiced by those administrators lower in the hierarchy is that decisions are held in abeyance, pending the signatures of section and division chiefs, inspectors-general, directors-general, and frequently the ministers themselves. One result of this hierarchical review of decisions, it is claimed, is to inhibit initiative and to encourage administrative timidity. A bureaucrat who wants to be absolutely sure of himself—who wants to avoid trouble or embarrassment—will react to each situation according to the

38 *Interview,* Number 35, *op. cit.,* p. 10.

rule book, leaving it to the person immediately above him in the hierarchy to exercise creative departures from stultifying routine.

In the years since administrative reform has become the subject of attention, some efforts, most of them weak and ineffective, have been made to encourage decentralization of authority. The so-called Lucifredi Decrees dealing with this problem were presumably passed to implement the reform. However, the bureaucrats who were interviewed in this study agree to a man that the decrees have not been implemented. They say that not even the law enacted early in 1957, which placed considerable emphasis on the need for delegating authority all the way down from the minister to the section director, has had a clearly discernible impact.[39] Directors-general and others who are defined as extremely jealous of their status and prerogatives are evidently unwilling to see formal authority slip out of their hands. The criticism that administrative reform, in almost all its facets, has thus far been either stillborn or a total fiasco is a widely held view in Italy.[40]

An official of the Ministry of the Treasury describes the 1957 Reform Statute as a "tragicomedy." He notes that there is widespread hostility to bureaucratic reform among many groups in the country. Included among the opposition "is the Bourbonic indifference of the higher bureaucrats, many of whom are actually hostile to scientific administration." [41] Another official, in the Ministry of Finance, claims that the obstacles to change are to be traced to the unification of Italy and the superimposition

[39] See Ignazio Scotto, "La Nuova disciplina del rapporto di pubblico impiego," in *Problemi della pubblica amministrazione* (Bologna, 1958), pp. 81 ff.

[40] For a criticism of the bureaucracy and its desperate need for reform, see Cesare Zappulli, "La Burocrazia vista da un giornalista," in *Problemi della pubblica amministrazione* (Bologna, 1960), pp. 203–10. Some of the examples of bureaucratic waste and irrationality cited by the author are not unlike those discovered in the U.S. federal bureaucracy by the Hoover Commission task forces.

[41] Personal memorandum to the author (July, 1958), p. 2.

on the Italian bureaucracy of a paternalistic administrative system with "the tendency toward the protection of the interests of privileged classes, the negation of private individual rights, and opportunism deprived of justice." He adds that notwithstanding the posture of the highest-level bureaucrats, there are many younger people in the bureaucracy who favor reform and who would like to see decisional authority more widely and substantially dispersed within the ministries.[42] A third official, a section leader in the Ministry of the Treasury, laments that delegation of authority and other reforms will never take place as long as the political leadership is unwilling to compel directors-general to accept change. Regarding these latter officials, most of whom date from the Fascist era, he says: "These directors-general and inspectors-general are often opponents of reform for ideological reasons. That is, they have never actually been able to accept the democratic state. They are very frequently opponents of the Republic. They are, in any case, likely to resent any effort on the part of the new political regime to suggest that the usages of the past are inefficient or otherwise wanting. . . . In the last analysis, the most impressive willingness on the part of a minister or other political representatives in the ministry to effect change will surely run up against the enormous power of inertia and sabotage that resides in the hands of the directors-general and the inspectors-general."[43]

I do not intend to challenge here either the assumption that Italian administration is highly centralized internally or that many top-level administrators—for ideological, psychological, or other reasons—are opposed to change. Directors-general who were interviewed in this study certainly agree that little actual delegation of authority has occurred, though they tend to ascribe this failure to the unwillingness of subordinates to accept greater responsibilities.

[42] *Ibid.*, p. 1.
[43] *Interview*, Number 16, *op. cit.*, pp. 1–2.

I do wish to suggest, however, that if the actual distribution of power in the bureaucracy mirrored the formal distribution of authority, interest-group leaders would be advised to limit their interaction to those occupying the very highest positions in the bureaucratic hierarchy. The fact is that no such restricted pattern prevails; any number of group leaders assure us that they effect contacts with officials at several bureaucratic levels. As a matter of fact, organizations such as Confindustria and the Italian Banking Association have developed an organizational pattern of status equals and counterparts who maintain close relations with bureaucrats at various levels.

The point is that, while authority is highly centralized in the bureaucracy, effective power is somewhat dispersed. It could not be otherwise. Thus the bureaucrats themselves recognize that a considerable amount of *de facto* decentralization exists and it is not alone those at the top who have the power to make important concessions to interest groups. It is this failure to recognize what exists in fact that results in a certain amount of disorientation, even chaos, in administrative behavior.

To paraphrase a number of bureaucrats who spoke to this point, it is of great utility for interest groups to seek the support of directors-general and inspectors-general. This is particularly the case where the group is attempting to prevent action—that is, to function as a veto group. One bureaucrat, summing up the importance of such a strategy, notes that "not very much that a director-general or inspector-general is opposed to can take place within a ministry." On the other hand, if it is positive action that a group seeks from the bureaucracy, all directive levels are of significance. To relate just one of many examples cited, a section director who is in charge of processing applications from private industrialists for financial credit to spur the industrial development of the South is in a key position either to facilitate or seriously to hamper the claims of any single group. Even when the actions of such an individual must be checked by twelve or more other officials, the cards can be stacked in favor of one line of action rather than another. Moreover, the mere ability of a bureaucrat to speed up or delay the ordinary administrative procedure is a power strongly respected by the groups themselves.

One perceptive bureaucrat suggests that it is the very extent of rigidity in the administrative hierarchy that increases the discretionary powers of the lower-level official who formally has none at all. If between such a bureaucrat and the minister there exist fifteen levels of formal approval, those near the bottom do not review decisions carefully because they assume that care will be taken at the top. Those at the top, on the other hand, also react in a completely formalistic way, either because they assume that underlings have done their work well or because they have too much to do to permit a substantive review.[44] The upshot is that, at least for the great majority of decisions that do not raise serious controversy, lowly officials have enough power to make them attractive targets for interest-group representatives.

Perhaps the best way to summarize this discussion is by pointing out that interest groups thrive in administrative situations that are muddy and confused. If this obtains, the Italian administrative hierarchy in its unreformed state is a striking example of susceptibility to interest group incursions. This is true not merely because of the gross discrepancies between formal authority and de facto power but also because of other characteristics that we shall turn to in a moment.

Bureaucratic centralization has a geographic dimension too. Little has been done so far to encourage the development of the regional autonomy anticipated by the Constitution. Where certain functions have been delegated to the provinces or municipalities, these latter are hamstrung in their functioning because they do not possess adequate

[44] *Ibid.*, p. 7.

revenue-raising powers.[45] In this type of setting, the local prefect takes on the qualities of omnipotency over the political and administrative activity that occurs within his province. While the field representatives of other ministries do indeed exercise some discretion and operating freedom, the single most important official to seek out as a means of exercising local influence remains the prefect.

Because of this situation, a number of respondents insist that any complete understanding of the role of interest groups, particularly *parentela* groups, in directing administrative policies would have to take the prefects into account. An official of the Ministry of Agriculture, for example, comments that in the implementation of land reform programs priests and bishops seek to intervene through the prefects. He notes that when direct efforts of this nature fail to yield the desired results, the clergy will transfer their intervention to Rome, but that this is not necessary very often. Although the respondent, a Christian Democrat, notes that not all members of his Party approve of such clerical interference in strictly governmental affairs and that it is a grave error for the D.C. to permit it, the practice nevertheless persists.[46]

A representative of I.R.I. notes that the *Cassa per il Mezzogiorno* (Fund for the Development of the South) has become a gigantic patronage organization which employs people and awards developmental contracts strictly on the basis of political considerations. While he is aware that this sort of behavior occurs in any society, he asserts that in Italy the Christian Democrats and Catholics have managed to raise it to a colossal scale.[47] An Italian writer with a deep understanding of the South echoes the generalization that through the activities of bishops and prefects the programs of land reform have become essentially

---

[45] For a scathing criticism of geographic centralization of administrative power and an argument for greater regional autonomy, see Massimo S. Giannini, "Il Decentramento nel sistema amministrativo," in *Problemi della pubblica amministrazione* (Bologna, 1958), pp. 155–83.
[46] *Interview*, Number 37, *op. cit.*, p. 7.
[47] *Interview*, Number 65, *op. cit.*, p. 2.

instruments of local patronage. Land is awarded, loans are made, credit is secured, fertilizer is distributed, and contracts are awarded on a fairly strict basis of loyalty to the Christian Democratic Party. He adds that this practice is certainly no secret. "The clergy and the party do not advertise this, but they have an interest in making the system known; that is, they wish to impress upon some of the recalcitrants the difficulty of making any economic progress if they persist in supporting political formations not approved by the Church. . . . This basic truth is so widely understood in the South today that families that wish to prosper will place family members in several of the political parties. Thus, one will go into Christian Democracy, another into the Communist Party, another to the Monarchist Party or Italian Social Movement as a means of hedging against all of the probable or possible political eventualities of the country." [48]

Enough has been said here to demonstrate not so much that Italy is unique as that the patterns of public administration at the local as well as national level do not seriously inhibit the application of bureaucratic pressure based on *parentela*. As far as the use of political criteria to influence placement, transfer, and promotion is concerned, the interview evidence is somewhat mixed. We have already noted, for example, the view of the Christian Democratic leader who emphasizes that on these matters the bureaucracy is something more than a passive element. In a similar vein, we have the assertion of an official of the Ministry of the Interior who insists that merit is so important on matters of tenure and promotion as to quite definitely limit the importance of *parentela* factors.[49] But statements from other bureaucrats we noted earlier contradict this position. Furthermore, it seems rather farfetched to assume that Communists and Socialists, say, would have equal chances as Christian Democrats to enter the very sensitive Ministry of the Interior and to rise to

[48] *Interview*, Number 33, *op. cit.*, p. 7.
[49] *Interview*, Number 4 (Rome, November 24, 1957), p. 2.

important positions there. On the basis of what we can learn from the data at hand, it seems reasonably clear that *parentela* considerations are fully operative at the highest bureaucratic levels. Indeed, legislation permits the President of the Republic to appoint directors-general and other top-level administrative officers on the recommendation of the Council of Ministers and without regard to questions of seniority. Presumably such key appointments are understandably matters of political patronage, and *parentela* groups may be presumed to be very much involved in the process. This surmise is confirmed by an official of the Ministry of Foreign Affairs who states that no top-level position in his Ministry is likely to be awarded until the person involved has been accepted by the Italian clergy. He holds that while this does not mean that the clergy dominate public administration, it is evidence that they are able to have a considerable impact on it.[50]

A further point concerning promotion, stressed by a number of bureaucrats, is that the criterion of comparative merit for promotion is a two-edged sword. On the one hand, it introduces a certain amount of needed flexibility into the system. Able young persons who might leave the public service for other employment may be kept in the system if their chances for professional mobility are not narrowly tied to considerations of seniority. On the other hand, comparative merit can be, and according to some has been, abused for political purposes. Thus, where merit is established not on the basis of examination but by standards that are much vaguer, individuals can move up to higher positions as a result of their strong connections with the dominant party or its *parentela* groups. It is doubtful that Catholic Action has made use of this weapon as strongly as interview responses suggest, but that it has been used to some extent in recent years is not in doubt. More important, perhaps, is the considerably widespread belief in the bureaucracy and interest-

[50] *Interview*, Number 7, *op. cit.*, p. 5.

group circles that successful administrative careers are not as open to outsiders as they are to those who have found some sort of accommodation within the Christian Democratic Party.

A final point on the bureaucracy's susceptibility to *parentela* pressure involves the differences that one can detect within the bureaucracy itself. Even though our evidence on this point is somewhat limited, it seems apparent that highly technical agencies are often less open to *parentela* pressure than other kinds of units.[51] For example, an official in the Comptroller General's office holds that the highly technical nature of its work protects it somewhat against group incursions. Another bureaucrat in the Ministry of Foreign Affairs cites the strong mystique and prestige of the Ministry as providing some protection against *parentela* pressures. He adds that the absence of such factors at the provincial and local levels is what provides the clergy and other Catholic groups with considerable ability to affect bureaucratic policy there.

Perhaps a basic difference should be drawn here between *clientela* and *parentela* influence. Where the basis of the group's approach is essentially the former, it is likely to be much more successful in the vertical, technical, highly specialized administrative agencies. Where, on the other hand, the basis of the intervention is *parentela,* the highly politicized agencies, such as prefectures, reform and development units, and sensitive ministries like Foreign Affairs and Interior are likely to represent the major sectors of successful intervention. It seems reasonably clear that the two kinds of approach we have described exist in fact, and that which ever one of

[51] I am aware that this suggestion conflicts with the views of Jean Meynaud, who holds that the more functionally specialized agencies are open to greater interest-group influence in France. Here, however, I am thinking primarily of *parentela* pressure, although I would repeat my caveat that the age or function of an administrative agency is not necessarily protection against *clientela* pressure either. See his "Les Groupes d'intérêt et l'administration en France," *Revue Française de Science Politique,* 7 (July–September, 1957), pp. 573–93.

them represents a group's central tendency will tell us a great deal about the group's ability to influence bureaucratic policy.

We can now turn to an examination of this question, as well as to other characteristics of the Italian bureaucracy that protect it from, or make it susceptible to, *clientela-* or *parentela*-based group intervention.

CHAPTER X · SCOPE AND LIMITS
OF BUREAUCRATIC INTERVENTION

WE have examined in some detail both the *clientela* and the *parentela* phenomena as they seem to bear on the ability of associational interest groups to make their weight felt in the bureaucracy. It is now evident that while elements of both relationships will be detected in the activities of most major interest groups, each group tends to display a central tendency. Thus Confindustria relies primarily on *clientela,* although pressures for greater *parentela* are evident. Catholic Action is a striking example of *parentela,* although in some limited contexts there are also *clientela* factors at work. In this chapter I wish to suggest which of these relationships seems to be of greater utility to the competing groups. I also wish to restore some balance to the total picture by suggesting that there are additional factors that make the bureaucracy vulnerable to the demands of interest groups and others that provide it with a certain capacity to resist or at least to manage the flow of demands that enter the bureaucratic sphere from other sectors of the polity.

PERCEPTIONS OF RELATIVE GROUP IMPACT

It is widely believed in Italy—and the belief is overwhelmingly confirmed by our interviews—that the single most powerful interest group operating in the political system is Catholic Action. Over half of the group leaders, four-fifths of the political leaders, and one-third of the bureaucrats interviewed identify Catholic Action as being in a class by itself in this regard. A national leader of Confindustria asserts that, from the vantage point of his Confederation, Catholic Action is more influential in public administrative circles than are even those trade

349

unions supported by the Christian Democratic Party.[1] One of C.G.I.L.'s officials tends to play down all groups except Catholic Action, arguing that because of the position it holds within the Christian Democratic Party, it is responsible for the increasing clericalization of Italian society and government.[2] A director of the Christian Democratic C.I.S.L. who has himself been a Catholic Action leader generalizes that Catholic Action is immensely powerful in the bureaucracy because it is increasingly able to influence bureaucratic appointments, determine who will be awarded major academic chairs in the universities, place its own people on state-owned radio and television organizations, and receive its quota of appointments to the directive boards of the state-controlled industries of I.R.I.[3] The editor of a political weekly, acknowledging that there has been great tension between Catholic Action and the Amintore Fanfani group, stresses that the tension grows out of the degree of control over the D.C. that Catholic Action managed to achieve between 1946 and 1958.[4] A director of one of I.R.I.'s major divisions claims that it is not Catholic Action that is conditioned by the D.C. or other Catholic organizations but really Catholic Action that sets limits on the behavior of others.[5] Many other statements that make similar points could be adduced. The general perception is aptly summarized by one group leader who remarks: "Catholic Action constitutes a fundamental problem for Italy. That organization is no longer merely spiritual or apostolic, but an enormous political and economic force in the country. It is an organization that succeeds in dominating important sectors of Italian society. It wants to control what is written in the newspapers, what kinds of books are published, what kinds of motion pictures are produced, what kinds of programs appear on television, what

[1] *Interview*, Number 98, *op. cit.*, p. 8.
[2] *Interview*, Number 94, *op. cit.*, p. 2.
[3] *Interview*, Number 6, *op. cit.*, p. 2.
[4] *Interview*, Number 32 (Rome, February 1, 1958), p. 4.
[5] *Interview*, Number 65, *op. cit.*, p. 8.

kinds of recreation we Italians engage in, what kinds of persons are elected to communal councils and the Parliament, what kinds of individuals will have the opportunity to make careers in the public administration—that is, it is interested in everything except spiritual things." [6]

As far as the intentions of Catholic Action are concerned, the above observation is reasonably accurate. In their interview responses, national leaders of most branches of the mammoth organization are quick to articulate that creating the proper kind of citizen—the "civic man"—is a central purpose of Catholic Action activity. In the single-minded pursuit of this goal it is apparent that Catholic Action, in one way or another, will seek to intervene anywhere in the society or the polity. This orientation can best be illustrated by an examination of some data concerning the public licensing of motion picture theaters in Italy.

A national leader of A.G.I.S. (Italian General Association of Entertainment) points out that for several years the Catholic unit within the Association has tried to increase its relative power position. He indicates that the general strategy is based not merely on the force of numbers that the Catholics can muster within the organization but particularly on the use of political and bureaucratic influence to increase Catholic weight in the entertainment industries. The degree of influence exerted in the postwar years can be adduced from information concerning the disposition, by the Ministerial Committee that grants licenses to motion picture theatres, of requests to operate such new enterprises, or to enlarge those already in existence. During the period October 1, 1954, to January 31, 1955, the Committee handled and disposed of 1,817 such requests as shown by Table 11.

The most striking aspect of this table is not that the number of parish church requests rejected is less than one-third the rejection level for private entrepreneurs, it is that, during the period covered, as many parish as private

TABLE 11: Disposition by Ministerial Committee of Requests to Open New Theaters or to Enlarge Existing Ones, October, 1945–January, 1955 [7]

Type of Organization	Requests	Granted		Rejected		New Theaters
		Number	Percent	Number	Percent	
Private enterprise	1,189	774	65.2	415	34.8	477
Parish churches	628	564	89.9	64	10.1	477

[7] Data extracted from Associazione Generale Italiana dello Spettacolo, *Relazione della presidenza al consiglio generale ed alle assemblee ordinarie delle associazioni di categoria aderenti* (Rome, 1956), pp. 56–57.

theaters came into existence. According to our A.G.I.S. respondents, this trend has been true for some years, and by 1958 fully one-third of all the motion-picture houses in Italy were those owned and operated by the parish churches. He adds that there is more than a quantitative aspect to consider, in the sense that the newer parish churches are no longer tiny, dingy places but full-blown and often elegant theaters that seat large numbers of people. At the beginning of this evolution—say, in 1953— the private theaters outnumbered the parish enterprises seven to one; the fact that in just a few years the ratio has changed so dramatically is said to have certain ominous long-run implications for the Italian motion-picture industry.[8]

It is apparent on close examination that the rules promulgated by the Presidency of the Council of Ministers and applied by the Ministerial Committee clearly favor the continued and disproportionate growth of parish theaters. For example, one general rule states that before a new theater can be authorized in a particular area, a five percent growth in motion-picture attendance must be demonstrated for the previous year. However, additional regulations stipulate that where there does not exist any theater, or where the only theaters in existence are privately run, new parish theaters can be authorized. This

[8] *Interview*, Number 18, *op. cit.*, pp. 6–7.

regulation alone is sufficient to provide organized Catholicism with the opportunity to achieve a position of unchallenged dominance in this activity.

A.G.I.S. leaders assert, and officials of Catholic Action agree, that the strategy here is to make it difficult or impossible to produce in Italy motion pictures that are not acceptable to Catholicism. By exercising strong control over the places where motion pictures are shown, Catholic organizations can achieve a degree of direction of what motion pictures are produced that has thus far eluded them. If the balance is very heavily tipped in Catholicism's favor, it is unlikely that such motion pictures as *Don Camillo* or *La Dolce vita* would ever again materialize. On the other hand, as the Italian film output of recent years suggests, Italian affluence may now be such that most Italians can afford to attend commercial theaters, without having to be dependent on cheaper parish theaters.

Catholic Action's position is that, in addition to meeting strict standards of morality, motion pictures should not focus on man's baser instincts, his social degradation, his hopeless economic plight, or his struggles with religion, society, and government. Motion pictures should be happy, not sad; they should amuse and uplift the spectator and not cast him into a mood of defeat and depression. In short, motion pictures should not be too realistic and should not dwell on themes that increase a sense of discontent. The point here, however, is not whether the Catholic Action view is right or wrong but that as a result of the influence the view can exercise on the Christian Democratic Party and the upper bureaucracy, an important medium of communication has to some extent fallen under the control of one of Italy's ideologically isolative and sectarian interest groups. It is to developments such as this that Italians—and the respondents in this study—point when they underline the power of Catholic Action and the integralist intentions of organized Catholicism in general.

It is significant that the image of Catholic Action as the most powerful organized group in the Italian polity is held not only by Catholicism's major detractors but also by other Catholic group leaders, conservative members of the bureaucracy, and leaders of Confindustria. Several of the latter openly express their fear that Catholic Action will eclipse the industrial Confederation in the Ministry of Industry and Commerce, making of that key administrative sector "yet another vehicle at the service of Catholic interests." Within Catholic Action itself there is frank and self-confident appraisal of the vast influence exercised by the organization. As an example of this, a national leader of *Gioventù Femminile,* the young women's segment of Catholic Action, asserts that Catholic Action is far more important in the legislature and the bureaucracy than the Christian Democratic C.I.S.L., or for that matter any other Catholic group. She indicates that this is true not only because of Catholic Action's greater size but also because the organization carries on an important educational function in connection with several million persons in Italy. Contrasting Catholic Action and C.I.S.L., she says: "C.I.S.L. *organizes* its members; Catholic Action *forms* its own, shapes new attitudes in them, requires its membership to adopt new attitudes, requires its membership to dedicate themselves to the kind of work that demands sacrifice; and it works out this program of indoctrination and action not merely through occasional meetings but through frequent regular meetings, through personal and profound contacts. Catholic Action imbues its membership with principles." [9]

This respondent adds that the best proof of the strength of the organization is that Communism considers it and not Christian Democracy or any other Catholic organization its greatest enemy. For this reason, she adds, it is probably Catholic Action and not the D.C. that, in a political emergency, would provide the greatest amount of

[9] *Interview,* Number 41 (Rome, January 31, 1958), p. 14.

cohesive opposition to a threat from the Communist Party.[10]

No other group operating in Italy is viewed by our respondents quite in the same light. Only one bureaucrat considers the Coltivatori Diretti the most powerful group in the bureaucracy, although several more caution that Paolo Bonomi's mass organization is not to be lightly treated. On the other hand, as many as seven of fifty-eight group leaders and Confindustria officials single out this organization as the most significant instrument for intervention in public administrative processes. The ministries of Agriculture and Labor are said to be particularly susceptible to Coltivatori Diretti demands, although power is said to be generalized throughout the bureaucracy.[11] On a number of occasions, however, the same respondents who single out this group for particular attention also note that its strength is largely based on the close ties it manages to maintain with Catholic Action and the Italian clergy.

As far as the trade unions are concerned, there is almost universal agreement that, regardless of their ideological orientation, they do not count for much in public administrative circles. To be sure, as we have previously noted, leaders of U.I.L. and C.G.I.L. speak of collusion between C.I.S.L., on the one hand, and D.C. ministers and upper-level bureaucrats, on the other. Some of this undoubtedly occurs, as do instances in which, when trade unions are entitled to formal representation on bureaucratic bodies, C.I.S.L. receives preferential treatment because of its *parentela* relationship to the governing political party. It is nevertheless of considerable interest that not a single bureaucrat or political leader interviewed in this study singled out the trade unions as interest groups

10 *Ibid.*, p. 16.
11 For an interesting criticism of the way in which the Coltivatori Diretti and Confagricoltura use the Italian bureaucracy for purposes of securing captive members and of compelling them to pay organizational dues, see Adolfo Battaglia, "Lo Stato in appalto," *Il Mondo*, 6 (December 21, 1954), p. 4.

that carry particular weight in Italian politics. This is all
the more curious when one stops to recall that C.I.S.L.
and C.G.I.L. have strong contingents in the legislature,
and when it is remembered that the unions have a large
number of grievances against Italian society and a great
many demands to make of it.[12]

The position of relative weakness is frankly recognized
by trade-union leaders, although the reasons they adduce
for it are often strictly ideological or polemical. C.G.I.L.
leaders, for example, regularly attribute trade-union weakness in the polity to the domination of society by monopoly capitalism and the 1948 decision of the Catholics to
destroy the labor organizational unity that emerged in
1945 at war's end. U.I.L. officials ascribe the weakness in
part to the same factors, but add that C.I.S.L.'s role of
serving as a foil for conservative elements within the D.C.
is greatly responsible for the inability of the labor confederations to mount a coordinated attack on the legislature and bureaucracy. C.I.S.L. spokesmen in turn lament
the sectarian, class-oriented philosophy and tactics of both
the other confederations, and claim that labor's weakness is a direct result of the unwillingness of C.G.I.L. and
U.I.L. to come to terms with the conditions of the twentieth century. Whatever may be the particular rationale
offered, it is fairly clear that union leaders by and large
recognize that their impact on the authoritative allocation of values in Italian society has been considerably
limited in recent years.

It is possible, of course, to exaggerate the weaknesses of
the unions, and it should therefore be understood that

[12] Space does not permit a detailed treatment of this important problem. The interested reader should consult my *The Italian Labor Movement: Problems and Prospects* (Ithaca, 1957). Cf. the series of articles that
appeared in *Mondo Economico* in the summer of 1957. Of particular
interest are: Paolo Cavezzali, "Nuovi Problemi e nuovi compiti per i
sindacati," *Mondo Economico*, 12 (July 6, 1957), pp. 8–9; the responses of
Giulio Pastore (C.I.S.L.) and Vittorio Foà (C.G.I.L.), *ibid.*, 12 (June 1,
1957), pp. 11–12, (June 29, 1957), pp. 8–9. Cf. the important article by
Gino Giugni, "Esperienze corporative e post-corporative nei rapporti di
lavoro in Italia," *Il Mulino*, 51–52 (January–February, 1956), pp. 3–17.

their influence over policy must be seen with reference to other groups with which the unions compete. Thus, relative to most of the associational interest groups in the country, all the labor confederations exert considerable influence over policy. Relative to each other, it is apparent that U.I.L. is the weakest union and that, notwithstanding C.G.I.L.'s greater numbers, it does not have the impact on policy that is true of a C.I.S.L., which remains, after all, a member of the Christian Democratic family. Moreover, with the "Opening to the Left" one might suppose that both C.I.S.L. and C.G.I.L. may count for more in both the legislature and the bureaucracy than has been true for most of the years since 1948.

One should add that, as a matter of operating style, the unions utilize weapons such as the strike or the demonstration that often compel both the political and bureaucratic officials to give some attention to union demands. Indeed, it is apparent from even a cursory examination of Italy's postwar history that extreme measures on the part of the trade unions were the only means available to force either the legislature or the bureaucracy to deal meaningfully, instead of superficially, with problems of great concern to organized labor. Reflecting this, as well as his intention to qualify comments concerning his organization's relative weakness, a leader of C.G.I.L. observes:

"We have at least been able in many instances to constrain the public administration and the Parliament to pay attention to what we say. The I.R.I. battle [i.e., *Sganciamento*], the battle over the petroleum law [i.e., regarding limits on foreign investments] are good examples of what I am talking about. This is also true of some of the issues that come before the Interministerial Committee on Prices where, on occasion, we have had to make very important national issues of the prices of such things as fertilizers and medicines. When this has happened, when we have fought well, the Committee has been compelled to reduce certain prices. As a consequence, I would repeat to you that we really do not view public administration as a series of completely closed doors. We do have some means of entering and of making our influence felt." [13]

Following Catholic Action, the group most frequently named as an exerciser of the greatest influence in bureaucratic circles is Confindustria. The way in which this allegation or perception is articulated differs as one moves from one ideological group to another, and depending on whether the respondent is a group leader, politician, or bureaucratic official. Some Communists and Socialists, for example, tend to cast the matter in strict and often simplistic Marxist terms. On their reasoning, the fact that Italy is a bourgeois, capitalistic society implies by definition that the industrial confederation will enjoy preponderant power not only in the bureaucracy but within the political system as a whole. Indeed, not only is the Italian polity presumably in the clutches of Confindustria, but the confederation itself is nothing more than the abject instrumentality of a handful of economic monopolies. Bureaucrats are seen as the lackeys and mouthpieces of these interests and the idea that either the bureaucracy or other associational interest groups might serve as sources of countervailing power is flatly denied. Between the leaders of Confindustria, on the one hand, and Catholic Action, on the other, there is said to exist the most occult and sinister kind of collusion, aimed at preventing any serious modification in the exercise of economic and political power or in the prevailing system of social stratification. For those who share this perception, seemingly liberal political orientations such as that represented by Amintore Fanfani, are said to be illusory. The only fountainheads out of which genuine change might flow are presumably left-wing revolution or the peaceful coming to power of the extreme left-wing parties.

[13] *Interview,* Number 94, *op. cit.,* p. 10. Another C.G.I.L. national official supports this view, adding that C.G.I.L. is too large for the bureaucracy to ignore and that, because of its size, the bureaucrats themselves are often in informal contact with leaders of the Confederation. *Interview,* Number 106, *op. cit.,* p. 1.

The above is a distilled composite of responses concerning Confindustria that one can expect from leaders of C.G.I.L. and from officials of the Communist and Socialist parties, as well as from some Radicals who initially broke with the Liberal Party precisely over the question of how much influence within it the representatives of or spokesmen for Confindustria manifested. However, there is another kind of response that one encounters when talking with bureaucrats or with Confindustria leaders themselves. Several officials of the Ministry of Industry and Commerce, for example, frankly assert that the dominant organized group interacting with the Ministry is clearly and without any doubt Confindustria. They generally add, however, that this is as it should be, in view of the fact that the Ministry exists to encourage industrial expansion, that Confindustria does in truth represent the vast majority of Italy's significant industrial enterprises, and that what the Ministry does in its daily operations is of prime concern to the industrial confederation and its members. In short, for all the clientelistic reasons we have previously explored, the administrators within the Ministry of Industry and Commerce expect that the weight of Confindustria over bureaucratic decisions will be considerable.

Of particular significance in the view of many respondents is the expertise that Confindustria can bring to bear on problems of concern to the bureaucracy. One of the confederation's leaders stresses that the bureaucracy, particularly the ministries of Labor and Industry, often turns to Confindustria on matters involving the interpretation of laws or the development and application of administrative regulations. Thus, while the approach of the confederation to the bureaucracy invariably has political implications, its ability to intervene at all is frequently based on the image of technical competence that the confederation has succeeded in implanting in bureaucratic circles.[14] An official of the Association of Italian Joint Stock

14 *Interview*, Number 85, *op. cit.*, p. 11.

Companies, which is closely tied to Confindustria, is even more emphatic on this score. He notes that his organization has achieved a widespread reputation for competence in fiscal matters and that for this reason the particular position that it, or Confindustria, assumes in these matters is likely to be accorded the greatest respect by the bureaucracy as well as by other sectors of government.[15] Although the empirical evidence does not support simplistic allegations concerning Confindustria's powers, it is reasonably clear that the confederation counts for something in bureaucratic circles and that in some administrative agencies it continues to be a more significant associational interest group than either the trade unions or Catholic Action.

If we were to compare in a general way the three categories of groups concerning which some illustrative information is supplied, we would probably have to conclude that, by and large, Catholic groups are the most powerful ones operating in the bureaucracy. Among these, Catholic Action seems predominant, although the Coltivatori Diretti are not to be ignored, particularly in the Ministry of Agriculture. After the Catholic groups, Confindustria continues to be important in bureaucratic circles, and, finally, left-wing groups such as C.G.I.L. and U.I.L. are of considerably less importance, even if not totally without influence.

This broad generalization, however, must be qualified in a number of ways that may or may not be apparent from what has already been said.

First, it should be obvious that when speaking about a group's influence over the bureaucracy, not the whole bureaucracy but particular and individual segments of it must be analyzed. The significant influence that Confindustria continues to exercise in the Ministry of Industry and Commerce probably spills over into the ministries of the Treasury, Finance, and Labor but is certainly not of the same magnitude. When Confindustria leaves the

---

15 *Interview*, Number 95, *op. cit.*, p. 5.

area of natural *clientela* relationship, both *parentela* and other *clientela* considerations undercut its influence. In this sense it is probably valid to assume, as did one of our previous respondents, that the bureaucracy constitutes the "feudal holdings" of some of the major interest groups functioning in the Italian political system.

Second, it is important to recognize that, to varying degrees, both Confindustria and Catholic Action, as interest groups, have been somewhat in decline since 1953. We have already noted that the industrial Confederation no longer enjoys the prestige in governmental circles that was true of the era of Angelo Costa and Alcide De Gasperi. Confindustria leaders, themselves, recognize this and are relatively free to admit that the confederation did not come through with as much electoral financing as had been promised the D.C. in 1953. Confindustria's leaders claim they were double-crossed when the D.C. in 1953 failed to elect more Christian Democratic Confindustria spokesmen; Christian Democrats argue that Confindustria blandly sought to support political parties that were at odds with the D.C. One response to this changed situation was Confindustria's experiment with the ill-fated Confintesa, a somewhat crude and clearly amateurish attempt by Confindustria to enter the legislative struggle in an open and unprecedented way. In any event, the experience of Confintesa as well as the running of editorial laments and bitter indictments in Confindustria's major newspaper, *L'Organizzazione industriale,* clearly reveal the agonies of a powerful interest in serious decline.[16]

To some extent, considerable decline is also true of Catholic Action since 1953. The great influence that the

16 See, for example, the following main editorials in *L'Organizzazione Industriale:* "Necessaria chiarezza di idee" (January 7, 1954), p. 1; Necessaria serenità di lavoro" (January 21, 1954), p. 1; "Considerazioni sull'immobilismo" (July 14, 1955), p. 1; "Motivi di confusione" (July 21, 1955), p. 1; Report of a meeting of the Executive Junta (November 17, 1955), p. 1; "Identificazione del sociale nell'economico" (June 21, 1956), p. 1; "Rapporto da salvaguardare" (February 2, 1956), p. 1. For some official governmental responses to Confindustria attacks see "Notiziario," supplement to *L'Organizzazione Industriale* (January 26, 1956), p. 4.

organization was able to exercise within the D.C.—and, through the Party, in the legislature and bureaucracy— was clearly based on the fact that in the earlier postwar years the electoral fate of Christian Democracy hinged on the organization and operation of Catholic Action and the Civic Committees. During the critical years when Fascism's fall created a power vacuum, and when genuine revolutionary ferment was in the air, these organizations were the only ones prepared effectively to compete with Communism and Socialism for the allegiance of the liberated Italian voters. Many of those who were interviewed remark that Italy would almost certainly have gone the way of Czechoslovakia had not organized Catholicism been available to meet the Communists head on in every diocese and parish where the latter sought to exert electoral prowess. Indeed, a leader of the National Civic Committee points out that the Civic Committees were created in February, 1948, precisely because the extreme Left emerged as the most powerful faction in the elections of 1946 and because the Vatican was most concerned about the relatively weak structure of the D.C. This respondent notes that while it is true that the D.C. did not possess a cellular structure that would permit it to compete effectively with the P.C.I., it could depend, from 1948, on the cellular structure provided by Catholic Action and the Civic Committees in all of the country's more than 20,000 parishes and over 300 dioceses.[17]

Without engaging in detailed examination, it is possible to say that between 1948 and 1953 the D.C. became heavily mortgaged to Catholic Action and the Civic Committees. No one will question that these were dominant organizations in the selection of D.C. candidates, the manipulation of preferential votes in favor of candidates acceptable to the Catholic Right, the naming of some Cabinet members, and the exercise of some control over bureaucratic careers and administrative decisions. Since the D.C. Congress of Naples of 1954, however, there has

17 *Interview*, Number 20, *op. cit.*, pp. 1–2.

occurred a gradual erosion of Catholic Action's power. De Gasperi's death led to a decline in the influence within the Party exerted by center and right-wing "notables" who maintained close ties with Catholic Action. As many observers note, the heavy mortgage was lifted in part because Amintore Fanfani sought systematically to create a party apparatus that would eventually make the D.C. less abjectly dependent on Catholic Action's far-flung capillary organization. While Catholic Action opposed the growth of indigenous party strength, it failed to stem the development and was also in turn made the captive of a situation wherein it could not heavy-handedly avoid support of the D.C. in electoral campaigns. Finally, the election of John XXIII to the papacy signaled something of a liberalizing tendency in the Vatican. Luigi Gedda, the ultraconservative president of Catholic Action and an obvious favorite of Pius XII, was replaced by a milder leader. Even the casual observer could detect that Catholic Action would no longer play quite the critical role in Italian politics that it had managed for over a decade. Thus in the realm of organized Catholicism—which, as we have noted, is certainly not as monolithic as many in Italy and abroad superficially claim—it is possible to detect that, while still a formidable interest group, Catholic Action counts for less today than it did just a few short years ago. The structure of group influence over legislative and bureaucratic decisions is not as rigid or immutable as some might fear or suppose.

It is also noteworthy that images of overwhelming Catholic Action power grow out of confusing Catholic Action activity with the direct intervention of the clergy into the political process. One very perceptive legislator notes that all interest groups tend to exaggerate their importance and that this is particularly true of Catholic Action. The point is that, in the final analysis, all Catholic organizations—Catholic Action as well as A.C.L.I., C.I.S.L., and D.C.—are dependent on ecclesiastical authority. It is perfectly permissible for Catholic groups to fight among themselves, and, indeed, the Vatican may actually encourage some of this kind of interaction. It is also acceptable that there be manifested some ideological variation among Catholic groups; the Vatican itself is not free of significant differences in this regard. What is really critical is the inability of any Catholic group to challenge seriously the power and authority of the clergy. Thus a Catholic who belongs to C.I.S.L. and is opposed to Catholic Action can and often is elected on a D.C. list notwithstanding this conflict. "But," says our legislator, "if one is really and substantially opposed to the Church, he simply does not get elected as a Christian Democrat." [18]

This respondent, as well as others, stresses the power over the political process that is exercised by priests and bishops, and cautions that these must not be confused with Catholic Action. Particular stress is laid on the capability of bishops to influence what happens administratively at the local level. A leader of C.I.S.L. asserts, for example, that when the labor confederation really wants something done locally, it invariably turns to a bishop for help. If, as is infrequently the case, the bishop is favorably disposed toward the union, he will intervene with the prefect, the provincial administration, or representatives of the national ministries. On some occasions, as has been noted, he may travel to the ministries at Rome in order to make his plea or demands.[19] A Socialist deputy adds that it is at the local and provincial levels that great influence is exercised by interest groups over public administration. It is here that national regulations are implemented, taxes collected, public works contracts awarded, ministerial regulations in the fields of agriculture, commerce, and labor enforced or ignored, and so forth. In general, he holds that the groups that are the most successful in directing the nature of local-level administration are those with the best access to the bishops.[20]

18 *Interview*, Number 101 (Rome, June 28, 1958), p. 4.
19 *Interview*, Number 6, *op. cit.*, p. 8.
20 *Interview*, Number 2, *op. cit.*, p. 2.

A leader of the Republican Party in Bologna notes, however, that it is often Catholic Action that has this favored access. Thus, when local or national administrators are recalcitrant, Catholic Action leaders have recourse "to the most expedient instrument of pressure. That is, they go to the bishop or cardinal of the area, who in turn makes it known to the political leaders or bureaucrats that he favors the request of the Catholic organization. To oppose a bishop in Italy today is likely to be disastrous for anyone rash enough to chance it." [21]

A respondent who has conducted considerable research into the Italian interest-group phenomenon indicates that the oft-cited example of bishops intervening in local politics and administration, or in the ministries at Rome, is not an exaggeration. As a matter of fact, given the important role in social welfare activities now exercised by the clergy, it is only natural that clerics should frequently intervene in government on behalf of their constituents. He notes that: "There is something about the way in which the political system has developed in this postwar period that makes it almost compulsory for an effective pastor or bishop to engage in this type of activity. That is, given the inefficiency of the bureaucratic system, and given the vital ward-heeler role engaged in by the Italian clergy, these are the individuals who must intervene in public administration on behalf of those who, at the level of the parish and the diocese, are closely identified with Christian Democracy." [22]

Whatever may be the forces that catapult clergymen into the bureaucratic process, it is obvious that their effectiveness or influence should not be confused with that of Catholic Action. To be sure, bishops can be the specific instruments through which Catholic Action asserts itself in bureaucratic circles. Nevertheless, one can conceptualize a considerable diminution in the powers of Catholic Action without extending the generalization to

21 *Interview*, Number 22, *op. cit.*, p. 7.
22 *Interview*, Number 47 (Rome, February 19, 1958), p. 8.

cover members of the clergy as well. Bishops are not exclusively at the service of Catholic Action; they sometimes do intervene on behalf of A.C.L.I., C.I.S.L., or other Catholic or Christian Democratic interest groups. They may also intervene for individual parishioners or on behalf of the official church itself.

For these reasons, among many, it is necessary to view the clergy as a separate category of interest in Italy. A leader of Catholic Action's National Presidency was careful to emphasize this fact, pointing out that there are many occasions when bishops and priests intervene directly in political and bureaucratic matters without mediating their activities through the organizational machinery of Catholic Action. "When they act in this fashion," he says, "they act not as officials or representatives of Catholic Action, but purely as individuals with an interest in having a particular administrative or legislative matter go in a particular direction rather than another." [23]

IDENTIFICATION OF BUREAUCRATS WITH INTEREST GROUPS

Obviously, the interaction between groups and the bureaucracy that we have examined in previous chapters does not imply that the public administrator is a passive element in the process. We have already noted that there is some validity to the proposition laid down in Chapter II, that bureaucratic agencies will differ in the degree to which they are penetrable by organized interest groups. In the same earlier chapter, we set out the proposition that decision makers in the bureaucracy will tend to favor those groups and group representatives with whom the bureaucrats share such things as ideological orientation, social class, education, life style, and so on. We can now explore what conclusions concerning this last proposition seem to be supported by our interview data.

The first thing to note here is that the evidence is somewhat mixed. If, as we noted in Chapter VIII, the

[23] *Interview,* Number 14 (Rome, December 12, 1957), p. 2.

interest group is not "respectable," the bureaucrat will tend to play down its significance, or even seek to ignore it when he can. If the group does have respectability—and this may mean a number of things, including wealth and high social status—there is definitely a tendency on the part of the bureaucrat to favor it. Thus it might be said that social status is of some importance, but we have little way of knowing exactly how important this factor may be as it applies to the individual group negotiator. The fact is that, even for the most proletarian of the interest groups, leadership tends to reside in the hands of men and women who hold university degrees and who are clearly members of the middle class. In almost all cases, those group leaders who interact with the bureaucrats are the latter's status equals. Very often they have had exactly the same university experiences, majoring in the ubiquitous field of jurisprudence. If status considerations are operative, therefore, they will probably reflect the status of group membership rather than that of group leaders.

Nevertheless, it is of some importance to explore what role, if any, various kinds of *identification* between bureaucrats and interest groups play in the interactive process. Assertions of the importance of identification are plentiful among our bureaucratic respondents. One of them, for example, in stressing that most administrators have fairly broad discretionary powers, adds that the typical administrator will certainly be influenced in his behavior by the extent to which he shares the values of an interest group or maintains close personal contacts with group leaders.[24] Another official, speaking of the Ministry of Industry and Commerce, notes that he and his colleagues maintain strong bonds of professional and personal friendship not only with the bureaucratic leaders of Confindustria but also with the representatives of Italy's major corporations.[25] Many of the views concerning

[24] *Interview*, Number 3, *op. cit.*, p. 4.
[25] *Interview*, Number 8, *op. cit.*, p. 3.

economic problems expressed by a director-general in the same Ministry are indistinguishable from the remarks that emanate from Confindustria leaders, and he frankly sees his role as requiring that he fully understand and empathize with Italian industrialists.[26] A Cabinet member with much direct experience in bureaucratic management asserts that it is the most natural of phenomena that public administrators should develop a sense of strong identification with those groups with which the bureaucrats' major activities are carried on.[27]

What the bureaucrats define as "natural" some interest-group leaders strongly protest. Left-wing groups, for example, see some sort of bourgeois conspiracy underlying the strong rapport that characterizes those in the Ministry of Industry and Commerce, on one side, and leaders of Confindustria, on the other. Trade-union leaders by and large complain that a sense of empathy of the bureaucrat toward organized labor simply does not exist, that bureaucrats in general identify with management groups, and that the trade unions are severely disadvantaged because of this. Laical group leaders can wax eloquent over the adverse consequences they suffer because allegedly increasing numbers of middle- and high-level bureaucrats owe their positions to Catholic Action and therefore tend to view problems and react to them as would Catholic Action leaders themselves. Comments such as these, of course, reflect the highly fragmented character of the interest-group structure as well as the extremely isolative and alienated nature of Italian political culture. The groups that are plugged into the administrative process tend to exclude competitors; the groups that are excluded tend to be excluded completely.

There are several subtypes of bureaucratic-group identification concerning which we can comment briefly. In some cases the subtype appears to be of central importance; in others its impact borders on the insignificant.

26 *Interview,* Number 38, *op. cit.,* p. 7.
27 *Interview,* Number 28, *op. cit.,* p. 2.

1. *Education.* Although identification by education is of little significance, there are several ways that the educational experiences of group leaders and bureaucrats do impinge substantially on the making of bureaucratic decisions. In the first place, the Italian bureaucracy greatly lacks top-level administrators who are technically trained. The bureaucratic elite consists overwhelmingly of persons trained in jurisprudence. Engineers, scientists, technicians, and other specialists capable of coping with the problems of a technological society are even scarcer in the bureaucracy than they are in the country at large. The relatively small number of scientifically trained graduates produced by Italian universities have naturally tended to filter into the industrial sector, where both the challenges and the rewards are greater than what the bureaucracy can offer.

A confrontation of the interest-group specialist with his less expert counterpart in the bureaucracy implies a clear disadvantage for the latter. One dimension of this phenomenon was highlighted when we discussed the lack of indigenous research facilities in administrative agencies and the tendency of the bureaucracy to be overly dependent on associational interest groups for information. Another dimension involves the use by interest groups of highly trained officials who make demands of the bureaucracy. Thus a leader of the Italian automotive industry's most important association (A.N.F.I.I.A.) stresses that when he approaches bureaucrats at Rome, he is usually accompanied by one or more specialists from the Milan office. According to this respondent, this kind of approach is tremendously advantageous in that it "is an excellent way to proceed to the education of members . . . of public administration who are extremely ill-informed regarding the technical details of the industries represented by our association." [28]

As we shall note in a subsequent section, the administrators are not without their own defenses against the

28 *Interview,* Number 1, *op. cit.,* p. 8.

onslaught of the expert. Indeed, it is possible to argue that the educational characteristics of the bureaucrats themselves constitute a potential source of defense. Let us note here exactly what this means.

If we were to compare the Italian with the French bureaucracy, one striking feature of the former would be the absence of the *grandes écoles* that are so significant in France in bureaucratic training. As Ehrmann notes, the French bureaucracy is a "splintered bureaucracy," with some of the specialized sectors highly permeable by organized interest groups.[29] According to Ehrmann's formulation, the very specialized and somewhat fragmented nature of the French bureaucracy increases its susceptibility to effective group pressure.

The situation in Italy is markedly different. The vast majority of those who fall into the "administrative class" category are members of the lower-middle and middle classes. Moreover, in almost every case their educational preparation has involved four years of university training in the field of jurisprudence. On both the class and educational (as well as regional origin) dimensions, the Italian bureaucracy is much more homogeneous than the French.

There are two ways of evaluating the consequences of this difference. One is to suggest that, where the bureaucracy is splintered—and where bureaucratic decisions require the participation of more than one bureaucratic sector—the very existence of strongly diverse bureaucratic traditions and orientations will provide a means of tempering the impact of any single *clientela* or *parentela* group's intervention. The French situation, for this type of decision, might be said to provide greater autonomy for the bureaucracy than is true of Italy.

To be sure, there are bureaucratic decisions in Italy that also require the participation of several agencies, and,

29 Henry W. Ehrmann, "French Bureaucracy and Organized Interests," *Administrative Science Quarterly*, 5 (March, 1961), pp. 549–50. The author makes the same point in his "Administration et groupes de pression," *Economie et Humanisme*, 123 (January–February, 1960), pp. 7–8 (reprint).

insofar as there do exist differences in orientation among bureaucrats, the same phenomenon may be operative. This would be true particularly of issues that serve to mobilize different *clientela* groups. Nevertheless, the structure of French bureaucracy offers more, in the sense that to the situation we describe is added a quantum of internal countervailing bureaucratic power and reciprocal bureaucratic control which grows out of the greater internal differentiation of French bureaucratic agencies and the differing styles of the various agencies.[30]

There is a second, and in my view preferable, way of evaluating this phenomenon. It applies not merely to bureaucratic decisions involving single agencies but to decisions of the bureaucracy in general. It is possible to argue that the greater homogeneity of the Italian bureaucrats increases the probability that they see themselves as involved in an essentially independent function within the political system. Independence would imply a commitment to resist pressures from forces external to the bureaucracy—forces, whether political or private, that would seek to use the bureaucracy as a mere instrumentality for the achievement of goals that are different from those that the bureaucrats themselves define as legitimate. In short, the suggestion here is that the educational and social homogeneity of the Italian bureaucracy makes it more capable than its French counterpart of resisting the attempts of the legislature, the Cabinet, or associational interest groups to harness the bureaucrats to their own goals.

To be sure, the situation is neither black nor white. We have already observed that a lack of scientifically trained public administrators may serve to the advantage of interest groups that overwhelm the bureaucrats with technical expertise. On the other hand, as we shall note below, training in jurisprudence leads many Italian ad-

[30] On this point, see Joseph LaPalombara and Gianfranco Poggi, "I Gruppi di pressione e la burocrazia italiana," *Rassegna Italiana di Sociologia*, 1 (October–December, 1960), pp. 44–45.

ministrators in search of the public interest. It causes them to emphasize the importance of the law and the need to enforce and interpret it rationally.

It would be difficult to overemphasize the importance of the orientation to rationality that grows out of the bureaucrat's education in jurisprudence. A great number of interest-group leaders, as well as the bureaucrats themselves, recognize this as a significant variable that impinges on administrative behavior. To be sure, not all of the comments in this regard are favorable. One administrator, for example, notes that the rationality-oriented Italians engaged in a mammoth effort to create a completely rational administrative system in which individual discretion is reduced to a minimum. Those who fashioned the administrative code are said to have brought into being the kind of situation wherein the sharp administrator is able, by referring to one or another section of the code, to support any decision he elects to reach in his work.[31] Another administrator, a leader of the National Productivity Committee who is deeply involved in the movement for bureaucratic reform, is extremely harsh in his evaluation of the juridical education of administrators and the formalized and legalistic structure of the bureaucracy. He notes that the rigidities of the law apply not merely to career patterns but also to the whole of administrative procedure: "Administrative acts in Italy are controlled from the standpoint not of accuracy or efficiency but of the legality of the act or the procedure No one in the bureaucracy is really concerned about whether administrative procedures are efficient or productive from the standpoint of cost. The legalistically minded bureaucrat wants all such actions to be legal—that is, to fall within the framework of the juridical order." [32]

31 *Interview,* Number 17, *op. cit.,* p. 3.
32 *Interview,* Number 52 (Rome, January 17, 1958), p. 2. The abortive and often ill-considered attempts of the National Productivity Committee to introduce stream-lined administrative procedures based on American principles of scientific management cannot be treated here. The experiment does depict quite dramatically the capacity of the Italian bureacracy

It is obvious enough that consequences like those cited do stem from the educational background of administrators. On the other hand, there are many who stress that the insistence on rationality has its positive and politically stabilizing side. A director-general emphasizes that not merely any demand—even from a highly favored *clientela* group—is likely to be accorded favorable treatment by his ministry. What the groups request must conform to a minimum framework of rationality, and it is grossly misleading to write about Italian public administration in any way that ignores this basic reality.[33] Similarly, another bureaucrat who laments the considerable influence that Confindustria exercises over his ministry is careful to add that the Confederation is under considerable pressure to convince the bureaucrats that its demands are rational.[34] An inspector-general who is completely aware of the great importance of *clientela* and *parentela* groups in the administrative process is also willing to acknowledge that the bureaucracy is strongly motivated to find the most rational solution possible for the problems with which it must deal.[35]

So important is the orientation to rationality on the part of bureaucrats that it is said to provide some limited access even to those left-wing groups which generally benefit neither from *clientela* nor from *parentela* factors. As one Christian Democratic leader sees it, "There is a strong tendency on the part of functionaries to seek rational choices. Thus groups of the Left who stress the objective conditions of a particular situation are prob-

---

to resist change, particularly when what is proposed is so alien to Italian traditions and culture.

One may also note here that one reason for Confindustria's technical superiority over the bureaucracy lies in its quite different basis of leadership recruitment. A national leader of the Confederation points out that, in its selection of young people for career-training programs, Confindustria gives preference to those who have graduated from faculties of economics and commerce. *Interview*, Number 55 (Rome, January 19, 1958), p. 5.

[33] *Interview*, Number 38, *op. cit.*, p. 8.

[34] *Interview*, Number 8, *op. cit.*, p. 6.

[35] *Interview*, Number 83, *op. cit.*, p. 10.

ably able to get the ear of many of these same functionaries." [36] In short, it seems apparent that, to some degree
at least, the educational background of the Italian bureaucrat can and sometimes does incline him toward behavior
that limits the powers of some groups but augments that
of other groups not normally able to articulate their interests in bureaucratic settings.

Finally, in order to restore some balance to the general
point I am making here, it should be acknowledged that
there exists more than one educational road to rationality
in administration. It is certainly possible, for example,
that the type of technical education that is typical of
certain French administrators might lead to another kind
of rationality. There are various kinds, as Max Weber
points out, and this factor alone should caution us not
to draw a single and rigid generalization from the observation that Italian administrators are educationally more
homogeneous than their counterparts in France.

This last point might be illustrated with a single concrete example. It seems relatively clear that the amount
of educational exposure in economics that is typical of
Italian bureaucrats is not only limited but also of a strong
pre-Keynesian flavor. This circumstance is most favorable
to Confindustria and other employer associations that
speak the same language. It is disadvantageous to the trade
unions whose leaders are oriented to Keynesian and post-
Keynesian economic principles. In France, on the other
hand, Keynesianism has evidently managed to penetrate
into certain administrative sectors which, in turn, use this
particular orientation to limit and condition to some
extent the orientations and predispositions of other administrative sectors. In other words, the more varied
rationalities of French administration would seem to make
the bureaucracy accessible to a greater variety of groups,
even if one price paid for this is the greater vulnerability
of the French bureaucracy to the requests and demands
of organized interest.

[36] *Interview*, Number 40, *op. cit.*, p. 15.

2. *Origin.* A second type of identification between bureaucrat and group leader may involve the origin of each of them. Typically in Italy, comments regarding the origins of the bureaucrats emphasize geographic region. It is widely believed, and empirical observation would certainly sustain, that Southern Italy produces a heavily disproportionate number of public administrators. The traditional South is the largely unindustrialized region where the sons of middle-class families have typically majored in jurisprudence and then found places in the bureaucracy. During the period encompassed by the field work for this study, 22,622 of the 33,169 students studying jurisprudence were located in Southern universities. By way of contrast, only 7,163 of the total of 19,694 students enrolled in the fields of mathematics and the physical and natural sciences were in Southern universities.[37] Southern university graduates, confronted with an economy that simply will not absorb all the budding lawyers, enter the bureaucracy in droves. A similar phenomenon operates at the lower levels of the bureaucracy, because the public service tends to afford a refuge for the excessive population produced in the South and clearly not accommodated by the private labor market.[38]

Despite the predominance of Southern Italians in the bureaucracy, we have little evidence that this structure works to the advantage of certain groups and to the disadvantage of others. Nothing said by any administrator suggests that bureaucrats prefer to deal with interest-group representatives who emanate from the South. Nor do the group leaders who are sensitive to the rules of bureaucratic interaction single out the necessity, or even the advisability, of sending Southern Italian negotiators to represent interest groups in the ministries and other

[37] Istituto Centrale di Statistica, *Annuario statistico italiano* (Rome, 1959), p. 106.

[38] It is apparent that neither emigration nor the private sector of the economy in the South is able to absorb the growth in population. We thus encounter the heavy in-migration from southern to northern locales that I discussed in Chapter II, above.

administrative agencies. Some non-Southern administrators lament the predominance of Southerners in their midst; some group leaders, particularly among industrialists from the North, despair over having to deal with a bureaucracy made heavy and cumbersome by the allegedly "Southern way" of dealing with problems. There is little question that many find extremely frustrating a bureaucratic system that combines a formal structure inherited from Piedmont and a set of attitudes and orientations to action inherited from the Bourbons. But we cannot say that origin in the regional sense is a variable that accounts for the differing access and influence that interest groups are able to develop in the realm of public administration. The situation might be different if there were a greater incidence of interest-group organization and membership in the South. It is noteworthy, however, that the very region that produces most of the bureaucrats is also the one in which associational interest-group organization and membership is the least well developed.

Nor do we find that origin—in the sense of interest-group leaders detached to administrative agencies—is of striking importance in Italy. The Italian bureaucracy normally involves a lifetime commitment to a career in the public service. It is not easy for interest groups to insert their leaders into the bureaucracy laterally and on a temporary basis. Some of our respondents do claim that interest groups such as Catholic Action manage to place their own people in bureaucratic positions, and some of these claims are undoubtedly true. This pattern, however, is a form of identification we shall discuss in a moment. Here it is necessary to emphasize that, except at the level of ministerial cabinets, associational interest groups rarely place their leaders in bureaucratic roles.[39]

[39] A significant exception to this generalization occurred when various industrial groups "loaned" some of their personnel to administrative agencies responsible for the management of Marshall Plan activities. See, for example, *L'Organizzazione Industriale*, 3 (June 17, 1948), p. 3; 3 (December 2, 1948), p. 1.

3. *Group membership.* Much more frequent is the case of the administrator who sees his job as a life career and who at the same time retains a position of membership or leadership in an associational interest group. This pattern now applies primarily to Catholic interest groups that are able to utilize *parentela* as a means of infiltrating the bureaucracy. Presumably, this factor would be particularly salient in the naming of interest-group members or leaders to regional and local administrative agencies.

Admittedly, the distinction between identification by *origin* and identification by *membership* is not hard and fast. We may note, for example, the remarks of a central ecclesiastical assistant of Catholic Action addressed to a 1953 meeting of diocesan leaders of G.I.A.C.—the Italian (male) Youth of Catholic Action. After having spoken of the continuing contemporary power of Freemasonry, and generally of "this bourgeoisie that remains in the state bureaucracy, remains in the economy, remains in the judiciary," Monsignor Sargolini concludes: "Well, then, dear friends, an electoral victory will not suffice to reform the world, to give us a Christian social order in Italy. It is a matter of reforming men, remaking them, and then *placing these same men a little bit all over. . . .* Here, then, is the function of Catholic Youth . . . to be a great breeding ground of men—men who will later then personally assume responsibility and *who will be placed* in all sectors." [40]

Obviously, an appeal of this kind may, if implemented, give rise to identification by both *origin* and *membership*. On the basis of the information at our disposal, however, the latter pattern seems to be the more important of the two. Placing group leaders on ministerial cabinets for relatively short periods may have some advantage but is usually a short-run strategy and, as we shall see, is subject to rather negative reactions from the permanent bureauc-

[40] Presidenza Centrale della Gioventù Italiana di Azione Cattolica, *Atti della quattro giorni presidenti diocesani GIAC* (Rome, n.d.), p. 9 (emphasis supplied—J.L.).

racy. Inserting one's leaders and members "a little bit all over," as Monsignor Sargolini recommends, is clearly a means of assuring long-term influence over bureaucratic decisions.

4. *Institutional mission.* I have in mind here the situation in which the bureaucrats identify the operation of a ministry with the achievement of the goals or desires of an associational interest group. It is this kind of identification that leads many of our respondents to claim that the Ministry of Industry and Commerce is a feudal holding of Confindustria, that bureaucrats in this agency think with the premises and through the logical formulations typical of the industrial confederation, and so forth. In several cases, of course, we encountered leaders within the Ministry who frankly state that their central mission is that of encouraging the growth and prosperity of private enterprise in any way that seems appropriate and possible.

This form of identification, then, is based on the bureaucrat's definition of the particular scope and purpose of his agency. As such, it constitutes one of the most important factors making for the development of a strong *clientela* relationship. One reason why the unions are not as effective as they might be in the Ministry of Labor and Social Security is that the bureaucratic leaders there see their purpose as regulatory rather than facilitative vis-à-vis the unions and labor in general. On the other hand, the Ministry of Agriculture's bureaucrats define their role as that of facilitating the growth and prosperity of agriculture. This sense of identification goes a long way toward explaining why the Coltivatori Diretti and Confagricoltura have been successful in effecting and maintaining a strong *clientela* relationship with this agency.

5. *Reference group choice.* It is extremely difficult to delineate the extent to which Italian bureaucratic decisions can be explained by the resort of the administrator to reference-group criteria. In essence, the reference-group type of identification would be operative whenever the

bureaucrat adopts, as an ideal type of behavior, the style of life or thought that he considers to be typical of the leadership of a particular associational interest group. It is not sufficient that the style of life or thought be *admired* by the administrators. Were this the case, we would expect a great many of the latter to favor C.G.I.L., because they are certainly free to express how much they admired the frank, aggressive, and essentially honest behavior of Giuseppe DiVittorio, who long directed the left-wing labor confederation's activities. In order for this kind of identification to matter, it is essential that the bureaucratic decision-maker adopt, consciously or unconsciously, the style and the behavior of a particular interest group.

Aside from the fact that reference-group identification is a very slippery concept, there is little in our interviews that warrants our including it as a salient variable accounting for bureaucratic responses to interest-group desires or demands. Quite obviously, there must be some of this phenomenon in any bureaucratic structure. When an inspector-general in the Ministry of Industry and Commerce notes that he and his colleagues are more sensitive to the needs of Confindustria than of any other group in Italy, one might say that for them the industrial confederation constitutes a significant reference group.[41] But, in general, this seems to be a less important variable than is apparently true in a country like France.

One important reason for the difference between the two countries is that there is evidently much less *pantouflage* in Italy. One or two of our respondents do mention instances of industries recruiting personnel out of the public bureaucracy, but such statements are striking because of their infrequency. Much more frequent are statements such as that made by a leading Italian industrialist who notes that, unlike the French situation, the relationship between Italian bureaucrats and industrialists is close. He points out that there are undoubtedly some few high civil servants who transfer to industrial manage-

41 *Interview*, Number 83, *op. cit.*, p. 11.

ment, just as there are some legislators who are secretly on industrial payrolls. The incidence of the latter pattern is probably greater; in any event the cases in which top-level and "hungry" public administrators are recruited into industries and interest groups that subsequently use them as a means of obtaining bureaucratic leverage are extremely rare. Thus one would not expect to find bureaucrats consciously using Confindustria or other industrial associations as reference groups on the expectation that they might eventually be recruited into positions of much greater remuneration.[42]

6. *View of the world.* The last type of bureaucratic-group identification we will mention involves a sharing of values and attitudes—a tendency on the part of the bureaucrat to view the world and its problems more or less exactly as do certain interest-group leaders with whom the bureaucrats interact. We suggested the importance of this variable when we discussed varying kinds of rationality and the fact that Italian bureaucrats tend to see economic problems as do the typical Italian industrialists and their associations. What is critical here is that some bureaucrats and interest-group leaders tend to reason in the same way, to develop the same categories for judging people and problems, and to lean toward essentially the same kinds of solutions for the problems that are brought to the bureaucracy's attention.

It is significant, for example, that a leading official of the Ministry of Industry and Commerce views the movement for bureaucratic reform as an effort on the part of the trade unions to gain additional leverage over the bureaucracy. He is opposed to unions, abominates the strike as a weapon in collective bargaining, and generally articulates the same attitudes toward organized labor that one

---

42 *Interview,* Number 45, *op. cit.,* p. 5. The reader might be reminded that recourse to reference groups as a means of explaining bureaucratic behavior opens up a Pandora's box of infinite regression. If a bureaucrat's action cannot be explained by his relationship to overtly organized and intervening interest, one begins chasing the phantom of his "reference groups."

encounters among Confindustria's leaders.[43] Another official of the same ministry, while noting that he and his colleagues generally see things very much as do their colleagues in Confindustria, assumes that the tendency of bureaucrats to react to problems as do their clientele groups is true of every sector of public administration.[44]

On the whole, what we encounter among Italian bureaucrats is an aversion to party politics, great hostility to organized labor, and even greater hostility of distrust expressed toward political leaders. Insofar as such views are prevalent, they serve strongly to identify the bureaucratic leaders with the industrialists and other economically privileged classes in the society. It is partly because the bureaucrats, themselves, strongly believe in the idea of a class war that the fragmentation and ideological conflict typical of Italian society at large is often reproduced in the bureaucracy. This factor also goes a long way toward revealing why the bureaucracy has been less effective as an aggregator of conflicting interests than one might justifiably expect within a political system that displays at least the trappings of democratic pluralism.

BUREAUCRATIC CAPACITY TO RESIST

I very much wish to avoid the impression that the Italian bureaucracy—or any bureaucracy, for that matter—is simply an object or target of interest-group assaults or a passive instrumentality in the political process. To be sure, we have touched on many of the bureaucracy's vulnerabilities to interest-group demands. *Parentela,* the lack of indigenous research and information-gathering resources, feeble merit systems, and similar factors are arrayed on one side of the ledger. But as we have already seen in part, such factors as the educational background of the bureaucrats may very well serve as a means of enforcing the independent role of the bureaucracy. Indeed, not even such phenomena as the inadequacy of research

43 *Interview,* Number 102, *op. cit.,* p. 6.
44 *Interview,* Number 83, *loc. cit.*

facilities are completely one-sided, for the bureaucrats are not, after all, completely ignorant, and, in contrast to many groups, they are relatively well endowed with expert knowledge.

In order to summarize what we have already learned in this regard and to add some additional information, it will be useful to list the variables that tend to strengthen the capacity of the bureaucracy to resist the demands of interest groups. Because we have already dealt with such factors as *education* and the particular *nature* of the agency involved, we need not discuss these any further. It is necessary to give some brief attention, however, to the role of the *public interest,* the *permanent nature* of the bureaucracy, and the *administrative role* itself as important conditioners of administrative behavior.

1. *The public interest.* It is now a commonplace to cast aside the "public interest" as a euphemism that masks the much more real or fundamental interests that govern administrative or other governmental behavior. Presumably, the concept is too abstract and ephemeral; its meaning has never been convincingly explicated; certainly it is not something that one can easily discover as the result of empirical investigation. Confusion is said to be further compounded in that those who deal with this concept often do so on the basis of widely varying philosophical and epistemological first premises.[45]

It is not my intention to enter the debate concerning the theory of the concept. Rather, I wish to note here that Italian administrators frequently have recourse to it—whatever its meaning—and that it can be and is used as a means of permitting the bureaucracy to resist the overtures of associational interest groups. As a director-general in the Ministry of Industry and Commerce phrases the matter: "One of the misconceptions currently abroad, particularly in the United States, is that functionaries are individuals who identify with and normally follow the

[45] For an excellent discussion of this and related problems, see Glendon A. Schubert, *The Public Interest* (Glencoe, 1961).

policies determined by certain associations or groups. I do not agree with this at all. I insist that there does exist a general interest and that it has been traditionally the responsibility of the public official to find it and to apply it to the best of his ability." [46]

This bureaucrat, as well as many others, stresses that the function of the bureaucracy is to apply the law. They tend to see the bureaucracy in two roles—one of which involves a high degree of interaction with interest groups and other branches of government, the other of which requires that the bureaucrat at some point step back from the fray and ask what the public interest in the situation may be.

Perhaps this matter can best be illustrated by stopping for a moment to consider the pattern whereby some of the major associational interest groups are accorded formal, corporative representation on certain bureaucratic bodies. We have already conceded that, to some extent, those groups so privileged enjoy an advantage over groups that do not have representation. As the bureaucrats view formal representation, however, it does not constitute a serious threat to administrative autonomy. For one thing, the minister is never under any formal constraint to accept the recommendations of advisory committees on which groups may be represented. For another, the representation of clientele groups on such bodies will make it easier for the ministry to enforce regulations in which the groups, themselves, have been intimately involved. In this regard, more than one administrator points out that it is of considerable advantage to them to have the groups represented so that they can learn the bureaucrats' points of view and be held responsible in part for what the bureaucracy does. [47]

For the interest groups involved, formal representation is virtually a two-edged sword. The group representatives

<hr>

[46] *Interview,* Number 103 (Rome, July 3, 1958), p. 6.
[47] In particular, on this point, *Interview,* Number 8, *op. cit.,* p. 2; *Interview,* Number 83, *op. cit.,* pp. 5, 9, 16.

themselves are constrained to phrase their demands in terms of some "public" or "general" interest. When the bureaucrats have recourse to this concept, the groups are scarcely in a position to demand that what they need or desire for themselves should override what the bureaucrats find to be more consistent with the public interest. This is not to say that the Italian administrator views himself as an oracle from whom periodic wisdom defining the parameters and specific content of the public interest emanates.[48] Rather the typical bureaucrat, as the foregoing pages attest, recognizes that he is intimately involved in a highly politicized process and that the concept of public interest is one of the few meaningful weapons he can utilize in order to assert a bureaucratic decision that is not tied to narrow, particularistic interest-group considerations. Thus one of them, in speculating about this problem, suggests that the bureaucrats in their search after the rationality of public interest are considerably aided by the very fact that there exist interest groups which make competing demands on the bureaucracy.

Needless to say, like most other factors involved in bureaucratic resistance to group pressure, the public interest will appear ludicrous if pushed too far in our analysis. Its significance must be judged in the light of everything else that has been discussed thus far. There are times when it can and is overridden by strong considerations of *clientela* or *parentela,* as well as by the interests of the bureaucracy in expediency, with which it can be easily confused. Nevertheless, if we assume, as we must, that the bureaucrat is also in search of elbow room in the interactive process, it would be foolish to write off the concept of public interest as a piece of legerdemain or cheap rationalization.

2. *The permanent nature of the bureaucracy.* To paraphrase a French observer, politicians are transients while bureaucrats are permanent residents. This axiom is of considerable importance to our understanding of the ca-

48 See Ehrmann, "French Bureaucracy," *op. cit.,* pp. 542, 545.

pacity of the bureaucracy to resist the intervention of interest groups, particularly those that rely primarily on the *parentela* pattern. This can best be illustrated by noting something about group intervention at the level of the minister and his personal Cabinet.

Although ministerial Cabinets will often contain members who are appointed from the permanent bureaucracy, the minister and his personal staff are chosen primarily on the basis of patronage considerations. By and large, ministers are unwilling to entrust the affairs of the ministries to permanent civil servants who are not personal friends and in whom they cannot place considerable trust. When the vicissitudes of coalition politics dictate that ministerial undersecretaries shall be persons in whom the minister cannot place complete confidence, he will isolate and neutralize these politicians, relying heavily on his personal entourage. The British institution of the permanent, neutral, and omnicompetent ministerial secretary is simply unknown in Italy, as it is unknown in France.

As Ehrmann notes for France, "Group representatives inclined to obtain 'flash' decisions rather than steady influence prefer turning to a sympathetic *cabinet,* especially when they regard members of the bureaucratic hierarchy as foes rather than friends." [49] Exactly the same pattern is discernible in Italy. Because ministerial Cabinet members are primarily political, because they will not hesitate to intervene in bureaucratic matters on behalf of their friends, they constitute an attractive target for groups that have failed to work out a strong *clientela* relationship.

In the short-run at least, such intervention often works in the sense that "flash" decisions are forthcoming. As one top-level bureaucrat puts it, those groups with the greatest access to the minister and his friends in the Cabinet are likely to be the most successful. He notes that "whenever an important question arises in the ministry, the functionaries cannot act on their own but must act in the name of the minister and with his approval. . . . Those

49 *Ibid.,* p. 544.

groups that wish to be effective must gain the attention of the political appointees in the bureaucracy." [50]

According to two other administrators, one important power that the Cabinet members have over the permanent bureaucracy involves the awarding of *premiums.* Evidently, it is not unusual in Italy for one ministry to perform a special piece of work for another. Often, when this happens, the ministry receiving the service awards a financial premium to the other. These premiums are then distributed down the line, so much for directors-general, a little less for inspectors-general, still less for division chiefs, and so on. Almost invariably, some of the money filters up to those bureaucrats who are in the minister's Cabinet, even if, as is usual, they have performed no actual service. According to our respondents, "They manage to do this simply by telling the people involved that they will not have the minister sign any authorization for the acceptance of the premium unless they, themselves, are included in the distribution of the funds." [51]

The corrupting potential of this practice is self-evident. If a minister refuses to authorize premiums unless members of his Cabinet share in the loot, he can just as easily refuse to authorize additional money for poorly paid bureaucrats who appear recalcitrant in the face of requests on behalf of *parentela* groups. In other words, the powers of the minister extend considerably beyond the role he and his staff might play in matters of assignment, transfer, and promotion.

On the other hand, this matter is far from one-sided. Several bureaucrats note that the average minister is very much aware of the concentrated, extensive, and autocratic powers of the directors-general. In most instances, they seek to avoid open breaks with these men, knowing that life at the top can become much more complicated—and

---

[50] *Interview,* Number 87, *op. cit.,* pp. 4–5.
[51] *Interviews* 111 and 111a (Rome, July 10, 1958), pp. 2–3. We will note more about Confindustria's preference for the bureaucracy in Chapter XI.

the operation of the ministry much more chaotic—as the result of failure to achieve a *modus vivendi* with the top-level permanent bureaucracy. Illustrating this point, a member of the Ministry of Foreign Affairs tersely observes, "If a minister really attempted to impose policies that are not viewed favorably by the professional bureaucrats, he would find himself talking to the wind." [52] He qualifies this by admitting that when a minister or undersecretary takes a personal interest in a matter, he is likely to prevail over the bureaucrats—or at the very least he will receive consideration that is special and not available to just anyone or any group representative. Nevertheless, where the bureaucracy decides to plant its feet, those who are viewed as only temporary power-holders in the ministry are not likely to make much headway.[53]

The same general and sometimes sullen resentment that the bureaucrat expresses against politicians he also reserves for interest-group leaders who seek to intervene through the ministerial Cabinets. Groups that have recourse to this strategy are viewed as not playing the game. They are invariably involved in an open or covert violation of that very rationality that Italian bureaucrats hold so dear. The very fact that a decision is obtained, or compelled, outside the "normal" bureaucratic process marks the group as unreliable and accords it less status inside the bureaucracy than is reserved for "respectable" groups that rely on *clientela*.

It may very well be that, after a long period of Christian Democratic hegemony, the resistant capacity of the Italian bureaucracy has been considerably eroded. This seems to be the meaning of the following observation by a leader of the Industrial Union of Lazio, a Confindustria affiliate: "I personally remember a number of directors-general who in the past came close to refusing to go along with the dictates of ministers and undersecretaries. They were the kinds of persons who, when they discovered that

[52] *Interview,* Number 7, *op. cit.,* p. 3.
[53] *Ibid.,* p. 4.

political appointments to the ministry were going to be made in any event, forthrightly stated that they would accept no responsibility for the action. The younger people, however, want to make a career and are spineless. We cannot count on the younger functionaries as we could count on the old generation." [54]

3. *The administrative role.* It is abundantly clear that the administrative role itself equips the bureaucrat to resist becoming the willing or easy prey of organized interest. Whatever may be a new recruit's origins or previous system of values, he is certain over time to identify with the bureaucracy as such—that is, with both the principled and the expedient interest of public administration. Only the exceptional person, with no commitment to the public service as a career and with psychologically reinforcing professional and other memberships outside the bureaucracy, can long resist the impact of the role he occupies in an organization.

It is impossible to record here the mountain of evidence available to support the above generalization. The very persons who criticize the unwillingness of the bureaucracy to accept change acknowledge that this conservatism is a source of strength in the bureaucracy itself. When bureaucrats in large numbers define their role as requiring the objective application of the law, they generally do so with great pride and with a sense of having to protect the bureaucracy—and therefore the nation—against the irrational and particularistic forces at large in the country. Those administrators who speak favorably about the role of precedent, about the sacred character of the administrative code, may present headaches for the modernizing elite, but they also constitute an integral part of that aspect of the bureaucracy that gives it internal stability, even at the cost, I might add, of fanning the fires of political instability in general.

Thus one administrator candidly points out that bureaucrats are very jealous of, and attached to, their own

[54] *Interview,* Number 98, *op. cit.,* pp. 7–8.

powers and will not sit idly by in the face of efforts to diminish or rearrange them.[55] Another stresses that the bureaucrat is trained over time to resist excesses. Thus he succeeded during the Fascist era in resisting Mussolini's efforts radically to remake the bureaucracy. Similarly, he is now inclined to display the same tenacious resistance to contemporary proposals—concerning the bureaucracy or public policy in general—that he considers equally excessive. "As far as I am concerned," he says, "bureaucracy represents tradition and continuity. It cannot be shoved left or right. It has the role of inhibiting all excesses in society, and preserving tradition." [56]

There are some group leaders and political officials in Italy who bitterly complain that what the bureaucrats call tradition are really the values and the attitudes developed during the Fascist era. The view of these critics is captured in the following comment in one of Italy's left-center periodicals: "Our bureaucracy, it is evident, does not love the state in which it lives and on which it lives. . . . In almost all functionaries . . . there is very much alive today a nostalgia for the Fascist period . . . that is, an epoch in which there did not exist parliamentary investigating committees." [57]

Once again, it is necessary to avoid extending the specific observation to the breaking point. Nostalgia for Fascism, even a Fascist mentality, there may be, and it may serve the bureaucracy well by affording it a basis for resisting the pressures of certain interest groups. On the other hand, such a system of values would in turn cause the bureaucracy to identify with industrial and other groups that brought Fascism into existence and helped to maintain it in power for more than two decades.

Nor should we glide lightly over the fact that Fascism did manage considerably to vitiate the independence of

55 *Interview*, Number 17, *op. cit.*, p. 2.
56 *Interview*, Number 102, *op. cit.*, p. 8.
57 Angelo Conigliazo, "Il Burocrate allo specchio," *Il Mondo*, 5 (January 10, 1953), p. 1.

a once relatively proud bureaucracy. At war's end, as one respondent of Cabinet rank remarks, Italy was confronted with a bureaucratic structure in which most of the leading personalities, as well as many of the younger ones who currently hold sway, were confused as to the bureaucracy's role. They certainly did not possess any clear conceptualization of what the appropriate behavior of a bureaucracy should be to avoid becoming largely instrumental for one particular ideological or religious group in the country.[58] Therefore, while there does exist some capacity to resist, we must come back to the realization that, on matters of vital policy, the bureaucracy has been and remains allied not with the society or polity as a whole but only with restricted, isolated, and highly antagonistic segments of it.

CONCLUSION

We can conclude this discussion by coming back to the structural principles of *clientela* and *parentela* with which we have dealt in several chapters. If, within each of these patterns, we were to ask which groups in Italy appear to be the most significant and influential, the answer (of surprise to no one at this point) would be Confindustria and industrial associations in *clientela* situations, Catholic Action and other Catholic associations in *parentela* settings. But we can ask, in addition, whether *clientela* or *parentela* is the more significant strategy for intervening in the bureaucracy. In responding to this query it is necessary to be analytical, because head-on confrontation of the two patterns in Italy is not as frequent as the empirical researcher and the reader might desire. To be sure, there are issues such as *Sganciamento* which suggest that, on vital and dramatic occasions, the strength of *clientela* gives way before considerations of *parentela*. It is also possible to note that, where a group such as the Coltivatori Diretti is both client and *parente,* it can and does overshadow an organization such as Confagricoltura. It

[58] *Interview,* Number 58, *op. cit.,* p. 8.

seems rather obvious that, in the best of all possible worlds, an interest group would seek to develop and to capitalize on both kinds of relationships.

Analytically, we offer the following proposition: the most productive strategy for a group to develop in the public administrative sector is one of *position*. In the long run, the ability to create and maintain fixed channels of access to the bureaucracy is more important than the ability, even on a vital issue, to exercise pressure through an agency that is outside the bureaucratic system. The strategic logic of the *clientela* relationship satisfies the requirements of this principle, whereas that of *parentela* does not. *Clientela* implies the existence of important and relatively permanent bridgeheads inside the system. It implies privileged access; the client group renders itself more or less indispensable to the bureaucratic agency; often its pressure activities are not even perceived by the bureaucrats for what they really are. Indeed, the protection of the *clientela* group's interest often becomes part of bureaucratic precedent and, as such, is protected by the bureaucrat's passionate attachment to precedent and tradition. In this regard it is worth recalling the view concerning Confindustria expressed by Giuseppe Bottai, Minister of Corporations, in 1930: "We have arrived at such a point of reciprocal esteem that we can consider the leaders of the Confederation as collaborators of the Ministry of Corporations, to whom we can accord complete confidence." [59]

This kind of rapport between Confindustria and the Ministry of Industry and Commerce has remained relatively unchanged. By comparison with it, even the massive support for its programs that Catholic Action can muster on a *parentela* basis seems to be inferior. To be sure, the quantum of *parentela* pressure that Catholic groups can sometimes generate is enormous, and in many cases irresistible. But this fact alone should not obscure the essentially fragile character of the influence that such

[59] *L'Organizzazione Industriale*, 10 (May 15, 1930), p. 186.

politically advantaged groups can exercise, when seen over a period of time.

Bureaucratic pressure based on *parentela* must be regenerated with each new issue and perceived each time by the public administrators. On each of these occasions, we may assume for our previous discussion that there will be some bureaucratic effort to exert its own capacity to resist. Where the bureaucrats are forced to concede to superior power, resentment against the group or groups involved almost inevitably follows. This kind of intervention creates neither a permanent connection with the bureaucracy nor a channel of access that both the bureaucrats and the group leaders view as normal and acceptable.

In other words, I am suggesting that all of the talk in Italy about priests, bishops, and even cardinals scurrying about ministerial corridors is a mark of long-range weakness rather than strength. It reveals that the power of Catholic groups is based on *issue orientation* rather than *position orientation*. It also indicates that, unlike a *clientela* group such as Confindustria, Catholic associations cannot depend on the automatic response of the bureaucrats. It seems to me significant that, throughout our interviews, Confindustria is mentioned primarily in the bureaucratic context, while Catholic Action and other Catholic groups are related primarily to the legislative process. Indeed, it is probably this very strategic inferiority in the bureaucratic sector that leads the latter groups to concentrate on the legislative arena. The same is true, let us add, for the left-wing groups that fail to achieve bureaucratic access because of their lack of "respectability." It is not merely a matter of chance or preference that C.G.I.L.'s intervention takes place primarily in the legislature.

It should also be underlined that the Italian bureaucrats are fully aware that Catholic organizations do not constitute a monolith, and that the country's hegemonic political party is a house of ideological contradictions, held together by the relatively weak pegs of confessionalism. To the extent that this division is reflected in Christian Democratic Cabinet changes, the money of *parentela* is almost as devaluated in Italy as it was under the French Fourth Republic when the parties played a game of musical chairs. To the extent that the hegemonic political force is not cohesive, to the extent that the bureaucrats do not see it as essentially monolithic, they can put into play their own "strategies of resistance and independence." The less that Christian Democracy is compact, the weaker will be the impact of *parentela* on the bureaucracy. Some freedom for the bureaucrat is implicit in a situation where he can rightly ask not merely whether a group is Catholic but whether it belongs to the Christian Democratic faction which currently holds the reins of political and governmental power.

As one would expect, Catholic groups are perfectly aware of the limitations of their strategy and of the superiority of a strategy of position orientation. Some of their leaders have begun to ask how they can add that orientation to their *parentela* advantages. This willingness to explore other avenues seems implicit in the three lines of operation developed by Catholic Action in recent years, namely to (1) systematically infiltrate the bureaucracy at all possible levels, (2) use political influence to affect the recruitment as well as the careers of key bureaucratic personnel, and (3) increase the weight of organized Catholicism in those associational interest groups that have already established a *clientela* relationship with the bureaucracy.

But the political process is full of interesting ironies and contradictions. While Catholic Action moves toward *clientela,* Confindustria begins to wonder whether position is enough and whether a little bit of *parentela* would not go a long way. It is to this phenomenon that we now turn in the concluding chapter.

393

CHAPTER XI · GROUP PERCEPTIONS
AND BEHAVIORAL CONSEQUENCES:
AN EPILOGUE

INTRODUCTION

WE have noted in some detail the patterns of interaction that characterize interest group relationships to the legislature and the bureaucracy. It will be appropriate and useful to close with an attempt to show that what group leaders and groups do in Italy is to a marked degree influenced by their perceptions of the realities that surround them. Because the bulk of my field interviews were conducted with leaders of Confindustria and Catholic Action, I shall confine myself to these two organizations, although my findings should be valid for interest-group leaders anywhere.

That an individual's behavior is in part conditioned by his frame of reference—that is, by the way be defines or structures the situation—is a frequent assumption of the literature of the social sciences. To put this differently, we can say that what the individual does is necessarily and in some measure a function of the way in which he perceives and evaluates the environment in which behavior occurs. As used by March and Simon, "frame of reference" applies to relatively long time-intervals during which a large number of remembered environmental events become stimuli that influence behavior.[1] The individual actor who responds to such stimuli is seen as a choosing, problem-solving, and decision-making organism. As a complex information-processing mechanism, he can

---

[1] James G. March and Herbert A. Simon, *Organizations* (New York, 1959), p. 11.

394

and does respond in varied ways to the environmental stimuli to which he is exposed.[2]

To be sure, environmental perception is not the only factor that is said to influence behavior. Some psychiatrists, for example, hold that much of human behavior is a resultant of forces that remain below the threshold of consciousness. Others stress the impact on behavior of formal organizational structure. Simon himself argues that to a considerable degree the structure of bureaucratic organization delimits the behavioral alternatives available to the bureaucrat.[3] Nevertheless, the environmental variable simply cannot be ignored: "The organizational and social environment in which the decision maker finds himself determines what consequences he will anticipate, what ones he will not; what alternatives he will consider, what ones he will ignore." [4]

According to this line of reasoning, behavioral choices are functions of a limited and simplified model of the real situation, the elements of which are never to be assumed as given but "are themselves the outcome of psychological and sociological processes including the chooser's own activities and the activities of others in the environment." [5] Thus the situation is subjectively defined. For each actor, definition includes some knowledge regarding one's own goals and values, as well as central assumptions concerning future events, alternative choices of action available, and presumed consequences of each alternative action.

2 Additional relevant works of March and Simon may be consulted as follows: March, "An Introduction to the Theory of Measurement of Influence," *American Political Science Review*, 49 (June, 1955), pp. 431–51; Simon, *Administrative Behavior* (New York, 1947); Simon, "Related Choice and the Structure of the Environment," *Psychological Review*, 63 (March, 1956), pp. 129–38.

3 See Simon, *Administrative Behavior, op. cit.*, Ch. 10. Cf. Robert K. Merton, whose "Bureaucratic Structure and Personality," *Social Forces*, 18 (1940), pp. 560–68, is a classic item in the literature.

4 March and Simon, *Organizations, op. cit.*, p. 139.

5 *Ibid.*

In earlier chapters, I described the political and social context in which interest-group activity occurs. Although these are perceptions that may properly be considered as my own—and therefore open to my own subjective distortion—it is important to understand that they materialize in part out of the responses provided by those who were interviewed in this study. When I describe Italy as badly integrated, highly fragmented and rent by extreme ideological conflict, I necessarily reflect the sum total of my own perceptions of that political culture. While I believe this perception to be reasonably accurate, the points I wish to make in this chapter can be established only if we have some inkling as to how those Italians who represent Confindustria and Catholic Action perceive that same setting.

PERCEPTIONS OF REALITY: CONFINDUSTRIA

Confindustria leaders view the environment in which they function as extremely hostile to the interests of businessmen and industrialists. They frequently lament that the nation fails to appreciate the vitally important role played by the entrepreneur. Without him, the argument runs, Italy would face disaster; the economy would flounder and drift in the direction of a less dynamic and less efficient statism. The entrepreneur is depicted as a complete social man, in whom the finest human virtues are incarnated and developed. *L'Organizzazione Industriale,* an official organ of the Confederation, put it this way a few years ago: "The industrialist is, socially speaking, the most complete and representative of men. He is the exponent of work—of creative work—which is the most noble of man's activities. In his own plant, he himself works tirelessly—more than any other. . . . He sees his plant the way the artist contemplates his major work. More than the purely economic man (like the financier) he has a more human vision of problems because he is in direct contact with labor. He is more human, more in line with reality and more sincere than the purely political man." [6]

More recently, on the occasion of his elevation to Confindustria's presidency, Furio Cicogna asserted that even the Italian industrialists who are driven primarily by the profit motive are gradually transformed into lovers of their creations, so much so, in fact, as to be willing to undergo untold sacrifices in the interest of their perfection.

This image of Italy's industrialists is certainly not the dominant one in the country, and Confindustria's leaders both understand and lament this. Because they correctly view Italians as holding a more tarnished image of the businessman, they view themselves as the custodians of the faith and strength of the entrepreneur, and they see as one of their crucial missions the need for modifying the public image in a more appropriate direction. Thus the pages of most confederal publications are replete with articles depicting the entrepreneur in the most favorable of terms. Short of a massive public relations effort (to which subject we will return below), a strong effort has been made since the War to convince Italians, and perhaps the industrialists themselves, that the entrepreneur is not merely exploitive, that he deserves better of his countrymen, and that, indeed, the country could not possibly do without him.

Confindustria leaders confess that they have not been markedly successful in their campaign. One reason for this, they claim, is that Italian society has drifted farther and farther away from the central values of economic liberalism. These values, to which Confindustria still rigidly adheres, are free, private enterprise; minimum interference in the economic sphere on the part of the State; political decisions based on the "iron law" of economics and not on social or political (i.e., demagogic) considerations; and a recognition that industrialists, not politicians,

[6] May 19, 1949, p. 3.

are the best judges of all decisions affecting the economy.

Confindustria is clearly tied nostalgically to these eighteenth-century tenets of classical liberalism. Curiously, references to such values, which are frequent, are generally unelaborated and primitive; little effort is apparent to fit them into the twentieth century in some modified and updated way. There is little evidence, for example, that Confindustria's leaders are aware that, following Lord Keynes, there has been an effort to restate classical economic theory. Confindustria is evidently satisfied to applaud any government action that seems to represent "a gradual and reasoned return to the principles of economic freedom" and to declare "how destructive state interference has always been to the natural equilibrium which would otherwise be created in the three necessary and sufficient forces of entrepreneur, capital, and labor." Looking at postwar Italian society, a vice-president of Confindustria was compelled to remark: "But, alas, how diverse the realities of today are from this harmonious picture which now represents for us industrialists almost a faraway dream, to which we turn our bewildered glance." [7]

Classical economic values are found to be under attack from many quarters of Italian society. One source of aggression is the government, for over a decade the domain of Christian Democracy. To Confindustria this means that the traditional hostility of some segments of Catholicism to capitalism can now be expressed in various ways ranging from legislative policies to administrative regulations. As we have already seen, this perception of the implications of Christian Democratic hegemony currently makes a great deal of sense.

Confindustria is also confronted with a society in which notions of class conflict, and behavior based on these notions, are clearly rampant. One of the Confederation's leaders spoke at considerable length on this theme. Unlike the United States, he points out, Italy is a society of class

[7] See *ibid.* (July 31, 1948), p. 1; Confederazione Generale Italiana dell'Industria (C.G.I.I.), *Annuario 1948* (Rome, 1949), p. 408.

war. Marxism in Italy developed in a period of wide-spread illiteracy; thus it has been translated into the most brutal and simplistic generalizations regarding the relationships between employers and employees. The hostility of the masses toward the employers is fostered not merely by Communist and Socialist organizations, from which one expects such behavior, but also by a number of Catholic groups, such as the trade unions, and by the left-wing of the Christian Democratic Party.[8]

The confederation spends a great deal of energy attempting either to refute or at least to temper ideas of class conflict. For example, it is regularly pointed out that there are three factors of production, including the entrepreneur, and not merely two, capital and labor; and since the principal one of these three factors is the entrepreneur, the well-being and development of the working class is necessarily tied to and dependent on his well-being. Private entrepreneurial activity is said to be a "permanent necessity" of production and of civilization; it cannot be replaced by any kind of Bolshevik revolution.

Continuing this line of attack, Confindustria takes the position that it is the working class, and not the entrepreneur, that is conservative. For this reason, it is dangerous to the needs of economic risk-taking and development to accede to the demagogically inspired demand that workers be given a share in the management of industries. In seeking new economic processes and opportunities, it is the entrepreneur, the industrialist, who is the revolutionary.[9]

Another Confindustria response to the class war ideas said to permeate Italian society is to argue that there exists an identity of interests between the worker and his employer. During the early postwar years, for example, when Italian industrialists were under bitter and telling

[8] *Interview,* Number 86 (Rome, May 22, 1958), p. 7.

[9] See *L'Organizzazione Industriale* (April 28, 1948), p. 1. For a recent restatement of this view, see the words of the last president of Confindustria, A. De Micheli, in *Il Mondo Economico* (February 18, 1961), p. 31.

attack by the Communist-dominated trade unions, the then confederal president, Angelo Costa, was able to say, "We are so certain of the coincidence of our interests with those of the workers that we are ready to accept for all problems solutions that are in the true interest of the workers." [10] Through the years, however, Confindustria has noted how difficult it is for the workers to accept this point of view, not only because of the nature of the masses but above all because the workers in Italy are callously manipulated by the trade unions and the political parties. These latter, often taking advantage of the unhappy situation in which the working class finds itself, poison the workers and public opinion; they demagogically create a climate of opinion toward industrialists which is cold-bloodedly "based on the false and damaging assumption of class war." Thus the same union leaders who in private recognize the validity of industrialists' arguments maintain in public a hostile attitude, aggravate feelings of class war, and instigate the workers against a "hypothetical enemy." The same irresponsible behavior is said to be characteristic of political party leaders—even those of non-revolutionary parties—with the result that the confederation's constant appeals for collaboration among the social classes fall on deaf ears and achieve no favorable response. Under the circumstances—so runs this conclusion—the confederation's actions must be based on the central assumption that the social system is uncompromisingly antagonistic to the employer class.

Beyond these generalized perceptions of the nature of Italian society, Confindustria leaders manifest very specific notions regarding the political system, the nature of the Italian power structure, the character of the bureaucracy, other organized groups, and so on. All these perceptions tend to influence the kind of organizational behavior that we shall touch on below.

As we have seen, Confindustria views political parties as essentially demagogic and irresponsible. This indict-

[10] C.G.I.I., *Annuario 1948* (Rome, 1949), p. 276.

ment extends not only to the Communist and Socialist parties but to the parties of the political Center as well. "Irresponsibility" in these latter is felt to be particularly damaging, since it is from the nonrevolutionary, bourgeois parties that the confederation expects to receive some support for its values and its public stances. Where this is not forthcoming, the confederation tends either toward dismal pessimism or toward half-hearted "solutions" which have thus far failed to receive the enthusiastic support of the industrialists.

From the practical standpoint, the confederation's problems are said to grow out of the modified nature of the Italian political system and power structure. Not only is the locus of overwhelming power seen as residing in a hegemonic Christian Democratic Party, but the Party is clearly understood to favor what we have described as *parentela* relationships with certain interest groups.

Confindustria leaders are careful to point out that Christian Democratic hegemony might not be so threatening if the internal character of the Party were not so subject to change. Thus, while the essentially conservative center faction of the party remained in control under the leadership of Alcide de Gasperi, Confindustria was able quietly to intervene in the political process. It was during the De Gasperi years that the confederation could continue and even expand the *clientela* relationships with the bureaucracy that were nurtured after World War I and which grew to enormously satisfying proportions during the Fascist era.

As the confederal leaders see it, the environment changed with the death of de Gasperi and the ascendancy of Amintore Fanfani. It is from the Christian Democratic forces around Fanfani that additional threats to industrial interests are said to emerge. We have already noted that manifestations of this threat were seen in the election of Giovanni Gronchi as President of the Republic, in the *Sgancimento* law affecting Confindustria's control of state-owned industries, and in the burgeoning, swashbuckling activities of E.N.I., particularly in the years of Enrico Mattei's leadership of that public corporation.[11] All of these fears, of course, were intensified when Amintore Fanfani and Pietro Nenni succeeded in effecting the "Opening to the Left." Confindustria's concern and outrage reached a fever pitch in 1962–63, when the Fanfani government, supported by the Socialists, proceeded to nationalize the electrical industry, one of the strongest and most conservative elements within the industrial confederation. The privileged access to the power structure, which reached its zenith under Fascism, has obviously sunk to an all-time low in the eyes of Confindustria's leadership.[12]

As they view the power structure, Confindustria leaders express concern even about Catholic Action. To be sure, there are some who emphasize the important electoral role played by the Catholic Action-inspired Civic Committees since 1948. Others stress the influence over the selection of D.C. candidates exercised by A.C.I. units in most provinces. Still others point to A.C.I.'s control of Catholic women and the now universally recognized crucial role that women play in assuring Christian Democratic electoral victories. Equally significant for some is the large number of D.C. deputies who have long backgrounds of training and experience in the ranks of Catholic Action. Whatever the particular factor selected, the general perception within the confederation is that A.C.I. is a force that anyone at the helm of the political system must reckon with.

[11] For a typical attack on E.N.I. by Confindustria's president, see *L'Informazione Industriale* (September 20, 1956), p. 1. For another criticism of increasing statism, see *ibid.* (November 1, 1956), p. 1.

[12] The pages of all Confindustria's publications (as well as Italy's conservative press in general) for the latter part of 1962 and the early months of 1963 are replete with violent attacks on Fanfani and Nenni regarding the nationalization of electricity. Mr. Cicogna, the current president of Confindustria, reiterates the concern over Italian society's failure adequately to appreciate the vital role of the industrialist and of private enterprise. In this regard, see the interesting editorial, "La Guerra della Confindustria," *Il Mondo* (March 12, 1963), p. 1.

Many of the same confederal leaders who recognize Catholic Action as a conservative influence in Italian society and politics, however, view the power of A.C.I. as a mixed blessing. On the one hand, Confindustria is happy to have so powerful an organization attempting to limit or prevent such things as state-controlled economic enterprise, strikes led by Catholic trade unions, cooperation between Christian Democrats and Socialists, etc. On the other hand, many Confindustria leaders are ideologically tied to the liberal state, and they bemoan what they perceive as the increasing clericalization of Italian society. Thus one finds them speaking, often without evidence, of the massive interference of Catholic Action with political and administrative decisions, of the growth of Catholic power over voluntary associations, and of the priests and bishops who crowd ministerial corridors on their errands of intervention in the public administrative process.

When confederal leaders compare Confindustria to Catholic Action and to other organized Catholic groups, they conclude that the Confederation is *outside* the power structure, that it is not really one of the competing groups within the Christian Democratic Party, and therefore that it cannot hope to intervene in the political process, as do some of the important organizations with which the confederation competes for influence. This understanding, coupled with other perceptions outlined above, results in a self-image of relative weakness; confederal leaders are quick to point out that Confindustria operates under significant disadvantages and that it is not nearly as powerful in Italian politics as many in Italy would suppose or claim.[13]

Thus Confindustria leaders do not find the general climate very reassuring. The society is perceived to be hostile, rent by class conflict; the political system is scored

[13] It should be noted that the bureaucratic (as distinguished from the political) leaders of Confindustria are careful not to push the notion of weakness too far. They obviously have an interest in persuading their industrialist leaders and organizational members that the existence of the Confederation makes a significant difference.

as largely corrupted by demogogic, opportunistic, and irresponsible party leaders who make their careers at the expense of industrialists; universal suffrage represents for these leaders the means whereby irrational masses—and particularly ignorant and priest-ridden women—bring antagonistic Catholic forces to power; mass groups with aims that contrast sharply with those of the Confederation are seen as trading heavily on *parentela* relationships to Christian Democracy; the country is held to be drifting more and more dangerously close to the shoals of collectivism; and few people, in or out of government, are said genuinely to understand the role, problems, and needs of the Italian businessman. All of this is interpreted as particularly ironic in view of the dramatic economic strides that the country manifests in recent years.

These are the assumptions and perceptions that go a long way toward explaining Confindustria's political behavior.

What of Catholic Action?

PERCEPTIONS OF REALITY: CATHOLIC ACTION

For several reasons, it is difficult to generalize about the content and meaning of the perceptions of reality manifested by the leaders of Catholic Action. In the first place, Catholic Action is officially described as the apostolic arm of the Catholic clergy and is by most measures completely subservient to the wishes of the Vatican. The top-level leaders of A.C.I. branches are never elected but chosen by the clergy; presumably, on all matters involving doctrine or policy—as opposed to action or methodology—it is the clergy, through the network of ecclesiastical assistants who oversee A.C.I. activities at all levels, that sets the direction of the organization. For this reason, it is necessary and logical to note reality perceptions as they are officially formulated and handed down by the Catholic hierarchy itself. Our interviews with both clerical and lay leaders of Catholic Action clearly indicate that the Catholic Church is anxious to assure that only limited freedom to interpret and evaluate reality is permitted. This simple and basic relationship of Catholic Action leaders and members to the clerical hierarchy is simply and pointedly stated by a leader of the *Movimento Laureati,* that branch of Catholic Action that recruits intellectuals and university graduates. "By taking out a membership card, one does not merely show one's interest in the Movement's activities. One also engages himself toward the Church hierarchy; he places himself at the disposition of the hierarchy in order to act according to the latter's direction." [14]

Secondly, and despite what I have just said, it is clear that Catholic Action is an immense organization consisting of units that are ideologically and temperamentally somewhat dissimilar. For example, there is a significant gulf that separates the extremely conservative *Unione Donne* (Union of Women) or the *Gioventù Femminile* (Young Women) from the Movimento Laureati or the F.U C.I. (Federation of Italian Catholic University Students). The former two units are less politically oriented than the latter, more exclusively tied to the apostolic rather than the secular dimension of Catholic Action. The latter organizations are self-consciously committed to the exploration of intellectual and political problems, much more determined to maximize the amount of freedom of philosophical as well as methodological initiative that can be expressed within the rather narrow confines of an admittedly authoritarian organization.

Thus the Movimento Laureati leader cited above is careful to distinguish his unit from others within Catholic Action. The Movement, he says, differs from other Catholic Action branches in the sense that it is willing openly to confront any problem, without the typical kind of Catholic Action prejudice that leads to choices on a completely a priori basis. Skirting very close to a basic criticism of the way in which Catholic Action is managed, he says: "The message of the gospel needs translation into

[14] *Interview,* Number 39 (Rome, February 4, 1958), p. 5.

a language that is differentiated according to the time and place in the total life of the Church in which an effort is made to communicate the message. It is the major responsibility of the priesthood, the ecclesiastical hierarchy, to guard the substantive integrity of the message. It is the duty of the lay members of the Catholic Church to elaborate that message so that it conforms to the exigencies of the time in which the elaboration takes place. It is specifically the task of the cultured or intelligent segment of the laity to conduct this elaboration." [15]

This claim for relative freedom of action is echoed by a national leader of F.U.C.I., who claims that his organization is somewhat separated from the rest of Catholic Action and that, like the Movimento Laureati, it experiences less interference from the Catholic clergy. He says: "F.U.C.I. has a spirit of its own that the other branches of Catholic Action, with the important exception of the Movimento Laureati, does not share. For example, F.U.C.I. places great emphasis on the rule of free discussion as the most important internal educational device. Free discussion is simply not permitted in the four great branches of Catholic Action [i.e., U.D.A.C.I., Union of Women; U.U.A.C.I., Union of Men; G.I.A.C., Young Men; and G.F., Young Women]. The other branches of Catholic Action are highly articulated organizations where a rigidly hierarchical and authoritarian method of leadership and membership relationships is maintained." [16]

He goes on to say that F.U.C.I. seeks an open dialogue with the laical forces of the country, that it seeks to liberalize the internal structure as well as the policy orientations of Catholic Action, and that it persists in these

[15] *Ibid.*, p. 13.

[16] *Interview*, Number 42 (Rome, February 24, 1958), pp. 1–2. In marked contrast to this statement is the assertion by a former national leader of *Gioventù Femminile*, who emphasizes that the organization does not have its own ideology, that it is abjectly dependent on the clergy, and that it confines itself to apostolic work, to political indoctrination, and to compelling its members to make a choice between the kitchen and the nunnery. *Interview*, Number 41, *op. cit.*, pp. 5–7.

two orientations notwithstanding opposition from the rest of Catholic Action or the discouraging fact that little headway has been made.

I cite these respondents not to suggest that each branch of Catholic Action is free to perceive realities as it chooses but to caution against easy generalizations and to emphasize that organized Catholicism is not an absolute monolith even in that organizational sector over which the clergy can and does exercise the most assiduous and pervasive control.

Thirdly, it is necessary to understand that, for many practical and operational purposes, Catholic Action is essentially what each bishop, operating at the level of the diocese, decrees that it will be. One of the most significant internal struggles within Catholic Action (which we cannot examine in detail) is between those who would centralize authority in the General Presidency (i.e., Secretariat) at Rome and others who wish to maximize both functional divisional and geographic autonomy. For the latter, there always tends to be entirely too much ideological and tactical direction from the Center; for the former, the long tradition of autonomy under the direction of local bishops is felt to be dangerous and chaotic. The point to bear in mind is that, even under the highly centralizing designs of Pope Pius XII and Luigi Gedda, who ran Catholic Action as tightly as possible, many bishops could and did interpret for themselves the most efficacious way of implementing in the diocese the evangelical and (unofficially) political mission of Catholic Action.

With these caveats in mind, we can examine the way in which Catholic Action "defines the situation." In doing so, certain facts about its ideology must be borne in mind. Of these, the most critical is that the main body of Catholic Action's ideology is not its own but emanates from the Catholic Church as A.C.I.'s sponsoring institution. While it is possible to analyze the utterances of A.C.I. leaders and to detect therein certain ideological orientations, the most striking thing about these men and women is that they see little need for ideological exploration; for them the totality of truth is embodied in the Catholic Church. This conviction leads to a rigid acceptance of utterances of the clergy and into a translation of these utterances into an operational code.

A second fact concerning A.C.I. ideology is implied in this last remark, namely that the ideology matters a great deal in the sense that the behavior of organizations and individuals is expected to conform to it. Indeed, because A.C.I. does not in theory—and probably not in fact either—have the right to fashion or modify its ideology, the ideology takes on absolute importance; any serious deviation from it would be fatal to the continuance of leadership, membership, or the organization itself. Even those leaders within Catholic Action who are the most daring in terms of expressing ideological freedom recognize that to go too far will either bring a serious indictment and possible expulsion by the clergy or will require that the "radicals" leave the organization. What hangs heavily over the whole organizational apparatus is the understanding that it exists to do the clergy's bidding and that the clergy will dispense with it whenever it should decide that it can or must dispense with Catholic Action. A similar pattern exists for many other interest groups that are merely party auxiliaries; some of the Communist Party front organizations would be striking examples. My generalization here is that, where this kind of relationship prevails, organizational leaders find themselves under great pressure to assure rigid behavioral conformance to the organization's external determined ideological premises.

Taking their cues from Catholic doctrine and the Italian clergy, A.C.I. leaders view the modern world in a wretched and almost condemned state. Social unrest, wars, immorality, and the threatening evil of Communism are seen as merely symptoms of a deeper moral disease which is in turn identified with the world's alienation from Christ as personified by the Catholic Church. Alienation itself is understood to stem primarily from the Protestant Heresy, which made the critical error of trying to accept Christ without accepting His Church. All other "errors," including liberal skepticism, unrestrained individualism, and Communism's militancy against all spiritual values are felt to be logically and historically connected to this initial deviation. The greatest evil now abroad is seen as any of the varied laical attempts to restrict the operations and the influence of the Church to the merely religious.

Equally condemned is the unrestrained devotion of the modern world to material goods as against spiritual values. Society is seen as a vast wasteland, where the only erect and prevailing sources of real values and truth reside in the Church. The simple and overriding reality is that the only remaining opportunity to transform the world from savage to human and from human to divine now lies in the world's conversion to the Catholic Church.[17]

This pessimism, however, is noncatastrophic. In Catholic Action's ideology there exists the firm conviction that the triumph of the Church over this continued rebellion and alienation of the modern world is certain to materialize in time, if not within our time. Catholic Action is identified by its leaders as one agent (indeed, the principal agent as far as the mobilization of the layman is concerned) working toward this great and necessary transformation.

The type of ideological conditioning to which Catholic Action members are subjected is typified by the following words, uttered in 1952 by Pope Pius XII to the convention of Unione Uomini at Rome:

"Today, not Rome only, nor Italy only, but the whole world is threatened. Oh, do not ask us who is the enemy and what dress he is wearing. He is everywhere and among everybody;

17 This is the essence of a speech by Pope Pius XII to which Luigi Gedda, Catholic Action's chief until recently, frequently pointed as the manifesto of his own policy line for A.C.I. Radio message of February 10, 1952.

he can be violent and shrewd. In these last centuries, he has tried to work the intellectual, moral, social disintegration of the unity in the mysterious organism of Christ. He has wanted nature but not grace; reason but not faith; freedom but not authority; at times authority but not freedom. The enemy has become more and more demanding, his demands more and more astonishingly open. First, yes to Christ but no to the Church. Then, yes to God but no to Christ. Finally, the blasphemous cry: God is dead; even: God never was. One has attempted, then, to build up the structure of the world upon foundations that we do not hesitate to call responsible for the threat now impending on mankind; an *economy without God,* a *law without God, politics without God.* The enemy is at work to make Christ a foreigner in the universities, in the school, in the family, in the administration of justice, in legislative activity, in the assemblies of nations where peace and war are deliberated upon."

What Pope Pius XII implies here is carried to a supposed logical historical conclusion by Catholic Action leaders. For example, after tracing laissez-faire Liberalism to romantic Socialism, Luigi Gedda has little difficulty in asserting that, "Over the centuries, today's Communism is the descendent of the Protestant Revolution." [18] Ecclesiastical Catholic Action leaders, such as Cardinal Siri, are capable of the same form of reasoning. Today's onslaughts on Catholicism can all be traced back to the initial error of the Reformation.

Thus no matter how detailed may be Catholic Action's recitation of the evils that beset mankind, the basic accusation and condemnation points back to the initial cause. The only logic that Catholic Action leaders understand is that present evils are simply current manifestations of the sin of not recognizing the Catholic Church and rejecting her teachings.

It is also necessary to stress that this view both reflects and reinforces an essentially exorcistic mentality, by which I mean that the social problems of modern society are

[18] *Atti della quattro-giorni presidenziale diocesana G.I.A.C.* (Rome, 1953), p. 81.

never examined in terms of their complex determinants and multiple dimensions; all current problems will be solved if only mankind will acknowledge its errors and return to moral sanity. That current social and economic problems are not easily guided or resolved by simple moral teachings fails to shake Catholic Action leaders from the conviction that the problems exist primarily because of a failure of mankind to recognize its moral responsibilities.

The pessimism with which the contemporary situation is viewed is qualified by two additional and critically important convictions. The first of these is that a still greater ruin threatens mankind; the second is that the threat can be stopped if adequate action is taken. Both feelings find expression in the following quotation from *Gioventù* a publication of the G.I.A.C.–Young Men of Catholic Action. "We feel we have entered the final act of our tragic, contemporary civilization, the act in which–as in the Greek tragedies–the catharsis that is the denouement is to take place. Only two forces are still alive and active on the stage of the world: Catholicism and Communism." [19]

It goes without saying that in this final and dramatic encounter, the greatest force on which the Catholic Church can draw for assistance is Catholic Action. This conviction on the part of A.C.I. leaders is echoed in the words of Pius XII uttered in 1940: "In such a grave hour of history . . . we set our sights upon Catholic Action and find in it grounds for hope. We trust that we shall find in Catholic Action, rallied tightly around the bishops and the Holy See, many devoted and fervent collaborators toward the great enterprise: Christ's return into the consciences, into the family hearths, into public custom, into relations between social classes, into public order, into international relations.[20]

As Catholic Action leaders view Italian society–and the

---

[19] In *Iniziativa*, 4 (January, 1951), p. 2.
[20] Quoted in Carlo Falconi, *La Chiesa e le organizzazioni cattoliche in Italia*, 1945–1955 (Milan, 1956), p. 364.

world—there exists a persistence among men not to recognize the Catholic Church as the sole and ultimate repository of truth and morality. Instead, there prevail competing ideologies that encourage class war and destroy mankind's innate brotherhood, as well as organizations that aid and abet anticlericalism and by so doing represent an open and direct threat to the security of Catholicism. It is therefore the duty of all Catholics, and particularly those who militate in the ranks of Catholic Action, to take whatever action is necessary to modify this reality. The members and leaders of Catholic Action see themselves as called upon particularly to express faithfulness in the Church, to assert the Church's presence in every way possible, to take action and to give testimony on the Church's behalf, to do apostolic work, to respond to massive assaults on the Church in kind, and to preach, disseminate, and implement the Church's message for Italian society (and the world), which is total. No segment of the society is to be left untouched, and herein lies the meaning of what Italians, often fearfully, identify as the "integralism" (*integralismo*) of Catholicism. It is in the ideological commitment to apply the total message of living reality that one can find the rationale for the way in which Catholic Action has developed as one of Italy's major interest groups.

BEHAVIORAL RESPONSE: CONFINDUSTRIA

Italian society's perceived hostility toward the industrial class encourages Confindustria to prefer political activities of low visibility. In the years since World War II, the pattern of quiet, unspectacular intervention in the bureaucratic sphere resulted from conscious choice and not merely from the demonstrated superior efficaciousness of *clientela* relationships. The Confederation's interest-group behavior of the postwar years stands in market contrast to what prevailed during the Fascist era. Then Confindustria openly supported the regime; Il Duce's praises were sung in all confederal publications; Italian industrialists in considerable numbers sat in the national legislature; and many of Confindustria's most prominent leaders were co-opted into important positions in the Fascist corporations.

As perceptions of the environment change, so does organizational and individual behavior. The wave of anti-industrial reactions that accompanied the fall of Fascism left an indelible impression on industrial leaders, and particularly on the more conservative bureaucrats who manage the day-to-day affairs of Confindustria. Thus, in our interviews, we found that most of these latter clearly prefer the kind of political intervention that does not expose the Confederation too openly to public scrutiny.

A particular manifestation of this posture is the Confederation's aversion toward public relations campaigns. One leader stresses that the public relations approach is appropriate for the United States, "where industrialists are respected heroes," but completely untenable in Italian society, where such activities would surely boomerang to the great disadvantage of the industrial class.

The confederal leader points out that more is involved here than the anti-Fascist reaction. Prior to the advent of Fascism, the problem of creating and developing Italian industry had often to be completely hidden from the public. The kinds of financial manipulations necessary to this development were such that they would not have been adequately understood by the masses. Thus there early developed a tendency to keep from the public the basic facts relating to the country's industrialization. This early period was then followed by the Fascist interlude during which the industrialists were under little pressure to communicate with the public at all. The industrialists were then in the driver's seat and did not have to bother too much about what the public might be thinking of the business community.[21]

21 *Interview*, Number 88 (Rome, May 22, 1958), p. 7. This respondent adds that "keeping oneself hidden" is part of the Italian's "national char-

Given this kind of background, it is obvious why many of Confindustria's leaders and members not only fail to see the need for a public relations campaign but are actually fearful of it. Beyond this genuine fear, there are confederal leaders who seem to be ethically opposed to the "Madison Avenue approach," and who insist that the confederation's responsibility is to educate the masses rather than manipulate them through the use of symbols and slogans. One leader asserts that "we do not want a superficial approach—the Hollywood approach—to the general public; instead, we find it our task to educate the masses, to form them, and to mold their thinking regarding certain problems that are of great interest to us."

In keeping with this latter philosophy, Confindustria does publish a newspaper, *Gazzetta per i Lavoratori,* designed for distribution to the workers, which stresses the important role of private enterprise and the necessity of maintaining harmony between management and labor. As a public relations function, tedious white papers are published, carefully and interminably documenting the position of the Confederation on issues of public policy affecting industry. The amateurishness of this direct approach to education is seen in a volume entitled *Creators of Labor,* which consists of photographs and unbelievably dull résumés of the pioneers of Italian industrial development. It is quite obvious that Confindustria's message gets across—if it does at all—primarily through the network of pro-business newspapers that are financially and/or ideologically identified with the Confederation.

Bureaucratic insistence on education is strongly enforced, however, by the firm conviction that a massive and open attack on the public would absolutely backfire. Thus: "If we descend to the demogogic level, we will surely lose the battle. We cannot beat the opposition at their own game at this level. Look at what happened to Confintesa. As a result of our experience there, we have

acter." It is therefore basically natural for the industrialist to try to keep himself hidden from the public. *Ibid.,* p. 8.

been told by the Christian Democratic Party to tend to our business of producing goods and services and stay out of politics. This is what is likely to happen again if we descend to the demogogic level." [22]

There are some nonbureaucratic Confindustria leaders who are strongly opposed to this view, on the ground that it reflects dangerous habits and methods of reasoning developed under Fascism. One of them points out that then the Confederation could ignore the public, because of the assurance that "there is someone in government who will take care of us." That this is no longer the case has only gradually dawned on many industrialists. As a result, there continues to prevail the dubious notion that the private sector will somehow survive, come what may.

Another reason for emphasis on education rather than propaganda, on quiet and indirect rather than open political activities, lies in the widespread philosophy of industrial paternalism. When the typical industrialist, in a family-owned firm, is not treating the worker as a chattel, he tends to assume the role of stern (occasionally indulgent) father. Reflecting this orientation, a former president of the Confederation says:

"I believe that we must operate at two levels. First there are the day-to-day tactics of the Confederation. These involve us primarily in the negotiation of various kinds of contracts. They are what I would call artillery tactics, according to which we try to shoot first.

"Then there is a second level—of long-range strategy. This requires a constant effort, in every way and through every possible means, to educate the public, to let the worker understand that he has a natural link with the industrialist. *If some of this is paternalism, what of it? A father wants the best things possible for his son.* We must convince the worker that it is industry that really seeks to defend the single worker's interests. We must break down class lines and all other barriers to communication. This is a difficult task but the one to which we are dedicating our energies." [23]

[22] *Interview*, Number 99 (Rome, June 30, 1958), p. 3.
[23] *Interview*, Number 122 (Rome, September, 1959), p. 10.

A third factor that we must note is that Italian industrialists fail to perceive realities in a like manner, lack a sense of class cohesiveness and are manifestly difficult to organize. Difficulties of organization can be traced back to the earliest years of Confindustria. Early confederal leaders like Gino Olivetti encountered great reluctance on the part of industrialists to organize nationally, and it was only with great difficulty that what began as the Turin Industrial League in the first years of this century became the Confindustria in 1910.[24] Moreover, up to the present day, Italy's two cultures dictate that Confindustria is much more meaningful north of Rome than south. By and large, the history of the confederation suggests that it is only in time of extreme threat, such as the occupation of the factories following World War I, that the industrialists have managed to come together in meaningful association.

It is also apparent that the industrialists do not evince a common political consciousness. A leader of the Italian Liberal Party, closely identified with Confindustria, stresses that the industrialists "do not feel or understand the need for common political action. There is not even a recognition that the industrialists in the country have certain interests in common." [25] The result is that industrialists support political parties ranging from social democracy on the Left to neo-Fascism on the Right. Furthermore, there is a tendency on the part of industrial giants like Fiat and Montecatini to have one foot inside and another foot outside the Confederation. Fiat, in the first place, does not agree with the conservative policies of Edison and other industries in the Lombardy Group. In the second place, the industrial giants are often strong enough to effect in their own way interaction with political parties,

[24] There is some conflict of opinion as to when Confindustria did come into existence. In 1956, A. De Micheli points to 1907 as the founding year. In the same year, an official of the Turin Industrial Union sets the date at 1910. The latter date seems more appropriate. See *L'Informazione Industriale* (September 12, 1956), p. 1, and (September 20, 1956), p. 1.

[25] *Interview*, Number 120 (Rome, July 12, 1958), p. 4.

other interest groups, and the various branches of government. Confederal leaders, both political and bureaucratic, do not condone the independence of action exerted by Fiat, Montcatini, and other large industries. Several of them assert that this kind of disintegrated approach to politics is exactly what increases the ineffectiveness of Confindustria vis-à-vis the other groups with which it competes. One leader, who strongly favored the Confintesa movement, describes it in part as an attempt by confederal personnel to have the medium and small industries condition the political behavior of the larger enterprises.[26] This attempt failed, of course, as did Confintesa itself.

Another aspect or dimension of Confindustria's low-visibility posture is the obvious reluctance of industrialists to run for public office. On the one hand, confederal leaders bemoan the considerable direct representation in Parliament achieved by the trade unions, Catholic Action, the Caltivatori Diretti, and other groups. They point out that members of Parliament think nothing of getting up openly to speak on behalf of labor, but that, were one to debate in favor of industry, he would be criticized and even ridiculed. This situation is described as in marked contrast to the Fascist period, when many, sometimes twenty or more, confederal officials held seats in the national legislature.

On the other hand, the industrialist is labeled as a person who loathes politics and who therefore shuns it for many reasons. He is described as distrusting associational activity (i.e., "he is a rugged individualist"); he is said to fear political retaliation in the event that an anti-industrialist party comes to power; he is supposed to understand that industrial candidates simply will not fare well under an electoral system that encompasses the triple obstacle of universal suffrage, proportional representation, and politically illiterate women who vote as they are

26 *Ibid.*, p. 3.

told by their priests. In short, the industrialist is not inclined to engage in battles he believes he will lose, nor is he well attuned to the requirements of Italy's rough-and-tumble political campaigns. Concerning this last point, one of them says: "Permit me to say that it disgusts us to have to combat the various tactics of the Communists in the public squares. We would be willing to do physical battle with them if necessary, but we do not like to have to compete with their political tactics. This does not represent lack of courage on the part of industrialists; it is simply an unwillingness to engage in the undignified activities of Italian politics." [27]

Or, as articulated by a recent president of the Confederation: "In this postwar period, the political war has been too venomous to permit industrialists to enter politics. . . . They just do not have the stomach for it. How can an industrialist come before a crowd of Italians who have been convinced by the Communists that they are nothing but exploiters?"

The preference for the political shadows rather than the spotlight dominated Confindustria's behavior from the War's end until 1955. Beginning in 1956 with the elevation of Alighiero De Micheli to the presidency, the situation changed. De Micheli's election was widely interpreted as a victory of the Milan industrial group over the Genoa group represented by Angelo Costa, his predecessor. Prior to his election, De Micheli had been uninterruptedly president of the important Lombardy Industrial Association (*Assolombardo*). It was generally assumed that he was in favor of organizational reform and that he would considerably shake up the Confederation.

De Micheli was not disappointing in this latter expectation. He launched for Confindustria an experiment in direct political action—Confinesta—that was unprecedented in the years after the War. He urged that industrialists come out into the open in defense of their interests; he recognized that the reliance on *clientela* relationships

27 *Interview,* Number 22, *op. cit.,* p. 7.

with the bureaucracy, and on the kind of behind-the-scenes deals developed by Angelo Costa, was no longer a reasonable response to the realities of Italian society. He could point to developments we have already noted as evidence for the assertion that the basic interests of the industrial class were in extreme danger.

The Confintesa formula was rather simple. Confindustria and the industrialists would place financial support behind conservative parties, primarily the Liberal Party led by Giovanni Malagodi. In addition, large sums would be spent on all sorts of electoral propaganda and a major effort would be made to persuade industrialists to run for office at the local, provincial, and, eventually, national levels. These men could compete as candidates not merely in the Liberal Party but also in others ranging from Christian Democracy on the Left to the neo-Fascist Italian Social Movement (M.S.I.) on the right.

It is widely conceded that the Confintesa experiment ended disastrously in the elections of 1956 and 1958. The Liberal Party, the locus of Confindustria support, fared very badly; the candidates in every party supported by Confintesa were generally not elected. Nevertheless, following the 1956 debacle, De Micheli tried to shore up industrialist morale. At Turin he assured his colleagues that Confintesa was not dead but very much alive; that it "might work to guarantee the existence of a middle class willing to defend itself, in the certainty that by defending itself it assures the Italian people not only of freedom of enterprise but of all civil liberties." He added that, "for the good of the Fatherland, we must not betray this expectation." [28]

Even following Confintesa's dismal showing in the 1958 general elections, those who supported De Micheli refused to see the writing on the wall. In September, 1959, one of Confindustria's leaders had this to say: "Several parties in some measure represent our interests. The Liberal party and a good portion of Christian Democracy fall into

[28] *L'Informazione Industriale* (September 20, 1956), p. 1.

this category. A few years ago a Christian Democratic candidate would have been frightened to come out in favor of free enterprise. This is no longer the case, and we are thankful for it. Moreover, the situation has improved in other sectors as well. Look at the Socialists and Communists who no longer speak of nationalization and socialization. . . . Even Fanfani—that fanatic Tuscan—will have to knuckle under to this particular circumstance."

Two years later, "that fanatic Tuscan," had brought about the "Opening to the Left" with the Socialist Party and forced through Parliament a law to nationalize the electric industry, despite the vocal protests of those in several parties who did speak up for private industrial interests. Less than two years later, De Micheli was replaced by Furio Cicogna as Confindustria's president. The election of this man, in his late seventies, must be understood as a repudiation of the unsettling dynamism that De Micheli brought to the position. Cicogna is an old Confindustria hand, having been elected from Confindustria to the Fascist Corporation in 1939. Although he, too, comes from the Assolombardo, there is little evidence that he shares De Micheli's views on direct political participation. His will probably be a return to the shadows—a development that will greatly please Confindustria's bureaucratic leaders.

For the truth is that the bureaucrats—as opposed to the political leaders—in the Confederation were greatly upset by De Micheli's policies. They have come to have a respect for and a vested interest in *clientela* relationships; they are convinced that, in the long run, it is solely access to the bureaucracy that will pay off for the industrialists. Some of them privately applaud Confintesa's failure. Others remark that until the time is more propitious, Confindustria had best concentrate on the bureaucracy, and on *clientela,* where disturbances from the left-wing of Christian Democracy can be minimized.

It is difficult to predict what patterns Confindustria's

intervention will follow in the future. The "radicals" are still very active and vocal, and, while they agree with the "conservatives" in the general definition of the situation, they are apparently no longer willing to rely on *clientela* for the protection of their interests. Yet the alternatives to this reliance are not reassuring. On the one hand, there is the prospect of more open support for the Liberal Party and other parties which at the moment do not count for much in the power structure. On the other hand, a Christian Democratic Party dominated by its left wing is not a very attractive place for most of Italy's industrialists. Nevertheless, circumstances and perceptions of them are such that the Confederation will feel increasing pressure to find new channels of political efficacy. The choices that are made in the future are certain to have more than a casual impact on the stability of Italian democracy.

BEHAVIORAL RESPONSE: CATHOLIC ACTION

Given the perceptions, ideology, and organizational self-image of Catholic Action's leaders, it is not surprising that they should seek to develop a form of operational activity that will leave no sector of society untouched. If the society is shot through with evil, evil itself must be eradicated wherever it is found; if the Catholic Church is besieged by enemies, they must be sought out and combated wherever they may lurk; if the message of the Church is total, applying to every facet of human existence, there is no sector of social organization and behavior that should remain ignorant of it.

One obvious implication of this formulation is that Catholic Action must be a mass movement. What began in the mid-nineteenth century as a relative handful of ardent young Catholics is now one of Italy's vastest organizations.[29] One national leader proudly asserts that

[29] In 1954, Catholic Action claimed the following, non-overlapping membership: Adult men, 285,455 in 12,224 units; young men, 556,752 in 15,706 units; adult women, 597,394 in 16,389 units; and young women, 1,215,977 in 19,026 units. See Presidenza Generale dell'Azione Cattolica Italiana, *Annuario della Azione Cattolica Italiana* (Rome, 1954).

A.C.I.'s three and one-half million members account for over six percent of the Italian population. In some of the regions of northern Italy, the proportion is much higher. Although membership falls off in the strongly left-wing central regions of Tuscany, Emila-Romagna, and Umbria, it is certain that Catholic Action is a factor to be reckoned with in all of the country's 311 dioceses and in most of the more than twenty thousand parishes they contain. Even after one discounts for natural membership figure exaggeration, it is certain that A.C.I. ranks as one of the top three interest groups in the country.

Moreover, as one of A.C.I.'s national leaders points out, those who are in the organization are *real* and dues-paying members. In addition, they understand that membership carries with it the responsibility to carry out assignments when they are given.[30] The criteria of selection and retention to membership are such that those who remain or survive to join an adult unit are highly militant and devoted followers.

Catholic Action philosophy would also argue for organization by sector. The four great branches of the organization recruit young men, young women, older men, and older women. In addition, there are three major branches that involve university students, college graduates and intellectuals, and teachers. There is considerable disagreement, however, as to whether there should be further functional divisions or subdivisions in the organization. For example, our interviews with leaders of the G.I.A.C. revealed considerable tension between those who manage the age-group divisions and others who are in charge of subunits dealing with industrial workers and rural inhabitants. At the time of this study at least, there existed the strong feeling that neither President Luigi Gedda nor the ecclesiastical hierarchy under Pius XII ap-

---

[30] *Interview*, Number 11 (Rome, December 12, 1957), p. 4. This respondent claims that until 1946 Catholic Action received no money from the Vatican. Presumably, until that time activities were financed by membership dues and other fund-raising devices. *Ibid.*, p. 6.

proved of functional divisions that were broken along social class lines. The line of "interclassism" is strong, and Gedda clearly did not want Italian Catholic Action to emulate class-conscious organizational patterns typical of French Catholic Action.

In a sense, this type of functional division is unnecessary. As we noted earlier, there now exist in Italy interest groups to cover every conceivable major social, professional, and economic category. Many of these groups maintain close liaison with Catholic Action branches and are to some extent influenced and guided by it. Nevertheless, there are Catholic Action leaders who feel that other Catholic groups lack the doctrinal purity and strong sense of devotion that marks A.C.I. For this reason, we can expect some pressure for greater functional articulation to continue.

Another possible implication of Catholic Action assumptions is that the work of the organization should be managed and integrated under a highly centralized national administration. Under the presidency of Luigi Gedda, a major effort was made to increase the powers of the General Presidency at Rome at the expense of territorial and functional units. One of Gedda's closest collaborators admits that the drive for centralization—the great emphasis on organizational structure—was a source of great internal tension and controversy. In support of the idea of greater centralization, this individual spoke of "compact unity" and "harmonious operations." In fact, he really meant that more critical policy and tactical decisions should be made at Rome and not left to the bishops in the dioceses or to the seven major divisions.[31]

What this respondent describes as the atomistic tendencies in A.C.I. are said to be traceable to the Fascist period. Throughout that era, in order to be able to offer more effective resistance to attempts of the Fascist government to interfere with Catholic Action activities, the Vati-

31 *Ibid.*, p. 10.

can decreed a major decentralization of the organization. This tactic would presumably have made it more difficult for the Fascists to wreck A.C.I. than if it were a highly centralized unit. The decision to effect organizational atomization is not unlike that followed by Communist parties when they are under direct and immediate assault.

Following World War II, Luigi Gedda attempted to reverse this trend. He ran into opposition, not only from lay leaders of Catholic Action but also from many bishops who had become key figures in diocese-level A.C.I. activities during two decades of Fascism. In this latter sense, the organizational controversy was caught up in the even more fundamental Catholic question of how much autonomy in fact is to be permitted the powerful bishops, on which foundation the organizational apparatus of world-wide Catholicism really rests. As several A.C.I. leaders are quick to assert, the bishops of Italy retain great power and cannot easily be directed from the A.C.I. General Presidency at Rome. For this reason, as well as for reasons of strong internal opposition, the Gedda drive for centralization never reached the degree of implementation to which he and his devoted associates and collaborators aspired.

One might compare this situation to the controversy within Confindustria over the manner and form of political participation. Just as Confindustria's bureaucrats are subtly able to oppose open political participation, the unit leaders of Catholic Action are able to resist centralization; just as Fiat and Montecatini are able to intervene politically in their own right and outside the Confederation, the bishops are able to guide Catholic Action units in their dioceses pretty much as they wish and dictate. Perceptions of reality at the national level may call for a particular organizational and behavioral response. However, local perceptions—or, in any case, interval organizational maneuvering—may make such a response impossible. This is only one of the bitter dilemmas that confronted Luigi Gedda.

Another source of tension within Catholic Action is whether and to what extent there should be intervention in politics. Another way of putting this question is to ask whether A.C.I.'s mission is essentially apostolic or whether the organization is to be the major secular arm of the Catholic Church. Catholic Action leaders, who share perceptions of reality, are divided on this question. When I asked one of the national ecclesiastical assistants how he would define the A.C.I. mission, he quickly replied that "the ends of Catholic Action are equated with the ends of the organized Church. . . . There is some feeling in the hierarchy that it has failed to bring about a day-to-day relationship with its flock. Catholic Action is construed as one of the means of evolving modern Christianity in terms of adopting the ends of the Church to the real conditions in which the Catholics find themselves in Italian (as well as other) society." [32] Many other lay leaders also emphasize the apostolic or evangelical purpose of A.C.I. They sharply shun the political or secular interpretation—namely, that A.C.I. is an important instrument for gaining and maintaining a certain amount of political power. While every unit of Catholic Action is conceded to be spending some time in the civic training of members (i.e., in their preparation for responsible participation in the country's political life), education is said to be as far as the organization goes in this direction.

Luigi Gedda responds in the same vein, holding that Catholic Action represents laical apostolic work adapted to modern conditions. He notes that it is the purpose of A.C.I. to learn to communicate the message and the teachings of the Church to the specialized categories of Italian society. Gedda adds, as do other leaders, that Catholic Action does not directly engage in politics, that this is prohibited by the A.C.I. constitution, as well as by the 1929 Concordat that was incorporated into the Constitution of the Italian Republic. "This means," he says, "that

[32] *Interview*, Number 24 (Rome, February 12, 1958), pp. 1–2.

Catholic Action's political activity is indirect. However, even if Catholic Action does not directly tell its members to vote for Christian Democracy, the members are conditioned to do so. This is a form of conditioned reflex—as in the case of Pavlov's dog." [33]

The view that Catholic Action is not directly involved in the political process is shared by almost no one outside the organization. A former leader of Catholic Action asserts that A.C.I., like all Catholic groups, aims at "integralism," which implies a total—and totalitarian—control of society. Catholic Action represents a new form of the Church's intervention in the political life of the country, after the Church lost the temporal power it exercised prior to Italy's unification. Another ecclesiastical assistant points to the essentially political origins of Catholic Action when he remarks: "Catholic Action came into existence with the precise goal or purpose of defending the liberty and rights of the Church against the incursions of eighteenth-century liberalism. The Church increasingly felt the need of defending itself against the attacks of liberalism run rampant." [34]

It is needless to pursue at any length the question whether Catholic Action is or is not directly in politics; it most obviously is. On the critical point of A.C.I.'s relationship to the directly political civic committees, it is widely understood that they were Luigi Gedda's creation. Moreover, a national leader of A.C.I. frankly admits the committees' origins in and ties to it, and adds that the National Civic Committee has no formal constitution, in order to avoid any difficulties concerning the Concordat's prohibition against Catholic Action's engaging in politics! [35]

The more pertinent question, then, is *how* Catholic Action should engage in politics. Until now, the major patterns have been direct representation in Parliament

[33] *Interview*, Number 113 (Rome, July 18, 1958), p. 2.
[34] *Interview*, Number 60 (Rome, January 14, 1958), p. 3.
[35] *Interview*, Number 20, *op. cit.*, p. 1.

and trading on *parentela* relationship to the D.C. However, as we have noted, *parentela* can be an ephemeral power base, not merely because the hegemonic Party may lose political control but also because an antagonistic faction may capture the Party. Fanfani represented the latter kind of threat for Catholic Action. Aldo Moro is less of a threat but still not completely reliable. Were one to go by the utterances of *Il Quotidiano,* A.C.I.'s semi-official and strident organ, Amintore Fanfani is no different from the Socialists and other forces of darkness loose in the society. Indeed, many Catholic Action leaders are frank to comment that, in their eyes, many of Christian Democracy's leaders are as morally reprehensible as the laical politicians of the country. The mission of integralism must be carried out within the D.C. as well.

Most of A.C.I.'s realists recognize that there is no complete alternative to continuing to capitalize on a *parentela* relationship with the D.C. No matter how strong men like Fanfani might be or remain, the Party apparatus cannot function under its own power and must continue to rely on the civic committees, Catholic Action militants in the parishes and dioceses, and the bishops. No matter how different from Pius XII Pope Paul VI may be, there is a limit to the extent that he can now compel Catholic Action to withdraw from the political scene. As long as Christian Democracy remains the strange amalgamation of groups that it is, a group like A.C.I. that is based on outright and unequivocal confessionalism is certain to make its weight felt in a Catholic party.

However, there are now strong pressures aiming at *clientela*—at establishing the kinds of relationships to the bureaucracy that would transcend the term of office of a single party or, indeed, compel that party to come to terms with the bureaucracy. Catholic Action leaders frankly want "our people" on committees that award university professorships, on committees that advise ministries, on boards that govern publicly controlled enterprise, and spread about in the bureaucracy itself. As one A.C.I.

representative who emphasizes *clientela* points out, "contacts with the ministries turn out to be particularly fruitful where the functionary involved comes from one of the Catholic Action branches." [36] For men and women who share an image of themselves as involved in a noble mission with religious overtones, the argument is very persuasive that no avenue of possible effectiveness in the execution of that mission should be left unexplored.

It may well be, as one former A.C.I. leader claims, that the behavior of the organization brings about in its members and others a complete blocking of effective discourse and interaction (*blocco e chiusura reciproca*), and that this phenomenon has a nefarious influence on Italian society. [37] It is also true that this type of *blocco* is one of the basic conditions of Italy, in which all the groups are compelled to operate. In these circumstances there is much to justify Catholic Action's implementation of the Church's unrelenting will to power. It is fair to say that because the secular State may permit the Church less control than previously, Catholicism's effort to maximize political power is undiminished. Catholic Action is clearly an important instrument for reaching this goal—not blindly, but on the basis of a fairly realistic appraisal of the limits on behavior, and on the attainment of power, imposed by any given situation. The Church can be and is often defeated, but it never relinquishes its claim to power. This is the *élan* that drives Catholic Action. It is also one of the critical reasons why the interest-group phenomenon in Italy does not yet contribute, as it might, to the maintenance of democratic stability.

[36] *Interview,* Number 25 (Rome, February 13, 1958), p. 9.
[37] *Interview,* Number 41, *op. cit.,* p. 8.

SELECTED BIBLIOGRAPHY

I. BOOKS

Adams, John C., and Paolo Barile, *The Government of Republican Italy*. Boston: Houghton Mifflin Company, 1961.

Almond, Gabriel A., and James S. Coleman, eds., *The Politics of the Developing Areas*. Princeton: Princeton University Press, 1960.

Associazioni Cristiane dei Lavoratori Italiani, *L'Azione sociale aclista*. Rome: Edizioni A.C.L.I., 1957.

Associazioni Cristiane dei Lavoratori Italiani, *Relazione generale della presidenza centrale: VI congresso nazionale*. Rome: Litostampa, 1957.

Azione Cattolica Italiana, *Annuario, 1954*. Rome: Presidenza Generale dell'Azione Cattolica Italiana, 1954.

Azione Cattolica Italiana, *Statuto*. Rome: Presidenza Generale dell'A.C.I., 1957.

Banfield, Edward, *The Moral Basis of a Backward Society*. Glencoe: The Free Press, 1958.

Bentley, Arthur Fisher, *The Process of Government*. Chicago: University of Chicago Press, 1908.

Braga, Giorgio, *Il Comunismo fra gli italiani*. Milan: Edizioni di Comunità, 1956.

Caizzi, Bruno, *Antologia della questione meridionale*. 2nd ed. Milan: Giulio Einaudi Editore, 1955.

Camera di Commercio del Comune e della Provincia di Roma, *Guida Monaci: Annuario generale di Roma e provincia*. Rome: Via Francesco Crispi, 10, 1956.

Candeloro, Giorgio, *L'Azione Cattolica in Italia*. Rome: Edizioni di Cultura Sociale, n.d.

Candeloro, Giorgio, *Il Movimento Cattolico in Italia*. Rome: Edizioni Rinascita, 1955.

Casucci, Costanzo, *Il Fascismo*. Bologna: Società Editrice Il Mulino, 1962.

Chiarelli, Giuseppe, *Il Consiglio Nazionale dell'Economia e del Lavoro*. Milan: Giuffrè, 1957.

Civardi, Luigi, *Compendio di storia della Azione Cattolica Italiana*. Rome: Coletti Editore, 1956.

Civardi, Luigi, *Manuale di Azione Cattolica*. Rome: Coletti Editore, 1951.

Comitato Nazionale per la Celebrazione del Primo Decennale della Promulgazione della Costituzione, Five Volumes on the Italian Constitution; I, *Discorsi e scritti sulla costituzione;* II, *Studi sulla costituzione;* III, *Studi sulla costituzione;* IV, *I precedenti storici della costituzione;* V, *L'attuzione della costituzione.* Milan: Giuffrè, 1958.

Compagna, Francesco, *I terroni in città.* Bari: Editori Laterza, 1959.

Compagna, Francesco, and Vittorio De Caprariis, *Geografia delle elezioni italiane dal 1946 al 1953.* Bologna: Società Editrice Il Mulino, 1954.

Confederazione Generale dell'Industria Italiana, *Annuario, 1962.* Rome: Tipografia Fausto Failli, 1962. (This annual review of Confindustria's activities is available for most of the years of the organization's history and is an invaluable primary data source.)

Confederazione Generale dell'Industria Italiana, *Il Distacco delle aziende a prevalente partecipazione statale dalle organizzazioni degli altri datori di lavoro.* 3 vols. Rome: Fausto Failli, 1958.

Confederazione Generale dell'Industria Italiana, *The General Confederation of Italian Industry.* Rome: Stampatore Apollon, 1957.

Confederazione Nazionale Coltivatori Diretti, *Relazione del presidente al VII congresso nazionale.* Rome: Ramo Editoriale degli Agricoltori, 1953.

Confederazione Nazionale Coltivatori Diretti, *Relazione del presidente al XI congresso nazionale.* Rome: Stabilimento Tipografico Ramo Editoriale degli Agricoltori, 1957.

Confederazione Nazionale Coltivatori Diretti, *Relazione del presidente al XII congresso nazionale, Vol. II, documentazione statistica.* Rome: Tipografia del Ramo Editoriale degli Agricoltori, 1958.

Confederazione Nazionale Coltivatori Diretti, *Relazione del presidente al XII congresso nazionale, Vol. I, Parte generale.* Rome: Tipografia del Ramo Editoriale degli Agricoltori, 1958.

Confederazione Nazionale della Piccola Industria, *Relazione del presidente confederale all'assemblea: 15 maggio 1954.* Rome: Eliograf, 1954.

Confederazione Nazionale della Piccola Industria, *Relazione del presidente confederale all'assemblea: 13 ottobre 1956.* Rome: Eliograf, 1956.

De Rosa, Gabriele, *L'Azione Cattolica: Storia politica dal 1874 al 1904.* Bari: Editori Laterza, 1953.

De Rosa, Gabriele, *L'Azione Cattolica: Storia politica dal 1905 al 1919.* Bari: Editori Laterza, 1954.

Dickinson, Robert E., *The Population Problem of Southern Italy.* Syracuse: Syracuse University Press, 1955.

Eckstein, Harry, *Pressure Group Politics: The Case of the British Medical Association.* Stanford: Stanford University Press, 1960.

Ehrmann, Henry W., ed., *Interest Groups in Four Continents.* Pittsburgh: University of Pittsburgh Press, 1958.

Ehrmann, Henry W., *Organized Business in France.* Princeton: Princeton University Press, 1957.

Falconi, Carlo, *La Chiesa e le organizzazioni cattoliche in Italia, 1945–1955.* Milan: Giulio Einaudi Editore, 1956.

Falconi, Carlo, *Gedda e l'Azione Cattolica.* Florence: Parenti Editore, n.d.

Falconi, Carlo, *Il Pentagono vaticano.* Bari: Editori Laterza, 1958.

Ferrari, Franco Luigi, *L'Azione Cattolica e il "Regime."* Florence: Parenti Editore, 1957.

Finer, Samuel E., *The Anonymous Empire.* London: The Pall Mall Press, 1958.

Gorresio, Vittorio, *Stato e chiesa.* Bari: Editori Laterza, 1957.

Guarneri, Felice, *Battaglie economiche.* 2 vols. Milan: Garzanti Editore, 1953.

Guérin, Daniel, *Fascism and Big Business.* New York: Pioneer Publishers, 1939.

Horowitz, Daniel L., *The Italian Labor Movement.* Cambridge: Harvard University Press, 1963.

Hyman, Herbert, *Political Socialization.* Glencoe, Ill.: The Free Press of Glencoe, 1959.

Istituto Centrale di Statistica, *Annuario statistico italiano,* all the volumes since 1950. Rome: Istituto Poligrafico dello Stato, annually.

Jemolo, Arturo Carlo, *Chiesa e stato in Italia negli ultimi cento anni.* Milan: Giulio Einaudi Editore, 1955.

Kogan, Norman, *The Government of Italy*. New York: Thomas Y. Crowell Company, 1962.

LaPalombara, Joseph A., *The Italian Labor Movement: Problems and Prospects*. Ithaca, N.Y.: Cornell University Press, 1957.

Magri, Francesco, *L'Azione Cattolica in Italia*. 2 vols. Milan: Editrice La Fiaccola, 1953.

Meynaud, Jean, *Les Groupes de pression en France*. Paris: Armand Colin, 1958.

Ministero dell'Industria e del Commercio, *L'Istituto per la Ricostruzione Industriale—I.R.I.* 3 vols. Turin: Unione Tipografico Editrice Torinese, 1955.

Nobis, Enrico, *Il Governo invisible*. Rome: Edizioni di Cultura Sociale, 1955.

Pergolesi, Ferrucio, *Lineamenti della Costituzione italiana*. Rome: Edizioni Cinque Lune, 1956.

Poggi, Gianfranco, *Il Clero di riserva*. Milan: Feltrinelli, 1964.

Potter, Allen M., *Organized Groups in British National Politics*. London: Faber and Faber, 1961.

Rodelli, Luigi, *I Preti in cattedra*. Florence: Parenti Editore. 1958.

Rossi, Ernesto, *Il Malgoverno*. Bari: Editori Laterza, 1955.

Rossi, Ernesto, *I Padroni del vapore*. Bari: Editori Laterza, 1955.

Rossi, Ernesto, *Lo Stato industriale*. Bari: Editori Laterza, 1953.

Rossi, Ernesto, Eugenio Scalfari and Leopoldo Piccardi, *Petrolio in gabbia*. Bari: Editori Laterza, 1955.

Sartori, Giovanni, ed., *Il Parlamento Italiano, 1946–1963*. Naples: Edizioni Scientifiche Italiane, 1963.

Simon, Herbert, *Administrative Behavior*. New York: The Macmillan Company, 1947.

Stewart, J. D., *British Pressure Groups*. Oxford: The Clarendon Press, 1958.

Truman, David B., *The Governmental Process*. New York: Alfred A. Knopf, 1951.

Webster, Richard A., *The Cross and the Fasces*. Stanford, California: Stanford University Press, 1960.

Weiner, Myron, *The Politics of Scarcity: Public Pressure and Political Response in India*. Chicago: University of Chicago Press, 1962.

Zappi Recordati, Antonio, *Struttura, compiti e funzioni della Confederazione Generale dell'Agricoltura Italiana.* Imola: Cooperativa Tipografico Editrice Paolo Galeati, 1958.

II. ARTICLES

Adams, John Clarke, and Paolo Barile, "The Implementation of the Italian Constitution," *American Political Science Review,* 47 (March, 1953), pp. 61–83.

Almond, Gabriel A., "A Comparative Study of Interest Groups and the Political Process," *American Political Science Review,* 52 (March, 1958), pp. 270–82.

Anonymous, "La 'Meridionalizzazione' della pubblica amministrazione," *Mondo Economico,* 10 (February 19, 1955), pp. 20–21.

Anonymous, "Sotto-governo," *Dibattito Politico,* 2 (March 6, 1956), p. 24.

Apter, David E., "A Comparative Method for the Study of Politics," *American Journal of Sociology,* 64 (November, 1958), pp. 221–37.

Ardigò, Achille, "Il Volto elettorale di Bologna," in Spreafico, Alberto, and Joseph LaPalombara, eds., *Elezioni e comportamento politico in Italia.* Milan: Edizioni di Comunità, 1962, pp. 801–49.

Ardigò, Achille, "Le Trasformazioni interne nelle campagne settentrionali e l'esodo rurale," in *Atti del IV Congresso Mondiale di Sociologia, Aspetti e problemi sociali dello sviluppo economico in Italia.* Bari: Editori Laterza (1959), pp. 39–54.

Barile, Paolo, "I Poteri del presidente della repubblica," in Comitato Nazionale per la Celebrazione del Primo Decennale della Promulgazione della Costituzione, Vol. III, *Studi sulla Costituzione.* Milan: Giuffrè (1958), pp. 133–83.

Beer, Samuel H., "Pressure Groups and Parties in Britain," *American Political Science Review,* 50 (March, 1956), pp. 1–23.

Beer, Samuel H., "The Representation of Interests in British Government: Historical Background," *American Political Science Review,* 51 (September, 1957), pp. 613–30.

Blanksten, George I., "Political Groups in Latin America," *American Political Science Review,* 53 (March, 1959), pp. 106–27.

Brown, Bernard E., "The Army and Politics in France," *Journal of Politics,* 23 (May, 1961), pp. 262–78.

Brown, Bernard E., "Pressure Politics in France," *Journal of Politics,* 18 (November, 1956), pp. 702–19.

Centro di Documentazione della Presidenza del Consiglio dei Ministri, "La Rinascita dell'Italia," *Documenti di vita italiana,* 3 (January–February, 1953).

Centro Italiano Ricerche Documentazione, "I Gruppi di pressione," *Tempi Moderni,* 3 (April–June, 1960), pp. 43–55.

Centro Italiano Ricerche Documentazione, "I Gruppi di pressione," *Tempi Moderni,* 3 (July–September, 1960), pp. 13–33.

Centro Italiano Ricerche Documentazione, "I Gruppi di pressione in Italia: conclusioni," *Tempi Moderni,* 3 (October–December, 1960), pp. 103–12.

Cervigni, C., and G. Galasso, "Inchiesta sul Partito Socialista Italiano," *Nord e Sud,* 3 (March, 1956), pp. 6–160.

Ciranna, Giuseppe, "Un 'Gruppo di pressione': La Confederazione Nazionale Coltivatori Diretti," *Nord e Sud,* 5 (January, 1958), pp. 9–39.

Cole, Taylor, "Three Constitutional Courts," *American Political Science Review,* 53 (December, 1959), pp. 963–84.

Compagna, Francesco, "Dopo i primi anni di esodo rurale," *Nord e Sud,* 8 (October, 1961), pp. 6–10.

Davis, Morris, "Some Neglected Aspects of British Pressure Groups," *Midwest Journal of Political Science,* 7 (February, 1963), pp. 42–53.

DeCaprariis, Vittorio, "Gruppi di pressione," *Nord e Sud,* 3 (December, 1956), pp. 66–69.

DeCaprariis, Vittorio, "Gruppi di pressione e società democratica," *Nord e Sud,* 8 (May, 1961), pp. 16–27.

DeMarchi, E., "Introduzione ai 'pressure groups,'" *Occidente,* 12 (1956), pp. 105–12.

D'Eufemia, G., "Aspetti giuridici dei gruppi di pressione," *Nord e Sud,* 6 (March, 1957), pp. 69–71.

Dogan, Mattei, "Le Comportement politique des Italiens," *Revue Française de Science Politique,* 9 (June, 1959), pp. 383–409.

Dogan, Mattei, "Le Donne italiane tra il cattolicesimo e il marxismo," in Spreafico, Alberto, and Joseph LaPalombara, eds., *Elezioni e comportamento politico in Italia.* Milan: Edizioni di Comunità, 1962, pp. 475–94.

Dogan, Mattei, "La Stratificazione sociale dei suffragi," in Spreafico, Alberto, and Joseph LaPalombara, eds., *Elezioni e comportamento politico in Italia*. Milan: Edizioni di Comunità, 1962, pp. 407–74.

Dominedò, F. M., "Saggio sul potere presidenziale," in Comitato Nazionale per la Celebrazione del Primo Decennale della Promulgazione della Costituzione, Vol. III, *Studi sulla Costituzione*. Milan: Giuffrè, 1958, pp. 201–27.

Ehrmann, Henry W., "French Bureaucracy and Organized Interests," *Administrative Science Quarterly*, 5 (March, 1961), pp. 534–55.

Ehrmann, Henry W., "Les Groupes d'intérêt et la bureaucratie dans les démocraties occidentales," *Revue Française de Science Politique*, 11 (September, 1961), pp. 541–68.

Ehrmann, Henry W., "Pressure Groups in France," *Annals of the American Academy of Political and Social Science*, 319 (September, 1958), pp. 141–48.

Eldersveld, Samuel J., "American Interest Groups: A Survey of Research and Some Implications for Theory and Method," in Henry W. Ehrmann, ed., *Interest Groups in Four Continents*. Pittsburgh: University of Pittsburgh Press (1958), pp. 173–96.

Ferrarotti, Franco, "L'Evoluzione dei rapporti fra direzioni aziendali e rappresentanti operai nell'Italia del dopoguerra," in *Atti del IV Congresso Mondiale di Sociologia, Aspetti e problemi sociali dello sviluppo economico in Italia*. Bari: Laterza Editori (1959), pp. 133–48.

Finer, Samuel E., "The Federation of British Industries," *Political Studies*, 4 (February, 1956), pp. 61–84.

Forcella, Enzo, "Azione Cattolica e Democrazia Cristiana," *Il Ponte*, 6 (June, 1950), pp. 606–13.

Giannini, Massimo S., "Il Decentramento nel sistema amministrativo," in *Problemi della pubblica amministrazione*. Bologna: Zanichelli Editore (1958), pp. 155–83.

LaPalombara, Joseph, "The Comparative Role of Groups in Political Systems," *SSRC Items*, 15 (June, 1961), pp. 18–21.

LaPalombara, Joseph, "La Confindustria e la politica in Italia," *Tempi Moderni*, 4 (October, 1961), pp. 3–16.

LaPalombara, Joseph, "I Gruppi di interesse in Italia," *Studi Politici*, 7 (January–March, 1960), pp. 11–35.

LaPalombara, Joseph, "Gruppi di pressione e pubblica amministrazione," in Luciana Praga, ed., *Problemi della pub-*

blica amministrazione. Bologna: Zanichelli Editore (1959), pp. 141–59.

LaPalombara, Joseph, "The Political Role of Organized Labor in Western Europe," *Journal of Politics,* 17 (February, 1955), pp. 59–81.

LaPalombara, Joseph, "The Utility and Limitations of Interest Group Theory in Non-American Field Situations," *Journal of Politics,* 22 (February, 1960), pp. 29–49.

LaPalombara, Joseph A., and John T. Dorsey, "On the French and Italian Bureaucracies," *PROD,* 1 (September, 1957), pp. 35–40.

LaPalombara, Joseph, and Gianfranco Poggi, "I Gruppi di pressione e la burocrazia italiana," *Rassegna Italiana di Sociologia,* 1 (October–December, 1960), pp. 31–55.

MacKenzie, W. J. M., "Pressure Groups: The Conceptual Framework," *Political Studies,* 3 (October, 1955), pp. 247–55.

Macridis, Roy E., "Interest Groups in Comparative Analysis," *Journal of Politics,* 23 (February, 1961), pp. 25–45.

Manzocchi, G., "Appunti sul fenomeno dei gruppi di pressione," *Vita e Pensiero,* 43 (January, 1960), pp. 48–51.

March, James G., "An Introduction to the Theory of Measurement of Influence," *American Political Science Review,* 49 (June, 1955), pp. 431–51.

Merton, Robert K., "Continuities in the Theory of Reference Groups and Social Structure," in Merton, R. K., *Social Theory and Social Structure.* Rev. ed., Glencoe, Illinois: The Free Press (1957), pp. 310–26.

Meynaud, Jean, "Essai d'analyse de l'influence des groupes d'intérêt," *Revue Economique,* 2 (1957), pp. 3–46.

Meynaud, Jean, "Les Groupes d'intérêt et l'administration en France," *Revue Française de Science Politique,* 7 (July–September, 1957), pp. 573–93.

Meynaud, Jean, "I Gruppi di interesse in Francia," *Studi Politici,* 4 (July–September, 1957), pp. 404–34.

Meynaud, J., and J. Meyriat, "Les Groupes de pression en Europe Occidentale," *Revue Française de Science Politique,* 9 (March, 1959), pp. 229–46.

Monypenny, Phillip, "Political Science and the Study of Groups," *Western Political Quarterly,* 7 (June, 1954), pp. 183–201.

Pedrazzi, Luigi, "Partiti politici e gruppi di pressione," *Il Mulino*, 36 (October, 1954), pp. 601–12.

Piazzi, U., "I Gruppi di pressione nella democrazia moderna," *Quaderni di Azione Sociale*, 10 (September–October, 1959), pp. 666–91.

Prandi, Alfonso, "L'Insegnamento politico della chiesa," *Il Mulino*, 11 (February, 1962), pp. 128–33.

Rossi-Doria, Manlio, "Aspetti sociali dello sviluppo economico in Italia," in *Atti del IV Congresso Mondiale di Sociologia, Aspetti e problemi sociali dello sviluppo economico in Italia*. Bari: Editori Laterza (1959), pp. 9–35.

Rothman, Stanley, "Systematic Political Theory: Observations on the Group Approach," *American Political Science Review*, 54 (March, 1960), pp. 15–33.

Sartori, Giovanni, "Gruppi di pressione o gruppi di interesse," *Il Mulino*, 8 (February, 1959), pp. 7–42.

Simon, Herbert A., "Related Choice and the Structure of the Environment," *Psychological Review*, 63 (March, 1956), pp. 129–38.

Sofri, Gianni, "Il Fascismo," *Il Mulino*, 11 (February, 1962), pp. 159–62.

Weiss, Ignazio, "Proprietà e finanziamento della stampa quotidiana italiana," *Tempi Moderni*, 3 (July, 1960), pp. 3–12.

Weiss, Ignazio, "Proprietà e finanziamento della stampa quotidiana italiana: una precisazione," *Tempi Moderni*, 3 (October–December, 1960), pp. 101–02.

Zappuli, Cesare, "La Burocrazia vista da un giornalista," in *Problemi della pubblica amministrazione*. Bologna: Zanichelli Editore (1960), pp. 203–10.

INDEX

access, attitudes of bureaucrats concerning, 289; structured nature of, 259–262; unequal nature of, 268–270
ACLI (Italian Association of Christian Workers), 108, 150, 211, 223; Catholic nature of, 332; *clientela* relationships of, 296–297; leadership, 225; origins, 224; relationship to Christian Democracy, 226; tensions with CISL, 225; trade union functions, 224–225
Adams, John Clarke, 69n, 110n, 112n
Adenauer, Konrad, 316
administrative agency, verticality of, 271–272
administrative reform, inadequacy of, 340–341; lack of seriousness of, 328–329; Lucifredi Decrees in, 340; need for, 279, 281, 340n; obstacles to, 279–281, 283; opposition to, 341; results of, 281
administrative specialists, 256
administrative specialization, early lack of in Italy, 278–279
Adrian, Charles, 25n
AGIS (Italian General Association of Entertainment), 351 ff.
agricultural consortiums, 236
Almond, Gabriel, ix, x, 13, 14n, 15n, 53n, 60n, 79
Ammassari, Paolo, 99n, 100n
ANCE (National Association of Building Constructors), 178, 217
Andreotti, Giulio, 88, 91, 215, 216n, 219, 244
ANFIIA, 202, 203, 302, 369
ANPI (National Association of Italian Partisans), 150, 152, 153, 197

anti-clericalism, as a fragmenting factor, 57–58
Apter, David, 16, 17n
Archibugi, Franco, xiv
Ardigò, Achille, 47n, 62
Article 17, 216, 324
Association for the Industrial Development of Southern Italy, *see* SVIMEZ
Association of Italian Joint Stock Companies, 211; origins of, 204; position regarding Article 17, 205–206; publications of, 204–205; reputation of, 204
associations, goals of, 127–143; leadership characteristics of, 155–161; membership characteristics of, 143–155, 162–164; number of, 128; political nature of, 142–143; student, 140–142; types of, 127–143; veterans, 137–138; women's, 138–140
Assolombardo (Lombard Industrial Association), 134–135, 164, 420
auditors, 169
authoritativeness, of groups, 297–302
Avanti!, 184

Baget-Bozzo, Giovanni, 8
Banfield, Edward C., 38n, 65n
banking association, 212
Barbera, Lidia, xiv
bargaining, hampered by fragmentation and isolation, 249
Barile, Paolo, 69n, 106n, 110n, 112n
Basso, Lelio, 4n
Battaglia, Adolfo, 355n
Beer, Samuel, 23, 256n
Benevento, Camillo, xiv
Bentley, Arthur Fisher, 13, 15, 17
Blanksten, George I., 15n, 54n

439